Refining Composition Skills

Rhetoric and Grammar

Fifth Edition

Regina L. Smalley

Mary K. Ruetten

Joann Rishel Kozyrev

HH | Heinle & Heinle
Thomson Learning™

AUSTRALIA • CANADA • DENMARK • JAPAN • MEXICO
NEW ZEALAND • PHILIPPINES • PUERTO RICO • SINGAPORE
SPAIN • UNITED KINGDOM • UNITED STATES

Acquisitions Editor: Eric Bredenberg
Associate Acquisitions Editor: Thomas Healy
Senior Marketing Manager: Charlotte Sturdy
Production Editor: Jeffrey M. Freeland
Senior Manufacturing Coordinator: Mary Beth Hennebury
Designer: Jean Hammond Design

Cover Designer: Elise Kaiser
Cover Image: PhotoDisc, Inc.
Illustrator: Len Shalansky
Compositor: Modern Graphics, Inc.
Printer: Von Hoffman Graphics

For permission to use material in this text, contact us:

web	www.thomsonrights.com
fax	1-800-730-2215
phone	1-800-730-2214

Pre-recorded material supplied by CNN®.
© 2000 Cable News Network, Inc.® All rights reserved.
© 2000 Turner Learning, Inc. All rights reserved.

Heinle & Heinle Publishers
20 Park Plaza
Boston, MA 02116

CANADA:
Nelson/Thomson Learning
1120 Birchmount Road
Scarborough, Ontario
Canada M1K 5G4

JAPAN:
Thomson Learning
Palaceside Building, 5F
1-1-1 Hitotsubashi, Chiyoda-ku
Tokyo 100 0003, Japan

UK/EUROPE/MIDDLE EAST:
Thomson Learning
Berkshire House
168-173 High Holborn
London, WC1V 7AA, United Kingdom

LATIN AMERICA:
Thomson Learning
Seneca, 53
Colonia, Polanco
11560 México D.F. México

SPAIN:
Thomson Learning
Calle Magallanes, 25
28015-Madrid, España

AUSTRALIA/NEW ZEALAND:
Nelson/Thomson Learning
102 Dodds Street
South Melbourne
Victoria 3205 Australia

ASIA (excluding Japan):
Thomson Learning
60 Albert Street #15-01
Albert Complex
Singapore 189969

Photo & Illustration Credits: p. 18, Michael LaJoie/Image Resource Bank; p. 35, Jonathan Stark/Image Resource Bank; p. 40, B. Bachman/The Image Works; p. 89, Mitch Wojnarowicz/The Image Works; p. 117, Jonathan Stark/Image Resource Bank; p. 145, Len Shalansky; p. 171, Joseph Sohm, ChromoSohm Inc./Corbis; p. 203, Michael LaJoie/Image Resource Bank; p. 231, Owen Franken/Corbis; p. 247, Michael Newman/PhotoEdit; p. 262, Karl Weatherly/Corbis; p. 285, Ralph A. Clevenger/Corbis; p. 300, Len Shalansky.

Text credits for this book appear on page iv, which constitutes an extension of this copyright page.

Library of Congress Cataloging-in-Publication Data

Smalley, Regina L.
    Refining composition skills : rhetoric and grammar / Regina L. Smalley, Mary K. Ruetten, Joann Rishel Kozyrev.—5th ed.
      p. cm.
    Includes index.
    ISBN 0-8384-0223-2 (alk. paper)
      1. English language Rhetoric.   2. English language—Textbooks for foreign speakers.   3.
English language—Grammar—problems, exercises, etc.   I. Ruetten, Mary K.   II. Kozyrev,
Joann.   III. Title.

PE1408 .S577 2000
808'.042—dc21

                                    99-087244

This book is printed on acid-free recycled paper.

Printed in the United States of America
   8   9   04

A Very Special Thank-You

The publisher and authors would like to thank the following coordinators and instructors who have offered many helpful insights and suggestions for change throughout the development of the new edition of *Refining Composition Skills*.

Wendy Ashby	University of Arizona, *Tucson, AZ*
Nancy Boyer	Goldenwest Community College, *Huntington Beach, CA*
Lynn T. Bunker	University of Houston, *Houston, TX*
Martha Compton	University of California, *Irvine, CA*
Linette Davis	Coastline College, *Fountain Valley, CA*
Mary Di Stefano Diaz	Broward Community College, *Davie, FL*
Kara Dworak	San Jose State University, *San Jose, CA*
Russell Faux	Newbury College, *Brookline, CA*
Gladys C. Highly	Grossmont College, *El Cajon, CA*
Kelly Kennedy-Isern	Miami-Dade Community College, *Miami Beach, FL*

Text Credits

Contents

Chapter 3   The Narrative Paragraph

When Princess Diana died, many people wrote poems, notes, and letters to leave at her memorial sites. In this clip, people reflect on why they were moved to write these messages.
In this excerpt, General Colin Powell, whose parents were born in Jamaica, tells the story of his visit to the village where his father was born and his first feelings upon meeting his extended family.
In this paragraph, Mary Kay Mackin reflects on Christmas holidays she has spent with her family and comes to a conclusion about the part she likes best.
In this essay, which first appeared in the *Los Angeles Times*, Elizabeth Wong tells of her painful experiences growing up in the bicultural atmosphere of Los Angeles' Chinatown. She describes the difficulty of being Chinese on the outside but American on the inside.

In this article, Bob Greene writes about the unwritten cultural rules in our lives. Greene gives multiple examples of the rules we follow without even thinking about them.

In this essay, which first appeared in Rose Del Castillo Guilbault's column for *This World*, she gives an example of the power of language. She shows how a particular Spanish word has come to have different meanings in different cultures.

This report examines the growth of the communication training industry and notes that women are often the target market for communication training seminars, tapes, and books. The clip includes a short interview with Deborah Tannen and other communication experts.

In this excerpt from her textbook *Polite Fictions*, Nancy Masterson Sakamoto explains the difference between Japanese and American conversation styles. She uses an analogy that compares each conversation style to a particular sport.

This excerpt from Deborah Tannen's book *You Just Don't Understand* examines the different ways that American men and women view decision making. She notes that the different notions of communication that women and men have can lead to conflict between couples.

This report shows people visiting a very special museum which houses a collection of new products that were unsuccessful. People in marketing often visit this museum to help them understand why products succeed and fail.

In this excerpt from his popular book *Doublespeak,* William Lutz examines the words that many advertisers choose to make misleading but legal claims for products they wish to sell.

In this excerpt from a college textbook, the authors explain Maslow's hierarchy of needs and show how advertisers can appeal to each type of need to influence consumers' buying behavior.

This clip features Hilgraeve, a small software company which has found its niche in communications software. The founders of the company talk about how their company got started and what they believe they must do to continue to be successful.

Chapter 12   The Argumentative Essay   275

Unit Three   Grammar Review   299

Appendices   381

Preface

Level and Aim of the Text

The fifth edition of **Refining Composition Skills** presents an integrated program of writing for high-intermediate and advanced students of English as a second or foreign language (ESL/EFL). It combines extensive practice in rhetorical strategies and techniques with a review of appropriate grammatical structures and verb tenses. With its extensive appendices, the text can further serve as a handbook for writing, grammar, and mechanics. The primary audience is the academically oriented ESL student; however, the text also can be useful in developmental writing courses for native speakers who could benefit from more guidance in writing compositions.

Flexibility of the Text

Refining Composition Skills can accommodate the needs of students of varying degrees of experience and levels of writing skills. Inexperienced writers will build a solid foundation in writing beginning with Unit One, which presents the basic paragraph patterns useful for high school- or college-level writing: narrative, descriptive, and expository. This unit covers developing and restricting topic sentences; organizing and developing effective, detailed support of the controlling idea; and outlining. Students who have had considerable practice composing the types of paragraphs presented in this unit may consider the chapters in Unit One a review. More experienced writers might begin the text with Unit Two, which focuses on the multiparagraph essay. This unit introduces the common patterns of exposition along with argumentation. Here the emphasis is on a strong thesis statement and appropriate and well-organized support. Another option for experienced writers is to review the writing process and the paragraph in Chapters 1 and 2 before or after starting essay writing in Unit Two. *Refining Composition Skills* contains enough material so that teachers can pick the chapters most appropriate for their students and thus design writing courses of varying difficulty.

Design of the Text

Except for Chapters 1, 2, and 6, which provide introductions to the writing process, the paragraph, and the essay, respectively, each chapter in **Refining Composition**

Skills focuses on a rhetorical mode of development and the conventions associated with that mode. Each chapter contains four basic components: getting started video and journal writing activities, reading selections, an introduction to the rhetorical pattern, and the relevant composition skills (devices for achieving coherence).

Each chapter (except Chapters 1, 2, and 6) begins with several thematically chosen readings with topics geared toward the interests of academically oriented ESL students. The readings are followed by comprehension/discussion questions intended to generate lively class discussions and provocative essay topics. In addition, each chapter topic is reinforced in the examples and exercises throughout the chapter. The reading passages also function as examples of the rhetorical modes and of professional writing, providing evidence that the principles of rhetoric apply in writing both outside and inside the classroom. The reading component allows for flexibility in teaching: Teachers who wish to focus on the academic content of the essays can begin with the introductory essays, and teachers who prefer the developmental approach can begin with the sections on rhetoric.

In the rhetoric section, the rhetorical patterns are carefully and clearly explained and illustrated, often with student samples that can be used as models early in the chapter. The section on composition skills introduces techniques for achieving coherence, such as the use of adverbial clauses and transitional expressions, and encourages the application of those skills in the writing of compositions, thus emphasizing the necessity for revision in the writing process. In addition, each chapter includes exercises for mastery of the composition skills. To further encourage revision and a focus on accuracy, the writing component in each chapter includes references to relevant grammar points in Unit Three, Grammar Review. To conclude the chapter, writing assignments of varying difficulty are included, including several "assignments from the disciplines," which are assignments typical of those students might encounter in a college-level content class.

Major Revisions in the Fifth Edition

One of the major changes in the fifth edition of *Refining Composition Skills* is the "Getting Started" section which begins each chapter. This section is designed to introduce students to the chapter theme and goals and help them activate schema which will enable to them to benefit more fully from the activities which follow this introduciton. Each "Getting Started" section includes journal writing prompts as well as a CNN Video Activity to go along with the CNN video available at no charge to teachers who adopt *Refining Composition Skills*. Teachers may select from these initial activities to appeal to a wide variety of learning styles and to prepare students for the activities they will encounter later in the chapter.

Other revisions in this edition include the inclusion of "Composition Skills and the Internet" activities which encourage students to explore the Internet as a source of both information and inspiration. Because of the changing nature of the Internet, references to URLs have been kept to a minimum, although there are some references to pages that seem to be reliable. In case one of the URLs does not work, keywords are always provided so that teachers and students can use their favorite Internet search tools to complete the activities. These "Composition Skills and the Internet" activities are designed to complement the text but can be skipped without losing continuity if Internet access or class time is limited.

Similarly, the new "Assignments from the Disciplines" at the end of each chapter can be used to simulate college-level writing assignments. However, if students do not have the background knowledge, time, or preparation to respond to these questions, teachers may elect to use the more general questions which precede the "Assignments from the Disciplines" or to refer to these assignments as examples of university writing requirements.

Other changes include the clear articulation of chapter goals at the start of each chapter, the inclusion of several new appendices, including peer review checklists, information on using others' words and ideas, and model letters. These new appendices are added to the comprehensive references provided in the appendices and the grammar review section, allowing the text to function as both a textbook and a writer's handbook. Finally, a number of the reading passages have been changed to continue to offer up-to-date readings which will be of interest to students.

With this edition, *Refining Composition Skills* retains its developmental, step-by-step approach to writing while providing greater emphasis on the reading/writing connection and the process of writing.

Articulation with *Developing Composition Skills*

Developing Composition Skills, an intermediate-level writing program, has been developed as a natural stepping stone to *Refining Composition Skills*. This intermediate-level text introduces students to the various rhetorical modes through an approach that affirms the interconnectedness of writing, reading, and grammar.

Acknowledgments

We would like to thank our reviewers, our colleagues, and our students for offering their valuable suggestions during the preparation of this and all editions of *Refining Composition Skills*. We are especially grateful to the editorial team at Heinle & Heinle for their support throughout the project; and to Jill Kinkade, developmental editor, for her diligent work and invaluable suggestions throughout the project.

Regina L. Smalley
Mary K. Ruetten
Joann Rishel Kozyrev

Unit One
The Paragraph

Chapter 1 The Writing Process

Theme

The Writing Process

Goals

Writing

To learn about the stages of the writing process

To practice techniques for generating ideas, such as keeping a journal, brainstorming, freewriting, WH-questions, and clustering

To understand the difference between revising and editing

Getting Started

Journal Writing:

A **journal** has a number of uses. First, it is a place for you to record your observations about the world and reflect on them. If you hear a conversation on a bus or witness an unusual occurrence in a dormitory, describe it in your journal and make some observations about it. What did you notice? What struck you? How can you connect this experience to your life? Thus, writing in your journal is a way of thinking on paper, a way for you to explore and discover what you think. The journal is a record of your ideas and insights about the world and serves as a storehouse for future writing material. Then, when you get a writing assignment, you can look back in your journal for topics, ideas, and materials and already have them at hand.

You may also do more directed writing assignments in your journal. For example, your teacher may ask you to respond to a reading passage, telling how you felt or what part of the passage was particularly significant to you; to reflect about your writing process, describing how you went about writing something; or to prewrite in preparation for another assignment.

In your journal writing, you will focus on ideas and insight. Write as much as you can, allowing your mind to make connections. Do not worry too much about grammatical correctness or style. Focus your energy on recording what you think.

Journal Writing: Choose one of the following topics and write in your journal for 20 minutes.

1. Describe yourself as a writer. How do you go about writing? What kinds of things do you like to write about? What do you dislike? What is hard for you? Easy?

2. Tell about your most successful writing experience. When did you write something that you were particularly proud of? Why were you proud of it? What does this experience say about you?

3. List a number of subjects or topics that you are interested in or know a lot about. Then choose one of these topics and write about it. What is it? What do you know about it? Why is it interesting? What does this interest suggest about you?

4. Recall an unusual occurrence you witnessed recently. What happened? Why did it happen? Why was it unusual? What did you make of it?

CNN® Video Activity: "The 37,000-Page Diary"

 Many people keep journals or diaries. Some write in them once a week, and others write every day. If a person keeps a diary for many years, however, reading back through the thoughts, ideas, and observations made over the years can tell a lot about the person's life and how he or she has changed. In this video, you will see an interview with Edward Robb Ellis, who has kept a diary since 1927. As you watch the video, try to answer these questions:

1. Why did Mr. Ellis start to keep his diary? Why has he continued?
2. What are some of the important events he has recorded in this diary?
3. Why is keeping this diary so important to Mr. Ellis?

Video Follow-up: Discussion Questions
After you watch the video, discuss journal writing and diary keeping with your classmates. Use these questions to guide your discussion:

1. Have you ever kept a journal or a diary? Why did you start? If you quit, why did you stop?
2. How do you think keeping a journal can help you become a better writer?
3. In this class, your teacher may ask you to keep a journal. What do you think you will like about this experience? What will be difficult for you?

The Process of Writing

This book is designed to help you become a better writer. In the following chapters, you will focus on writing paragraphs and essays using different types of development. In this chapter, however, you will focus on the **process of writing**, the way writers actually go about the task of writing. While different writers approach the process in different ways, all writers go through a general sequence of stages called **prewriting**, **drafting**, and **revising**. You will work through these same stages as you complete your paragraphs and essays.

When you get an assignment for a paragraph or essay, use one of the following invention techniques to help you get started:

Prewriting

In the **prewriting** stage, writers take time to think about their topic and generate ideas. They also spend some time focusing and planning the piece of writing.

Generating Ideas

Sometimes you are frustrated because you cannot think of anything to say about a topic. In this section, you will learn a number of strategies and techniques for generating ideas. Use these techniques when you first begin to think about your topic and then anytime you feel your flow of ideas drying up.

Invention Techniques

Brainstorming

A **brainstorm** is a sudden insight or connection. Brainstorming is a way to associate ideas and stimulate thinking. To brainstorm, start with a word or phrase and let your thoughts go in whatever direction they will. For a set period of time, do not attempt to think logically but write a list of ideas as quickly as possible, putting down whatever comes to mind without looking back or organizing. After the set time is up, look over what you have listed to see if any of the ideas are related and can be grouped. If so, the groupings suggest a topic or area of support. You can use brainstorming to focus on a particular topic or to develop more examples or ideas for your essay in progress.

Following is an example of a brainstorm. The writer has marked with an asterisk the ideas she could use to write a physical description of her grandmother.

MY GRANDMOTHER

*small	energetic
*wrinkled	*skinny
*short	*spots on hands
slippers	drives old car
strange vegetables	*twinkle in eye
apple trees	homemade bread
clean clothes	*not much?
*glasses	*hair in bun

EXERCISE 1·1   As a class, choose one or two of the following topics to brainstorm, and work quickly for 15 minutes. After you have finished, arrange your ideas in groups on your own. Then compare and contrast your groups with those of your classmates. You will note that different writers will explore different aspects of the topic.

family	a problem	computers
travel	a memory	television
education	a fear	automobiles

Freewriting

Freewriting is writing without stopping. It means writing whatever comes to your mind without worrying about whether the ideas are good or the grammar is correct. Its purpose is to free up your mind to let it make associations and connections. So when you freewrite, do not interrupt the flow of your ideas. Write them as they come to you. Do not censor any thoughts or insights. Do not go back and reread. Do not cross anything out. When you freewrite, set a goal: for example, a time limit of 15 minutes or a number of pages in your journal. Then write continuously until you reach your goal. After you have finished, reread what you have written and look for interesting ideas or insights that might be useful to you in your writing.

Following is an example of freewriting from which the writer could develop a paragraph about a vivid memory.

A Memory

I remember a time I got lost. I was a little girl—maybe seven years. Gone shopping with my family—my parents were doing something—I don't remember what and I walked away—I don't know why. Maybe I saw something or got bored. Then I just remember sitting on the counter by the sales clerk and I was crying. I was wearing a blue dress. the clerk was talking to me and saying things like—don't worry, it's OK, we'll find your mama. That's all I remember. I don't remember if my parents found me or what—I guess they did. I don't know how they noticed I was gone.

EXERCISE 1·2   Choose one of the following topics and freewrite for five minutes.

a recent trip	the environment
a family member or friend	your job
a familiar place	an American custom
a custom in your country	an important site in your country

WH- Questions

When newspaper reporters write articles, they try to answer the following questions in the first sentence of the report: **who**, **what**, **when**, **where**, **why**, and sometimes **how**. You can use these same questions to generate material for your writing. Asking these questions allows you to see your topic from different points of view and may help to clarify your position on the topic. To use this technique, write out as many WH- questions as you can. Then answer them as fully as you can.

Here is an example of WH- questions used for invention. It is the first part of a list of questions that one writer, Carlos, developed. Carlos started with a sentence containing the bare facts he wanted to write about and then developed a number of WH- questions about each fact. After completing his list of questions, Carlos answered them. He used the information generated in his answers to write his essay.

My uncle	(WHO)
was laid off from his job	(WHAT)
at the hospital	(WHERE)
last April	(WHEN)
because of the recession.	(WHY)

1. **Who** is my uncle, really? What kind of a person is he? What do people think of him?
2. **What** happened exactly? **How** and **when** did it happen? **Why**? Who was present? What did my uncle say when he found out?
3. **Where** does my uncle work? Where is this place? What do I know about the location? What department does he work in? What does he do there?

EXERCISE 1·3   Choose one of the topics listed in Exercises 1-1 or 1-2 or choose your own topic. Then write as many WH- questions as you can on the topic and answer them.

Clustering

Clustering is making a visual map of your ideas. It frees you from following a strictly linear sequence; thus it may allow you to think more creatively and make new associations. To use this technique, begin with your topic circled in the middle of a sheet of paper. Then, draw a line out from the circle and write an idea associated with the topic. Circle this idea and from it draw lines and write ideas associated with it. Continue to map or cluster until you cannot think of any more ideas. When you have finished, study your map to find new associations about your topic and to see the relationship of ideas.

Here is an example of clustering. From this prewriting, the writer could develop an essay about the benefits or problems with advertising.

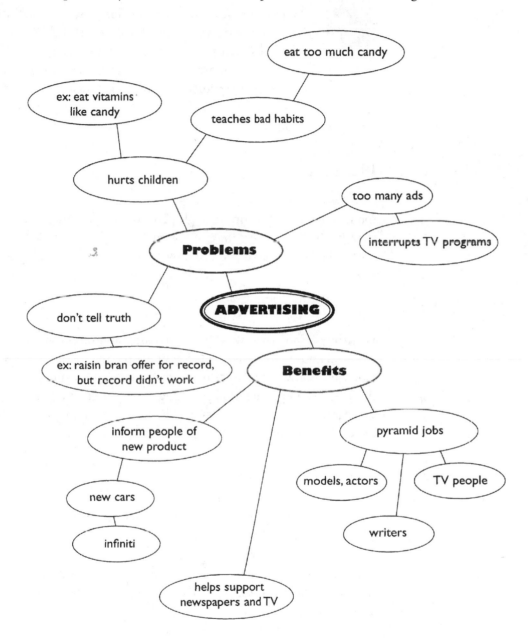

EXERCISE 1·4   Choose one of the topics listed in Exercises 1-1 or 1-2 or choose your own topic. Then use clustering to map your ideas about it. Start with your topic in the middle of the page and work out from there.

Internet Activity: Composition Skills and the Internet

 Where do you think professional writers get their ideas? What are their writing habits? Do they really revise what they write? The website http://www.inkspot.com/poll has asked writers to respond to these and other questions; go to this site to read their answers. If you need more strategies and suggestions for ways to get ideas, use an Internet search tool and do a keyword search for "writer's block." Report to your class about the information you find.

Planning

After writers have generated ideas about their topics, they focus their ideas on a main point and develop a rough plan for the paragraph or essay they are going to write. In the chapters that follow, you will learn how to focus ideas in controlling sentences. You will also study how to organize and develop ideas effectively.

Drafting

Drafting is the actual writing of the paragraph or essay. Once you have gathered material and made a rough plan, you are ready to write. As you write a first draft, you will follow the general plan you have mapped out. While writing your first draft, focus on getting your meaning down on paper; do not be overly concerned with grammatical correctness at this stage. Depending on the length of the piece of writing, you may write it in one or several sittings.

Revising

The first draft of a piece of writing is really just a place to start. After it is completed, the real work of writing can begin. Successful writers know that writing is mostly revising. Thus, as you write, you will want to spend time revising your papers. Revising is usually broken down into two parts: **revising**, or changing the content and organization of the paragraph or essay, and **editing** the sentences and words in it.

Revising is really rethinking or reseeing your paper. During prewriting and drafting, you were mostly concerned with finding ideas and getting them down. Now, you will need to shift from suspending judgments to making them. Now, you will need to evaluate your writing. To help you evaluate your drafts, you will find **revision checklists** in each of the following chapters. The questions in the checklists will help you decide whether your writing is sufficiently focused and developed.

It is also helpful to ask someone else to read your draft and give you feedback. For this purpose, you will find **peer review checklists** in Appendix I. You and your classmates can use these to respond to each other's writing. Following are guidelines for being an effective peer reviewer:

1. Think of the writing as work in progress.
2. Think of yourself as a coach or guide, not a judge.
3. Look at the big picture. Do not just focus on grammatical or spelling errors.
4. Comment on what the writer has done well. Be specific.
5. Comment on the weak parts of the writing. Be specific.
6. Be honest but tactful in commenting on the writing.

In addition to your own evaluation and the evaluation given by your peers, your teacher may also give you feedback on a draft. Once you have received feedback, you can decide what kinds of changes to make. Following are the major ways you will revise:

1. **Add**. You may need to add material to support your ideas or add sentences and phrases to connect ideas.
2. **Cut**. You may need to get rid of parts that are not relevant to the topic or repeat what has already been said.
3. **Replace**. You may need to replace parts you have cut.
4. **Move material around**. You may want to change the order of sentences or paragraphs.

In the Coherence sections of the following chapters, you will study ways to revise and improve your drafts.

Editing

In revising, you were concerned with focusing and supporting your ideas—that is, with the content of your paper. Once you are basically satisfied with the content, you will want to turn your attention to the form, with how you expressed your ideas. At this point, you may need to rephrase or **edit** some of your sentences. Rephrase sentences that are not clear or not precise. Then check your sentences to make sure they are grammatically and mechanically correct.

The Grammar Review section of this textbook contains explanations and exercises on troublesome grammar points. You may want to review the areas of grammar that give you trouble.

As a last step, **proofread** your paper. Read the paper to find any errors in grammar, spelling, mechanics, or punctuation.

Finally, remember that the writing process is flexible. You do not move through the stages of the process in a rigid, lockstep fashion. Instead, you will move back and forth between the stages, perhaps going back to prewrite for some more material after you have revised or rewriting a paragraph that you have just drafted.

You *do* need to discover the best way for *you* to prewrite, draft, and revise. Some people spend more time prewriting than others; some people spend more time drafting and revising. There is no one right way. As you continue to refine your composition skills, you need to develop your own individual method.

Chapter **2** Introduction to the Paragraph

Theme

Introduction to the Paragraph

Goals

Writing

To restrict the topic of a paragraph

To formulate and improve the topic sentences of paragraphs

To develop a paragraph with supporting information and ideas

To revise paragraphs to increase unity and coherence

Reading

To recognize the topic and topic sentence of a paragraph

Getting Started

Journal Writing: Choose one of the following two questions, and write about it in your journal.

1. How do you react to comments that teachers and peers make about your writing? How do you feel when a paper is returned to you with comments? Pleased? Disappointed? Motivated to improve? Can you usually use these comments to make your writing better or not?
2. Was your first impression of your college campus or classroom positive or negative? What appealed to you? What concerned you? Do you think your first impressions were accurate?

CNN® Video Activity: "Learning to Read and Write"

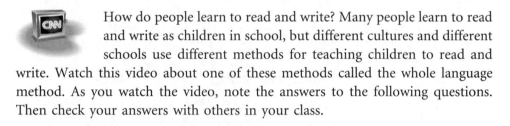 How do people learn to read and write? Many people learn to read and write as children in school, but different cultures and different schools use different methods for teaching children to read and write. Watch this video about one of these methods called the whole language method. As you watch the video, note the answers to the following questions. Then check your answers with others in your class.

1. Make a list of the different ways children in this class are learning to improve their reading and writing skills.
2. How are these methods similar to and different from the methods used by your teachers when you were a child learning to read and write?
3. What do you think are the advantages of the whole language method of improving your language as compared with more traditional methods of learning?

Video Follow-up: Discussion Questions
After you have watched the video, use your notes to help you think about the following questions. Discuss your opinions with your teacher and your classmates.

1. How do you think adults and children learn to read and write differently?
2. Which of the methods described in this video and in your notes might be useful to you and your classmates as adults who are trying to improve your reading and writing? What other methods might be useful?
3. Which of these methods do you think works better for children than for adults? Why?

What is a Paragraph?

What is a paragraph? You probably know that a paragraph is a group of sentences and that the first sentence of this group is indented; that is, it begins a little bit more to the right of the margin than the rest of the sentences in this group. But it is not enough to say that a paragraph is a group of sentences. How do these sentences relate to each other? How does a paragraph begin and where does it end? What constitutes a good paragraph? These are the questions we answer in this first unit.

The Topic of a Paragraph

To begin with, a *paragraph* is defined as a group of sentences that develops one main idea; in other words, a paragraph develops a topic. A *topic* is the subject of the paragraph; it is what the paragraph is about. Read the following paragraph, which is *about* the habit of smoking cigarettes.

> Smoking cigarettes can be an expensive habit. Considering that the average price per pack of cigarettes is about $2.50, people who smoke two packs of cigarettes a day spend $5 per day on their habit. At the end of one year, these smokers have spent at least $1,825.00. But the price of cigarettes is not the only expense cigarette smokers incur. Since cigarette smoke has an offensive odor that permeates clothing, stuffed furniture, and carpeting, smokers often find that these items must be cleaned more frequently than those of nonsmokers. Although it is difficult to estimate the cost of this additional expense, one can see that this hidden expense does contribute to making smoking an expensive habit.

EXERCISE 2·1   Study the following paragraphs to find their topics. Write the topic for each paragraph in the space provided.

1. A final examination in a course will give a student the initiative to do his or her best work throughout the course. Students who are only taking notes and attending classes in order to pass a few short tests will not put forth their best effort. For instance, some of my friends in drama, in which there is no final examination, take poor notes, which they throw away after each short test. Skipping classes also becomes popular. Imagine the incredible change a final examination would produce. Students would have to take good notes and attend all classes in order to be prepared for the final examination.

   —*Suzanne Gremillion*

   This paragraph is about _____.

2. Another reason why I like the beach is its solitary atmosphere. At the beach, I have no witness but the beach, and I can speak and think with pleasure. No one can interrupt me, and the beach will always be there to listen to everything I want to say. In addition, it is a quiet place to go to meditate. Meditation requires solitude. Many times when I am confused about something, I go to the beach by myself and find that this is the best place to resolve my conflicts, solve problems, and think.

—*M. Veronica Porta*

This paragraph is about _____.

3. Weird stuff seems to go with major comets. When a comet appeared in A.D. 60, the people of Rome assumed it meant the impending death of their still new emperor, Nero. He responded by exiling a potential rival. When another comet turned up just four years later, ancient historians say he ordered the execution of dozens of nobles. It is said that Moctezuma II saw a comet in 1517 that foreshadowed the downfall of the Aztec empire. In 1910, a wave of hysteria swept over the United States amid reports that Earth was about to pass through Halley's tail.

—William R. Newcott, "The Age of Comets."
National Geographic, 192: 6 December 1997. p. 105.

This paragraph is about _____.

4. When we make attributions about ourselves or about others, we tend to attribute the behavior in question to either *internal* or *external* forces. When you see someone crash his car into a telephone pole, you can attribute that unfortunate piece of behavior either to internal or external causes. You might conclude that the person is a terrible driver or emotionally upset (internal causes), or you might conclude that another car forced the driver off the road (external cause). If you fail an exam, you can attribute it to internal causes such as stupidity or a failure to study, or you can attribute it to external causes such as an unfair test or an overheated room.

—John P. Houston, *Motivation* (New York: Macmillan, 1985), p. 255.

This paragraph is about _____.

Prewriting: Planning

Although sometimes you are assigned topics to write about, often these topics are too general to be developed adequately in one paragraph. Therefore, you will need to *restrict* your topic: that is, you will need to narrow down your topic to a more specific one. Suppose, for example, that you are asked to write about your favorite place, and you choose a country such as Mexico. Although you could easily write several sentences naming all the things you like about Mexico, it would be more interesting for your reader if you narrowed down the topic *Mexico* to a particular place in Mexico, such as the Great Temple in the Aztec ruins. Your topic should be narrowed down as much as possible. Look at how the topic *Mexico* is narrowed here:

Of course, there are many other ways to narrow the same topic. For example:

Now let us suppose that you are asked to write a paragraph about drugs. Obviously, the topic *drugs* is far too broad for specific development in one paragraph; the topic needs to be narrowed down, or restricted. Observe here how the topic *drugs* can be restricted:

D R U G S

Marijuana

Effects of Smoking Marijuana

Effect on Memory

This paragraph, then, will discuss *one* of the effects of smoking marijuana: memory loss. Like most topics, this one can be narrowed down in several ways. Observe:

M A R I J U A N A

Reasons People Smoke It

Peer Pressure As a Reason

This paragraph will discuss one of the reasons people smoke marijuana: peer pressure.

EXERCISE 2·2   Fill in each line that follows by narrowing down the topics given. For the last one, select your own topic, and then narrow it down.

1. _____ Cigarettes _____

   _____ Effects of Smoking Cigarettes _____

   _____ Effects on Health _____

   _____ Effects on Lungs _____

2. _____ Cigarettes _____

   _____ Cigarette Smokers _____

_____ Types of Cigarette Smokers _____

_____

3. _____ Technology _____

_____ Computers _____

_____ Three Uses of Computers _____

_____

4. _____ Fatal Diseases _____

_____ Cancer _____

_____

_____

5. _____ My Hometown _____

_____

_____

_____

6. _____

_____

_____

_____

The Topic Sentence

The topic of a paragraph is usually introduced in a sentence; this sentence is called the *topic sentence*. However, the topic sentence can do more than introduce the subject of the paragraph. A good topic sentence also serves to state an idea or an attitude about the topic. This idea or attitude about the topic is called the *controlling idea*; it controls what the sentences in the paragraph will discuss. All sentences in the paragraph should relate to and develop the controlling idea. To illustrate, let us look at the following topic sentence to identify the topic and the controlling idea:

Smoking cigarettes can be an expensive habit.

In this sentence, the topic is the *habit of smoking cigarettes*; the controlling idea is that smoking can be *expensive*. A paragraph that develops this topic sentence should demonstrate that smoking cigarettes can indeed be an expensive habit. Reread the paragraph on page 13 and see if it develops the idea of *expensive*.

Of course, there are many other controlling ideas one could have about the topic of smoking cigarettes. Indeed, one of the most popular is that smoking is hazardous to health. See how this idea is developed in the following paragraph:

Smoking cigarettes is hazardous to your health. Several years ago, a United States government study was released that linked the intake of tar and nicotine, found in cigarettes, with the development of cancer in laboratory animals. The evidence was so overwhelming that the United States government required cigarette manufacturers to put a warning on the outside of each package of cigarettes which says, "Warning: The Surgeon General has determined that cigarette smoking is hazardous to your health." Aside from the most serious and dreaded disease, cancer, cigarette smoking also can aggravate or promote other health problems. For example, smoking can increase the discomfort for people with asthma and emphysema. It can give one a "smoker's cough" and contribute to bronchitis. Finally, recent studies have shown that cigarette smokers are more susceptible to common colds and flu. Whether you get an insignificant cold or the major killer, cancer, smoking cigarettes is hazardous. Is it worth it?

EXERCISE 2·3 Study the topic sentences that follow. Circle the controlling idea and underline the topic in each sentence. Note: The controlling idea and the topic may be expressed in more than one word. The first one is done for you.

1. Another way to reduce the rate of inflation is to balance the federal budget.

2. A final advantage Martina Navratilova had on the court was her constant aggressiveness.

3. A properly planned science fiction course should include a unit on political implications.

made illegal

4. Einstein's unsuccessful attempt to get nuclear weapons banned° was dissappointing to him.

5. One of the biggest problems with athletic scholarships is that more attention is paid to sports than to education.

misleading

6. Some seeming English-Spanish equivalents are deceptive°.

dangerous

7. Another reason air pollution is hazardous° is that it damages the earth's ozone layer.

8. Savings bonds are also a safe investment.

9. Although bright, Maria is a very shy girl.

10. Another problem for students is finding a part-time job.

Improving the Topic Sentence

As indicated, a topic sentence introduces the topic and the controlling idea about that topic. However, it is not enough merely to have a topic and a controlling idea. The controlling idea should be clear and focused on a particular aspect. For example, consider the following topic sentence:

Drinking coffee is bad.

This sentence has a topic—*drinking coffee*—and a controlling idea—*bad*—but they are vague. In what way is coffee bad? For whom or what is it bad? Is drinking only a little coffee bad, or is drinking a lot of coffee bad? As you can see, this topic sentence leaves a lot of questions that probably cannot be answered effectively in one paragraph. The sentence needs more focus, and that focus can come from the controlling idea:

Drinking over four cups of coffee a day can be harmful to pregnant women.

In this version, the topic itself is narrowed down some more, and the controlling idea is more precise.

EXERCISE 2·4   Study the following groups of sentences. Circle the number of the better topic sentence in each pair. The first one is done for you.

1. There are many things that make learning the English language difficult.
2. What makes English particularly difficult to learn is pronunciation.

3. Enrolling in college is not an easy task
4. Registration at State College is a painful process.

5. *Gone with the Wind* may be an old movie, but it is still a good movie.
6. The acting in *Gone with the Wind* was superb.

7. The wide variety of merchandise makes Sears convenient.
8. The home repair department in Sears is convenient.

9. The architecture in Chicago reflects trends in modern design.
10. Chicago is an interesting city because of its history, architecture, and sports activities.

EXERCISE 2·5   Read the following weak topic sentences. Rewrite each one to make it more specific. You can narrow down the topic and/or the controlling idea. The first one is done for you.

1. The Honda Civic is an excellent automobile.

   The Honda Civic is economical to maintain.

2. My hometown is a wonderful place.

3. Many improvements are needed at this school.

4. Exercise is good for you.

5. Driving a car can be hazardous.

6. Computers are useful.

_____

7. There are many interesting things to do at the park.

_____

8. Watching television is bad for you.

_____

Recognizing the Topic Sentence

A topic sentence, then, serves to introduce the topic and the controlling idea. But where should the topic sentence be placed in the paragraph? Generally, because the topic sentence does introduce, it is a good idea to place it at or near the beginning of the paragraph. However, depending on the kind of paragraph it is in, the topic sentence may be placed near the middle or even at the end of the paragraph. Sometimes neither the topic nor the controlling idea is explicitly stated in one sentence; this does not mean, however, that a topic and controlling idea are not present. In this kind of paragraph, the topic and controlling idea are implied; that is, they are clearly suggested in the development of the paragraph. However, it is usually a good idea to state topic sentences clearly, not only to be certain that the idea is clear but also to help control the development of the paragraph.

EXERCISE 2·6   Study the following paragraphs. In the space provided, write out the topic sentence for each paragraph, underlining the topic and circling the controlling idea. If the topic sentence is implied, write one out.

1. Another interesting area of research has to do with the distinction between intrinsic and extrinsic motivation. We are intrinsically motivated when we do something "for the fun of it," or for no other reason than to perform the behavior. We sing in the shower, not because we expect applause or because we are trying to earn money, but merely because we like to do it. We do crossword puzzles, paint pictures, and look at the sunset because it is intrinsically rewarding to do so. We don't expect any external reward. Extrinsic motivation, on the other hand, refers to situations in which we do act because we expect some external reward. We may only show up at the office because we need the money. We may only go to school to please our parents. We may be exceptionally polite to a particular individual because we want something from her.
   —John P. Houston, *Motivation* (New York: Macmillan, 1985), p. 268.

Topic Sentence: _____

_____

2. In 1944, the United States signed a treaty with Mexico guaranteeing that country 1.5 million acre-feet of Colorado River water a year. But the big division of the Colorado's precious water had occurred in 1922 under the Colorado River Compact, signed by the seven states along the river and the federal government. What makes the agreement shaky—some describe it as "a house of cards"—is that it is based on an overly optimistic estimate of the river's average flow. About 15 million acre-feet of water were originally apportioned to the states; actually, the average annual supply is only 13.8 million. In addition, the Compact did not take into account Mexico's right to any Colorado River water at all, so the 1.5 million acre-feet later guaranteed to Mexico widen the gap between demand and supply. The Colorado is, in short, overbooked.
   —Adapted from David Sheridan, "The Colorado: An Engineering Wonder Without Enough Water." *Smithsonian* 13 (February 1983): pp. 46–47.

   Topic Sentence: _____

   _____

3. Tigers are generally believed to have evolved in southern China more than a million years ago and then to have prowled westward toward the Caspian Sea, north to the snow-filled evergreen and oak forest of Siberia, and south across Indochina and Indonesia, all the way to lush tropical forest of Bali. Their modern history is admittedly dispiriting. Into the 1940s, eight supposed subspecies persisted in the wild. Since then, however the tigers of Bali, the Caspian region, and Java have vanished, and the South China tiger, hunted as vermin during the regime of Mao Zedong, seems poised to follow them into extinction; fewer than 30 individuals may now survive outside zoos, scattered among four disconnected patches of mountain forest, probably too few and far between to maintain a viable population ever again.
   —Geoffrey C. Ward, "Making Room for Wild Tigers." *National Geographic* 192 (December 1997): p. 13.

   Topic Sentence: _____

   _____

4. Anyone who saw him once never forgot his nose and his body. The first time anyone saw him, they were very surprised. The second time, they looked at his nose with admiration, as if it were a valuable treasure. His nose, which was longer than Barbra Streisand's, occupied most of his face. When he smiled, nothing but his nose was visible. He was recognized by it even in a

crowd. The treasure made one think that in his previous life he had been a collie or an anteater. In addition, his nose was as thin as a razor. If he had flown like a jet, he could have divided the clouds. His body was also very skinny. He looked as if he had not eaten for ten days. He was a heavy eater, but one couldn't imagine where he kept food in his body. Finally, on a windy day, he was blown away and gone, like Mary Poppins.

—*Nobutaka Matsuo*

Topic Sentence: _____

_____

5. We write because we want to understand our lives. This is why my closets are filled with boxes and boxes of musty old journals. It is why I found pages of poetry under my stepdaughter Kira's mattress when she went off to camp. It is why my father tells me he will soon begin his memoirs. As John Cheever explains, "When I began to write, I found this was the best way to make sense out of my life."

—Lucy McCormick Calkins, *The Art of Teaching Writing*
(Portsmouth, New Hampshire: Heinemann, 1986), p. 3.

Topic Sentence: _____

_____

6. Sometimes on Friday, our Sabbath day, my father would take us to the Old City, marked by the Bab el-Metwalli, or Gate of the Holy Man, named after the Sufi sheikh who reportedly sat there centuries before, performing miracles for passersby. For all that Cairo is my hometown, I never ceased to marvel at the sights and the exotic history that made up my city. The streets of the Old City, far too narrow for automobiles, were choked instead with the traffic of horses, donkeys, and even people laden down with loads of fresh vegetables, firesticks, vases of copper, and brass to be sold in the bustling Khan el-Khalili bazaar. Cairo had been the greatest trading center in the world for centuries, and it was here in the caravanserai of the Khan el-Khalili that medieval traders from all over the Arab world had unloaded their camel trains. It was near here also that the Fatimid sultans had kept a zoo for the giraffes, ostriches, and elephants sent to them as tribute from kingdoms in Africa.

—Jehan Sadat, from "Growing Up in Cairo,"
in *Woman of Egypt* (Simon and Schuster, 1987).

Topic Sentence: _____

_____

Formulating the Topic Sentence

Prewriting: Generating Ideas

Thus far, you have been given topics and controlling ideas to recognize and improve, but often you must find your own controlling idea. Once you have found a manageable topic for a paragraph, you need to examine that topic more closely to determine your own feelings or attitudes about it.

To decide on the controlling idea and what you want to say about a topic, begin by using one or more of the prewriting techniques for generating ideas you learned in Chapter 1. For example, suppose you are asked to write about a place in your country, and you narrow that broad topic down to a certain resort. The following is one example of a brainstorm on the topic:

> Topic: Lehai Resort
> Notes:
> - Pretty sandy beaches, palm trees along the shore, clear turquoise water, gorgeous mountains
> - Tourists swarming everyplace, new hotels cropping up every month; one hotel blocks the view of the sea from the road, many tourist shops
> - Resort provides many jobs, brings in $1 million in revenue from tourists, has attracted some new companies to the city

The list could, of course, be expanded. Once you have brainstormed your ideas, look through the list for something striking. For example, you might realize that the resort has provided economic benefits to the local area. Or, you might find that you want to write about the beauty of the resort area. Several ideas could emerge from this brainstorming session. Here are a few:

> Lehai Resort is set in one of the most scenic coastal areas in the world.
> Lehai Resort has been ruined by the excessive influx of tourists.
> Lehai Resort has brought direct and indirect economic benefits to our area.

EXERCISE 2·7   Choose one of the following topics or one of your own and brainstorm the topic. After writing everything that comes to mind on the topic, sort through the list and choose an idea that interests you. Write a topic sentence that has a controlling idea. In the space provided, write your topic sentence, underline the topic and circle the controlling idea. If necessary, narrow the topic down further. If your teacher suggests, you may repeat this process for another one of the topics.

superstitions	pollution
an interesting custom	your major
a memorable teacher	an important decision

_____

_____

_____

_____

Support

Prewriting: Planning

Once you have generated ideas and formulated a controlling idea about your topic, the next step is to extract from your prewriting notes the material you can use to develop the paragraph. This material is used to support the opinion or attitude expressed in your topic sentence. It serves to back up, clarify, illustrate, explain, or prove the point you make in your topic sentence. Most often we use factual detail to support a point. Such detail may include facts from resource material, such as magazines, journals, and books, or details about things you or others have observed. Basically, support comes from the information you used to arrive at the view you have expressed in your topic sentence.

When you are examining your notes to find support for your topic sentence, you may find it necessary to add material to your notes. Let's take as an example the topic sentence "Lehai Resort has nearly solved our local employment problem." From the notes on this topic, we might extract "Lehai Resort provides many jobs" and "has attracted some new companies to the city." These two bits of information can serve as the basis for more notes and support. To generate more notes at this stage, you may find it useful to ask WH- questions (see Chapter 1, p.6), such as "What are the companies that have opened up? How many jobs have they brought to our city? How else has the resort provided jobs? What are those jobs? What was the employment situation before the resort opened? What is the employment rate now?" The answers to these questions will serve as a foundation for the support for your paragraph. Your revised notes might be as follows:

> Unemployment rate in 1990 = 35%; in 2000 = 8%
> Hotel jobs: Statler Hotel, 100
>   Modern Inn, 50
>   New Wave Spa, 35
> Five new shops on Beach Highway for tourists—15 new jobs
> New companies (since 1992):
>   Jones Batiking
>   Mary's Dollworks
>   Julio's Tour Guide Service

J & M Corporation
Menk's Manufacturing Company

Now you are ready to write the support out as sentences and list them under your topic sentence in outline form, grouping related details together. For example, for the Lehai Resort example, your paragraph outline might look like this:

Topic Sentence:
Lehai Resort has nearly solved our local employment problem.

Support:

1. The unemployment rate has dropped from 35% in 1990 to 8% in 2000.
2. The tourist industry has created many jobs.
   a. Three new hotels have opened up.
      1) The Statler Hotel employs 100 local residents.
      2) The Modern Inn hired 50.
      3) The New Wave Spa has 35 new workers.
   b. Five new shops have opened on Beach Hwy., for a total of 15 jobs.
   c. Tourist-related industries have opened up: Jones Batiking, Mary's Dollworks, and Julio's Tour Guide Service.
3. The resort has attracted two nontourist companies: J & M Corp. and Menk's Mfg. Co.

Such an outline is useful in two ways: It provides a means for quickly checking your sentences to see if they deal with the topic, and it serves as a guide for checking whether the sentences are logically arranged. Here is an outline of the paragraph on page 13:

Topic Sentence:
Smoking cigarettes can be an expensive habit.

Support:

1. Cigarettes cost about $2.50.
2. The average smoker smokes two packs a day.
3. The annual expense for this smoker is $1,825.00.
4. The smoker must also pay for extra cleaning of carpeting, furniture, and clothes.

Obviously, not all the sentences in the original paragraph are listed or recorded verbatim. For example, the sentence "But the price of cigarettes is not the only expense cigarette smokers incur" is omitted here. This sentence certainly relates to the topic and the controlling idea, but its main function is to provide a link in the sentences; it joins the section discussing the price of cigarettes with the section dealing with the hidden expense of cigarette smoking. This type of sentence is called a *transition.* (Transitions are discussed at length in the following chapters.) Also omitted from the outline is the last sentence: "Although it is difficult to estimate the cost of this additional expense, one can see that this hidden expense does contribute to making smoking an expensive habit." This type of sentence, which summarizes the main idea in the paragraph, is called the *concluding sentence.* Not all paragraphs need concluding sentences, but they are useful for ending the development of the support smoothly.

How you organize your sentences within a paragraph will depend on your topic and purpose. In the following chapters, you will learn how to support various kinds of topics and how to organize that support. At this stage, it is important to understand that the material you use to write the sentences in your paragraph should directly support the view you express in your topic sentence.

EXERCISE 2·8   Study the paragraph about cigarette smoking on page 18. In the space provided, write the topic sentence, circle the controlling idea, and outline the support given in the paragraph. Write the concluding sentence if there is one.

Topic Sentence: _____

_____

Support:

1. _____

2. _____

3. _____

4. _____

Conclusion: _____

_____

EXERCISE 2·9   Using the material you brainstormed in Exercise 2-7, write the topic sentence and circle the controlling idea in the space provided. Then study your notes and decide on relevant support. If you do not have enough support, generate more by using another prewriting technique (for example, WH- questions). Then list the support in sentence form.

Topic Sentence: _____

_____

Support:

1. _____

2. _____

3. _____

4. _____

5. _____

Unity

Each sentence within a paragraph should relate to the topic and develop the controlling idea. If any sentence does not relate to or develop that area, it is irrelevant and should be omitted from the paragraph. Consider the topic sentence discussed earlier in this chapter:

Smoking cigarettes can be an expensive habit.

If a sentence in this paragraph had discussed how annoying it is to watch someone blow smoke rings, that sentence would have been out of place, since it does not discuss the expense of smoking.

A paragraph that has sentences that do not relate to or discuss the controlling idea lacks *unity*. Note the following example of a paragraph that lacks unity:

Another problem facing a number of elderly people is living on a reduced income. Upon retiring, old people may receive a pension from their company or Social Security from the government. The amount of their monthly checks is often half the amount of the checks they received when they were employed. Suddenly, retirees find that they can no longer continue the lifestyle that they had become accustomed to, even if that lifestyle was a modest one. Many find, after paying their monthly bills, that there is no money left for a movie or a dinner out. Of course, sometimes they can't go out because of their health. Maybe they have arthritis or rheumatism and it is painful for them to move around. This can also change their lifestyle. Some older people, however, discover that the small amount of money they receive will not even cover their monthly bills. They realize with horror that electricity, a telephone, and nourishing food are luxuries they can no longer afford. They resort to shivering in the dark, eating cat food in order to make ends meet.

The topic of this paragraph is "another problem facing a number of elderly people," and the controlling idea is "living on a reduced income." Therefore, all of the sentences should deal with the idea of the problem of living on a reduced income. In the paragraph, though, there are three sentences that do not discuss this particular topic: "Of course, sometimes they can't go out because of their health. Maybe they have arthritis or rheumatism and it is painful for them to move around. This can also change their lifestyle." These sentences should be taken out of this paragraph and perhaps developed in another paragraph.

EXERCISE 2·10   Read the following paragraphs. Underline the topic sentence in each paragraph and cross out any sentences that do not belong in the paragraph. There may be one or more irrelevant sentences.

1. Since the mid-1960s, there has been a tremendous increase in the popularity and quality of Latin and South American novelists; in fact, some call this literary movement "El Boom." Mexico has produced, for example, Carlos Fuentes, who wrote *The Death of Artemio Cruz*. The 1967 Nobel Prize for Literature was awarded to the Guatemalan novelist Miguel Ángel Asturias. Argentina has given us numerous impressive writers, such as Jorge Luis Borges, Julio Cortázar, Luisa Valenzuela, and Manuel Puig, whose *Kiss of the Spider Woman* was made into a film. William Hurt won the Oscar for Best Actor for his role in that movie. Another recent novelist who has impressed the world is Chile's Isabelle Allende (*The House of the Spirits*). The list could go on, but probably the biggest name associated with this movement is Gabriel García Márquez, a Colombian whose enormously popular *One Hundred Years of Solitude*, published in 1967, helped him earn the 1982 Nobel Prize for Literature.

2. One of the most acclaimed and beloved of Japanese animators is Hayao Miyazaki, whose *Nausicaa of the Valley of Wind* (given the more comfortable English title *Warriors of the Wind* . . .) was a hauntingly beautiful fable about ecology, the power of love, and hope. The same director made the enchanting children's fantasy *My Neighbor Totoro*, the story of two young country girls and their encounters with forest spirits and other odd entities. Miyazaki's evocation of an ethereal countryside, a Japan of quiet beauty that seemed to some no longer to exist, brought many an adult viewer to tears of nostalgia and regret. This surprises some people who think that animation is only for children.

   —Adapted from: Lee Server, "Anime," *Asian Pop Cinema* (1999), p. 88.

3. The most obvious problem with being unemployed is not having the money you need for daily life. Most people need money just for the necessities—paying the rent and buying food. And even though buying clothes may not be a necessity, it is still important. If you don't have a job, who is going to give

you the money for rent and food? Maybe you have an uncle or a cousin who will let you borrow a little bit of money for a month or two, but most people can't afford to pay for other people's rent. So, if you don't have a job, you will have trouble paying the rent and buying food.

4. I would not want to live to be 500 years old if I was the only really old person, if everyone else died at the normal time. One reason is that people would always keep coming to me and asking questions about the past. They would want to know when this happened and that happened and did such-and-such really happen. They would keep bothering me. I think now sometimes old people do not like being bothered. The other reason is that it would be too sad. If everyone else died at the normal time, I would have to watch all my friends and family die. I would not want to see my children die or my grandchildren. I would be like a freak.

Coherence

We have seen that a paragraph must have a topic and controlling idea, support, and unity. Another element that a paragraph needs is *coherence*. A coherent paragraph contains sentences that are logically arranged and that flow smoothly.

Logical arrangement refers to the order of your sentences, which varies depending on your purpose. For example, if you want to describe what happens in a movie (that is, the plot), your sentences would follow the sequence of the action in the movie, from beginning to end—in that order. If, on the other hand, you want to describe the most exciting moments in the movie, you would select a few moments and decide on a logical order for discussion—perhaps presenting the least exciting moments first and the most exciting last to create suspense. (In the following chapters, we study the various principles for ordering ideas and sentences.)

A paragraph can be incoherent even when the principle for ordering the ideas is logical. Sometimes, as students are writing, they remember something that they wanted to say earlier and include it as they write. Unfortunately, this sentence often ends up out of place. Study the following paragraph, in which one or more sentences are out of order:

Although Grants Pass, Oregon, is a fairly small town, it offers much to amuse summer visitors. They can go rafting down the Rogue River. They can go swimming in the Applegate River. Lots of people go hunting for wild berries that grow along the roadsides. Campers will find lovely campgrounds that are clean. There are several nice hotels. Tourists can browse through a number of interesting shops in town, such as antique stores. One fun activity is shopping at the open market where local folks sell produce grown in their gardens. Grants Pass has a lot of places to eat, ranging from a low-calorie dessert place to lovely restaurants. Some of these restaurants offer good food and gorgeous views. One store to visit is the shop that sells items made from Oregon's beautiful myrtlewood. Fishing in the area is also a popular activity. Water sports are by far the main attraction. As you can see, Grants Pass offers a lot to do in the summer. If you want to give your family a nice, wholesome vacation, try visiting Grants Pass.

The paragraph seems to have a principle of organization: The first half is devoted to activities in the areas just outside of the city itself, and the last half discusses activities within the city. However, toward the end of the paragraph, the writer seems to throw in a few sentences as an afterthought. Three sentences—"One store to visit is the shop that sells items made from Oregon's beautiful myrtlewood," "Fishing in the area is also a popular activity," and "Water sports are by far the main attraction"—are out of place. This paragraph could be revised as follows:

Although Grants Pass, Oregon, is a fairly small town, it offers much to amuse summer visitors. Water sports are by far the main attraction. Visitors can go rafting down the Rogue River. They can go swimming in the Applegate River. Fishing in the area is a popular activity. Lots of people go hunting for wild berries that grow along the roadsides. Campers will find lovely campgrounds that are clean. There are several nice hotels. Tourists can browse through a number of interesting shops in town, such as antique stores. One store to visit is the shop that sells items made from Oregon's beautiful myrtlewood. One fun activity is shopping at the open market where local folks sell produce grown in their gardens. Grants Pass has a lot of places to eat, ranging from a low-calorie dessert place to lovely restaurants. Some of these restaurants offer good food and gorgeous views. As you can see, Grants Pass offers a lot to do in the summer. If you want to give your family a nice, wholesome vacation, try visiting Grants Pass.

The order of the sentences in this revised version is improved, but it is still not completely coherent, for the sentences do not always flow smoothly.

Smooth flow refers to how well one idea or sentence leads into another. Smooth flow can be achieved through sentence combining and through the use of certain expressions, called transitions, that provide the links between ideas. Some transitional expressions include *for example, to begin with, in contrast, however, also,* among many others that we will cover throughout this text. Note how the addition of some expressions and the combining of some sentences improve the coherence of this paragraph:

> Although Grants Pass, Oregon, is a fairly small town, it offers much to amuse summer visitors. Water sports are by far the main attraction. Visitors can go rafting down the Rogue River or swimming in the Applegate River. Fishing in the area is *another* popular activity. Lots of people also go hunting for wild berries that grow along the road-sides. *In addition,* there are lovely, clean campgrounds where campers can park their vehicles. *For those who prefer to stay in town,* Grants Pass offers several nice hotels. In town, tourists can browse through a number of interesting shops, such as antique stores and the shop that sells items made from Oregon's beautiful myrtlewood. *Another* fun activity is shopping at the open market where local folks sell produce grown in their gardens. *And finally,* Grants Pass has a lot of places to eat, ranging from a low-calorie dessert place to lovely restaurants, some of which offer good food and gorgeous views. As you can see, Grants Pass offers a lot to do in the summer. If you want to give your family a nice, wholesome vacation, try visiting this charming town.

The expressions *another, also, in addition, and finally* bridge the gaps in ideas. Some of the sentences have been combined as well. Combining sentences and adding transitions make the ideas and sentences easier to follow.

If the sentences are not logically arranged or if they do not connect with each other smoothly, the paragraph is *incoherent*. Coherence is an important quality of writing.

EXERCISE 2·11   Study each of the following paragraphs, in which one or more sentences are out of order. Revise these paragraphs for greater coherence by arranging the sentences in logical order.

1. In the hotel business, computers ease the load at the front desk. With a computer, a clerk can make a reservation easily and quickly, without the use of cards, racks, or registration books. So when guests come in to register, their reservations can be checked, and they can be given available rooms without much fuss or bother. The hotel business is just one type of enterprise that has profited by the invention of computers. And with a computer, the clerk can get an instant update of the room status. This tells the clerk which rooms are available to guests.

2. Political conventions in America attract all kinds of people besides dele-gates. You are sure to see an artist or two doing chalk portraits of the

candidates on the sidewalks. Groups who wish to attract attention to their political and social causes demonstrate outside the convention halls. The pro-life people,° the pro-choice people,° the supporters of nuclear energy, those against nuclear energy, and the pro-gays and anti-gays are probably the most common groups. Others just like to poke fun at the candidates. For instance, at most conventions you will find at least a couple of people wearing masks of their favorite or least favorite candidates. Others dress in costumes and carry signs with outrageous° comments about the candidates or the political process. Another social-political group is the one advocating more civil rights and better economic opportunities for minorities. No matter who they are or what their reasons are for going to the conventions, these people always add color to the sometimes boring conventions.

people who want abortion to be illegal

people who want abortion to be legal

ridiculous, incredible

3. An example of this kind of prejudice happened to me when I was in the fourth grade. I remember one time when all the students were being allowed to choose a book they wanted to read. When it was my turn to choose a book, she laughed at me and said, "Oh, that one is too hard for you. I'll choose one for you." I was so embarrassed. I thought that she should not embarrass me in front of the class like that. My teacher treated me as if I was about two grade levels below my classmates. My family had just moved here from California, and she did not think I was up with the rest of my class.

EXERCISE 2·12 Study the following paragraphs, which lack both unity and coherence. For each paragraph, rearrange the sentences for coherence and omit any sentences that do not belong.

1. First of all, teenagers work for their own current expenses. For example, my cousin Celia works at a clothing store and buys all her own clothes. Last week, she bought herself a nice leather jacket. And one of my friends bought himself a used car just from the money he made after school. Young people want to make money for their future. Young people want to buy clothes, and they want to save money to buy a car or a stereo or a television. An example of this is saving money for an education after high school. My cousin Robert is doing this for his future. He also told me that he is saving some money to set up a household after marriage.

2. The driving lesson I got from my fiancé was a very distressing one. I started off very well until my fiancé started getting bossy. I did one wrong thing so he started shouting at me. The little incident occurred when he wanted me to make a U-turn in the middle of the street. As I was trying to do that, I turned the wheels too hard and the wheels hit the end of the curb. My fiancé started yelling at me as if he were crazy. So I calmly put the car in park and

started to get out to let him drive since I obviously wasn't doing it the way he wanted. But he grabbed my arm and told me to finish getting the car out of the middle of the street. Oh, I forgot to tell you that when the tires hit the curb, the car stopped in the middle of the street. I guess that was why he was worried. My fiancé also tried to teach me to play tennis and he shouted at me then, too. He also wanted me to move the car because there were cars coming in both directions. I decided after this incident that my fiancé was not the right person to teach me to drive.

3. The way women are shown in TV commercials today has changed compared with 20 years ago. Twenty years ago, commercials mostly showed women as brainless housewives. In those commercials, women were concerned about getting the best laundry detergents, the softest toilet paper, or the tastiest soup. They were portrayed as sort of dumb and silly, as if the most important thing in the world was getting hamburger on sale. Women in commercials today are not just housewives. They are shown as professional working people, too. For example, in one telephone commercial, a woman with a briefcase is saying goodbye to her child and husband as she is about to catch a plane. In commercials today, women are shown as housewives, but they are not portrayed as so dumb. For example, the woman in the Dristan commercial I saw last night seemed like a normal, intelligent person. I think the same difference is true for ads in magazines.

Internet Activity: Composition Skills and the Internet

 Do you need more help with topic sentences, paragraph support, unity, or coherence? There are many Online Writing Labs (OWLs) on the Internet which offer additional advice and practice with these and other composition skills. Find out if your school has an OWL. If it doesn't, do a keyword search for "online writing labs" or visit the OWL at Purdue University at http://owl.english.purdue.edu/.

EXERCISE 2·13 Writing Assignment   Write a paragraph using the topic sentence and support you developed in Exercise 2-9. After you write the paragraph, consult the checklist at the end of the chapter.

EXERCISE 2·14 Assignments from the Disciplines   Following are some topics which are typical of writing assignments in college-preparation or college success classes. Use one of the prewriting techniques you learned in Chapter 1 to generate ideas and support. Then, decide on a controlling idea and choose the details that will support it. Finally, write the paragraph.

1. Many students feel anxious before a test. Write a paragraph describing what students can do to combat test anxiety.
2. Choose a major or profession you have chosen or in which you are interested. Write a paragraph explaining what one skill or quality is most important for success in this major or profession.

Composition Skills

Revision

Peer Review
When you have finished writing the first draft of your paragraph, give it to a classmate to read and review. Use the peer review checklist in Appendix I to respond to each other's drafts.

Revision Checklist for the Paragraph
Use these questions to help you to give suggestions to your peers and to revise your essay.

1. Is your topic sufficiently narrowed down?
2. Does your paragraph have a topic sentence? If not, is the topic sentence implied?
3. Does your paragraph have a clear, focused controlling idea?
4. Is your paragraph unified; that is, do all of the sentences support the controlling idea?
5. Is your paragraph coherent; that is, are the sentences logically arranged and do they flow smoothly?

Chapter **3** The Narrative Paragraph

Theme

Personal Reflections

Goals

Writing

To write a narrative paragraph

To organize ideas using chronological development

To write a topic sentence with a strong controlling idea

To manipulate supporting sentences to convey an attitude

To increase coherence through adverbial clauses of time and sequence

Reading

To read and reflect on writers' personal experiences and discoveries about themselves

Grammar

To review adverbials of time and sequence, prepositions in time expressions, adverbial clauses of time, and simple past vs. past progressive and past perfect tenses

Getting Started

Journal Writing: Choose one of the following two questions, and write about it in your journal.

1. Think about an important, exciting, or humorous thing that happened to you or a friend. In your journal, tell this story.
2. What is a famous holiday or event that happens in your hometown every year? Why is this event or holiday important? What do people do during this celebration? How does the celebration make you feel?

CNN® Video Activity: "Messages for Princess Diana of England"

 When Princess Diana of England died, many people wrote poems, notes, and letters to leave at her memorial sites. Why do you think people felt a need to write about Princess Diana or write messages to her family even though they didn't know the princess or her family personally? As you watch this video, make a note of the comments made by each person featured in the video. Then, compare their reactions. How were their responses to Diana's death the same and different?

Video Follow-up: Discussion Questions
1. Do you remember Princess Diana's death? Did you have any feelings similar to those of the people portrayed in the video?
2. Do you remember the passing of any other person who was important to you? What were your feelings then?
3. Looking back now on these experiences, what are your reflections on those times?

Readings: Personal Reflections

Through reflecting on events in our lives, we come to understand ourselves and the world around us. Perhaps you remember a specific incident from childhood or adolescence that had a significant impact on you or taught you something about yourself. Through reflecting on events like these, we make important personal discoveries.

In the readings that follow, the writers recount important events that led to personal understanding or discoveries. As you read, determine what each writer discovered.

Reading ①

From "My American Journey"
by Colin Powell

In this excerpt, General Colin Powell, whose parents were born in Jamaica, tells the story of his visit to the village where his father was born, and his first feelings upon meeting his extended family.

1   We piled into jeeps provided by the Jamaican government and headed north into the interior°. We turned onto a dirt road that cut through the red earth like a gash°. Handsome homes gave way to humble cottages. The road dwindled° to a path, and we finally had to get out and walk. We had been on foot for about fifteen minutes when, out of nowhere, the "custus"—the local government head—and the police chief and several other officials appeared and greeted our party. We walked behind them across gently rising fields to a crest, then started down a rutted° trail into a small valley where something quite magical happened. People seemed to emerge out of nowhere. Soon, about two hundred people surrounded us, young and old, some colorfully dressed, some in tatters,° some with shoes, some barefoot. All at once, the air was filled with music. A band appeared, youngsters in black uniforms playing "The Star-Spangled Banner."

2   "The children are from the school your father attended," the custus informed me. The musicians then shifted to calypso tunes as familiar to me as our national anthem. The crowd began clapping, reaching out to Alma and me, taking our hands, smiling and greeting us. From a distance, a smaller group started toward us. The crowd parted to let them pass. I was choked with emotion. This was my family. No one needed to tell me. Some I had met before. As for the others, it was in their faces, in their resemblance to each other, in their resemblance to me. We had arrived at Top Hill, land of my father's birth. They embraced me and started introducing themselves, Aunt Ivie Ritchie, Cousin Muriel, Uncle Claude, Cousin Pat, in a blur of faces and family connections.

the center of the island
a deep cut
became smaller and smaller

having lots of holes

old, worn out clothing

EXERCISE 3·1 Comprehension/Discussion Questions

1. Why did General Powell and his wife, Alma, visit Top Hill, Jamaica?
2. What happened during their trip to Top Hill? Tell the story.
3. How far does General Powell have to travel to get to Top Hill? What details from the paragraph support your answer?
4. What different groups of people greet General Powell and his wife? How does Powell react to each group?

5. How does General Powell know that the last group of people are his family?

6. General Powell says he "was choked with emotion" when he met his extended family. Why do you think he reacted this way? How do you think you would have reacted?

7. Have you ever had an experience like this? Do you remember travelling to a place where one of your parents lived or meeting your extended family for the first time? Tell the story.

8. Have you ever taken an important trip or met an important person? What were your emotional reactions? Tell the story.

9. Examine the two paragraphs in this passage. Do the paragraphs have implied or stated topic sentences? Write the topic sentence for each paragraph. Do the topic sentences you have written have controlling ideas? What are they?

Reading ②

"The Best Part"
by Mary Kay Mackin

In the following paragraph, Mary Kay Mackin reflects on Christmas holidays she has spent with her family and comes to a conclusion about the part she likes best.

look forward to

enjoying each other's company

delight in

In my family, we eat Christmas dinner about four o'clock in the afternoon. That means we spend almost all day preparing the dinner and anticipating° it; it also means that the members of my family traditionally spend this time together. When I think about it, this fellowship° is really the best part of Christmas Day for me. On Christmas morning, my parents and sisters and brothers and I have a light breakfast and open the gifts we have bought for each other. While the younger children begin playing with their new toys, my brother and I settle in the living room to talk and wait. Since we are both music lovers, we often play our new tapes or CDs or discuss the latest albums. We relish° the fact that we have nothing to do but wait for the events of the day to unfold. While we take it easy in the living room, my mother and father spend their time together cooking all the family favorites. We can almost tick off the hours by the aromas that come out of the kitchen: first, the sweet, tangy smell of apple pie, then the pungent aroma of my father's special sweet potato dish, and the rich, nutty smell of my mother's asparagus casserole. Around noon, my oldest sister and her husband with their three children come bursting in the front door. Now, there is more talking, more opening presents, more children playing with new toys on the living room floor. Pretty soon, someone suggests a walk to the park or a singalong around the piano. The activity in the kitchen increases as my father stirs the gravy and my mother

help

puts the finishing touches on the festive table setting. The rest of us pitch in°
with the last-minute jobs of filling the water glasses and pouring the wine.
Finally, the whole family sits down, my father says a brief prayer, and we begin
talking again.

EXERCISE 3·2 Comprehension/Discussion Questions

1. What is the best part of Christmas for Mackin?
2. What details does she give to support this idea?
3. Are the details convincing? Specific?
4. Does the paragraph have a topic sentence? If so, what is it? What is the
   controlling idea?
5. Think of a holiday that you have enjoyed again and again. What is the best
   part of it each time for you? Why?

Reading ❸

"The Struggle to Be an All-American Girl"
by Elizabeth Wong

In this essay, which first appeared in the *Los Angeles Times*, Elizabeth Wong tells of her painful experiences growing up in the bicultural atmosphere of Los Angeles' Chinatown. She describes the difficulty of being Chinese on the outside but American on the inside.

1   It's still there, the Chinese school on Yale Street where my brother and I used to go. Despite the new coat of paint and the high wire fence, the school I knew ten years ago remains remarkably, stoically° the same.

without emotion

2   Every day at 5 P.M., instead of playing with our fourth- and fifth-grade friends or sneaking out to the empty lot to hunt ghosts and animal bones, my brother and I had to go to Chinese school. No amount of kicking, screaming, or pleading could dissuade° my mother, who was solidly determined to have us learn the language of our heritage.

to talk out of

3   Forcibly, she walked us the seven long, hilly blocks from our home to school, depositing our defiant tearful faces before the stern principal. My only memory of him is that he swayed on his heels like a palm tree, and he always clasped his impatient twitching hands behind his back. I recognized him as a repressed maniacal child killer, and knew that if we ever saw his hands we'd be in big trouble.

4   We all sat in little chairs in an empty auditorium. The room smelled like Chinese medicine, an imported faraway mustiness.° Like ancient mothballs or dirty closets. I hated that smell. I favored crisp new scents. Like the soft French perfume that my American teacher wore in public school.

staleness

5   There was a stage far to the right, flanked° by an American flag and the flag of the Nationalist Republic of China, which was also red, white and blue but not as pretty.

bordered

6   Although the emphasis at the school was mainly language—speaking, reading, writing—the lessons always began with an exercise in politeness. With the entrance of the teacher, the best student would tap a bell and everyone would get up, kowtow,° and chant, "Sing san ho," the phonetic for "How are you, teacher?"

bow

7   Being ten years old, I had better things to learn than ideographs° copied painstakingly in lines that ran right to left from the tip of a *moc but*, a real ink pen that had to be held in an awkward way if blotches were to be avoided. After all, I could do the multiplication tables, name the satellites of Mars, and write reports on *Little Women* and *Black Beauty*. Nancy Drew, my favorite book heroine, never spoke Chinese.

Chinese picture symbols used to form words

to detach from association

sellers of goods
obscene

ordinary

confused, unintelligible speech
make an approving sound

simplified speech, usually a mixture of two or more languages

tripped over . . . stumbled in speaking

8   The language was a source of embarrassment. More times than not, I had tried to disassociate° myself from the nagging loud voice that followed me wherever I wandered in the nearby American supermarket outside Chinatown. The voice belonged to my grandmother, a fragile woman in her seventies who could outshout the best of the street vendors.° Her humor was raunchy,° her Chinese rhythmless, patternless. It was quick, it was loud, it was unbeautiful. It was not like the quiet, lilting romance of French or the gentle refinement of the American South. Chinese sounded pedestrian.° Public.

9   In Chinatown, the comings and goings of hundreds of Chinese on their daily tasks sounded chaotic and frenzied. I did not want to be thought of as mad, as talking gibberish.° When I spoke English, people nodded at me, smiled sweetly, said encouraging words. Even the people in my culture would cluck° and say that I'd do well in life. "My, doesn't she move her lips fast," they would say, meaning that I'd be able to keep up with the world outside Chinatown.

10   My brother was even more fanatical than I about speaking English. He was especially hard on my mother, criticizing her, often cruelly, for her pidgin° speech—smatterings of Chinese scattered like chop suey in her conversation. "It's not 'What it is,' Mom," he'd say in exasperation. "It's 'What *is* it, what *is* it, what *is* it!'" Sometimes Mom might leave out an occasional "the" or "a," or perhaps a verb of being. He would stop her in mid-sentence: "Say it again, Mom. Say it right." When he tripped over his own tongue,° he'd blame it on her: "See, Mom, it's all your fault. You set a bad example."

11   What infuriated my mother most was when my brother cornered her on her consonants, especially "r." My father had played a cruel joke on Mom by assigning her an American name that her tongue wouldn't allow her to say. No matter how hard she tried, "Ruth" always ended up "Luth" or "Roof."

12   After two years of writing with a *moc but* and reciting words with multiples of meanings, I finally was granted a cultural divorce. I was permitted to stop Chinese school.

13   I thought of myself as multicultural. I preferred tacos to egg rolls; I enjoyed Cinco de Mayo more than Chinese New Year.

14   At last, I was one of you; I wasn't one of them.

15   Sadly, I still am.

EXERCISE 3·3 Comprehension/Discussion Questions

1. What did Elizabeth Wong and her brother do every day after school?
2. What was their attitude about this activity? How do you know?
3. Who wanted them to do this? Why?
4. According to Wong, what kind of man was the school principal?

5. Wong compares the smells of the Chinese school with those of the public school. What smells does she remember of each? How do these smells suggest her attitude toward each?

6. Wong compares what she learns at each school. What does she learn at Chinese school? At public school? In her opinion, which is more important? Why?

7. According to Wong, what was her grandmother like? What was Wong's attitude toward her? Why?

8. What was her brother's attitude about speaking English? How did Wong's brother treat his mother when she spoke English? How do you account for this behavior?

9. Explain the problem Wong's mother had with her American name, "Ruth."

10. Wong sees herself as multicultural. What does she mean? What examples does she give to prove this? Are these examples surprising? Why?

11. Who are the "you" and "them" in paragraph 14?

12. Explain the significance of the last sentence. What is Wong's attitude as an adult toward Chinese school?

13. Wong and her brother resented being forced to attend Chinese school. Do you think their mother was right in making them go? Why, or why not?

14. Wong describes the clash of two cultures and the conflicts that can occur from it. Do you think it is possible for someone to maintain connections with his or her original culture and at the same time become an "all-American"? What does one gain or lose in becoming completely Americanized?

EXERCISE 3·4 Vocabulary Development When you read, you often do not know the meanings of all the words in the essay. Even so, you often do not look up words in your dictionary but try to guess at the meanings of the words from the context, the words and sentences surrounding the unknown word. In this exercise, you will practice guessing at the meaning of words in context.

A. Following is a paragraph from Elizabeth Wong's essay. First, underline all the words you do not know and choose five to write on the blanks below. Then read the paragraph again and guess the meaning of each word. Write in the blank what you think the word means. Finally, check with your classmates and/or the dictionary to confirm your guesses. The first one is done as an example.

Forcibly, she walked us the seven long, hilly blocks from our home to school, depositing our defiant tearful faces before the stern principal. My only memory of him is that he swayed on his heels like a palm tree, and he always clasped his impatient twitching hands behind his back. I recognized him as a repressed maniacal child killer, and knew that if we ever saw his hands we'd be in big trouble.

1. __*defiant*__   *angry, resistant* _____

2. _____   _____

3. _____   _____

4. _____   _____

5. _____   _____

B. Now use each of your words in a sentence of your own.

Writing

Present Narration

There are several ways to organize sentences in paragraphs. The arrangement of sentences and details depends on the writer's purpose. Suppose, for example, that you are asked to write about a typical morning at school. Obviously, you would not begin by telling what you do when you get home; instead, you would begin with what you do first and end with what you do at the end of the morning. In short, you would arrange your ideas according to the *time* in which they occurred. Likewise, to explain a process (how to do something), you would begin by explaining what to do first and finish by explaining what to do last. Ordering your sentences and ideas in order of time is referred to as *chronological* development.

There are principally two types of writing that require chronological development: narration and process description. (Process analysis is discussed in Chapter 10.) Although narration usually refers to the telling of a story, the term is used here to describe the relating of an experience. That experience may be in the past (past narration) or it may be a typical experience (what people usually do) or it may be going on now (present narration).

Ordering your sentences and ideas chronologically is not hard, as you know. However, it can be difficult to make your paragraph unified—in other words, to decide what to include and what to omit and to select a controlling idea for your paragraph. Imagine that you received a letter from your cousin back home who is very curious about American customs. If you lived in New Orleans, you might decide to write to your cousin about the famous Mardi Gras celebration. Your narration might begin like this:

For many, Mardi Gras day begins on St. Charles Avenue with the Rex Parade. By nine o'clock, the avenue is lined with people dressed in all kinds of costumes. At around ten o'clock, the parade begins. First there is the sound of sirens. The police on motorcycles always lead the parade to clear the street. Then a band usually marches by. At this time, the people start clapping and swaying to the music. Next come the masked men on horseback. Finally, the first float arrives carrying men in costumes and masks. Immediately, everyone rushes toward the float. They wave their hands and yell, "Throw me something, Mister!" The men generally throw beads and coins at the crowd. Then the float passes, but soon another one comes and the people do the same thing over again. After about an hour, the parade passes by and the first part of Mardi Gras day ends.

The writer has narrowed down the topic to the Rex Parade on Mardi Gras day. The sentences are arranged logically in chronological order, which is appropriate for the topic. The paragraph, then, is coherent. The paragraph is also unified; all of the sentences discuss what people do during this parade. But is the author's attitude about the event clear? Not really. The cousin back home would have a difficult time determining the author's attitude about this topic. Of course, the writer does not *have* to tell what he feels about this experience, but a controlling idea would help the reader get a clearer image of what that experience is like. The paragraph can be improved by revising it to have a strong controlling idea:

When people here talk of Mardi Gras, they use the expression "Mardi Gras Madness." This delightful madness begins for many on St. Charles Avenue with the Rex Parade. By nine o'clock, the avenue is lined with people of all ages in colorful costumes, from cavemen to Supermen. They stroll among the crowd and chat with friends and strangers alike. Some dance and some drink. At around ten o'clock, the excitement mounts as the parade begins. First there is the welcome sound of sirens. The police on motorcycles always lead the parade to make a path through the jubilant crowd. Then a band usually marches by, playing a popular tune such as the theme from *Star Wars*. At this time, people start clapping and dancing to the music. Next come the masked men on horseback. They wave and the crowd waves back. Sometimes a girl goes up and kisses one of the riders! Finally, someone usually shouts, "There it is!" It is the first float carrying men in costumes and masks. Immediately, everyone rushes toward the float. They wave their hands and yell, "Throw me something, Mister!" The men throw beads and souvenir coins to the excited crowd. Usually, they catch the coins, but sometimes one hits the ground. Then several people rush to retrieve it, pushing and shoving if necessary. Then the float passes, but soon another one comes and the madness continues in the same way.

After about an hour, the parade passes by and the first part of Mardi Gras day ends.

By adding a topic sentence with a strong controlling idea ("delightful madness"), the writer clearly establishes his attitude about the parade. In addition, the writer has changed some of the sentences and added some details to make sure that the support shows the delightful madness at the Rex Parade.

Internet Activity: Composition Skills and the Internet

 To see pictures and videos of some of the many parades that take place at Mardi Gras time, point your browser to www.mardigras.com or do a keyword search for "Mardi Gras." Look through this site, and then choose one picture or video that you like. Write a paragraph describing the picture or video you have chosen.

EXERCISE 3·5   Reread the preceding paragraph and underline the specific changes the writer has made. What effect do these changes have on the paragraph?

EXERCISE 3·6   To practice manipulating supporting sentences to convey an attitude, rewrite each of the following sentences in two ways. In the first version, assume that the controlling idea is "enjoyable." In the second version, assume that it is "awful." Study the following useful expressions. Select from this list or add other expressions and details.

Topic Sentence: Fumiki enjoys his morning routine.
Useful Expressions:

jumps out of bed	happily
leaps out of bed	cheerfully
savors the flavor	carefully puts on
sips	selects with care
peaceful	sunlight

Topic Sentence: Nobutaka considers his morning routine awful.
Useful Expressions:

drags himself out of bed	wearily
forces himself to get out	grumbles
gulps the tea down	depressing
throws on his clothes	glare of the sun
annoying	

1. He gets out of bed.

   Fumiki: _____

   Nobutaka: _____

2. He puts on his clothes.

   Fumiki: _____

   Nobutaka: _____

3. He opens the curtains.

   Fumiki: _____

   Nobutaka: _____

4. He drinks some tea.

   Fumiki: _____

   Nobutaka: _____

5. He says "Good morning" to his neighbor.

   Fumiki: _____

   Nobutaka: _____

EXERCISE 3·7 Writing Assignment Using the information in Exercise 3-6, write a paragraph about either Fumiki or Nobutaka. You should add more information to support the controlling idea in your topic sentence.

EXERCISE 3·8 Writing Assignment Using one of the prewriting techniques you learned in Chapter 1, generate material about the morning or evening routine that you or a close friend follows. Then decide on a controlling idea and write a paragraph.

EXERCISE 3·9 Writing Assignment Choose one of the following topics.

1. Reread the paragraph on page 45 about the Rex Parade. The actions described in that paragraph are typical; that is, people do these things each year at the parade. People act differently at other kinds of parades. Think of a parade that is held in your country each year (such as an Independence Day parade). Make a list of the things people do before and during the parade. From that list, think of a controlling idea about your topic. Then write a paragraph about what people usually do at the parade. Be sure that the sentences all support the controlling idea.

2. Reread the paragraph on page 39 about the best part of the Christmas holiday. Think of a holiday that you have celebrated many times. Brainstorm about what typically happens during that holiday. Then, decide on a controlling idea and write a paragraph.

Composition Skills

Coherence

Adverbials of Time and Sequence

The sentences in both of the paragraphs on the Mardi Gras celebration are arranged in chronological order. Each of the paragraphs is a short narration. A narration, as noted earlier, tells a story or describes a sequence of events. It is important in narrative writing to show the reader the time relationship between sentences and ideas; clarifying the time relationship helps to achieve coherence. After all, if any of the sentences could be switched around without any significant change in meaning, the paragraph is not coherent. In the revised paragraph about the Rex Parade, the following adverbial expressions of time and sequence tie the sentences together logically, thus clarifying the time sequence.

> By nine o'clock . . .
> At around ten o'clock . . .
> First . . .
> Next . . .

In your paragraphs, using adverbials of time and sequence will give your writing coherence.

Grammar Review

If you want further review of grammatical structures that will help you achieve coherence and grammatical accuracy in your writing, see the Grammar Review Unit. The following sections are designed to coordinate with the narrative paragraph:

> Adverbials of Time and Sequence, pages 306–307
> Prepositions in Time Expressions, pages 307–309

These sections give practice with these structures in the context of the narrative paragraph.

EXERCISE 3·10   Think of a person you know who has a job that you are interested in, perhaps electrical engineering, nursing, or teaching. Write a sentence that tells the kind of job it is. Then answer the following questions. If you can not answer the questions, you could interview the person to get the information.

Example: My friend Li Ling is a photographer.

1. Does she like her job?
2. How does she get to work?
3. What time does she arrive at work?
4. What is one thing she does every day?
5. What is one thing she does not do very often?
6. What is one thing she sometimes does?
7. What is one thing she never does?
8. What does she like most about her job?
9. What does she like least?
10. At what time does she leave work?

EXERCISE 3•11 Writing Assignment   Using the information you generated in Exercise 3-10, make some notes about your friend's job. Add any information that comes to mind. From the material, find a controlling idea. Write a paragraph about what your friend generally does at work.

EXERCISE 3•12 Writing Assignment   Write a paragraph describing a typical morning in the life of a working person in your country, such as a doctor, farmer, businessperson, or computer programmer.

Past Narration

We have been concentrating on narrative paragraphs that describe a sequence of events in the present time. Just as common, if not more so, is narration that takes place in the past. Suppose, for example, that you were asked to describe a significant moment in your life. First, sum up the significance of this moment in one sentence. Then arrange your sentences logically and include only the sentences that relate to the topic. Study the following narration and see how the sentences are arranged, if it has a controlling idea, and if it has unity and coherence.

> One summer day when I was sixteen, my friend Steve and I were taking a new shortcut through the woods to visit another friend who lived in the country. His house was about five miles away by the road, but we figured the shortcut would cut it to only three. After we had hiked about halfway, we came to a creek. We studied it for a moment, thinking what to do. It was about 15 feet wide and, we guessed, 6 or 8 feet deep; we had to either swim across or walk perhaps miles out

of our way trying to find a bridge. Steve, a devil-may-care type, quickly took off his boots and trousers, tied them all together and threw them across the creek, plunged in without further ado, and had soon swum to the other side—dripping wet, to be sure, but already needling me for still being on the wrong side of the creek. Not a good swimmer, I hesitated: How deep was the water? Could I dog-paddle across without sinking? The longer I delayed, the more energetically Steve taunted me for being "chicken." Finally I gathered my nerve, took a deep breath, and, fully dressed, jumped into the creek. The result was predictable: my boots instantly became waterlogged and dragged me down beneath the surface; I could barely move my legs and began floundering helplessly, rapidly getting panicky. Fortunately for me, Steve quickly understood the situation. As I flailed about in the water, he leapt back into the creek and dragged me out safely on the other side. Ever since that day so many years ago when I almost drowned, I have had a healthy fear of any body of water more than 3 feet deep.

EXERCISE 3·13   On a separate sheet of paper, answer these questions about the preceding paragraph:

1. Where in the paragraph is the topic sentence located? Why do you think the author placed the topic sentence there?
2. What is the controlling idea?
3. Is the paragraph coherent? Is it unified? Explain.
4. Make an outline of this paragraph.

EXERCISE 3·14 Writing Assignment   Choose one of the following topics.

1. Think of a memorable experience you have had—it could be frightening, sobering, or amusing. Using one of the prewriting techniques you learned in Chapter One, generate material on the topic. Then, make an outline (review pages 25–26) of the sequence of events in your experience. What is the point of your narration? Make the point your controlling idea and write a topic sentence.
2. Think of a time when you had to do something against your wishes. Generate material and make an outline of the sequence of events in your experience. You may wish to refer to Elizabeth Wong's essay, "The Struggle to Be an All-American Girl," on pages 41–42.

Composition Skills

Coherence

Adverbial Clauses of Time

Time sequence is conveyed by terms like *after, first, then,* and *until* followed by noun phrases or time expressions. Although these expressions help to achieve coherence in chronologically developed paragraphs, a more sophisticated technique for achieving coherence involves adverbial clauses of time.

Note how the author uses adverbial clauses of time in the paragraph about the scary experience:

> One summer day *when I was sixteen,* my friend Steve and I were taking a new shortcut through the woods to visit another friend who lived in the country.
> *After we had hiked about halfway,* we came to a creek.
> *As I flailed about in the water,* he leapt back into the creek and dragged me out safely on the other side.

To improve coherence in your narrative paragraphs, use adverbial clauses of time.

Internet Activity: Composition Skills and the Internet

 Biographies are the stories of people's lives. You can read the stories of thousands of people at http://www.biography.com/. Use the search option to find an interesting biography. Is the narration in the past tense? Is it coherent? Because these paragraphs must give a lot of information in very little space, words like adverbials are often omitted. This means that the coherence of most of these paragraphs could be improved. Choose a biography and improve its coherence by adding adverbials and adverbial clauses of time. Turn in the original paragraph with its Web address along with your rewrite.

Grammar Review

If you want further review of grammatical structures that will help you achieve coherence and grammatical accuracy in your writing, see the Grammar Review Unit. The following sections are designed to coordinate with the narrative paragraph:

> Adverbial Clauses of Time, pages 306–309
> Verb Tense Review: The Simple Past, the Past Progressive and the Past Perfect, pages 362–367

In addition to practice with these grammatical structures, you will find additional writing assignments focused on the narrative paragraph.

EXERCISE 3·15 Writing Assignment   Following are some topics for your final writing assignment. Choose one that interests you and use one of the prewriting techniques you learned in Chapter 1 to generate ideas and support. Then, establish the sequence of events in your narrative and decide on your controlling idea. Also decide if your controlling idea should appear at the beginning or at the end of your paragraph. Remember to use adverbial clauses of time for coherence. Finally, since you are writing a past narrative, decide which of the past tenses to use. With these concerns in mind, write the paragraph.

1. Relate an incident in your life when you learned a lesson or made an important discovery.
2. Think of a significant historical event that took place in your lifetime, such as the fall of the Berlin Wall, a devastating earthquake or other natural disaster, or an important political event. Write a paragraph about what you were doing on that day when you heard the news of the event.

EXERCISE 3·16 Assignments from the Disciplines   Following are some topics for your final writing assignment which are typical of college writing assignments. For your final writing assignment, you may choose one that you have studied, or consult a textbook or the Internet to find the answer. Then, follow the directions for Exercise 3-15 to write your answer.

1. From Marketing—Marketers know that when a new product is introduced, it will go through a life cycle. Throughout this life cycle, the amount of the product that people buy changes, and the product's life ends when it is no longer needed. Choose a product and write a narrative paragraph that chronologically describes each stage of this product's life.
2. From Biology—As living things live, they move through different stages that start with conception and end with death. Choose one of the following organisms and write a paragraph which chronologically outlines the stages of the organism's life cycle: (a) moss, (b) a butterfly, (c) a chicken, (d) a human being.

Composition Skills

Revision

Peer Review

When you have finished writing the first draft of your paragraph, give it to a classmate to read and review. Use the peer review checklist in Appendix I to respond to each other's drafts.

Revision Checklist for the Narrative Paragraph

Use these questions to help you to give suggestions to your peers and to revise your essay.

1. A narrative paragraph relates a story or incident. Does your paragraph tell a story?
2. A narrative paragraph presents the sequence of events in a story in chronological order. Are your ideas and sentences arranged in chronological order?
3. Does your paragraph have a clear topic sentence or an implied topic sentence?
4. Does your paragraph have a clear, focused controlling idea?
5. Is your paragraph unified; that is, do all of your sentences support the controlling idea?

Chapter 4 The Descriptive Paragraph

Theme

People and Places

Goals

Writing

To organize and write paragraphs describing places and people

To organize ideas using spatial organization

To use modifiers to make details vivid and specific

To increase coherence by using adverbials of place and adjective clauses

Reading

To read and discuss descriptions of people and places

To comprehend the details of a description, including the sounds, smells, sights, and feelings associated with a person or place

Grammar

To review adverbs of place, adjectives, participles as adjectives, passive vs. active voice, adjective clauses

54

Getting Started

Journal Writing: Choose one of the following two questions, and write about it in your journal.

1. What people have had a great influence on your life? Think of one of these people and write about him or her in your journal. How did he or she influence you? What characteristics does this person have that you admire?
2. Where do you usually study? Is this place clean or messy? Quiet or noisy? Crowded or private? Write a description of this place, and tell why you prefer to study there.

CNN® Video Activity: "Yosemite National Park"

 Yosemite National Park is one of the most frequently visited national parks in the United States. People enjoy visiting it to see its beautiful waterfalls, large trees, and beautiful natural formations. However, people who visit Yosemite will find it difficult to be alone with nature because there are so many other people visiting the park with them. As you watch the video, make a list of adjectives, adverbs, and other descriptive phrases which describe (1) the nature in Yosemite, and (2) the people in Yosemite.

Video Follow-up: Freewriting

Choose two locations near your home or your school. One should be a place where you can be alone or where you can be near nature. The other should be a crowded place with many people. Sit in each place for about 15 minutes and write about what you see. Share your writing with your classmates or your teacher.

Readings: Important People, Important Places

Our lives are filled with places, people, and events. We remember certain important places from our childhood and from our current lives—perhaps a particular room or outdoor scene. Often when we think of that place, we not only see it in detail but we also smell the smells and hear the sounds associated with it. We remember what important event happened there. So, too, with people. Certain people are important in our lives—our parents, family members, teachers, others—and again, when we think of a particular person, we see the details and hear the sounds of that individual and remember, even with just a feeling, his or her impact on our lives.

In the following two readings, Jade Snow Wong remembers a particular person, and Tom Huth describes a memorable place. As you read the selections, try to answer this question: What important characteristics do the writers remember about the people and places they are describing?

Reading

"Uncle Kwok"
by Jade Snow Wong

In this reading selection from *Fifth Chinese Daughter*, the author's autobiography about growing up in San Francisco's Chinatown, Jade Snow Wong presents a memorable portrait of her Uncle Kwok. She describes his physical appearance and his actions from the time he enters the Wong factory (which also serves as the family's home) until he gets settled at his job. As you read the selection, try to discover Wong's attitude toward Uncle Kwok.

1   Among the workers in Daddy's factory, Uncle Kwok was one of the strangest—a large-framed, awkward, unshaven man whose worn clothes hung on him as if they did not belong to him. Each afternoon around three-thirty, as some of the workers were about to go home to prepare their early dinners, Uncle Kwok slowly and deliberately ambled° in through the Wong front door, dragging his feet heavily, and gripping in one hand the small black satchel° from which he was never separated.

2   Going to his own place at the sewing machine, he took off his battered° hat and ragged coat, hung both up carefully, and then sat down. At first Jade Snow was rather afraid of this extraordinary person, and unseen, watched his actions from a safe distance. After Uncle Kwok was settled in his chair, he took off his black, slipperlike shoes. Then, taking a piece of stout cardboard from a miscellaneous° pile which he kept in a box near his sewing machine, he traced the outline of his shoes on the cardboard. Having closely examined the blades of his scissors and tested their sharpness, he would cut out a pair of cardboard soles, squinting° critically through his inaccurate glasses. Next he removed from both shoes the cardboard soles he had made the day before and inserted the new pair. Satisfied with his inspection of his renewed footwear, he got up, went to the waste can some seventy-five feet away, disposed of the old soles, and returned to his machine. He had not yet said a word to anyone.

3   Daily this process was repeated without deviation.°

4   The next thing Uncle Kwok always did was to put on his own special apron, homemade from double thicknesses of heavy burlap° and fastened at the waist by strong denim ties. This long apron covered his thin, patched trousers and protected him from dirt and draft. After a half hour had been

Margin glossary:
walked in a leisurely way
a small bag for carrying clothes, books, or other articles
worn, beaten up

having various kinds

looking with eyes partly closed

change

coarse cloth made of hemp used for making sacks

walked carelessly or idly

extreme care about details

consumed by these chores, Uncle Kwok was ready to wash his hands. He sauntered° into the Wong kitchen, stationed himself at the one sink which served both family and factory, and with characteristic meticulousness,° now proceeded to clean his hands and fingernails.

5   It was Mama's custom to begin cooking the evening meal at this hour so that the children could have their dinner before they went to the Chinese school, but every day she had to delay her preparations at the sink until slow-moving Uncle Kwok's last clean fingernail passed his fastidious° inspection. One day, however, the inconvenience tried her patience to its final limit.

not easy to please, excessively careful

convincing

6   Trying to sound pleasantly persuasive,° she said, "Uncle Kwok, please don't be so slow and awkward. Why don't you wash your hands at a different time, or else wash them faster?"

7   Uncle Kwok loudly protested the injustice of her comment. "Mama, I am not awkward. The only awkward thing about my life is that it has not yet prospered!" And he strode off, too hurt even to dry his hands finger by finger, as was his custom.

EXERCISE 4·1 Comprehension/Discussion Questions

1. What is the main point that Wong makes about Uncle Kwok? In which sentence is this point clearly established?
2. What are some of the physical details that Wong gives to describe Uncle Kwok?
3. How does Uncle Kwok dress?
4. How does he move? Find five words that describe the way he moves.
5. Describe Uncle Kwok's daily routine. What does he do first? Next? Next?
6. What is Wong's mother's attitude toward Uncle Kwok?
7. What words would you use to describe Wong's attitude toward her uncle?
8. What does Uncle Kwok's statement in paragraph 7 explain about his behavior? Does it help us to understand Uncle Kwok better? If so, how?
9. In the first paragraph, Wong describes Uncle Kwok as "strange." What makes him strange to her? What makes any person strange?

EXERCISE 4·2 Vocabulary Development   In describing Uncle Kwok, Wong uses adverbs of manner to tell about his actions. Adverbs of manner usually end in *-ly* and tell how something is done. Note these examples from the first paragraph of the essay:

Uncle Kwok *slowly* and *deliberately* ambled in through the Wong front door.

Slowly and *deliberately* tell how Uncle Kwok ambled or walked. In describing his walk, these words also help to indicate his character. Thus, they help us to understand Uncle Kwok better.

1. In the following phrases and sentences from the Wong reading, underline the adverbs of manner. Then tell what aspects of Uncle Kwok they help to convey.

    a. dragging his feet heavily (par. 1)

    b. he took off his battered hat and ragged coat, hung both up carefully (par. 2)

    c. Having closely examined the blades of his scissors and tested their sharpness (par. 2)

    d. he would cut out a pair of cardboard soles, squinting critically through his inaccurate glasses (par. 2)

2. The following adjectives all help to describe Uncle Kwok. Make them into adverbs of manner by adding -*ly*. Write the adverb in the blank provided. The first one is done for you.

    a. slow *slowly* _____

    b. awkward _____

    c. meticulous _____

    d. fastidious _____

    Now use each of the preceding adverbs in a sentence to describe a particular action of Uncle Kwok.

    a. *Uncle Kwok sauntered slowly to the sink to wash his hands.*

    b. _____

    c. _____

    d. _____

3. Wong relates some of Uncle Kwok's actions without a descriptive adverb. If she had used adverbs with the following actions, what words do you think she might have used? From your knowledge of Uncle Kwok's character, add an appropriate adverb to each of the following actions. Try to use a variety of adverbs. The first one is done for you.

    a. *tightly* _____ gripping in one hand the small black satchel (par. 1)

    b. Going _____ to his own place at the sewing machine (par. 2)

    c. he _____ traced the outline of his shoes on the cardboard (par. 2)

d. he _____ put on his own special apron (par. 4)

e. He sauntered _____ into the Wong kitchen (par. 4)

f. he proceeded _____ to clean his hands and fingernails (par. 4)

Reading **2**

From "Beyond the Sun"
by Tom Huth

In this excerpt from an article which appeared in *Traveler* magazine, Tom Huth describes Finnish Lapland as he saw it on a cross-country skiing trip one winter. In order to describe the beautiful snow-covered land he saw, Huth uses many similes and metaphors. For more information about similes and metaphors, see Exercise 4-4 after the reading.

path

piled
a picture made of small pieces of colored glass or stone
scratched
branches
in prayer

piles
moving up and down
falling asleep
short and fat

1   It's colder now. There's a rosy blush of color behind the clouds massed low in the southern sky, near where the sun might be. The trail cut a swath° fifteen feet wide through a deep evergreen forest, and I fall into the easy meditative rhythm of flatland skiing: kick-slide, kick-slide, kick-slide. It warms me up right away.

2   When the lodge is well behind me, with only the forest ahead, I at last stop and look around. What kind of magic is this? A minimalist world. Nothing but spruce trees mounded° with snow, a vast and enclosing mosaic° etched° solely in grays and whites. Candle spruce, the trees are called—tall and slender, their boughs° held close to their trunks for protection against the winter's weight, lowered in supplication.° Without a winter sun, without much wind, the snow that falls here doesn't melt or blow away, as it does back in Colorado, where I usually ski. Instead, it stays on the trees, bending the smaller ones over like so many nuns with their heads bowed in prayer. On the tops of the trees the snow clumps° into knobs that look like bobbing° human heads, like drunks falling asleep at a bar, like legions of friendly ghosts nodding off° to dreamland. And the smallest trees of all are but stubby° white thumbs lost entirely beneath the snow.

3   Without direct sunlight, there are no shadows here, no lines, no sharp distinctions. The daylight lies as a graying caress upon the soft, undisturbed patterns of free-fallen snow. It's a scene so easy on the eyes, so at peace with itself, that the skier opens wide to take it all in. Winter's wonderland discovered: the Forest White.

EXERCISE 4·3 Comprehension/Discussion Questions

1. What is the main idea that Huth wishes to convey about this place?
2. How would you describe the atmosphere of the part of Lapland that Huth is skiing through? Make a list of three adjectives which describe this atmosphere.
3. Explain what Huth means by, "I fall into the easy, meditative rhythm of flatland skiing." (par. 1).
4. What does the writer mean when he says, "What kind of magic is this? A minimalist world." (par. 2)? What details does he give to support this idea?
5. What does the writer mean when he says, "It's a scene so easy on the eyes, so at peace with itself, that the skier opens wide to take it all in."?
6. Huth describes the snow-covered trees in Finnish Lapland in detail. In your own words, describe what you think these trees must look like.
7. The author contrasts this place with Colorado, where he usually skis. How is this place different?
8. What do you think are the most memorable points of this landscape for the writer? Are these same points the most memorable for you as a reader?
9. Because the sun is never actually visible while Huth is skiing, he is very careful to explain the effect that this indirect light has on the landscape. Find five words or phrases in the article which describe the light in this place.
10. How does Huth feel about this place? How do you feel about this place after reading this description of it?

EXERCISE 4·4 Vocabulary Development

When writing a description, writers must use words to describe what they see, smell, hear, taste, and feel. The description is successful if it is so vivid that it recreates these sensations for the reader. One way to recreate these sensations with words is to use similes and metaphors to compare the thing being described with something familiar to the reader. The expression *like + noun phrase* is called a simile and is a valuable tool for descriptive writing. This expression makes a comparison between things that do not otherwise seem similar.

> *Example:* The tree wears the snow like a white fur coat.

Metaphor is a comparison that uses only the linking verb "to be," but does not use the words *like* or *as*.

> *Example:* The snow on the tree is a white fur coat that protects it from the winter.

Similes and metaphors are often used in poetry; however, you can use them in your writing, especially when you do not know a vocabulary word or when you just want to add an extra touch. For example, imagine describing someone's eyes that were green with specks of brown in them—a deep hazel. If that person had just been crying, the description could be, "Her eyes look like the forest after a rainstorm—dark green and brown and moist." Obviously, original comparisons can be overdone, but it is a good idea to try to use fresh, interesting comparisons once in a while.

In paragraph two, Tom Huth uses several similes and one metaphor to describe the trees he sees as he skis in Lapland. He also uses one simile in paragraph three to describe the effect of the light on the snow. Find these similes and the metaphor and write them on the lines below. Which ones paint the most vivid picture for you?

_____

_____

_____

_____

_____

_____

EXERCISE 4·5   Complete each of the following sentences with a noun phrase. Try to use a noun phrase that is creative.

1. Bill's outfit is quite colorful. In it he looks like _____

2. What beautiful hair you have! Your hair looks like _____

3. It's raining very hard. It sounds like _____

4. Just look at these "dishpan" hands. They look like _____

5. What an ugly car! It looks like _____

EXERCISE 4·6 Writing Assignment   Listen to the radio, television, recordings, or other people for interesting similes. Write down at least five.

Writing

Narrative paragraphs describe a sequence of events or tell a story; in other words, they describe an experience. The logical arrangement of ideas and sentences in a narrative paragraph is chronological—according to time order. But if you were asked to describe how something looks—a place, a thing, or a person, obviously, time order would not be logical. When you are describing the way something looks—its physical appearance—it is not time but space that is important. Therefore, you should arrange your sentences and details according to where the objects being described are located. This type of organization is called *spatial organization*. In a descriptive paragraph, you must make the location of the objects being described very clear.

Description of a Place

In describing a room, what should you describe first? The walls? The floor? Unlike the chronologically developed paragraph, there is no set pattern for arranging sentences in a descriptive paragraph. It is not necessary to begin with one area and then proceed to another area. Nevertheless, the sentences should not be randomly arranged. The description must be organized so that the reader can vividly imagine the scene being described. Imagine that you are describing a scene for an artist to paint. Would you have the artist paint the ceiling white and the bed blue and then go back and put posters on the walls before painting the walls? Of course not! Those directions might irritate the artist. The same applies to describing for the reader, for you are the describer with words, and your reader is the painter who mentally recreates what you are describing in the paragraph.

The arrangement of the details in a descriptive paragraph depends on the subject. The selection and the description of details depend on the describer's purpose. Suppose that your cousin wrote and asked you to describe your room. Remember that your cousin is very interested in what you think about your life in the United States. You might write your description like this:

> My dormitory room is on the second floor of Bienville Hall. It is a small rectangular room with a white ceiling and green walls. As you enter the room, straight ahead you will see two large windows with gold curtains. My bed, which is covered with a red and gold bedspread, is under the windows. On your left, against the wall, there is a large bookcase filled with books. Close to the door, a desk and chair sit next to the bookcase, with a small woven wastepaper basket underneath the desk. There are several posters on this wall. The one that is over the bookcase shows an interesting scene from our country. The one that is over the desk is of my favorite singer. To your right, built into the wall opposite the bookcase and desk, is a closet with sliding doors. Behind you on your right and somewhat behind the door, is a dresser with a mirror over it.

Examine this description. Is the location of the objects in the room clear? Are the details arranged logically? The answer to both of these questions is yes. The objects are clearly arranged and the description is easy to follow. The paragraph is both unified and coherent. But is the controlling idea about the room clear?

What impression is conveyed about the room? Would your cousin know if you liked the room or not? Probably not. To make the paragraph more interesting, you can add a controlling idea that states an attitude or impression about the place being described. After all, your cousin does want to know how you feel about your room. This paragraph could be revised to include a strong controlling idea. Read the following revised version and locate the topic sentence with the controlling idea:

> My dormitory room, on the second floor of Bienville Hall, is small and crowded. The dark green walls and dirty white ceiling make the room seem dark, and thus even smaller than it is. As you walk into the room, you are stopped short by my bed, which fills half of the room. The two large windows over the bed are hidden by heavy dark gold drapes. Against the wall on your left, pushed into a corner behind the head of the bed, is a large bookcase that is crammed with papers, books, and knickknacks. Wedged in between the bookcase and the wall opposite the bed is a small gray metal desk. It has a brown wooden chair that seems to fill the left end of the room. Stuffed under the desk is a woven wastepaper basket overflowing with paper and debris. The wall above the bookcase and desk is completely taken up with two small posters. On the right-hand side of the room is a narrow closet with clothes, shoes, hats, tennis racquets, and boxes bulging out of its sliding doors. Every time I walk out of the door, I think, "Now I know what it is like to live in a closet."

This revised version is quite different from the original one, even though both versions describe the same room. The addition of a topic sentence with a strong controlling idea has dictated not only what is included, but also how the objects in the room are described. A strong controlling idea gives the paragraph focus. Reread the preceding paragraph and underline the changes from the earlier version. These changes reinforce the controlling idea and give a clear idea of what you think about your little room.

EXERCISE 4·7 Writing Assignment   Rewrite the preceding paragraph using "comfortable" as the controlling idea in the topic sentence. Change the description to show that the room is comfortable. Feel free to add or delete details as necessary.

EXERCISE 4·8 Writing Assignment   Think of a room in your dormitory, apartment, or house. Make a list of the objects in the room. Then think about how you could describe them. What will you use for a controlling idea? Plan your paragraph and then write it.

The arrangement of the details in your description depends on your subject and purpose. When painting a picture with words, you can begin from left to right, from right to left, from top to bottom, or from bottom to top. Note how Alfred Kazin does this in the following description of his family's kitchen.

The kitchen held our lives together. My mother worked in it all day long, we ate in it almost all meals except the Passover *seder,* I did my homework and first writing at the kitchen table, and in winter I often had a bed made up for me on three kitchen chairs near the stove. On the wall just over the table hung a long horizontal mirror that sloped to a ship's prow at each end and was lined in cherry wood. It took the whole wall and drew every object in the kitchen to itself. The walls were a fiercely stippled whitewash, so often rewhitened by my father in slack seasons that the paint looked as if it had been squeezed and cracked into the walls. A large electric bulb hung down the center of the kitchen at the end of a chain that had been hooked into the ceiling; the old gas ring and key still jutted out° of the wall like antlers.° In the corner next to the toilet was the sink at which we washed, and the square tub in which my mother did our clothes. Above it, tacked to the shelf on which were pleasantly ranged square, blue-bordered white sugar and spice jars, hung calendars from the Public National Bank on Pitkin Avenue and the Minsker Progressive Branch of the Workman's Circle; receipts for the payment of insurance premiums, and household bills on a spindle. . . .°

—Alfred Kazin, "The Kitchen," from *A Walker in the City.*
Copyright 1951, 1979 by Alfred Kazin. Reprinted by permission of
Harcourt Brace Jovanovich, Inc.

*stuck out, protruded/
a deer's horns*

a pointed stick

Sometimes, though, the description can focus on some object that dominates the scene or on something that is unusual in the scene. In this case, it may be desirable to focus on that object and describe it first, since it is the first thing noticed. In the paragraph describing a room, for example, the first thing the writer describes is the first thing the viewer sees: the walls, ceiling, and the bed straight ahead.

Read the following description of a backyard and note the organization of the details. What is the controlling idea in the description?

Our backyard is dominated by a huge old live oak tree. The base of the trunk measures approximately ten feet around. The thick muscular trunk rises solidly for about 8 feet and then separates into four main branches. From these, the lower branches spread out horizontally over the ground, reaching into the neighbors' yards. The main branches continue to rise, up and up, where they compete with each other for air and sunlight. From these heights, the neighborhood cardinals and blue jays sing to each other, keeping a sharp eye out for cats. As the birds sway in the wind, they look as if they are riding a ship across a gently swelling ocean. From these heights, too, it is easy to see the variety of shrubs and sweet-smelling flowers lining the two long sides of our rectangular yard, the small walkway along the back of the house, and the back fence that runs along the alley.

Here the author describes not only what he or she sees but also the sounds and smells in the backyard. Describing what can be perceived with the senses—sights, sounds, smells, touch, taste—makes the scene even more vivid and interesting.

EXERCISE 4·9 Writing Assignment   Choose one of the following writing assignments.

1. Choose a room or place to describe. Concentrate on using several senses for your description.
2. Find a picture of a room or a house. Decide on a controlling idea and write a paragraph describing it. Submit the picture with your paragraph.

Internet Activity: Composition Skills and the Internet

 People often talk about a Web page as if it were a place; for example, you might hear someone say something like this: "My favorite *site* on the Web is the virtual museum. I love to *go* there and look at the art. It's a great *location*. You should *visit* it sometime."

Activities
1. Find a magazine or Web site that reviews Web sites. What principle of organization does the writer of the review use to describe the site?
2. Choose a Web site that you enjoy visiting, and write a description of it. What principle of organization will you use?

Composition Skills

Coherence

Adverbs of Place
Details in descriptive paragraphs are organized spatially to give the reader a clear picture of the scene being described. Clarifying the spatial relationship helps to achieve coherence. These spatial expressions are called *adverbs of place*; most of them are prepositional phrases (preposition + noun phrase). Some of the expressions used to clarify space relationships include:

on the second floor	on the righthand side	along the back of the house
straight ahead	against the wall	underneath the desk
under the windows	above the bookcase	opposite the bed
on your left	next to the toilet	from these heights
over the table	in the corner	

Here are some other expressions that clarify space relationships:

> *Behind the chair* is a guitar.
> *On top of the refrigerator* is a plant.
> The desk is *adjacent to the bookcase.*

EXERCISE 4·10   Study the following paragraph, and underline the adverbs of place. How do they help the paragraph achieve coherence?

So this was to be our home for the summer. My husband and I had rented a cabin on a ranch in Colorado and here we were. As we opened the front door of Spruce Tree Lodge, my first impression was of a dim, cool place inviting us to relax. With some lights on, I was relieved to notice on the wall in front of me the traditional white cabinets, small electric stove, and humming refrigerator that marked a functional kitchen. At least we weren't going to be doing all our cooking over a campfire! I noticed against the paneled wall to my left a small sofa made of tan naugahyde.° Even though it was not chic,° it spoke of years of comfort and service. Beside it, on a table in the corner, perched a funky old lamp made from a piece of unfinished pine. Both table and lamp were straight out of Salvation Army, but the mood they created was just right for long afternoons of reading novels. On the wall to my right were two big windows with a view of the trees and mountains outside. How glorious! We could sit on the sofa and drink in the timelessness of the mountains while the fir and spruce trees moved in the gentle lull° of the wind. In the middle of the room, straight ahead, stood a sturdy oak table with heavy, massive legs and a smooth, worn top. It would serve as desk, table, and catchall. My husband was already trying out the padded chairs, made of dark brown naugahyde, that were pulled up around the table ready for use. We smiled. Yes, the cabin would do very nicely.

imitation leather
fashionable

soothing sound

Using adverbs of place when you write descriptive paragraphs will give your writing coherence.

Modification: Specific Details
The details in a descriptive paragraph should not only be logically arranged but also vivid. As a painter with words, you want to give the reader as precise a picture as possible; otherwise, the reader will have only a vague sense of what

you are describing. To make the details more vivid, you need to modify them. (*Modify* means to restrict or narrow down the meaning.)

Nouns can be modified in three ways: by adding adjectives, by adding adjective and prepositional phrases, and by adding clauses. Each time a modifier is added to a noun, the class to which it belongs is restricted. For example, consider the word *book*. The word *book* describes a rather large class. A book can be large, small, green, old, or new; it can be a textbook or a novel. The word *book*, therefore, does not conjure up a precise image in the reader's mind. If the adjective *red* is added, then the class of books is restricted to those that are no other color but red; if *paperback* is added, the class of books is further restricted to those that are red paperback books. The class can be restricted even more by adding an adjective clause and a prepositional phrase: a red paperback book *that has a torn page in the middle.* Now the reader has a clear image of the book.

Always strive to make details specific. Vague descriptions do not allow the reader to really see the object. Specific details make your writing clearer and more interesting.

Grammar Review

If you want further review of grammatical structures that will help you achieve coherence and grammatical accuracy in your writing, see the Grammar Review Unit. The following sections are designed to coordinate with the descriptive paragraph.

Adverbs of Place, pages 305–306
Adjectives, pages 300–304
Participles as adjectives, pages 301–303
The Passive Voice vs. the Active Voice, pages 372–373

EXERCISE 4·11   Choose one of the following writing assignments.

1. Write a paragraph describing your favorite place, either indoors or outdoors. Since you are writing just one paragraph, be sure to narrow down the area you are going to write about. For example, if this place is a park, choose just one small area of the park.
2. Using the reading "Beyond the Sun" as an example, write a description of a place that you have visited. Be sure to narrow down the area that you describe and begin with a controlling idea. Try to use a few similes or metaphors to make your description richer and more interesting.

Description of a Person

In college writing, occasionally it will be necessary to describe an animate subject, such as a person, animal, or insect. For example, in a biology class, it might be necessary to describe the Cro-Magnon human or perhaps even a certain species of butterfly. In a sociology class, it might be necessary to describe a typical middle-class person. How would you describe a person? Depending on the subject or assignment, you could describe the person's physical appearance, behavior, or both. At this point, the discussion will be restricted to physical appearance, since the principle of organization is spatial, for the most part.

You can describe a person's appearance in many ways. You can tell about the person's style of clothing, manner of walking, color and style of hair, facial appearance, body shape, and expression. You can also describe the person's way of talking. Just what you select to describe depends on your topic and purpose. For example, how would you begin to describe your girlfriend to your cousin? Her hair? Her eyes? Her voice? Remember, you are the painter with words, so you want your description to be vivid, coherent—logically arranged so that your cousin can envision the face of your girlfriend. Look at the following description and see if you can get a good image of what Marie looks like:

> Marie has long black hair that falls down to her shoulders and surrounds her diamond-shaped face, which is usually suntanned. She has dark brown eyebrows over her blue eyes, which are rather large. Her nose is straight, and on the left side of the bottom of her nose, by her nostril, is a small mole. She has a small mouth, with lips that are usually covered with light pink lipstick. Her teeth are straight and white.

Is this paragraph coherent? Do you get a good picture of Marie in your mind's eye? Yes, the paragraph is coherent and the picture is clear—as far as it goes. But is the young lady attractive or plain? Does she have a regal appearance, or does she look rather ordinary? It is difficult to tell what the author's attitude is about the girlfriend's appearance; there is no real controlling idea here. In addition, the picture the author has painted with words is rather vague. Is Marie's hair curly or straight? Is her complexion smooth or blemished? Is her nose long? Are her lips thin or full? Are her teeth large or are they in proportion? Does she have an overbite? Are her eyebrows arched, or are they thick and straight? There are a lot of descriptive details the author has not included; as a result, his picture is not very vivid. Let us see how this description can be improved:

> Marie is as beautiful as any Hollywood star. Her thick, wavy, long black hair gracefully falls down to her shoulders and surrounds her exquisite,

diamond-shaped face. A golden suntan usually highlights her smooth, clear complexion. Her slightly arched chestnut brown eyebrows draw attention to her deep blue eyes, which remind me of a lake on a stormy day. Her eyes are large, but not too large, with thick eyelashes. Her nose is straight and neither too long nor too short. A small black mole on the left side of her mouth adds to her beauty. And her mouth! It is a small mouth that looks delicate and feminine. Her lips are rather thin, but not too thin; her light pink lipstick adds another touch of beauty. When she smiles, which is often, her well-formed and even, white teeth brighten up her whole face. There is nothing but extraordinary beauty in the face of Marie.

Now can you tell what the attitude is about the girlfriend's appearance? Yes, indeed! In this version, we get a vivid image of Marie through the eyes of her friend. The paragraph has a strong controlling idea—*beautiful*—and has much more specific descriptive detail than the first version.

EXERCISE 4·12 Writing Assignment   In the preceding paragraph, underline the changes the author has made. Do these changes support the controlling idea? Then outline the paragraph on a separate sheet of paper.

EXERCISE 4·13 Writing Assignment   Using the same descriptive detail as the original paragraph about Marie, write a paragraph that describes Marie as plain. Make any changes that you feel necessary.

When describing a person, you are not obliged to describe every single detail about the person's appearance. Sometimes it is better to focus on one or two outstanding features that convey something about the person's character. Read the following description of a young boy. What is the general impression you get about him from this description?

Wallace

The two most impressive things about him were his mouth and the pockets of his jacket. By looking at his mouth, one could tell whether he was plotting° evil or had recently accomplished it. If he was bent upon malevolence, his lips were all puckered up,° like those of a billiard player about to make a difficult shot. After the deed was done, the pucker was replaced by a delicate, unearthly smile. How a teacher who knew anything about boys could miss the fact that both expressions were masks of Satan I'm sure I don't know. Wallace's pockets were less interesting than his mouth, perhaps, but more spectacular in a way.

planning

squeezed together and wrinkled

round and fat
buttocks

stuck out

small tools

The side pockets of his jacket bulged out over his pudgy° haunches° like burro hampers. They were filled with tools screwdrivers, pliers, files, wrenches, wire cutters, nail sets, and I don't know what else. In addition to all this, one pocket always contained a rolled-up copy of *Popular Mechanics,* while from the top of the other protruded° *Scientific American* or some other such magazine. His breast pocket contained, besides a large collection of fountain pens and mechanical pencils, a picket fence of drill bits, gimlets,° kitchen knives, and other pointed instruments. When he walked, he clinked and jangled and pealed.

—Richard Rovere, "Wallace," *The New Yorker,* 4 Feb. 1950

EXERCISE 4•14   On a separate sheet of paper, answer the following questions about the preceding paragraph.

1. What is the general impression you get about Wallace?
2. What is the topic sentence? Is the controlling idea stated or implied?
3. Look up the following words in the dictionary and answer these questions:
   a. *pucker*—When do people pucker their lips?
   b. *unearthly*—What does Wallace's "unearthly" smile suggest that he has done?
   c. *bulge*—Where do you often find bulges?
   d. *pudgy*—Does this word suggest an ugly image or a cute image?
   e. *haunches*—Where are haunches located?
   f. *picket fence*—Draw a picket fence.
   g. *clink, jangle, peal*—Name at least one other thing for each of these words that makes the same sound.

In addition to using colorful verbs, nouns, and adjectives, the author of "Wallace" makes his description even more vivid by using similes to convey what Wallace looks like:

". . . his lips were all puckered up, like those of a billiard player."

"The side pockets of his jacket bulged out over his pudgy haunches like burro hampers."

EXERCISE 4•15 Writing Assignment   Choose one of the following topics and write a paragraph of description. Plan the paragraph carefully. Be sure you have a controlling idea that is supported with vivid, descriptive language. Try to use a comparison with *like*.

1. Review the model paragraph that describes Marie on pages 68–69. Write a description of the most beautiful or the most unattractive person you know.

2. Review the model paragraph about Wallace on pages 69–70. Write a description of a person that focuses on only one or two features. Here are some useful vocabulary words and expressions for this exercise.

FACIAL EXPRESSIONS	FACIAL SHAPES	EYES
scowl	round	beady
frown	broad	smiling
smirk	narrow	snapping
worried	heart-shaped	flashing
pained	moon-shaped	empty
blank	angular	staring
vivacious	oval	hard
delicate	flat	sad
lively		bulging
peaceful		
placid		

VOICE	MOUTH	EYEBROWS
booming	full-lipped	thick
rasping	thin-lipped	arched
squeaky	set	neatly plucked
harsh	sensuous	uneven
growling		
deep		
melodious		

OTHER EXPRESSIONS

crow's feet	protruding forehead	bony face
knitted brow		

Composition Skills

Coherence

Adjective Clauses
Chapter 3 emphasizes two ways of improving coherence in chronologically developed paragraphs: using time sequence markers, such as *first* and *after that*, and

using adverbial clauses of time. In this chapter, the emphasis has been on achieving coherence in spatially organized descriptive paragraphs by using adverbial phrases of place. Another technique for improving coherence is the use of the adjective clause.

An *adjective clause* (sometimes called a *relative clause*) modifies a noun and, like an adverbial clause, is a dependent clause that cannot stand alone as a sentence; it must be connected to an independent clause. But unlike adverbial clauses, which can be placed either at the beginning or at the end of a sentence, an adjective clause can be placed *only after the noun it modifies*; it can never be placed at the beginning of a sentence.

The subordinators that introduce adjective clauses include *who, whom, whose, that,* and *which.* Less common adjective clause subordinators are *when, where,* and *why.* Observe the use of adjective clauses in some of the passages you have read thus far:

It's a small mouth *that looks delicate and feminine.*

From these heights, too, it is easy to see the variety of shrubs and sweet-smelling flowers *that line the two long sides of our rectangular yard.*

As you walk into the room, you are stopped short by my bed, *which fills half the room.*

You have learned that a coherent paragraph is one that has logically arranged sentences and ideas; in addition, in order for a paragraph to be coherent, the sentences should flow smoothly. *Smoothly* is the key word here. If the sentences in a paragraph are mostly short and if the sentences contain a lot of repeated words, the paragraph is choppy. To illustrate, look at this description of a famous character in fiction:

One of the ugliest creatures in literature is the monster in the novel *Franken-stein, The Modern Prometheus.* The novel was written by Mary Shelley in the nineteenth century. The monster was created by Victor Frankenstein when he was a student at a university. The monster has flowing black hair. The hair is lustrous.° The monster has pearly white teeth. These fine features form a horrid contrast with his other features. He has yellow skin. The skin barely covers his facial muscles. His complexion is shriveled.° The monster has hideous,° watery, almost colorless eyes. The eyes seem to be almost the same color as the sockets. They are set in the sockets. Even uglier, perhaps, are his lips. His lips are straight and black.

shiny

wrinkled and old
very ugly

Does the paragraph have a controlling idea? Yes, the controlling idea is that the monster is one of the *ugliest* creatures in literature. Is the paragraph unified? Yes, it describes the monster as ugly. Are the sentences and ideas logically arranged?

Yes, the paragraph provides an organized description of the monster's face. But do the sentences flow smoothly? No. The paragraph has too many short sentences and too many repeated words and phrases. Adjective clauses can improve this paragraph:

> One of the ugliest creatures in literature is the monster in the novel *Frankenstein, The Modern Prometheus,* which was written by Mary Shelley in the nineteenth century. The monster, which was created by Victor Frankenstein when he was a student at a university, has flowing lustrous black hair. The monster has pearly white teeth. These fine features form a horrid contrast with his other features. He has yellow skin that barely covers his facial muscles. His complexion is shrivelled. He has hideous, watery, almost colorless eyes which seem to be almost the same color as the sockets that they are set in. Even uglier, perhaps, are his lips, which are straight and black.

By combining a few sentences using adjective clauses, some of the repeated words have been eliminated and the sentences flow more smoothly. More revisions of the paragraph can be done to make it flow even more smoothly, of course, but it is evident here that the use of adjective clauses helps achieve coherence.

EXERCISE 4·16   Underline all the changes in the preceding revised version. Do the changes improve the coherence of the passage?

Grammar Review

If you want further review of grammatical structures that will help you achieve coherence and grammatical accuracy in your writing, see the Grammar Review Unit. The section on Adjective Clauses, pages 322–327, is designed to coordinate with the descriptive paragraph.

EXERCISE 4·17 Writing Assignment   Following are some topics for your final writing assignment. Choose one that interests you, and use one of the prewriting techniques you learned in Chapter 1 to generate ideas and support. Then, decide on a controlling idea and choose the details that will support it. Finally, write the paragraph.

1. Think of a strange-looking creature from a movie or photograph. Write a paragraph describing its face or another part of it, such as its hands.
2. Assume you have a pen pal in another country. Write a paragraph to your pen pal describing your physical appearance. You might want to describe

your face, or you may prefer to describe one or two of your outstanding features.

EXERCISE 4•18 Assignments from the Disciplines   Following are some topics for your final writing assignment which are typical of college writing assignments. For your final writing assignment, you may choose one that you have studied or consult a textbook or the Internet to find the answer. Then, follow the directions for Exercise 4-17 to write your answer.

1. From Management—One of the most important tasks of a manager is to lead the company in the right direction, but not everyone finds it easy to be a leader. According to current management theory, what are the traits of an effective leader? Write a paragraph describing an effective leader.
2. From Literature—The main character of a classic tragedy is an admirable person with one tragic flaw. Choose a well-known tragic character from a novel or play and describe the character, including both the admirable qualities and the tragic flaw.

Composition Skills

Revision

Peer Review
When you have finished writing the first draft of your paragraph, give it to a classmate to read and review. Use the peer review checklist in Appendix I to respond to each other's drafts.

Revision Checklist for the Descriptive Paragraph
Use these questions to help you to give suggestions to your peers and to revise your essay.

1. Descriptive writing uses sensory details to paint a picture of a place, a person, or an object. Does your paragraph use sufficient vivid detail?
2. The controlling idea of a descriptive paragraph is often an attitude or an impression about the subject. Does your paragraph have a clear, focused controlling idea?
3. Is the controlling idea in your paragraph contained in a clear topic sentence? An implied topic sentence?
4. The details and support of the controlling idea in a descriptive paragraph often follow spatial organization or some other logical format. Are the topic sentence and details logically arranged in your paragraph?
5. Is your paragraph unified; that is, do all the sentences support the controlling idea?
6. Is your paragraph coherent; that is, do the sentences flow smoothly?

© CNN®

Chapter **5** The Expository Paragraph

Theme

Arts and Entertainment

Goals

Writing

To organize and write an expository paragraph

To use information, explanation, examples, facts, or illustrations to support a generalization

To use transitions to increase coherence

Reading

To learn about and discuss the attitudes, activities, and problems of artists from different parts of the world

To identify main ideas and support for main ideas in expository paragraphs

Grammar

To review present perfect vs. simple past tense and definite and indefinite articles

Getting Started

Journal Writing: Choose one of the following two topics, and write about it in your journal.

1. What kinds of movies or books do you like? Choose one movie or book that is your favorite and write about why you like it.

2. Choose a photograph, painting, or other piece of artwork that appeals to you. Look closely at the artwork, then write about it for 20 minutes. You may write about why you like it, you may describe it, or you can tell a story inspired by the artwork.

CNN® Video Activity: "The Artwork of Petroglyphs"

People have told stories and created artwork for thousands of years. Sometimes, we can even see these ancient art works in caves and on rocks. In this video, you will see some artwork that was created by native people who lived in North America as much as 2,000 years ago. An anthropologist will explain what we now think these symbols meant to the people who painted them. As you watch the video, try to answer these questions:

1. How old is the oldest petroglyph at this site?
2. For what two reasons did these Native American artists select this site?
3. In modern times, how do archeologists determine what a petroglyph means?
4. Why did these ancient people make these drawings?

Video Follow-up: Creating Pictographs
Think of a story from your culture or from your childhood, or use the library or Internet to find an ancient story or myth. Create a "pictograph" that could symbolize the story. Show the pictograph to your classmates and tell the story.

Internet Activity: Composition Skills and the Internet

To see more examples of art created by ancient people, do a key word search for "petroglyphs" on the Internet search tool of your choice. Choose one example which you find to be the most interesting, and write either a description of the petroglyph or a narrative telling the story you think the petroglyph might represent.

Readings: Arts and Entertainment

When we look for entertainment, we often pick up a popular paperback book or go out to the latest Hollywood movie. Chances are, the stories and images in them show mainstream American culture. However, many people, especially minorities and those from other countries, feel that these stories and images do not accurately reflect their experience. To remedy this situation, writers and filmmakers from other countries are depicting the lives and interests of people in their home countries and attempting to gain some recognition in the United States as well as at home. In the following readings, you will read about the attitudes and activities of artists from different parts of the world. As you read them, try to answer these questions:

1. What makes these artists unique?
2. How do these artists display their cultural identity?

Reading **1**

From "Survival"
by Margaret Atwood

Margaret Atwood, born in 1939, is a well-known Canadian novelist and poet. In the following reading, taken from the introduction to her 1972 book *Survival: A Thematic Guide to Canadian Literature*, Atwood describes her reading experiences as a youth. She explains that even though she was almost unaware of Canadian authors, she found delight in the few she did read.

1   I started reading Canadian literature when I was young, though I didn't know it was that; in fact I wasn't aware that I lived in a country with any distinct existence of its own. At school we were being taught to sing "Rule Britannia" and to draw the Union Jack; after hours we read stacks of Captain Marvel, Plastic Man and Batman comic books, an activity delightfully enhanced by the disapproval of our elders. However, someone had given us Charles G. D.

cried with pity
sad

Roberts' *Kings in Exile* for Christmas, and I sniveled° my way quickly through these heart-wrenching° stories of animals caged, trapped and tormented. That was followed by Ernest Thompson Seton's *Wild Animals I Have Known*, if anything more upsetting because the animals were more actual—they lived

ordinary

in forests, not circuses—and their deaths more mundane:° the deaths, not of tigers, but of rabbits.

2   No one called these stories Canadian literature, and I wouldn't have paid any attention if they had; as far as I was concerned they were just something else to read, along with Walter Scott, Edgar Allan Poe and Donald

choosing carefully

Duck. I wasn't discriminating° in my reading, and I'm still not. I read then primarily to be entertained, as I do now. And I'm not saying that apologetically:

I feel that if you remove the initial gut response from reading—the delight or excitement or simply the enjoyment of being told a story—and try to concentrate on the meaning or the shape or the "message" first, you might as well give up, it's too much like all work and no play.

3   But then as now there were different levels of entertainment. I read the backs of Shredded Wheat boxes as an idle pastime, Captain Marvel and Walter Scott as fantasy escape°—I knew, even then, that wherever I lived it wasn't *there*, since I'd never seen a castle and the Popsicle Pete prizes advertised on the comic book covers either weren't available in Canada, or cost more—and Seton and Roberts as, believe it or not, something closer to real life. I *had* seen animals, quite a few of them; a dying porcupine was more real to me than a knight in armor or Clark Kent's Metropolis. Old mossy dungeons and Kryptonite were hard to come by where I lived, though I was quite willing to believe they existed somewhere else; but the materials for Seton's stick-and-stone artifacts° and live-off-the-land recipes° in *Wildwood Wisdom* were readily available, and we could make them quite easily, which we did. Most of the recipes were somewhat inedible, as you'll see if you try Cattail Root Stew or Pollen Pancakes, but the raw ingredients can be collected around any Canadian summer cottage.

4   However, it wasn't just the content of these books that felt more real to me; it was their shapes, their patterns. The animal stories were about the struggle to survive, and Seton's practical handbook was in fact a survival manual: it laid much stress on the dangers of getting lost, eating the wrong root or berry, or angering a moose in season. Though it was full of helpful hints, the world it depicted was one riddled with° pitfalls, just as the animal stories were thickly strewn with° traps and snares. In this world, no Superman would come swooping out of the sky at the last minute to rescue you from the catastrophe; no rider would arrive posthaste° with a pardon from the King. The main thing was to avoid dying, and only by a mixture of cunning, experience and narrow escapes could the animal—or the human relying on his own resources—manage that. And, in the animal stories at any rate, there were no final happy endings or ultimate solutions; if the animal happened to escape from the particular crisis in the story, you know there would be another one later on from which it wouldn't escape.

5   I've talked about these early experiences not because I think that they were typical but because I think that—significantly—they weren't: I doubt that many people my age had even this much contact, minimal and accidental though it was, with their own literature. (Talking about this now makes me feel about 102, because quite a lot has changed since then. But though new curricula are being invented here and there across the country, I'm not convinced that the *average* Canadian child or high school student is likely to run

---

getting away from reality

items made from materials found in the woods

directions for meals made with plants found in the woods

full of

full of

immediately

across much more Canadian literature than I did. *Why* this is true is of course one of our problems.)

6   Still, although I didn't read much Canadian writing, what I did read had a shape of its own that felt different from the shapes of the other things I was reading. What that shape turned out to be, and what I felt it meant in terms of this country, became clearer to me the more I read.

EXERCISE 5·1 Vocabulary Development   Atwood uses a number of allusions and references to people, places, literature, and aspects of culture. In order to better understand the essay, try to identify the following allusions.

1. Paragraph l: "Rule, Britannia," the Union Jack, Captain Marvel, Plastic Man, Batman, Charles G. D. Roberts, Ernest Thompson Seton
2. Paragraph 2: Walter Scott, Edgar Allan Poe, Donald Duck
3. Paragraph 3: Shredded Wheat, Popsicle Pete, a knight in armor, Clark Kent's Metropolis, old mossy dungeons, Kryptonite, Cattail Root Stew, Pollen Pancakes

EXERCISE 5·2 Comprehension/Discussion Questions

1. When Atwood was young, what sense of national identity did she have?
2. What nationality were the writers Charles G. D. Roberts and Ernest Thompson Seton? What did each one write about? How did Atwood feel when she read them for the first time?
3. What was Atwood's main reason for reading as a young person? As an adult?
4. What is Atwood's opinion about reading for the "message"?
5. For what purpose did Atwood read Captain Marvel and Walter Scott? How was reading Seton and Roberts different for her? Why?
6. What do you think the book *Wildwood Wisdom* is about? Why does Atwood mention it?
7. What is Atwood's point about the "shapes" and "patterns" of Seton's and Roberts' books in paragraph 4? What was their view of life? Did it correspond to Atwood's own?
8. Does Atwood think that most Canadians have a good sense of their national literature? Explain. Has the situation changed since her youth? What influence has reading Canadian literature had on Atwood?
9. Have you had an experience similar to Atwood's? If so, be ready to explain it to the class.
10. Does the reading have a stated thesis sentence? If not, summarize the thesis in a sentence.
11. How does Atwood support her thesis? Give specific examples of support.

Reading ②

"Jackie Chan"
by Lee Server

The Hong Kong movie business has a long history, and Hong Kong films are produced on a wide variety of subjects and in many genres. However, the genre that is best known outside of Hong Kong is the kung fu film, which was made famous in western countries by the actor Bruce Lee. In more recent years, a new style of action film from Hong Kong has crossed international borders. These movies combine fast-moving action films with comedy, and they star the Hong Kong actor, Jackie Chan. In this excerpt from his book *Asian Pop Cinema* (1999), Lee Server examines Chan's acting style, stuntwork, and personality to discover what makes these films so successful.

---

very excited

enjoys

falls

driving crazily
police in old movies

protective railing
nearby

pushed inward

1   Jackie Chan's manic° optimism makes getting bones broken look like fun. He revels in° mishaps, highlighting them as "bloopers" run during the end credits, the outtakes of dangerous pratfalls° and sudden injuries and the van careening° to the hospital like a clip from a Keystone Kops° chase. Filming *Armour of God* at a castle in rural Yugoslavia, the actor took a leap from a forty-foot parapet° to the branch of an adjacent° tree—and missed. His body flew downward through space, slamming into the rocks below. A portion of the right side of his skull imploded° and his ears and nose poured blood like an open faucet. Doctors barely managed to save his life. His fractured skull left a permanent crater-like indent at the top of his forehead. "I don't do special effects," he once said. "It's not like Superman, Batman. Everybody can be Superman . . . but nobody can be Jackie Chan!"

poor

a poor boy in a
Charles Dickens novel
difficult
inability to be defeated
formed

2   Born in Hong Kong in 1954, Jackie as a child was given over by his impoverished° parents to the care of the Peking Opera Academy, a performing arts school that had much in common with Oliver Twist's° boyhood home. Under these mean° circumstances his extraordinary performing skills, agility, and indomitability° were forged.° He worked steadily in kung fu pictures, doing stuntwork and small roles, playing the punching bag for other actors, including Bruce Lee. After a few false starts Chan got one last shot at stardom, in something called *Snake in the Eagle's Shadow*, about a martial arts student and his disreputable old teacher. In this one Jackie presented himself as the anti-Bruce. The action was still dazzling and intense, with Jackie showing as much lightning speed and dexterity as Lee, but his scenes caused the audience

shake with fear

to laugh and jump in their seats rather than groan and shudder.° *Snake* was a hit, and the next one, the exhilarating *Drunken Master,* made him a superstar.

modest

3   Jackie's good-natured, self-effacing° persona, and demystified kung fu

pleasing

films irritated some fans of the genre, but most Asian moviegoers responded enthusiastically to his ingratiating° charisma. After a misstep in America, Jackie returned to Hong Kong and began producing a steady stream of huge hit films: *Project A, Wheels on Meals, Operation Condor,* etc., expanding the scope and impact of Hong Kong movies. He shifted the focus of his action films from

fighting

fights to stunts (though not without plenty of amazing Jackie-style hand-to-hand° as well), admitting the influence of the silent screen's athlete-clowns, Buster Keaton and Harold Lloyd. The canvas for the stuntwork grew larger with every film, utilizing planes, trains, motorcycles, wind tunnels, and epic car chases, such as the one that opens *Police Story*, destroying a whole neigh-

noisy fight

borhood in the melee.° They were as big as the Hollywood product, but always had that edge: no matter how elaborate the daredevil and action scenes,

putting his life and body in danger

Jackie never forgot the human factor—his own charismatic presence, front and center, risking life and limb.°

EXERCISE 5·3 Comprehension/Discussion Questions

1. What are the unique qualities of a Jackie Chan film? How are Chan's films different from other films from Hong Kong?
2. In the first paragraph, the author quotes Chan: "I don't do special effects," he once said. "It's not like Superman, Batman. Everybody can be Superman . . . but nobody can be Jackie Chan!" What does he mean by this?
3. In paragraph 2, the author compares Jackie Chan's acting to that of another famous kung fu actor, Bruce Lee. According to the author, how is Chan similar to Lee? How are they different?
4. Why did Chan's films irritate some people? What type of person was most likely to be irritated?
5. Throughout the passage, the author mentions experiences from Chan's background and other artists that influenced his work. Make a list of these influences and note how each affected Chan's style and acting ability.
6. How have Chan's films changed since his first big hit?
7. What is the main idea of this passage? Is it stated in a sentence? If not, summarize the main idea in a sentence.
8. How does the writer support this main idea? What kind of support is used?
9. In paragraph 1, the author tells a story about how Chan was seriously injured while he was filming in Yugoslavia. What do you think was the author's purpose in telling this story?

EXERCISE 5·4 Vocabulary Development Following are a number of words related to film and filmmaking. Find each word listed in the article, and try to determine

its meaning. Compare your answers with your classmates', and write out a short definition for each term.

Paragraph 1:   reel _____

                bloopers _____

                end credits _____

                outtakes _____

                clip _____

                special effects _____

Paragraph 2:   stuntwork _____

                stardom _____

Paragraph 3:   moviegoers _____

                hit films _____

                silent screen _____

Writing

The organization and content of a paragraph are determined by the topic and the controlling idea of that paragraph. A topic sentence must be supported with details organized chronologically in a narrative paragraph and spatially in a descriptive paragraph. Not all topics are best developed into narrative or descriptive paragraphs, however. Let us suppose, for instance, that you are asked to develop the topic sentence, "Going to college can be expensive." The controlling idea is, of course, *expensive.* What kind of support would you use for this topic sentence? Obviously, the topic sentence does not suggest that you tell a story or describe a scene or a person; rather, it suggests that you support the controlling idea with information, explanation, facts, or illustrations. A paragraph that explains or analyzes a topic is an *expository paragraph.* (*Expository* comes from the term *expose*, meaning "to reveal.") Although explaining a topic can be done in several ways, the most common approach to developing an expository paragraph requires using specific details and examples. (In subsequent chapters, other methods of developing expository paragraphs and essays are discussed.)

No matter what type of paragraph you are writing, you will need specific details and examples to support the controlling idea in your topic sentence. The controlling idea is the word or phrase in the topic sentence that states an *idea* or an *attitude* about the topic; this idea or attitude is frequently referred to as a *generalization.* A generalization is a statement that applies in most cases to a group of things, ideas, or people. A generalization can be a value judgment or an opinion ("Mr. Mantia is a nice person") or a factual statement ("The English language has borrowed many terms from the French").

EXERCISE 5·5 Study the following sets of sentences carefully. In the space provided, write a topic sentence that contains a pertinent generalization.

1. Topic Sentence: _____
   Support: a. Antarctica appears frozen in time, an icy world surrounded by frigid seas where winds of 100 mph are not uncommon.
   b. Temperatures regularly plunge to −100°F or below.
   c. Giant crevasses can open in the ice, swallowing people and machines.
   d. Sudden storms often blend ground and sky into one snowy blur that hopelessly disorients the most skilled aviators.*

2. Topic Sentence: _____
   Support: a. Many products on grocery store shelves are conspicuously labeled "cholesterol free."
   b. Two books, Robert E. Kowalski's *The 8-Week Cholesterol Cure* and Dr. Kenneth H. Cooper's *Controlling Cholesterol*, have been major best-sellers this year.
   c. Oat bran, which moderately lowers cholesterol levels, is selling so fast that some manufacturers are working around the clock to meet the demand.
   d. During the recent presidential campaign, doctors released medical reports with the leading candidates' cholesterol levels.

3. Topic Sentence: _____
   Support: a. Approximately $161 million were lost when lightning struck an Atlas-Centaur rocket carrying a navy satellite as the rocket rose from the launch pad at Cape Canaveral.
   b. A one-day delay in the launch of the Space Shuttle because of the threat of lightning costs $3 million.
   c. If an overnight delivery service has to clear its loading docks because of the threat of lightning, it does so at a cost of $1,000 per minute.
   d. Millions of dollars were lost in New York City when lightning

---

* Adapted from "Scramble on the Polar Ice," by Wolf Von Eckardt and reported by Walter Galling, *Time*, 22 Feb. 1982, p. 64.

caused a major blackout that resulted in large-scale vandalism and looting.

4. Topic Sentence: _____

   Support: a. Frogs live both in water and on land, so disturbances to either of these two habitats can affect the health and number of frogs in an area more quickly than that of other animals.

   b. Frog skin allows both water and oxygen to pass through, which means if the air or water is contaminated, the contaminants can easily enter and damage the frog's body.

   c. Frogs do not have protection such as scales or hair, so they are exposed to damage from the environmental factors such as ultraviolet radiation more than fish or mammals are.

   d. Frog eggs also easily absorb contaminants from the water and can be disturbed by environmental damage. Either of these problems can cause birth defects and low birth rates among frogs before other animals' offspring are affected.[*]

5. Topic Sentence: _____

   Support: a. A robotic helicopter named CYPHER can take off, fly, and land by itself; a human operator only needs to tell the helicopter where to go.

   b. A robot named IT can simulate human emotions. For example, when humans are near, the robot will smile.

   c. Engineer Jon Price has developed a robot named Sarcos which can imitate human movement when it is connected to an operator through sensors and a computer.

   d. Mark W. Tilden, a robotics expert, builds small solar-powered robots that seek out light and will even push similar robots out of the light to get more for themselves.

   e. Scientists predict that someday robotic cars will use video camera "eyes" to drive by themselves, with little or no help from the human passengers inside.[†]

Support of the Generalization

Specific Details

The topic sentence "Going to college can be expensive" should yield a paragraph that provides some information or explanation about the controlling idea—expensive. The topic sentence might be developed as follows:

[*] Adapted from Patrick Stewart, "The Call of the Wetlands." *Green Teacher*, 55. (Spring-summer 1998) p. 23.

[†] Information from Curt Suplee. "Robot Revolution." *National Geographic* 192, (July 1997) p. 76–95.

> Going to college can be expensive. Everyone knows that tuition and room and board aren't cheap, but there are other expenses that make going to college even more expensive. For instance, the cost of books and supplies is high. In addition, there are all kinds of special fees tacked onto the bill at registration time. Students usually have to pay for parking and even for adding and dropping courses after registration. The fees never seem to end.

Does this paragraph effectively demonstrate that going to college can be expensive? Although the writer mentions a few of the expenses that students must incur, the writer has not provided the reader with enough hard evidence to support the controlling idea—*expensive.* Specific details would help support this statement more strongly. Just as specific descriptive details help to support the controlling idea in a description and make the description more vivid and interesting, specific details help "prove" or support the generalization in an expository paragraph. This paragraph can be improved by using specific detail:

> Going to college can be expensive. Everyone knows that tuition and room and board can cost anywhere from $3,000 to $15,000 per term, but there are other expenses that make going to college even more expensive. For instance, books typically cost between $200 and $400 each term. Supplies, too, are not cheap, for as any student knows, paper, notebooks, writing utensils, and the many other supplies needed usually cost more at the college bookstore than at a local discount department store. For instance, a package of notepaper costing $1 at a discount store might cost $2 at a college bookstore. In addition, there are all kinds of special fees tacked onto the bill at registration time. A student might have to pay a $30 insurance fee, a $15 activity fee, a $10 fee to the student government association, and anywhere from $20 to $100 for parking. If a student decides to add or drop a course after registration, there is yet another fee. The fees never seem to end.

Instead of just referring to the expenses of attending college, in this revised version the writer uses specific details—in this case, factual details—to illustrate or prove the generalization.

In expository writing, then, the writer is like a lawyer who is trying to prove a point; a lawyer cannot make generalizations without giving proof to support his or her statements. Good proof is factual detail.

EXERCISE 5·6   To illustrate the difference in the support given in the two paragraphs about the expense of college, make an outline of each paragraph. On the left side of your paper, write the outline for the first version of the paragraph; on the right side, write the outline for the revised version. Then compare the support. For example:

INEFFECTIVE SUPPORT
Tuition and room and board aren't cheap.

EFFECTIVE SUPPORT
Tuition and room and board can cost anywhere from $3,000 to $15,000 a term.

EXERCISE 5·7   Study the following bits of information about the mythical town of Decasia, Illinois.

> January 3: Rose's Giant Boutique moves to the Town Mall shopping center.
> January 23: Heartland Department Store moves to the Town Mall.
> February 1: Thirty-six potholes are counted on Main Street.
> February 15: Fire destroys Boolie's Restaurant.
> March 3: During the night someone paints "The Killers" on four buildings.
> March 16: An "adult" (pornographic) bookstore moves into the building formerly occupied by Rose's Giant Boutique.
> April 5: The elegant Chandler Theater closes down.
> May 3: The famous Chez Pierre restaurant closes down for lack of business.
> June 15: Forty potholes are counted on Main Street.
> July 3: Bus service is discontinued.
> August 1: The remains of Boolie's Restaurant are condemned.
> August 15: Shank's Men's Clothing Store moves to the Town Mall in the suburbs.
> September 2: An "adult" movie theater opens at the old Chandler Theater.
> October 12: Three more buildings have "The Killers" painted on them.
> November 3: All of the windows of the old Heartland Department Store are shattered by stones.
> December 1: A pawnshop opens where Chez Pierre used to be.

Using the information from this list, rewrite the weak support given below and provide strong support for the topic sentence given. You do not have to use all the information provided. Write out the topic sentence and the strong support on a separate sheet of paper.

Topic Sentence:

The downtown area of Decasia is rapidly decaying.

Support:

1. Many of the stores are moving out.
2. Some of the buildings are unsightly.

3. The street is in bad shape.
4. Several sleazy places have opened up.

But support should not only be specific; it should be relevant as well. All of the supporting sentences in a paragraph should relate to the controlling idea in order for the paragraph to be unified.

EXERCISE 5·8 Study the following groups of topic sentences and details. For each topic sentence, circle the letter of the detail that does not support the generalization (controlling idea).

1. Smoking cigarettes is unhealthy.
   a. Studies have indicated that cigarette smoking increases the risk of cancer.
   b. Smokers have a higher rate of respiratory diseases such as emphysema and bronchitis.
   c. Studies have also shown that cigarette smokers have a higher rate of heart attacks.
   d. Moreover, cigarette smoke stains the teeth.
2. In the 1960s, nuclear power was expected to provide most of the additional electrical energy needed for the United States for the rest of the century. The West Coast seemed ideal for locating future nuclear power plants.
   a. Much of the coast is sparsely populated, so if a radiation leak occurred, it would affect only a few people.
   b. The urban centers requiring most of the electric power are close enough to the coast so that the costs of building power lines and transmitting electricity could be kept to a minimum.
   c. The West Coast is one of the most active earthquake areas in the United States, with the San Andreas fault running the length of the state of California.
   d. The ocean water from the Pacific Ocean would provide an efficient means of cooling a nuclear reactor—a major consideration since two-thirds of the heat generated by a nuclear power plant is wasted heat that must be dispersed.
   e. Because of the mountainous coastline, power plants could be constructed out of reach of potential floods.*
3. Polar bears are not considered to be endangered because in the 1960s, five countries worked together to insure their survival.
   a. Norway outlawed the hunting of polar bears.
   b. In the United States, the Marine Mammal Protection Act insures that only the natives of Alaska can hunt polar bears.

* Adapted from Charles C. Plummer and David McGeary, *Physical Geology,* 2nd ed. (Dubuque, Iowa: Wm. C. Brown, 1982), p. 292.

    c. In Greenland, the native Inuit hunt only 100 to 150 bears each year for food and clothing.

    d. The Soviet Union made the hunting of polar bears illegal as early as 1955.

    e. In the 1960s, Canada began research which led to a quota system designed to prevent overhunting of the bears.

    f. In recent years, poaching in Russia has increased, and researchers worry that oil spills in the Arctic Ocean may cause polar bears numbers to decrease.*

4. There are examples of behavior suggesting that animals can process information and make judgments.

    a. James Gould of Princeton University points out that honeybees, fed sugar water that is gradually moved away from the hive, anticipate where the food will be placed.

    b. Seagulls break open shellfish by dropping them on hard surfaces, flying low when their target is small.

    c. At the Yerkes Regional Primate Research Center in Atlanta, chimpanzees have been conditioned to communicate through symbols and are able to distinguish between signs that mean food and those that refer to nonedible items.

    d. The chimps also have demonstrated self-awareness. One chimp, while watching itself on a television monitor, directed a flashlight beam into its mouth, apparently curious about what its throat looked like.

    e. One of the most widely held misconceptions is that dolphins have an authentic language.†

Examples

Since factual details are not always available and since not all generalizations can be "proven," other kinds of support are necessary for the expository paragraph. The most common kind of support is *examples*. By definition, an example is an item that represents a group of things, people, or ideas. In other words, an example is a specific representative of a general category. An example of a horror movie is *The House of Wax*; an example of a tennis player is Bjorn Borg. In short, examples make the controlling idea—the generalization—clearer and more convincing and therefore are an effective means of support.

EXERCISE 5·9 Complete the following sentences, drawing on personal experiences and observations. The first one is done for you.

---

* Adapted from John L. Eliot. "Polar Bears: Stalkers of the High Arctic" *National Geographic,* 193. Jan. 1998, p. 60.

† Adapted from "Birds May Do It, Bees May Do It," *Time,* 2 May, 1983, p. 55.

1. An example of a dangerous drug is <u>*cocaine*</u>.

2. An example of a famous rock-and-roll singer is _____.

3. An example of a difficult course is _____.

4. Albert Einstein is an example of a _____.

5. Driving while under the influence of alcohol is an example of _____.

It is not usually sufficient just to name an example; often it is necessary to explain the example to show how it relates to and supports the generalization. For instance, notice the simple generalization in this topic sentence: "Tornadoes can be devastating." The topic is *tornadoes* and the controlling idea (generalization) is that they can be *devastating*. It would be insufficient to support that generalization by simply stating, "Take, for example, the tornado that hit Wichita Falls, Texas, in 1979." That does not really show that the tornado was devastating; in reality, the tornado might have caused very little damage. It is necessary to add an explanation of that example: "This tornado destroyed an entire block of homes and damaged many other houses and places of business. In addition, the tornado caused the death of several people." Now the reader is convinced that the example is relevant. The paragraph might conclude by discussing one or two more examples:

Tornadoes can be devastating. Take, for example, the tornado that hit Wichita Falls, Texas, in 1979. This tornado destroyed an entire block of homes and damaged many other houses and places of business. In addition, the tornado caused the death of over 20 people. More recently, in 1982, at least 25 tornadoes hit Arkansas, Texas, Mississippi, and Florida, killing 26 people, injuring over 300, and causing more than $50 million in property damage. In 1984, the town of Barneveld, Wisconsin, was leveled by a tornado that killed 7 and injured about 200. Even though not all tornadoes cause such massive devastation, if they touch down in populated areas, you can expect considerable damage.*

The explanation of an example does not have to be lengthy; sometimes all you need to do is add a few words. Consider another example:

Generalization:

The cost of living has been rising lately.

Support:

The average one-bedroom apartment goes for $650 a month.

Does this example really show that the cost of living has been rising lately? After all, there may have been no change in the average monthly rent for several years. The writer could add a clause to explain the example:

The average one-bedroom apartment goes for $650 a month, *whereas only two years ago it went for $475.*

Using this same generalization, the writer might discuss four or five additional examples to show that the cost of living has been rising, but among those examples should be at least one that provides information about a specific case. In other words, it is useful to provide specific detail for support.

Here is how the support might look for this generalization:

The cost of living has been rising lately.

1. The average one-bedroom apartment goes for $650 a month, whereas only two years ago it went for $475.
2. The cost of regular gasoline has increased from $1.15 a gallon to $1.35 a gallon in only six months.
3. When I first came to this town three years ago, it cost 25 cents to use the public telephone, but now it costs 35 cents.
4. In addition, my water bill has increased $2 in three months, even though my water consumption has not gone up.

* Information from "The Winter That Refused To Die," *Time*, 19 April, 1992, p. 24.

5. Finally, my cable television bill has just jumped up another $1.35 per month for basic service.

EXERCISE 5·10   In the preceding sentences, underline the part that clarifies its support of the generalization.

EXERCISE 5·11   For each of the following topic sentences, circle the controlling idea (generalization), and then write out two examples that support that idea. Be sure that the examples are adequately explained. For the second example, use a specific incident. The first one is done for you.

1. Mr. Morales (displays kindness) wherever he goes.

    a. *When he is on the bus, he talks to people who look sad. He tells them funny stories that invariably make them smile.*

    b. *Last week when he heard that his neighbor was sick, he made some soup and delivered it to her, along with a bouquet of flowers.*

2. There are several things you can do to reduce pollution.

    a. _____

    b. _____

3. Some things definitely need to be changed at this school.

    a. _____

    b. _____

4. I have learned a lot about _____ in the last year.

    a. _____

    b. _____

5. You can find some unusual items at the bookstore.

    a. _____

    b. _____

EXERCISE 5·12 Writing Assignment   Select one of the following writing assignments.

1. Choose one of the generalizations in Exercise 5-11. Develop a paragraph with examples drawn from personal experience.

2. Make a generalization about writers or filmmakers from your country. Develop the paragraph with examples.
3. The devastation from such natural disasters as floods, tornadoes, hurricanes, hailstorms, or droughts is awesome. Write a paragraph giving examples of the devastation caused by a natural disaster.

Illustrations and Anecdotes

It is not always necessary to give several examples to support the controlling idea; sometimes one example that is explained in greater detail will suffice to support the controlling idea. This kind of extended example is useful, not so much for "proving" the statement in the generalization but for illustrating it; therefore, this kind of example is called an *illustration*. Study the following paragraph:

The Internet has dramatically altered the way many people perform numerous tasks, and recently it has become an important tool used by those working for political and humanitarian reform. The ongoing struggle for democracy in Indonesia underscores the power of the Internet. Last spring, protesters bypassed the state-controlled media there by posting a Web site containing a database that kept track of the corruption of then president Suharto. People across the country were continually adding information about the accumulated wealth of the president and his children, knowledge of which fueled an already inflammatory situation. Students also relied on the Internet to coordinate their demonstrations, which eventually led to Suharto's resignation.

—*adapted from* Alden M. Hayashi "The Net Effect."
Scientific American (January 1999), p. 21

What is the controlling idea in this paragraph?

Another type of illustration is an *anecdote*. An anecdote is a brief story that dramatizes the point made in the generalization. In other words, it is a brief narrative. (To review the narrative paragraph, return to Chapter 3.) Study the following paragraph and note its organization:

There is a story, possibly apocryphal, about a psychologist who shut a chimpanzee in a soundproof room filled with dozens of mechanical toys. Eager to see what playthings the ape would choose when he was all alone in this treasure house, the scientist bent down on his knees and put his eye to the keyhole. What he saw was one bright eye peering through from the other side of the aperture. If this anec-

dote isn't true, it certainly ought to be, for it illustrates the impossibility of anticipating exactly what an animal will do in a test situation.
—Frank A. Beach, "Can Animals Reason?" *Natural History*, March 1948

What is the topic sentence of this paragraph? How are the sentences arranged?

Composition Skills

Coherence

Organization of Details and Examples

When a paragraph contains several details and examples, it is necessary to consider the order of their presentation. Unlike narratives, whose sentences logically are ordered chronologically, and descriptions, whose sentences are logically organized on a spatial principle, the sentences in the expository paragraph follow no prescribed or set pattern of organization. The ordering depends on the subject and often on the author's logic. There are, however, some common patterns that might be considered guidelines.

Order of Importance: Saving the Best for Last
Often, when you are developing a topic sentence with details and examples, one of the examples is more impressive than the others. Since readers generally remember what they read last, and since it is a good idea to leave a good impression on the reader, it is wise to place the most impressive example at the end of the paragraph. Study the following paragraph, and note that the last example is the most startling one:

A search through etymologies will reveal other examples of words which have narrowed in meaning since their early days. *Barbarian* was originally a vague designation for a foreigner of any kind; garage, when it was borrowed from France, meant "a place for storage." In the United States, *lumber* has specialized to mean "timber or sawed logs especially prepared for use," but in Britain the word still retains its more general meaning of "unused articles," which are stored, incidentally, in a *lumber room*. *Disease* originally meant what its separate parts imply, *dis ease*, and referred to any kind of discomfort. The expression "to give up the ghost"° and the biblical reference to the Holy Ghost may be the only remnants of an earlier, more general meaning for *ghost*, which once meant "spirit" or "breath." Now *ghost* has specialized to mean "a specter or apparition" of some kind. Perhaps the most startling specialization has taken place with the word *girl*; even as late as Chaucer's time, it was used to mean "a young person of either sex."
—Richard R. Lodwig and Eugene F. Barrett,
The Dictionary and the Language (New York: Hayden, 1967), p. 159

to die

Order of Familiarity: From the More Familiar to the Less Familiar   When the details in the expository paragraph are mostly factual, it is common to begin with the most obvious or familiar detail and move toward the less obvious or less familiar detail. This is the pattern of the following paragraph about the expenses of smoking cigarettes. The writer begins with details that most people would consider when thinking about expense: the price. Then the writer discusses the less obvious or familiar expense of smoking cigarettes: the cleaning expenses. Read the paragraph and note how the writer connects the more obvious expense to the less obvious expense:

> Smoking cigarettes can be an expensive habit. Considering that the average price per pack of cigarettes is about $2.50, people who smoke two packs of cigarettes a day spend $5 per day on their habit. At the end of one year, these smokers have spent at least $1,825. But the cost of cigarettes is not the only expense cigarette smokers incur. Since cigarette smoke has an offensive odor that permeates clothing, stuffed furniture and carpeting, smokers often find that they must have these items cleaned more frequently than nonsmokers do. Although it is difficult to estimate the cost of this additional expense, one can see that this hidden expense does contribute to making cigarette smoking an expensive habit.

Order of Time: From the Past to the Present   When the details and examples in a paragraph are taken from history or are events that have taken place in the past, it is often a good idea to order the examples according to chronology.

> The seventeenth century was a period of great advances in science. For example, early in this century, Galileo perfected the telescope and in 1609 published "The Sidereal Messenger," in which he reported the results of his observations of the Milky Way, the moon, and the planet Jupiter. Only a few years later, the Dutch scientist Anton van Leeuwenhoek performed pioneering research with the microscope, discovering among other things that weevils, fleas, and other minute creatures come from eggs rather than being spontaneously generated. Not long after this, William Harvey, an English physician, discovered the method by which blood circulates in humans and other animals and in 1628 published his findings in the historic treatise "On the Motion of the Heart and Blood in Animals." Finally, in the 1660s, Isaac Newton discovered the law of gravitation and the laws governing the physics of light, and he also invented differential calculus.

EXERCISE 5·13 Study the following topic sentences and their supporting details. Rearrange the support so that each detail is in its most logical position. Remember, there is no set order, but you must be able to justify your choices.

1. China has suffered from some of the worst disasters in history.
   a. The worst disaster of all time occurred in 1931, when the Huang He River flooded, killing 3.7 million people.
   b. On January 24, 1556, 830,000 people died in an earthquake.
   c. In 1642, 300,000 Chinese perished as a result of flood waters.
   d. In 1887, the Huang He River flooded, causing the death of 900,000 Chinese.
   e. The year 1927 saw another devastating earthquake, killing 200,000 people.
   f. There was an earthquake in Tangshan in 1976 that killed 242,000 people.
   g. In 1982 and 1983, over 1,700 people died from floods.
2. American women have been fighting for equal rights for over 100 years.
   a. In 1920, the Nineteenth Amendment to the Constitution was adopted. This amendment gave women the right to vote.
   b. In 1976, the U.S. military academies admitted women for the first time.
   c. Women began to fight for better working conditions in New York in 1868.
   d. In 1978, Congress passed the Pregnancy Disability Bill, which makes pregnancy an insurable disability.
   e. Women were still fighting to get the Equal Rights Amendment passed in 1980.
   f. Congress passed an act forbidding discrimination on the basis of sex by employers of 15 or more employees in 1964.
   g. Only in the 1990s did researchers begin to study the health conditions of women as frequently as those of men. Women were also more frequently included in trials of new medicines.
3. Some people think that enjoying work is more important than the amount of money earned.
   a. Mary Bright, an Atlanta cab driver, has an annual income of $17,800. She is fifty-three and has been driving a taxi since 1981. She says, "I love it."
   b. Bob Jones, a fifty-five-year-old patrol officer in Boston, has been on the job twenty-five years. He likes it a lot and thinks his salary of $29,000 is just fine. "Everything about it is great except for the politicians," he says.
   c. Susan Smith helps build homes in Concord, New Hampshire, for $15,000 a year. It's enough for her to get by on while she pursues a second profession in art.
   d. Al Johnson of Wyoming could be making more doing maintenance on the government's Minuteman missile system. Instead, he makes $19,000 a year as a photographic technician for the Wyoming Fish and Game Dept.
   e. Sixty-year-old Roberta Howell is a senior food service aid at Tampa General

Hospital in Florida. Although she could make more in New York, she is satisfied with the $22,000 she earns per year and loves her home in Tampa.

4. Any household repair, no matter how complicated, is made easier if you use the right tool for the job.

   a. To make holes in wood and for marking the place where a screw or nail goes in, you can use the scratch awl. It is about 6 inches long and has a wooden handle shaped like a 25-watt light bulb.

   b. A claw-hammer is useful because its curved prongs pull out tacks and nails.

   c. Side-cutting, square-nosed pliers are used for cutting and stripping wires.

   d. A smaller tack hammer is designed to hammer in tacks or headless nails on surfaces that are easily bruised by a larger striking force.

   e. Needle-nosed pliers have long and narrow noses that allow you to apply strong pressure for bending or straightening metal objects even in hard-to-reach areas.

   f. A gimlet, which looks like a long corkscrew, is used for drilling the start of a hole before inserting the screw.

   g. Of course, you always need a good set of screwdrivers of varying sizes, along with a Phillips head screwdriver.*

EXERCISE 5·14 Writing Assignment   Choose one of the following topics.

1. Every culture has proverbs. Some popular ones in the United States are "The early bird catches the worm" and "A stitch in time saves nine." Think of a popular proverb in your country and translate it into good English. Using the proverb as your topic sentence, write a paragraph with an anecdote from your life that shows the truth of this statement.

2. Tell an anecdote of something that happened to you when you were involved in your favorite leisure-time activity or entertainment.

Transitional Words and Phrases

Not only should sentences and ideas in a paragraph be logically arranged, but they should flow smoothly as well. Expressions such as *next, then, after that,* and the like signal time sequence; expressions such as *above, farther on, next to,* and so forth signal location. These types of words and phrases help to achieve coherence by establishing the relationship between sentences in a paragraph. Because they provide transitions—links or connectors—between ideas and sentences by signaling what is going to follow, they are called *transitional words and phrases.* Here the focus is on some transitions to be used to achieve coherence in the expository paragraph developed by example.

---

* Adapted from J. Flanagan, "Tools for the Task." *The Consumers' Almanac,* 1989 (1988), p. 100.

- *An example of, the most significant example.* These expressions are used to identify the example in the sentence; this approach is probably more commonly used for illustrations.

  An example of a brilliant scientist is Albert Einstein.

It is also a good way to clarify the significance of the example, especially when your paragraph goes from least important to most important:

  The most startling example of a word that has specialized in meaning is *girl.*

  One of the best-known examples of fish destruction in the United States took place in 1955 . . .

- *Another example, an additional example.* These expressions are used to introduce the second or third example for the same generalization when the examples are equally significant.

  Another example of a brilliant scientist is Georg Ohm.

- *To illustrate.* This infinitive phrase is used to introduce an illustration and is generally placed at the beginning of the sentence:

  To illustrate, let us look at a topic sentence to identify the topic and controlling idea.

- *For example, for instance.* These expressions are the most frequently used transitional words for introducing examples and illustrations. They occur most often at the beginning of a sentence, but they can be placed in the middle of the sentence (after the introductory phrase, after the verb phrase, or after the subject) and at the end.

  Take, *for example,* the tornado that hit Wichita Falls. (after the verb)

  In the paragraph describing a room, *for example,* the author begins with the first thing the viewer sees . . . (after the introductory phrase)

  For instance, let us say that you made the simple generalization in this topic sentence: Tornadoes can be devastating. (beginning)

  Let us say, *for instance,* that you made the simple generalization . . . (after the verb)

  Let us say that you wrote a long letter, *for example.* (end)

- *First, second, next, then, last, finally.* These transitional expressions, also used to indicate chronological order, can be used to signal examples, especially when the examples are given in time order. They can also be used when it is established that a limited number of things are to be discussed; these terms signal the progression of the discussion.

There are several things that I do not like about registration. *First,* it takes too long. The entire process takes the average student three hours. *Second,* it is too impersonal. No one knows your name, not even the counselors who stamp their names on your registration card. *Next,* I do not like the atmosphere where registration is held. The constant sound of voices is irritating and so are the fluorescent lights, which make everyone look a little sick. And *finally,* I do not like the way it is organized. First-year students always get in last; consequently, they end up with classes at inconvenient times.

- *To begin with.* This expression can often be used instead of *first.*
- *Also, furthermore, moreover, in addition, besides that.* These expressions are used to number or to include more information about an idea already stated.

This tornado destroyed an entire block of homes and damaged many other houses and places of business. *In addition,* the tornado caused the death of over 20 people.

This tornado destroyed an entire block of homes and damaged many other houses and places of business. *Moreover,* the tornado caused the death of over 20 people.

Also, the tornado caused the death of over 20 people.

Besides that, the tornado caused the death of over 20 people.

Furthermore, the tornado caused the death of over 20 people.

These expressions can be placed at the beginning of a sentence or at the beginning of an independent clause joined to another independent clause. In the latter case, you need to punctuate as follows:

This tornado destroyed an entire block of homes; *in addition,* it caused the death of over twenty people.

The expressions *moreover* and *also* can occur after the subject:

The tornado, *moreover,* caused the death of over 20 people. (use commas)

The tornado *also* caused the death of over 20 people. (no commas)

Special Note: *besides*

Besides means approximately the same as *in addition*; that is, it indicates a supplement to a point just started. However, *besides* is usually considered less formal. It is generally a good idea to use *in addition* in formal essays.

- *Finally, in conclusion.* These expressions signal the last example or the conclusion of a paragraph:

In conclusion, although I do not like the registration process, I know that at this point I have no choice but to go through with it.

Remember, there are many ways to achieve coherence; do not rely entirely on one way. Try to use a variety of coherence devices—a mixture of clauses, phrases, and transitional expressions. Do not overdo the use of transitions; it could be repetitious. Generally, two or three transitional expressions in a paragraph are sufficient.

EXERCISE 5·15 Which of the transitions in the preceding lesson would be appropriate in the following blanks? Make a list of those that fit in each blank.

Although the United States has become an advanced technological country, many old-fashioned superstitions still remain. _____, when walking down a street in New York City past ingeniously built skyscrapers, you might see a sophisticated New Yorker walk around instead of under a ladder. Of course, he or she knows that walking under a ladder brings bad luck. Or, should a black cat wander from a back alley to that same bustling street, some people would undoubtedly cross to the other side of the street to avoid letting a black cat cross their paths. _____, it is true that most buildings in the United States do not have a thirteenth floor and many theaters do not have a thirteenth row. Again, we all know that 13 is an unlucky number. _____, if you take a drive through Pennsylvania Dutch country, you will see large colorful symbols called hex signs attached to houses and barns. Of course, the people who live there say they are just for decoration, but sometimes I wonder.

EXERCISE 5·16 Using transitions studied in the preceding lesson, add transitions to the following paragraphs wherever appropriate.

1. In the past several years, we have become much more aware of hazardous conditions in the environment. Scientists recently reported that ozone, the natural shield protecting us from the sun's ultraviolet rays, has declined significantly. They noted that a hole in the ozone layer over Antarctica has developed and blamed the widespread use of certain chemicals for the ozone decrease. Scientists have warned us about the greenhouse effect, the gradual warming of the earth because the heat from the sun's rays is prevented from radiating back into space by a blanket of artificial gases. The chief gas in the greenhouse effect is carbon dioxide, a byproduct of burning fossil fuels in cars and factories. Waste disposal has become a significant problem. We not

only have tons and tons of household garbage to get rid of, but we also have hazardous waste from nuclear facilities and plants. While all of these are significant problems that must be solved in the near future, at least we are now more aware of them.

2. When surnames began appearing in Europe 800 years ago, a person's identity and occupation were often intertwined. A surname was a direct link between who a person was and what the person did. Taylor is the Old English spelling of tailor, and Clark is derived from clerk, an occupation of considerable status during the Middle Ages because it required literacy. The names Walker, Wright, Carter, Stewart, and Turner indicate occupations. A walker was someone who cleaned cloth; a wright was a carpenter or metalworker; a carter was someone who drove a cart; a steward was a person in charge of a farm or estate; and a turner worked a lathe. One of the few occupational surnames reflecting the work of women is Webster, which refers to a female weaver.*

Internet Activity: Composition Skills and the Internet

 Do you need additional help or practice with transitional words and phrases? There are many web pages that address this topic. Do a key word search for "transitional words and phrases" or visit your favorite OWL (Online Writing Lab).

Grammar Review

If you want to review grammatical structures that will help you achieve coherence and grammatical accuracy in your writing, see the Grammar Review Unit. The following sections are designed to coordinate with the expository paragraph:

Verb Tense Review: The Present Perfect vs. the Simple Past, pages 367–369.
Definite and Indefinite Articles, pages 313–317.

EXERCISE 5·17 Writing Assignment   Choose one of the following writing assignments.

1. Develop a topic sentence about your early reading experiences. Then write a paragraph of support using examples and details or an anecdote.

---

* Information from *The Times Picayune*, 17 June, 1984, sec. 3, p. 5.

2. Develop a topic sentence about your favorite leisure activity. Write a paragraph using appropriate support.

3. Develop a topic sentence about superstitions in your country. Then write a paragraph using appropriate support.

4. Develop a topic sentence about polluting the environment. Support it with specific examples in a paragraph.

5. In many languages, names have a particular significance. Write a paragraph explaining your culture's attitude about people's names. Support it with details and examples.

6. Make a generalization about a person you know, and then write a paragraph supporting that generalization with examples or an anecdote. For instance, you might begin with, "My little brother has done some amusing things." You could support this generalization with an illustration, an anecdote, or perhaps you could give several examples of amusing things he had done.

EXERCISE 5•18 Assignments from the Disciplines   Following are some topics which are typical of college writing assignments. Choose one that you have studied, or consult a textbook or the Internet to find the answer. Then, answer the question in a paragraph. Use the revision checklist to revise your paragraph.

1. From Accounting—An important part of any accounting system includes internal controls. What are internal controls and why are they important to a business? Use examples to support your answer.

2. From Anthropology—In a paragraph, explain the concept of reciprocity and support your explanation with examples from two or more cultures.

Revision

Peer Review
When you have finished writing the first draft of your paragraph, give it to a classmate to read and review. Use the peer review checklist in Appendix I to respond to each other's drafts.

Revision Checklist for the Expository Paragraph
Use these questions to help you to give suggestions to your peers and to revise your essay.

1. An expository paragraph supports the controlling idea with explanation, facts, and illustrations. Does your paragraph use sufficient details and examples?

2. The controlling idea, or generalization, of an expository paragraph conveys the writer's attitude about the topic. Does your paragraph have a clear, focused generalization?

3. The organization of details and support of the generalization in an expository

paragraph depends on the subject and the writer's logic. Are the generalization and support logically arranged in your paragraph?

4. Is your paragraph unified; that is, do all the sentences support the controlling idea?

5. Is your paragraph coherent; that is, do the sentences flow smoothly?

© CNN®

The Essay

Chapter 6 Introduction to the Essay

Theme

Introduction to the Essay

Goals

Writing

To understand the purpose for and characteristics of the three parts of an essay: introduction, developmental paragraphs, and conclusion

To identify and improve thesis statements

To identify and evaluate introductory paragraphs

To identify topics for developmental paragraphs and write the appropriate topic sentences

To understand the purpose for and characteristics of conclusions

To write an outline to plan essays and/or determine if an essay is well organized

Getting Started

Journal Writing: Choose one of the following two questions, and write about it in your journal.

1. What are the differences between writing assignments in college and writing assignments in high school? What are the differences between college teachers and high school teachers?
2. How do you feel before you take a test? What kinds of tests do you prefer? Multiple choice? True/False? Short answer? Essay? Why do you prefer this type of test?

CNN® Video Activity: "A Case of Plagiarism of Romance Novels"

 Plagiarism, which is using someone else's writing as if it were your own, is considered a serious offense in academic classes. If a professional writer plagiarizes the work of another writer, the plagiarizer may have to pay a lot of money in damages, and his or her reputation and career will probably be ruined. This video tells one story of plagiarism. Janet Dailey, who writes romance novels, admitted to plagiarizing work from Nora Roberts, also a romance novelist. Watch the video once to find out what happened when Dailey's plagiarism was discovered. How do you think Dailey felt? How about Roberts? What were the consequences of plagiarism?

Watch the video again, and pause the video when the words used by the two authors are shown on the screen. Notice that Dailey didn't copy the words exactly, but just used some of the words and ideas written by Roberts. Compare the original words with the plagiarized words. What percentage of the work is plagiarized? Are you surprised that this is considered plagiarism?

Video Follow-up: Gathering Information about the Consequences of Plagiarism

After you watch this video, find out what the consequences of plagiarism are for students. Most schools have an academic honesty policy that describes the consequences of plagiarism and other forms of cheating. Look at the academic honesty policy for your school. Answer these questions:

1. What are the consequences of plagiarism?
2. Why do teachers want students to avoid plagiarism?
3. How can students avoid plagiarism if they want to include others' ideas in papers they write?

For more information on ways to avoid plagiarism, see Appendix II: "Using other people's words and ideas."

Internet Activity: Composition Skills and the Internet

 Colleges and universities look on plagiarism as a very serious offense. Use a search tool on the Internet to search for the terms "plagiarism" or "academic honesty." How many pages did you find? Choose two or three of these pages and compare them. Are the policies similar? Are the consequences of plagiarism the same? How do they differ? Write a paragraph describing the results of your search.

Introduction to the Essay

Emphasis thus far has been on writing paragraphs with good, detailed support. Since a paragraph develops only one idea, the topics being developed are necessarily quite limited. Often, however, topics are too complex or too broad to be developed in a single paragraph. In this case, it is necessary to write an *essay*. An essay is a group of paragraphs that develops one central idea. How are the paragraphs organized in an essay? How many paragraphs are there in an essay? How does an essay begin and end? These are questions this unit will answer. Unlike the paragraph, the essay is a more formal composition. Each paragraph in an essay has a designated function:

1. Introduction. The introduction is usually one paragraph (sometimes two or more) that introduces the topic to be discussed and the central idea (the thesis statement) of the essay.
2. Developmental paragraphs. These paragraphs develop various aspects of the topic and the central idea. They may discuss causes, effects, reasons, examples, processes, classifications, or points of comparison and contrast. They may also describe or narrate.
3. Conclusion. This paragraph concludes the thought developed in the essay. It is the closing word.

How many paragraphs an essay contains depends entirely on the complexity of the topic; some essays have only two or three paragraphs, whereas others may have 20 or 30. However, for most purposes, the essays written for first-year college English courses contain from four to six paragraphs, with an introductory paragraph, several developmental paragraphs, and a concluding paragraph.

The Thesis Statement

The essay, like the paragraph, is controlled by one central idea. In the essay, the sentence containing the central idea is called the *thesis statement*. The thesis statement is similar to the topic sentence in that it contains an expression of an attitude, opinion, or idea about a topic; unlike the topic sentence, however, the thesis statement is broader and expresses the controlling idea for the entire essay. In fact, each of the developmental paragraphs should have a controlling idea that echoes or relates to the controlling idea—the central idea—in the thesis statement.

Here are a few points to remember about the thesis statement:

1. The thesis statement should be expressed in a complete sentence. Since the thesis statement is the main statement for the entire essay, it should express a complete thought; therefore, it should be expressed in a complete sentence. And since it makes a statement, it should not be written as a question.

   Not a thesis statement:
   My fear of the dark.

   Thesis statement:
   My fear of the dark has made my life miserable.

2. A thesis statement expresses an opinion, attitude, or idea; it does not simply announce the topic the essay will develop.

   Not a thesis statement:
   I am going to discuss the effects of radiation.

   Thesis statement:
   The effects of radiation are often unpredictable.

3. A thesis statement should express an opinion; it should not express a fact. Since the thesis statement expresses an attitude, opinion, or idea about a topic, the thesis statement is really a statement that someone could disagree with. The thesis statement, therefore, is a statement that needs to be explained or proved.

   Not a thesis statement:
   Cows produce milk.

   Thesis statement:
   The milk cows produce is not always fit for human consumption.

   Not a thesis statement:
   There are many advantages and disadvantages to going to college. (Not an arguable point.)

   Thesis statement:
   The advantages to going to college far outweigh the disadvantages.

4. A thesis statement should express only one idea toward one topic; if a thesis statement contains two or more ideas, the essay runs the risk of lacking unity and coherence.

Not a thesis statement:
>   Going to college in the Midwest can be fun, and I have found that living in a suburb of a large city is the best way to live while at college.

Thesis statement:
>   Going to college in the Midwest can be fun.

EXERCISE 6·1 Study the following statements carefully. If the statement is a thesis statement, write yes in the blank; if it is not a thesis statement, write no.

1. ____ The advantages of majoring in engineering.

2. ____ I would like to discuss my views on the Olympic Games.

3. ____ Students should be allowed to manage the bookstore.

4. ____ When I first came to the United States, I wasn't used to eating in fast-food places, and I was amazed at the shopping centers.

5. ____ Why do I want to be a lawyer?

6. ____ The differences between Mandarin and Hunan dialects.

7. ____ Knowing a foreign language can be beneficial to anyone.

8. ____ This advertisement attempts to appeal to the readers' sense of patriotism.

9. ____ I am going to describe my home.

10. ____ There are many similarities and differences between New York and Hong Kong.

EXERCISE 6·2 Study the following statements, which are not thesis statements. Rewrite each of the sentences to make it a thesis statement. The first one is done for you.

1. I am going to explain why I decided to go to college.

    Choosing to go to college was a difficult decision. _____

2. The hazards of storing chemical wastes.

    _____

    _____

3. There are many similarities and differences between life in the country and life in the city.

   _____

   _____

4. New York City is the largest city in the United States.

   _____

   _____

5. Universities in the United States should require more humanities courses; they should also have more social activities.

   _____

   _____

The Introduction

The thesis statement is the main statement for the entire essay. But where should the thesis statement be placed? Although there is no law that requires the thesis to be placed in any particular place in the essay, the thesis statement is usually in the introductory paragraph. After all, the thesis is the statement that the developmental paragraphs are going to explore. But where in the introduction should the thesis statement be placed? Before we answer this question, let us look at the characteristics of an introductory paragraph.

1. An introductory paragraph should introduce the topic. Do not forget that the introductory paragraph is the first thing that a reader sees. Obviously, this paragraph should inform the reader of the topic being discussed.
2. An introductory paragraph should indicate generally how the topic is going to be developed. A good introductory paragraph should indicate whether the essay is going to discuss causes, effects, reasons, or examples; whether the essay is going to classify, describe, narrate, or explain a process.
3. Generally speaking, an introductory paragraph should contain the thesis statement. This is a general rule, of course. In more sophisticated writing, the thesis statement sometimes appears later in the essay, sometimes even at the end. In some cases, too, the thesis is just implied. For college essays, however, it is a good idea to state the thesis clearly in the introduction.
4. Ideally, an introductory paragraph should be inviting; that is, it should be interesting enough to make the reader want to continue reading. Since the introductory paragraph functions to introduce the topic and since the introductory paragraph should be inviting, it makes good sense not to put the thesis statement right at the beginning of the introductory paragraph. Not

only should you introduce the topic before you state an opinion about it (the thesis statement), but you should try to entice the reader to continue after reading the first sentence. Stating an opinion about something in the first sentence is not usually very inviting; in fact, if readers disagree with the opinion, it may very well discourage them from reading your essay. Therefore, it is generally a good idea to place the thesis statement at or near the end of the introductory paragraph.

Prewriting: Planning

Since the introduction is the first paragraph the reader reads, it is often the first paragraph the student plans and can be, therefore, the most difficult. There are many ways to begin an essay. In this text, we discuss four basic types of introductions: (1) the "Turnabout," in which the author opens with a statement contrary to his or her actual thesis (Chapter 9); (2) the "Dramatic Entrance," in which the author opens with a narrative, description, or dramatic example pertinent to the topic (Chapters 10 and 11); (3) the "Relevant Quotation," in which the writer opens with a quotation pertinent to the topic (Chapter 11); and (4) the "Funnel."

The Funnel approach is perhaps the most common type of introductory paragraph. It is so called because the ideas progress from the general to the specific just as a funnel is wide at the top and narrow at the bottom. The approach is to open with a general statement about the topic and then to work toward the more specific thesis statement at or near the end of the introduction. Not only should the opening statement be general, it should be congenial as well; do not alienate the reader. See how this technique is applied in this introductory paragraph.

> Traveling to a foreign country is always interesting, especially if it is a country that is completely different from your own. You can delight in tasting new foods, seeing new sights, and learning about different customs, some of which may seem very curious. If you were to visit my country, for instance, you would probably think that my people have some very strange customs, as these three examples will illustrate.

In this introductory paragraph, the writer introduces the general topic of "traveling to a foreign country" in the first sentence and narrows down that topic to a more specific aspect—the customs in the writer's country. The thesis statement comes at the end with the central idea being *strange*. Illustrations should appear in the developmental paragraphs.

Just how general should the introductory paragraph be? One way to avoid beginning too generally or too far back is to have one key word in the first sentence reappear in the thesis statement, or if not the word itself, a synonym of the word or an idea. In the preceding paragraph, *visit* echoes *traveling* and the word *country* appears in the first and last sentences.

Here is another example of this type of introduction, taken from a popular science magazine:

> America is a throwaway society. From both industrial and municipal sources, the United States generates about 10 billion metric tons of solid waste per year. Every five years the average American discards, directly and indirectly, an amount of waste equal in weight to the Statue of Liberty. Municipal solid waste alone accounts for 140 million metric tons per year. The municipal solid waste produced in this country in just one day fills roughly 63,000 garbage trucks, which lined up end to end would stretch 600 kilometers, the distance from San Francisco to Los Angeles. The repercussions of our waste habits, however, stretch to every city. Let us demonstrate by example.
>
> —P. O'Leary, P. Walsh, and R. Ham, "Managing Solid Waste,"
> *Scientific American* 6 (Dec. 1988): p. 36. Copyright ©1988
> by Scientific American, Inc. All rights reserved.

EXERCISE 6·3   Study the following introductory paragraphs. Underline the word or words that appear in the first sentence and are restated in the thesis statement.

1. Computers are advanced machines that can store and recall information at very high speed. Computers are easy and interesting to use; however, some people are afraid of computers. I used to be afraid of computers, too, because of the fear of failure and because I knew nothing about programming. But actually I have learned that the procedures of working on computers are very easy.

   —Nader Alyousha

2. When we were very young, we believed that parents could do no wrong. Indeed, they seemed to us to be perfect human beings who knew all the answers to our problems and who could solve any problems that we had. However, as we grow older, we find that parents can make mistakes, too.

3. We live in an era where television is the national pastime. Since the invention of the television set, people have been spending more of their free time watching television than doing anything else. Many of the television addicts feel that this particular pastime is not a bad one; indeed, they argue that people can learn a great deal watching television. I am sure that if you look long and hard enough, you can probably find some programs that are educationally motivating. But, for the most part, I say that watching television is a waste of time.

   —Pamela Moran

4. Today's children are our future men and women. They will become the dominant force one day. If they receive proper guidance and have a nice

childhood, they will contribute immeasurably to our society after they have grown up. In other words, today's children are going to have a significant impact on our society in the future; therefore, parents should not neglect the proper conditions that children need during their childhood.

—Chun Lee

5. When we see a blind person nearing a street corner or a door, many times we try to help by opening the door or taking the person's arm and guiding him or her across the street, and while we do that, some of us talk to the blind person in a loud voice, as if the blind person is not only helpless but also deaf. Rushing to help a blind person without asking if that person needs help and speaking loudly are just two of the inappropriate ways people react to blind people. If you want to help a blind person whom you perceive as in need of help, you should bear in mind the following tips.

EXERCISE 6·4 On pages 108–109 are the characteristics of a good introductory paragraph. Using those characteristics, evaluate the following introductory paragraphs. Does the paragraph introduce the topic? Does it indicate how the topic is going to be developed? Does it contain a thesis statement? Is it inviting? If one or more of these are missing, write the missing element on separate paper. Some of the paragraphs may be good introductory paragraphs.

1. We are all familiar with the image of the fat, jolly person, right? Unfortunately, this is an inaccurate stereotype. Fat people are not always so happy.

2. "We are moving to the city!" These are the words of many villagers today. When they are asked to give reasons for their movement, they simply reply that life in the city is more developed than that in the village. In the city, there are communication, transportation, education, and medical services. Also there are more chances for jobs. I positively agree with these people, but have these people thought about their lives and health? Have they thought about the danger that might happen to their children? It might not be during the first six months of living, but in the future when the city becomes more inhabited by different people of different nationalities and when the streets get crowded with cars. Although the village is lacking some of the services mentioned above, it is still the best type of environment for me to live in.

—Habeeb Al-Saeed

3. I would like to tell you about my hometown, Hlatikulu, Swaziland. It is a small town of only 8,000 people. The main industries there are farming and working for the government, since it is the capital of the southern region.

4. Last year, my cousin, Julio, went to a bank to apply for a job. As you know, when you apply for a job, you must be ready to answer a lot of ambiguous questions. Some of the questions that an interviewer may ask you include: educational background, previous jobs, and salaries you earned. The problem

with Julio was that he wasn't prepared for the questions. The interviewer asked Julio a lot of things that he couldn't answer. Because Julio wasn't prepared for the interview, he didn't get the job. If you do not want to be in that situation, you may want to follow these steps.

—Mauricio Rodriguez

EXERCISE 6·5 Writing Assignment   Following are six possible thesis statements. For each one, use one of the prewriting techniques given in Chapter 1 and generate some information on the topic. Then choose the three topics you like best and write introductory paragraphs.

1. My country has some of the most beautiful sights you will ever see.
2. Speaking more than one language is a great advantage.
3. The AIDS virus is a worldwide problem.
4. Watching television is not a waste of time.
5. I can suggest several improvements needed at this school.
6. The New Year is one of the happiest occasions. (You may choose a favorite holiday in your country.)

The Developmental Paragraphs

Developmental paragraphs, which range in number in the typical student essay from about two to four, are the heart of the essay, for their function is to explain, illustrate, discuss, or prove the thesis statement. Keep in mind these points about the developmental paragraphs:

1. Each developmental paragraph discusses one aspect of the main topic. If, for example, you were asked to write a paper about the effects of smoking cigarettes on a person's health, then each paragraph would have as its topic an effect.
2. The controlling idea in the developmental paragraph should echo the central idea in the thesis statement. If your thesis statement about the effects of smoking cigarettes is "Cigarette smoking is a destructive habit," then the controlling idea in each paragraph should have something to do with the destructiveness of the effects.
3. The developmental paragraphs should have coherence and unity. The order of your paragraphs should not be random. As you have seen in the last three chapters, there are various ways to order the sentences in a paragraph; similarly, there are various ways to order your paragraphs. The same principles apply as you learned in Chapter 5, and additional strategies will be presented in this chapter. Just as your sentences need to flow smoothly, the train of thought at the end of one paragraph should be picked up at the beginning of the next

paragraph; this can be achieved through the use of transitions. Again, much attention will be devoted to transition use in this text.

Prewriting: Planning

In Chapter 2, you learned how to write a restricted topic sentence from your prewriting notes. The same technique can be used to arrive at a thesis statement; you need simply to remember that the thesis statement is more general than a topic sentence. After all, each developmental paragraph does discuss an aspect of the main topic expressed in the thesis statement. Once you have decided on your thesis, you need to break the thesis down logically into topics for your paragraphs. These topics are, in essence, supporting points for your thesis. Let us say, for example, that you wanted to write about the beautiful sights in your country—perhaps to persuade people to visit them or simply to inform your reader about your country. After you have taken considerable notes on the topic, you might come up with this thesis statement: "My country has some beautiful sights." The main topic of the essay is "sights in my country" and the central idea is "beautiful." The main topic then needs to be broken down into topics for paragraphs, perhaps two to four. Logically, the topics would be sights, with one sight perhaps discussed per paragraph, and the controlling idea for each of these topics should be something akin to "beautiful," such as "charming," "lovely," "enchanting," "glorious," and so on. We could illustrate this breakdown as follows for an essay about beautiful sights in Mexico:

$$\boxed{\text{MEXICO HAS SOME BEAUTIFUL SIGHTS}}$$

$$= \boxed{\text{beach at Progreso}} + \boxed{\text{Aztec Ruin}} + \boxed{\text{Monument}}$$

Just how you break down your thesis into topics depends on your thesis statement. There are several principles for logically breaking down your thesis. You can break it into topics according to causes, effects (benefits, advantages, disadvantages, results), steps in a process, types (kinds, categories, classes), examples, points of comparison and contrast, and reasons; these are the basic principles, and those that we will cover in depth in this text. One way to break your thesis down logically into topics is to turn your thesis statement into a question, keeping in mind what your topic and central idea are. The answers to this question might help you come up with possible topics for your developmental paragraphs; they can also help you determine a strategy for organizing your essay. (These strategies, or patterns of organization, are discussed in great detail in subsequent chapters.)

Here are some thesis statements and possible breakdowns into topics for the developmental paragraphs:

1. **Thesis Statement:**
   The village is the best environment for me to live in.

   Question:
   What makes it a good environment?

   Answers:
   The cooperation among people.
   Its lack of pollution.
   Its security.

   The central idea in the thesis statement is *best environment*, so this is a logical basis for the breakdown. Each paragraph would discuss a different element of the environment that is attractive to the writer.

2. **Thesis Statement:**
   In order to make a good impression at a job interview, you should prepare well for the interview.

   Question:
   What should you do to prepare for the interview?

   Answers:
   Plan your answers to the possible questions.
   Plan and prepare what you are going to wear.
   Make sure you arrive on time.

   The central idea in the thesis is *prepare well*. Here the writer chose to break down the thesis into the steps of a process.

3. **Thesis Statement:**
   Watching television is not a waste of time.

   Question:
   Why isn't it a waste of time?

   Answers:
   Because it is a valuable educational tool.
   Because it helps us to relax.
   Because it provides something for our family to discuss.

   With the central idea of *not a waste of time*, the writer's approach here is to discuss the reasons television is not a waste of time—in other words, to discuss the advantages of having television.

4. **Thesis Statement:**
   New York and Hong Kong are more alike than people think.

   Question:
   In what ways are they alike?

   Answers:
   They are both enormous.
   They both have lots of different ethnic groups.
   They are both port cities.

   In this breakdown, the writer selected points of similarity to develop the thesis.

5. **Thesis Statement:**
   Students should be allowed to manage the bookstore.

   Question:
   Why should they be allowed to manage it?

   Answers:
   Because it would benefit the students.
   Because the bookstore would benefit.
   Because the school would benefit.

   In this essay, the student discusses the reasons for allowing students to manage the bookstore, and in this case the reasons are the benefits.

EXERCISE 6·6 Following are thesis statements, each with two supporting topic sentences. Study the thesis statements and their supporting topic sentences to determine the logic or the principle behind the breakdown. Then fill in a topic sentence for each.

1. **Thesis Statement:**
   The city is the place for me to live.

   Topic Sentences:
   1. I like its excitement.
   2. I like the availability of resources.

   3. _____

2. **Thesis Statement:**
   Smoking cigarettes is harmful to your health.

   Topic Sentences:
   1. Heavy cigarette smoking can cause throat diseases.

2. Smoking can damage the lungs.

3. _____

3. **Thesis Statement:**
   Jogging isn't the only way to improve your circulation.

   Topic Sentences:
   1. Many have found cycling an excellent aerobic exercise.
   2. Another way to improve your circulation is to swim.

   3. _____

4. **Thesis Statement:**
   A foreign student enrolled at an American university often finds that his or her life isn't such a happy one.

   Topic Sentences:
   1. The complex registration procedure is frustrating.
   2. It is difficult to make friends.

   3. _____

5. **Thesis Statement:**
   Taking a foreign language should be required in high school.

   Topic Sentences:
   1. Students can learn about other cultures.
   2. It can help in business in the future.

   3. _____

EXERCISE 6·7   Study the following thesis statements. On a separate sheet of paper, brainstorm on two of them. Then write out at least three possible topic sentences for the two thesis statements.

1. Learning English isn't so easy.
2. My country has some of the most beautiful sights you will ever see.
3. Being unemployed can cause people to lose their self-respect.
4. You can see some unusual people on the bus.
5. Logging on to the computer is not a difficult task.
6. Students whose native language is not English may face many problems that English speakers do not encounter.
7. People go to shopping centers for many reasons.
8. Athletic teams bring universities a number of advantages.

Read the following student essay about sights to see in Quebec, Canada. Try to find the central idea for the essay; then try to find the controlling idea for each of the developmental paragraphs.

My Favorite Sights

In each country in the world, there are always some beautiful sights to see. They might be a monument, a garden, or a cathedral. Every country is proud of them, and everyone is interested in talking about them. In my country, three important points of interest attract a great number of tourists all year. No portrait of these sights is complete without mentioning their historical and seasonal aspects. Because of these aspects, Quebec is a place where you can find some of the most interesting sights you will ever see.

Old Quebec City is the living witness of our history. The first example is the church Notre-Dame des Victoires. Located at the bottom of Cap Diamant, this church was the first one built in North America. It commemorates the establishment of Quebec in 1608. It is a modest and charming church, constructed of stones and dominated by a single belfry from where you can still hear authentic chimes ringing. Another example is the Ramparts. Originally, they were long fortifications all around the city with three main doors to enter in. Now, the three doors are renovated and part of the fortifications is preserved, offering a harmonious blend of history and innovation. Finally, the focal point of Old Quebec City is the Plaines d'Abraham. It is a very large hill from which we can have a scenic view of the Saint Lawrence River and the city. It was on this site that our founders won many battles but, unfortunately, lost the most important one. Nevertheless, the spot is now a wonderful park where is still present, with its many cannons, a past which is not so far away. Regardless of the season, those three points are colorful: red in autumn, white in winter, light green in spring, and dark green in summer.

From the Plaines d'Abraham, it is easy to discover the majestic Saint Lawrence River. This beautiful broad river was the open door for our founders. Traveling in canoes, they established the first three cities in the lands drained by the Saint Lawrence: Quebec, Montreal, and Trois-Rivières. They must have been impressed with the clear, sweet water, the tree-studded islands, and the banks lined with pine and hemlock. Today, the river is an exceptional waterway extending 1,500 miles into the interior. Like the Mississippi River, it is, in every season, the location for great activities. Although the most important one is commercial, pleasure and sport are considerable: for example, boating, water-skiing, and fishing. These are particularly popular in summer. Furthermore, even though there are 3 to 5 feet of ice on the river in the winter, the Saint Lawrence is still navigable.

On the north shore of the Saint Lawrence River, five miles from Quebec, the famous Montmorency Falls are located. These beautiful falls were discovered by a French explorer in the sixteenth century. About 350 feet high, and with frothing, foaming sheets of water, they are the highest falls in North America. During the summer, it is popular to go to one of the huge park areas near the falls to admire their cascades. At night, it is possible to hear and see a lovely sound and light show. During the winter, the main activity is at the bottom. The small drops of vapor in the air form a huge, round block of ice at the bottom of the falls which becomes bigger and bigger. This strange sight draws a lot of children and adults who spend time climbing up and down.

Is it possible to find a country where the beauty, the history, and the variety in the scenery are combined in such perfect harmony? Of course, our four seasons mean four different aspects of the same sight. I don't know if it is because I am far from my country, but I am convinced that Quebec has some of the most beautiful sights that I have ever seen.

—Louisette Caron

EXERCISE 6·8   On a separate sheet of paper, answer the following questions about the preceding essay.

1. What is the main topic of the essay? What is the central idea?
2. What are the subtopics? What are the controlling ideas for the subtopics?
3. Are the paragraphs descriptive, narrative, or expository, or are they a combination?

In general, *interesting* is considered rather vague and general for a controlling idea; however, in "My Favorite Sights," Caron clarifies what she means by *interesting*: interesting for history and beauty during the seasons. In choosing *interesting* as a controlling idea, restrict its meaning by clarifying what you mean by this word.

Sometimes the writer chooses to present part of the thesis statement in the introduction and the rest of it later in the essay, often in the conclusion. This approach is useful when the writer wants to build up to a point rather than stating it prematurely. The following essay is an example of this approach. The writer gives a generalized thesis statement at the end of the introductory paragraph and specifies what the generalized thesis statement means in the conclusion. As you read the essay, underline the two parts of the thesis statement.

Why People Save Books

Many people who like to read also save the books they have read. If you walk into any home, you are likely to see anywhere from a single bookshelf to a whole library full of all kinds of books. I know a family whose library has shelves reaching up to their ceiling; they keep a ladder for climbing up to the high books. Obviously, they have collected books for many years and though they rarely actually open the books again, they keep them on the shelves, dusted and lined up neatly. Why do people save their books? There may be several reasons, but three stand out.

One reason people save their books is to use them as reference materials. People whose job training included studying a lot of textbook material may save some of those books for future reference. A doctor, for instance, may keep his *Gray's Anatomy* and his pharmacology books; an English teacher will hold on to *The Norton Anthology of British Literature* and other anthologies and novels for reference; a lawyer usually keeps her case books. But it isn't only the professionals who save their books. People who like to cook keep recipe books. Those interested in electronic equipment hold on to their books about stereos, computers, videotape machines, and the like. Many families keep encyclopedias and almanacs handy for their children to use for school. Having your own reference book available is so much more convenient than running to the library every time you want to check a fact.

Another reason some people save books is to make a good impression. Some think that a library full of the literary classics, dictionaries, and books about art, science, and history make them look well read and therefore sophisticated. Of course, this impression may be inaccurate. Some have never bothered to read the majority of those books at all! In fact, a few people even have libraries with fake books. Also, some people like to reveal to visitors their wide range of tastes and interests. They can subtly reveal their interests in Peruvian art, Indian music, philosophy, or animals without saying a word.

While some people may keep books for practical reference and for conveying an impression, I suspect that there is a deeper reason. People who enjoy reading have discovered the magic of books. Each book, whether it's *The Treasury of Houseplants* or *Murder on the Orient Express*, has transported the reader to another place. Therefore, each book really represents an experience from which the reader may have grown or learned something. When I sit in my study, I am surrounded by my whole adult life. *The Standard First Aid and Personal Safety* manual, in addition to providing information, reminds me of the first-aid course I took and how more assured I felt as a result. *Bulfinch's Mythology* brings the oral history of Western civilization to my fingertips, reminding me of my link with other times and people. Of course, all of the novels have become part of the mosaic of my life. In short, saving books makes me feel secure as I hold on to what they have given me.

In fact, if you think about it, security is at the bottom of all these reasons. It's a secure feeling to know you have information at hand when you need it. There is a kind of security, even though it may be false, in knowing you make a good impression. Finally, books that you've read and kept envelop you with a warm and cozy cloak of your life.

EXERCISE 6·9   On a separate sheet of paper, answer the following questions about the preceding essay.

1. What is the main topic of the essay?
2. The generalized thesis can be stated as, "People save books for three reasons." What is the central idea about those reasons?
3. What are the subtopics (reasons)? What are the controlling ideas for the subtopics?
4. What kind of paragraph is each developmental paragraph?
5. Identify specific details in each of the developmental paragraphs.

The Conclusion

Just as the introductory paragraph functions to open the essay discussion by introducing the topic and the central idea (thesis), so the concluding paragraph wraps up the discussion, bringing the development to a logical end. If the developmental paragraphs have done their job—that is, developed the thesis—then the conclusion should follow logically.

But what does one *say* in the conclusion? What is said depends entirely on what was developed in the essay. However, there is a standard approach to writing concluding paragraphs. Here are some points about conclusions:

1. A conclusion can restate the main points (subtopics) discussed. This restatement should be brief; after all, you have already discussed them at length.
2. A conclusion can restate the thesis. Generally, to avoid sounding repetitious, it is a good idea to restate the thesis in different words. The restatement of the thesis is really a reassertion of its importance or validity.
3. A conclusion should not, however, bring up a new topic.

For example, an essay about the most interesting places to visit in Mexico could conclude as follows:

> There are, of course, many more things to visit while you are in Mexico, but the beach at Progreso, the Aztec ruin, and the famous monument represent some of the more significant and beautiful sights to see. When you go to Mexico, visit these sights and you will be guaranteed a fond memory after you go home.

A concluding paragraph about allowing students to manage the bookstore might look like this:

> Providing jobs for students, jobs that would help cut the cost of managing the bookstore and providing on-the-job experience—which can only enhance the university's reputation for graduating knowledgeable students—are excellent reasons for allowing students to manage the bookstore. In fact, it is amazing that such a system is not in practice now.

EXERCISE 6·10   Reread the essay "My Favorite Sights" by Louisette Caron on pages 117–118. Then answer the following questions on a separate sheet of paper.

1. Are the main points in Caron's essay mentioned in the conclusion?
2. If not, does the conclusion seem appropriate, anyway? Why?
3. If yes, what are the main points she restates?

EXERCISE 6·11   Following are thesis statements, their supporting topic sentences, and conclusions. Study each conclusion to determine if it logically concludes. If the conclusion is not appropriate, write *not good* in the blank, and write the reason it is not good in the space provided. If the conclusion is appropriate, simply write *logical* in the blank.

1. **Thesis Statement:**
   Watching television is not a waste of time.

   a. It is a valuable educational tool.
   b. It provides entertainment to help us relax.
   c. It provides something our family can have in common to discuss.

   Critics of television will continue to put down the "boob tube." But, because of its educational value, its entertainment value, and its provision of things we can discuss together, our family is going to continue watching television for a long time, and so should others. Indeed, watching television is a good way to spend one's time.

   _____

   _____

2. **Thesis Statement:**
   Communicating in a foreign language can create some embarrassing misunderstandings.

   a. Mispronouncing words can lead to real embarrassment.
   b. Misunderstanding what someone says to you can create amusing problems.
   c. Misusing vocabulary words can really make you blush.

   Everyone who speaks a foreign language is bound to have misunderstandings from time to time. What you need to do is go to the laboratory as often as you can to improve your language skills. The people there are very nice, and they will help you with your grammar and pronunciation.

   _____

   _____

3. **Thesis Statement:**
   Television commercials are entertaining.

   a. The Coca-Cola commercial is a good example of an entertaining commercial.

    b. The Chevrolet commercial is as good as any situation comedy.

    c. The Fritos commercial is particularly amusing.

If you do not have a television, you are certainly missing out on the fun of commercials. There are also a lot of entertaining programs to see. In addition, the news programs can keep you informed about the world. Indeed, everyone should have a television set.

_____

_____

4. **Thesis Statement:**

    My reasons for coming to State University center around the services it provides.

    a. State University offers a superior program in my major.

    b. In addition, the university has high-quality academic resources.

    c. State also offers quality student services.

    d. The recreational activities make State even better.

The challenge of a diversified and excellent program, the academic resources, the student services, the recreational activities, and the low tuition are the reasons I decided to come to State University. I really think I made a wise decision. If you are looking for a quality education at a reasonable price, then consider State as the place to enroll.

_____

_____

5. **Thesis Statement:**

    In order to make a good impression at a job interview, you should prepare well for the interview.

    a. The first thing you should do is plan your answers to the possible questions the interviewer might ask.

    b. Then you should carefully plan and prepare what you are going to wear.

    c. Finally you should make sure that you arrive on time.

As you can see, it is necessary to be well prepared for the job interview. Having the answers ready, being properly dressed, and being on time can all help to make a good impression on the interviewer. If you follow these steps, you will find yourself sitting behind the desk at that coveted job in no time at all.

_____

_____

The Outline

Prewriting: Planning

One way to determine if an essay is well organized and if the paragraphs discuss the thesis statement is to outline the essay. In Unit One, the paragraph outlines were essentially topic sentences with the supporting sentences written out on separate lines. In outlining an essay, however, you do not need to write out all the sentences in the paragraphs. An outline is the skeleton of the essay; it is the structure around which the details and explanations are organized.

There are many ways to write outlines for essays. It is not necessary to follow any strict outline form. For example, technically, in an outline if there is a "1" there must be a "2," and if there is an "A" there must be a "B." When you are asked to write formal outlines for formal papers, you should follow this rule; but for most other purposes, an outline can be informal. Here is a suggestion for an outline form for planning your essay:

Thesis Statement:
  Write out the thesis statement in a complete sentence.

I. Write out the first developmental paragraph topic sentence.
   A. Identify the support. This can be a detail or an idea that the paragraph will discuss.
      1. Mention any additional detail about "A."
      2. If appropriate, mention another detail about "A."
   B. If you have another detail or example you are going to discuss in this paragraph, mention it here.
II. Write out the next topic sentence.
   A. Support.
   B. Support.
III. Write out the next topic sentence.
   A. Support.
      1. Detail if necessary.
   B. Support.

A quick glance at such an outline should reveal if the paragraphs are unified and coherent. Study the following outline of Caron's essay:

Thesis Statement:

   Because of these aspects, Quebec is a place where you can find some of the most interesting sights you will ever see.

I. Old Quebec City is the living witness of our history.
   A. Historical aspects.
      1. Notre-Dame des Victoires.
      2. Ramparts.
      3. Plaines d'Abraham.
   B. Seasonal aspects—beautiful in all seasons.

II. From the Plaines d'Abraham, it is easy to discover the majestic Saint Lawrence River.
   A. Historical aspects.
      1. Open door for our founders who established cities.
      2. Today, the river is an exceptional waterway.
   B. Seasonal aspects.
      1. The location for great activities in every season, particularly boating, water-skiing, and fishing in summer.
      2. The river is navigable in winter.

III. On the north shore of the Saint Lawrence River, five miles from Quebec, the famous Montmorency Falls are located.
   A. Historical aspects.
      1. Discovered by a French explorer in the sixteenth century.
      2. Highest falls in North America.
   B. Seasonal aspects.
      1. During the summer
         a. Go to park to admire falls.
         b. Sound and light show.
      2. During the winter-play on the block of ice.

Supporting details can be expressed in words or phrases in an outline.

EXERCISE 6·12   Reread "Why People Save Books" on pages 119–120 and write an outline using the form given on page 124.

EXERCISE 6·13   Following are some topics for your final essay. Using one of the prewriting techniques you learned in Chapter 1, generate a great deal of material on your chosen topic. Then find a central idea on which to base your thesis statement and decide on supporting points. Write an informal outline and then the first draft of your essay. Use the Revision Checklist at the end of the chapter to evaluate your essay.

   1. What are some noteworthy or interesting (unusual, beautiful, historically significant) sights in your country or hometown?

2. What are some of the areas where computers are being used? Write about some of the uses of computers. Or, discuss another important invention, such as satellites.

3. Write an essay explaining why you think people save books or some other objects. For example, many people save stamps, coins, dolls, even toys!

EXERCISE 6•14 Assignments from the Disciplines   Following are some topics that are typical of writing assignments in college-preparation or college success classes. Choose one of the topics, then follow the directions for Exercise 6-13 to write your answer.

1. Colleges and universities require students to take liberal arts courses so that graduates will have a basic understanding of disciplines other than the one in which they major. Liberal arts courses also help students to develop a better understanding of how people think and communicate. If you could design the liberal arts requirements at your college, what would you include? Write an essay explaining your choices.

2. Time management is an important skill for college students to master. Write an essay which outlines three or more techniques students can use to effectively manage their time.

3. Almost everyone encounters obstacles which must be overcome to achieve a goal. What is the biggest obstacle which stands between you and your college goals? Write an essay describing this obstacle and what steps you have taken to overcome it.

Composition Skills

Revision

Peer Review
When you have finished writing the first draft of your essay, give it to a classmate to read and review. Use the peer review checklist in Appendix I to respond to each other's drafts.

Revision Checklist for the Paragraph
Use these questions to help you to give suggestions to your peers and to revise your essay.

1. Is your introduction inviting? Does it introduce the topic?
2. Does your essay have a clear thesis?
3. Do your topic sentences support the thesis?
4. Does the support in your paragraphs support the topic sentences?
5. Does your conclusion end the discussion logically?
6. Is your essay coherent? Unified?

© CNN®

Chapter (7) The Example Essay

Theme

The Power of Culture and Language

Goals

Writing

To select examples to support a thesis and use these examples to write an essay

To understand how extended examples and numerous examples can effectively support a thesis statement

To learn how to avoid hasty generalizations

To use transitions between paragraphs

To use repetition of key words and phrases to increase coherence

Reading

To learn about and discuss examples of the power of culture and language in our lives

To identify examples in an essay and determine how they support a thesis

Grammar

To review gerunds and infinitives and noun clauses

127

Getting Started

Journal Writing: Choose one of the following two questions, and write about it in your journal.

1. What are some examples of unacceptable behavior in your culture? In American culture? Have you ever experienced an uncomfortable situation because someone from your culture or from mainstream American culture behaved in an unacceptable way?
2. What aspects of your culture have been misunderstood by another culture? What do people from this other culture need to know so that they can understand your culture better?

CNN® Video Activity: "The Lost Language of the Juaneno Tribe"

 How closely are language and culture related? Is it possible to be a part of a culture without knowing the language? In this video, you will see how the members of a tribe of Native Americans are trying to learn a language that no one speaks. This is the language of their ancestors, and many of them feel that it is important to try and bring this language back to life. As you watch the video, listen for answers to these questions:

1. How are these people trying to learn the language? What materials are they using? Who is their teacher?
2. Why did this language die out? Why didn't the people who knew the language teach it to their children?
3. Why do these people feel that it is important to learn this language, even though none of their ancestors who once spoke it are alive any more?

Video Follow-up: Sharing Your own Experiences
Many languages and cultures have changed throughout the years, but these days, because of TV and international travel, cultures seem to be changing faster. Think about some element of your native culture or language that has been changing or disappearing. Tell your class about it. Are there any movements in your country to revive this element of the culture or language? Do you think these movements will be successful?

Readings: The Power of Culture and Language

Both the culture we live in and the first language we learn to speak are powerful forces in shaping our behavior and worldview. From them we determine how to act in the world and how to make sense of it. Usually, we are unaware of the power of language and culture until we experience firsthand a different culture or learn to speak a different language. These activities help us to gain a perspective on our own culture and to see some of its unspoken but powerful rules. They also make us aware that, when two cultures meet, one culture can misunderstand or misinterpret the other.

The two selections that follow use examples to show the power of culture and language in our lives. As you read the essays, try to answer these questions:

1. What kinds of rules do we follow every day without thinking about them? Do these rules help us to live in society or do they cause problems?
2. What problems can happen when two cultures have different ideas about what kind of behavior is acceptable? What can happen when mistranslations of words and concepts occur?
3. How has your culture shaped your behavior?

Reading **1**

"How Unwritten Rules Circumscribe Our Lives"
by Bob Greene

Bob Greene's newspaper columns and articles are collected in *Johnny Dead-line Reporter: The Best of Bob Greene* (1976) and *American Beat* (1983). In the article reprinted here, Greene writes about the power of unwritten cultural rules in our lives. As you read the essay, consider these questions:

1. Are Greene's examples confirmed by your own experiences in American culture?
2. Would these same examples be true in your culture?
3. Can you think of additional examples of unwritten cultural rules?

---

1   The restaurant was almost full. A steady hum of conversation hung over the room; people spoke with each other and worked on their meals.

2   Suddenly, from a table near the center of the room, came a screaming voice:

3   "Damn it, Sylvia . . . ."

very loudly

4   The man was shouting at the top of his voice.° His face was reddened, and he yelled at the woman sitting opposite him for about 15 seconds. In the crowded restaurant, it seemed like an hour. All other conversation in the room stopped, and everyone looked at the man. He must have realized this, because

suddenly

as abruptly° as he had started, he stopped; he lowered his voice and finished whatever it was he had to say in a tone the rest of us could not hear.

surprising

5   It was startling° precisely because it almost never happens; there are no laws against such an outburst, and with the pressures of our modern world you would almost expect to run into such a thing on a regular basis. But you don't; as a matter of fact, when I thought about it I realized that it was the

seen

first time in my life I had witnessed° such a demonstration. In all the meals I have had in all the restaurants, I had never seen a person start screaming at

very loudly

the top of his lungs.°

speak loudly

6   When you are eating among other people, you do not raise your voice;° it is just an example of the unwritten rules we live by. When you consider it, you recognize that those rules probably govern our lives on a more absolute basis than the ones you could find if you looked in the lawbooks. The customs

no organization

that govern us are what make a civilization; there would be chaos° without

falling apart

them, and yet for some reason—even in the disintegrating° society of 1982—we obey them.

7   How many times have you been stopped at a red light late at night? You can see in all directions; there is no one else around no headlights, no

police car

police cruiser° idling behind you. You are tired and you are in a hurry. But you wait for the light to change. There is no one to catch you if you don't, but you do it anyway. Is it for safety's sake? No; you can see that there would be no accident if you drove on. Is it to avoid getting arrested? No; you are alone. But you sit and wait.

8   At major athletic events, it is not uncommon to find 80,000 or 90,000

grandstands, seating area in sports arena

or 100,000 people sitting in the stands.° On the playing field are two dozen athletes; maybe fewer. There are nowhere near enough security guards on hand to keep the people from getting out of their seats and walking onto

all together

the field en masse.° But it never happens. Regardless of the emotion of the contest, the spectators stay in their places, and the athletes are safe in their part of the arena. The invisible barrier always holds.

9   In restaurants and coffee shops, people pay their checks. A simple enough concept. Yet it would be remarkably easy to wander away from a meal without paying at the end. Especially in these difficult economic times, you might expect that to become a common form of cheating. It doesn't happen very often. For whatever the unwritten rules of human conduct are,

pay, do the right thing

people automatically make good° for their meals. They would no sooner walk out on a check than start screaming.

10   Rest rooms are marked "Men" and "Women." Often there are long lines at one or another of them, but males wait to enter their own washrooms, and women to enter theirs. In an era of sexual egalitarianism,° you would

equality

expect impatient equality people to violate° this rule on occasion; after all,

go against

there are private stalls inside, and it would be less inconvenient to use them than to wait. . . . It just isn't done. People obey the signs.

11   Even criminals obey the signs. I once covered a murder which centered

around that rule being broken. A man wanted to harm a woman—which woman apparently didn't matter. So he did the simplest thing possible. He went to a public park and walked into a rest room marked "Women"—the surest place to find what he wanted. He found it. He attacked with a knife the first woman to come in there. Her husband and young child waited outside, and the man killed her. Such a crime is not commonplace,° even in a world grown accustomed to nastiness.° Even the most evil elements of our society generally obey the unspoken rule: If you are not a woman, you do not go past a door marked "Women."

usual, normal

badness, evil

12　I know a man who, when he pulls his car up to a parking meter, will put change in the meter even if there is time left on it. He regards it as the right thing to do; he says he is not doing it just to extend the time remaining—even if there is sufficient time on the meter to cover whatever task he has to perform at the location, he will pay his own way. He believes that you are supposed to purchase your own time; the fellow before you purchased only his.

money left for waiter or bartender, gratuity

13　I knew another man who stole tips° at bars. It was easy enough; when the person sitting next to this man would depart for the evening and leave some silver or a couple dollars for the bartender, this guy would wait until he thought no one was looking and then sweep the money over in front of him. The thing that made it unusual is that I never knew anyone else who even tried this; the rules of civility° stated that you left someone else's tip on the bar until it got to the bartender, and this man stood out because he refused to comply.°

good manners

conform, go along

14　There are so many rules like these—rules we all obey—that we think about them only when that rare person violates them. In the restaurant, after the man had yelled "Damn it, Sylvia" and had then completed his short tirade,° there was a tentative aura° among the other diners for half an hour after it happened. They weren't sure what disturbed them about what they had witnessed; they knew, though, that it violated something very basic about the way we were supposed to behave. And it bothered them—which in itself is a hopeful sign that things, more often than not, are well.

outburst, angry speech

feeling of uncertainty

EXERCISE 7·1 Comprehension/Discussion Questions

1. What is Greene's thesis in "How Unwritten Rules Circumscribe Our Lives"?
2. What are some of the examples he gives to support it?
3. Are all of his examples equally strong? Do any of them strike you as unconvincing?
4. Why is it important that the laws discussed by the writer are *unwritten*? Do you agree that these laws govern our lives more strongly than written ones?

5. Which of the laws given by the writer are true in your culture? Give examples to support your answer.

6. Can you give additional examples of unwritten laws in any culture?

7. In your view, which unwritten laws mentioned in the essay seem basic to life in any civilized society and which seem relatively minor matters of form or taste? Explain your answers.

8. Where does Greene first state his thesis? Does he state it again? If so, where? Do you think his organization is effective?

9. Are the author's examples selected from a broad enough range of experience to support his thesis effectively?

10. Why are so many of Greene's examples exceptions, that is, examples of people who do not follow the unwritten laws?

Internet Activity: Composition Skills and the Internet

 As the Internet has grown, an Internet culture has developed. When you are sending e-mail or joining a newsgroup, you need to know the "rules of the Internet" and the culture of the group you are joining. The term "netiquette" has come to mean the "etiquette" or rules of the Internet. To learn more about this, do a keyword for "netiquette." Then, test your knowledge of Internet culture by taking this "Netiquette quiz" http://www.albion.com/netiquette/netiquiz.html. Then, discuss this question with your classmates: Why are the rules for appropriate behavior on the Internet often written down so clearly? Why don't people usually write down the rules for cultural behavior?

EXERCISE 7·2 Vocabulary Development   The following idiomatic expressions are used in Greene's essay. Study the sections of the reading in which the expressions occur. From the context clues or surrounding information, determine the meaning of each idiomatic expression. Then use each one in an original sentence.

1. at the top of his voice (par. 4)

_____

2. at the top of his lungs (par. 5)

_____

3. run into (par. 5)

_____

4. raise your voice (par. 6)

_____

5. nowhere near enough (par. 8)

_____

6. make good (par. 9)

_____

Reading ②

"Americanization Is Tough on *Macho*"
by Rose Del Castillo Guilbault

Rose Del Castillo Guilbault, born in Sonora, Mexico, is a syndicated writer for Pacific News Service. In this essay, which first appeared in her column for *This World* (1989), a weekly magazine of the *San Francisco Chronicle*, Guilbault gives an example of the power of language. She shows how a particular Spanish word has come to have different meanings in different cultures. As you read this essay, consider these questions:

1. What are the various meanings for the word *macho*?
2. What examples does Guilbault use to make her point?
3. What is the problem with the American use of the word *macho*?

the U.S./Mexican border

Americans of Spanish descent

spoken by European Jews

believes he is superior to women

unfaithful, has many women

the most perfect

1   What is *macho*? That depends which side of the border° you come from.

2   Although it's not unusual for words and expressions to lose their subtlety in translation, the negative connotations* of *macho* in this country are troublesome to Hispanics.°

3   Take the newspaper descriptions of alleged mass murderer Ramon Salcido. That an insensitive, insanely jealous, hard-drinking, violent Latin male is referred to as *macho* makes Hispanics cringe.

4   "Es muy macho," the women in my family nod approvingly, describing a man they respect. But in the United States, when women say, "He's so macho," it's with disdain.

5   The Hispanic *macho* is manly, responsible, hardworking, a man in charge, a patriarch. A man who expresses strength through silence. What the Yiddish language° would call a *mensch*.

6   The American *macho* is a chauvinist,° a brute, uncouth, selfish, loud, abrasive, capable of inflicting pain, and sexually promiscuous.°

7   Quintessential° *macho* models in this country are Sylvester Stallone, Arnold Schwarzenegger and Charles Bronson. In their movies, they exude

* See explanation of connotation/denotation in Exercise 7-4.

toughness, independence, masculinity. But a closer look reveals their *machismo* is really violence masquerading as courage, sullenness disguised as silence and irresponsibility camouflaged as independence.

8   If the Hispanic ideal of *macho* were translated to American screen roles, they might be Jimmy Stewart, Sean Connery and Laurence Olivier.

9   In Spanish, *macho* ennobles Latin males. In English it devalues them. This pattern seems consistent with the conflicts ethnic minority males experience in this country. Typically the cultural traits other societies value don't translate as desirable characteristics in America.

uncertainties

10   I watched my own father struggle with these cultural ambiguities.° He worked on a farm for twenty years. He laid down miles of irrigation pipe, carefully plowed long, neat rows in fields, hacked away° at recalcitrant weeds and drove tractors through whirlpools of dust. He stoically worked twenty-hour days during harvest season, accepting the long hours as part of agricultural work. When the boss complained or upbraided him for minor mistakes, he kept quiet, even when it was obvious the boss had erred.

chopped

unimportant

11   He handled the most menial° tasks with pride. At home he was a good provider, helped out my mother's family in Mexico without complaint, and was indulgent with me. Arguments between my mother and him generally had to do with money, or with his stubborn reluctance to share his troubles. He tried to work them out in his own silence. He didn't want to trouble my mother—a course that backfired,° because the imagined is always worse than the reality.

came back to hurt him

12   Americans regarded my father as decidedly un-*macho*. His character was interpreted as nonassertive, his loyalty non-ambition, and his quietness, ignorance. I once overheard the boss's son blame him for plowing crooked rows in a field. My father merely smiled at the lie, knowing the boy had done it, but didn't refute it, confident his good work was well known. But the boss instead ridiculed° him for being "stupid" and letting a kid get away with a lie. Seeing my embarrassment, my father dismissed the incident, saying, "They're the dumb ones. Imagine, me fighting with a kid."

made fun of

13   I tried not to look at him with American eyes because sometimes the reflection hurt.

14   Listening to my aunts' clucks of approval, my vision focused on the qualities America overlooked. "He's such a hard worker. So serious, so responsible." My aunts would secretly compliment my mother. The unspoken comparison was that he was not like some of their husbands, who drank and womanized.° My uncles represented the darker side of *macho*.

was promiscuous

15   In a patriarchal society, few challenge their roles. If men drink, it's because it's the manly thing to do. If they gamble, it's because it's how men relax. And if they fool around,° well, it's because a man simply can't hold back so much man! My aunts didn't exactly meekly sit back, but they put up with these transgressions because Mexican society dictated this was their lot in life.

are promiscuous

Latin women

word meanings

16   In the United States, I believe it was the feminist movement of the early '70s that changed *macho*'s meaning. Perhaps my generation of Latin women was in part responsible. I recall Chicanas° complaining about the chauvinistic nature of Latin men and the notion they wanted their women barefoot, pregnant and in the kitchen.* The generalization that Latin men embodied chauvinistic traits led to this interesting twist in semantics.° Suddenly a word that represented something positive in one culture became a negative prototype in another.

17   The problem with the use of *macho* today is that it's become an accepted stereotype of the Latin male. And like all stereotypes, it distorts truth.

18   The impact of language in our society is undeniable. And the misuse of *macho* hints at a deeper cultural misunderstanding that extends beyond mere word definitions.

EXERCISE 7•3 Comprehension/Discussion Questions

1. What is the thesis of Guilbault's essay?
2. What is the meaning of the word *macho* to Hispanics? To Americans?
3. What people are given as examples of the American meaning? How do these examples support Guilbault's definition of the American meaning of *macho*?
4. What people are given as examples of the Hispanic meaning? How do these examples support Guilbault's definition of the Hispanic meaning of the word?
5. Guilbault includes a discussion and examples of "the darker side of *macho*." What does this phrase mean? Who are the examples of it?
6. Does including the section on the darker side of *macho* strengthen or weaken her main point? How?
7. Guilbault says that the misuse of the word *macho* stereotypes Latin males. What does she mean?
8. In paragraph 9, Guilbault says, "Typically the cultural traits other societies value don't translate as desirable characteristics in America." Do you agree? Be prepared to support your answer with examples.
9. Can you think of a word, phrase, or concept from your language/culture that changed in meaning when incorporated into another language/culture? Explain the various meanings of the word.

EXERCISE 7•4 Vocabulary Development   Words have both connotations and denotations. Connotations are the implications, suggestions, or emotional associations of words from the point of view of the speaker. These associations can be favorable

---

* *barefoot, pregnant* and in the *kitchen*—a phrase used to suggest that women should be dependent on men and fulfill only their traditional role of mother and housewife.

or unfavorable. For example, the word *home* tends to have favorable connotations, suggesting warmth, love, and family. The word *shack*, while still a place to live, has negative connotations, suggesting dirt and poverty.

Denotations are the established, or dictionary, meanings of words. They do not imply or suggest favorable or unfavorable meanings. In contrast to *home* and *shack*, the word *house* is denotative. It means a dwelling place and does not suggest anything more.

In Guilbault's essay, she investigates the positive and negative connotations of the word *macho*. To describe men, she uses a number of other words that have connotations. Phrases and sentences from her essay are listed below. For each italicized word, determine if, in this context, the word is used with positive connotations, negative connotations, or simple denotation. Mark your choice in the space provided.

	DENOTATION	CONNOTATION POSITIVE	NEGATIVE
1. *hard-drinking*, violent Latin male (par. 3)			
2. manly, responsible, *hard-working* (par. 5)			
3. uncouth, selfish, *loud* (par. 6)			
4. selfish, loud, *abrasive* (par. 6)			
5. *sullenness* disguised as silence (par. 7)			
6. *translated* to American screen roles (par. 8)			
7. he *stoically* worked twenty-hour days (par. 10)			
8. *accepting* the long hours (par. 10)			
9. he kept *quiet* (par. 10)			
10. his character was interpreted as *nonassertive* (par. 12)			
11. my *vision* focused (par. 14)			
12. who drank and *womanized* (par. 14)			

Writing

The way you develop your topic depends on what the topic is and on what you want to say. Let us suppose, for example, that you are asked to write about the difficulties of being a foreign student. How could you develop this topic? You would probably want to develop it with examples that illustrate the difficulties. Could you adequately cover this topic in a single paragraph? Probably not. The topic is simply too broad. You will need to write a longer essay to cover this topic adequately. How to organize and develop the examples for such a topic in the multiparagraph essay is the focus of this chapter.

Number of Examples

Just how many examples you use in an example essay depends on the topic. Some topics require numerous examples, whereas others can be effectively developed with three or four extended examples (illustrations). For instance, the thesis statement "San Francisco has some of the most unusual sights in California" does not commit the writer to giving numerous examples; after all, the claim is only that this city has "some" unusual sights. Therefore, three or four extended examples should suffice. As you read the following essay about a student's first year in the United States, determine if the writer provides enough examples.

Americans Are Friendly to Strangers

I came to the United States one year ago and I had no idea about life in the United States and American traditions, except that life was complicated and people are strange. At the time I arrived at J.F. Kennedy airport, I felt very happy because I am fond of traveling around the world. Coming to America had been one of my dreams, so I could go to Jamaica or any island in the Caribbean. A few minutes later, however, I felt afraid. I asked myself why I had come to this strange world and what I was doing here. The reason for that was what I remembered my friends in Saudi Arabia saying about Americans and how they treat strangers. After I attended college, however, I discovered the opposite of what I had expected.

Even though American social relations are complex, hard to form, and hard to maintain, I managed to bridge the gap, and I was able to have close friendships with some Americans. For example, the first semester I attended college, I became friends with one of the American students who used to attend math class with me. We used to study together, go to parties together, and he used to help me a lot with my English. Even though he transferred to another university, we always keep in touch with each other. From my experience, I have come to understand that Americans are generally verbal and long, silent periods are uncomfortable to them. So, when I sit with Americans, I start a conversation with them by talking about the weather, sports, or about teachers' skills in the classroom. I think conversations make a friendly atmosphere among people.

The second example that proved to me that I had the wrong idea about Americans was when my wife and I drove across the country from New Orleans to San Diego. When I told my friends that my wife and I were going to drive across the United States and if they wanted to they could join us, they said, "It is dangerous to drive across America. You might get killed by one of the truck drivers or get robbed." However, we didn't pay attention to them because we wanted to find out what America is really like and how people treat strangers.

On the way from San Antonio to El Paso, our car stopped because it ran out of fuel. We got out of the car and waited for anyone to give us a ride. Ten minutes later, a truck driver pulled off the road. I approached him carefully and I asked him, "Could you please give us a ride to the nearest gas station?" He asked me why. I said, "Our car ran out of gas and we have to get some." He said, "The nearest station is thirty-five miles away and you might not find anyone who can drive you back to your car." Then he came up with a solution to our problem. He towed our car to the nearest station. When we reached it, I took a fifty dollar bill from my pocket and handed it to him, but he wouldn't accept it. He told me that he helped me because we needed help.

In general, Americans are friendly to strangers. From my experience, a person who treats people well will put them in a position where they have to respect him in return, but if he treats them badly they will treat him in the same way. Human beings are born with a good nature and they will not behave badly unless they are forced to. I think a person should judge people by dealing with them, not by listening to his friends.

—Nader Alyousha

EXERCISE 7·5 On a separate sheet of paper, answer the following questions about the preceding essay.

1. What is the thesis statement? What is the central idea?
2. How many examples does the writer give? Are the examples explained adequately?
3. Are there enough examples?

4. Are the examples relevant?
5. Are the paragraphs coherent and unified?
6. How are the paragraphs organized?

An outline of Nader Alyousha's essay might look like this:

Thesis Statement: Americans are friendly to strangers.

I. I was able to have close friendships with some Americans.
   A. One example is a student in my math class during my first semester.
      1. We studied together.
      2. We went to parties together.
      3. He helped me with my English.
      4. We still keep in touch.
   B. I begin friendships by starting a conversation about . . .
      1. The weather.
      2. Sports.
      3. Teachers' skills in the classroom.
II. I had the wrong idea about Americans.
   A. An example is our trip across the country.
      1. My friends said it was dangerous.
      2. When we ran out of gas, a stranger helped us.
         a. He towed our car.
         b. He wouldn't accept any money.

Conclusion: People will treat you well if you treat them well.

Some topics require numerous examples for adequate development. For instance, suppose the thesis statement is "Our city streets are in terrible condition." Would three extended examples of streets in bad condition be sufficient to develop this thesis statement? Probably not. Asserting that all—or even most—of the city streets are in terrible condition based on only three or four examples would be rather unwise; after all, a city has many streets and, in this case, most of them may in fact be in good condition. A generalization such as "Our city streets are in terrible condition" based on an insufficient number of examples is called a *hasty generalization*; in other words, it is a generalization made too hastily before examining enough evidence. Making such a generalization without giving sufficient examples for support sacrifices credibility with the reader. In short, thesis statements that state or imply "most" or "all" may need numerous examples for adequate support; thesis statements that are more moderate, stating or implying "some" or "a few," can often be supported with fewer, but more developed, examples.

Choice of Examples

Since an example is a "representative member" of a class or category, the examples you use to develop the thesis statement should be representative examples, examples that fairly support the thesis. Let's say, for instance, that you were writing an essay about the items found in mail-order catalogs, and in planning the essay you noticed that there were many items that were ridiculous. So, you might have arrived at the thesis statement, "Many items offered in mail-order catalogs are just superfluous, absurd trifles." If you used for your examples only items of one type, such as toys, clearly the examples would be unfairly chosen—not representative of most of the items offered in these catalogs. To be fair and effective, the examples should be from a range of areas. Study the following essay to determine if the examples are sufficient in number and if they are fairly chosen.

Useless Trifles

For many years, people living in remote areas relied on the Sears or Montgomery Ward's catalogs to purchase the necessities of life. These "wish books," as they were often called, helped people to improve the quality of their lives. Nowadays, nearly every household in the country receives a barrage of various catalogs selling everything from electric golf carts to padded coat hangers. The descriptions of these items suggest that they, too, will help improve the quality of our lives by providing convenience, comfort, and/or shortcuts to improve our appearance. But so often, these items are just superfluous, absurd trifles.

Whoever does the cooking has a great deal of work to do, and anything to ease that workload is certainly appreciated by any home-maker. Unfortunately, some of these clever items that claim to save time might actually end up making us waste time. Take, for example, devices to save time cutting. A specially designed cutter will slice six pieces of pie at the same time, each piece the same size. Another device cuts an apple in thin slices and removes the core all in one shot. Still another removes the corn from the cob, easily and quickly. Although these devices may save time in the actual cutting, just think of how much time the person lost trying to find the device in the first place and then cleaning it up afterward! The same problem applies to a hand-sized electric drink mixer. It might save the host or hostess some muscle, but not aggravation when he or she finds the batteries are dead and there are none in the house.

Certainly anyone would also appreciate items that make our lives more comfortable, but some of the items for the bathroom border on the absurd. For about $8 you can buy an inflatable pillow to rest against in the bathtub. (It's held secure by suction cups.) An inch-thick foam rubber pad will cushion you from the hard bottom of the tub as you bathe. Of course, if it gets mildew on it, it might be better located in the trash can. Finally, you can sit in comfort on the toilet on a plush toilet seat cover and listen to music from a radio built into a toilet paper container.

Comfort and convenience are carried to extremes in the area of personal care. Without any real effort at all, or so the ads in these catalogs claim, you can go to bed and wake up feeling and looking better. After taking special pills to melt away excess pounds, you can crawl into your bed and let it massage you all night long. (A curious electric device makes the bed vibrate.) In addition, you can rest your head on a wedge-shaped pillow that is supposed to help you sleep better. To protect your hairstyle while you sleep, you can don a special cap. To keep your chin from sagging, you can wrap a band around your face, under your chin, and up over the front part of your head. Finally, to prevent your eyes from getting puffy, all you need to do is slip on a water-filled face mask. Of course, if you wake up to find your mate gone, do not be surprised!

All of these items, whether they are designed to help us in the kitchen, comfort us in the bathroom, or improve the way we look and feel, are for the most part unnecessary. Rather than improve the quality of our lives, such items detract from it by wasting our time and money and cluttering up our cupboards and closets. And cluttering up our coffee tables and end tables are those stacks of catalogs offering more such useless trifles.

EXERCISE 7·6   On a separate sheet of paper, answer the following questions about the preceding essay:

1. What is the thesis statement? The central idea?
2. What are the topic sentences? The controlling ideas?
3. Does each of the paragraphs develop an aspect of the thesis statement?
4. Are there enough examples in the essay? Are the examples representative?
5. What is the principle of organization of the paragraphs? Why, for example, does the writer discuss items for personal care last?
6. Is the conclusion logical?
7. Make an outline of this essay.

EXERCISE 7·7   Following is information on the dumping of hazardous chemical wastes in the United States.*

Read the thesis sentence and the examples in the list. On the line next to each example, identify whether the example is complete, incomplete, or not an example.

Thesis:
Dangerous chemical substances are polluting our water supplies.

_____ 1. Pine Barrens, New Jersey—135-acre Jackson Township Dump. One hundred wells poisoned by chemicals from dump, causing kidney problems: One man had one kidney removed. His daughter died of kidney cancer when nine months old.

_____ 2. Elizabeth, New Jersey—50,000 barrels of hazardous chemicals exploded in abandoned dump and spread toxic fumes.

_____ 3. Love Canal, New York—landfill area. Chemicals were dumped in landfill. Contamination seeped into water supply. Twelve hundred houses and a school nearby. High incidence of cancer, birth defects, and respiratory and neurological problems.

_____ 4. The United States generates about 77 billion pounds of hazardous waste per year—much of it is dumped indiscriminately.

_____ 5. Massachusetts—22 towns have contaminated water supplies.

_____ 6. Michigan—300 places where wastes have polluted ground water.

_____ 7. Carlstadt, New Jersey—Fire in paint factory spread smoke and fumes over city. Citizens temporarily evacuated.

_____ 8. Pennsylvania—Wastes poured in abandoned mine shafts and tunnels in hills above Susquehanna River. Seeped into river, which is the water supply for a number of towns.

_____ 9. Kentucky—Outside Daniel Boone National Forest, 200 containers loaded with dangerous solvents were dumped without permission.

_____ 10. Now substances that are very dangerous are beginning to show up in our water supply.

_____ 11. Charles City, Iowa—Deep wells 30–40 miles downstream from chemical dump are contaminated.

* Information from Ed Magnuson, "The Poisoning of America," *Time*, 22 Sept. 1980, pp. 58–69.

EXERCISE 7·8 Writing Assignment   Choose one of the following writing topics. Before you begin planning and drafting your essay, use one of the prewriting techniques you learned in Chapter 1 to generate ideas about your topic. After gathering ideas, focus on a controlling idea and thesis statement. Next, choose examples to support your thesis. Make a brief plan for the essay. Write the essay.

1. Review the essay "Americans Are Friendly to Strangers" on pages 137–138. Write an essay about the Americans you encountered when you first came to this country. Were they friendly or not? Give examples to support your thesis.

2. On page 139 is a suggested thesis, "Our city streets are in terrible condition." Using this as your thesis, write an essay about the streets in the city where you live. If you think something else needs improvement, write an essay giving examples to illustrate your thesis. You could choose the food in the cafeteria, the buildings on campus, or even some aspect or item in your neighborhood or your country.

3. Do you or your family get mail-order catalogs? Write an essay about the items in these catalogs that you find particularly interesting. Review the essay on pages 140–141.

Composition Skills

Coherence

Organization of Examples
The examples and details in an expository paragraph can be organized according to time, familiarity, and importance. In an example essay, the principle of organization is essentially the same. For example, the author of the essay about friendly Americans chose to organize his examples according to both time and importance, whereas the writer of "Useless Trifles" chose to begin with the least interesting examples and end with the most interesting ones—those that are personal.

Transitions Between Paragraphs
Developmental paragraphs in the example essay must be connected so that they flow smoothly. Just because a paragraph introduces an additional aspect of the topic does not mean that the shift from one topic to the next should be abrupt; indeed, the shift should be smooth so that the reader understands clearly the progression of thought. Remember, just as a paragraph is incoherent if the sentences can be switched around without significant change in meaning, an essay is incoherent if the paragraphs can be switched around without significant change.

   There are two ways to connect the paragraphs in an essay: (1) with transitional expressions and (2) with the repetition of key words and phrases.

Transitions to Introduce Examples

In the first developmental paragraph of an example essay, there are several phrases that can be used to introduce the first example or group of examples:

Take, for example, this topic.

One example of a person who is kind is my neighbor.

One area of town where there are examples of improvement is uptown.

First, consider the case of Mr. Martinez.

To begin (To begin with), consider my roommate.

In the second developmental paragraph, the examples can be introduced in a variety of ways:

Another example of a good teacher is Mrs. Hahn.

An additional example is Mr. Ming.

Second, consider Mr. Jones.

Next, consider Ms. Evans.

In the last developmental paragraph, you can use the same type of transitions as above, but in an example paragraph that introduces the most important or most significant example, you should indicate its importance in the beginning of the paragraph:

Still another example of a good teacher is Ms. Lin.

Third, consider Main Street.

Finally, there is the problem of air pollution.

The most important example of a helpful person is my advisor.

The most significant (interesting) example of air pollution is provided by Los Angeles.

To see how these types of transitions can be used to connect paragraphs, study the following essay.

Words That Camouflage

People use words, of course, to express their thoughts and feelings. And as everyone knows who has tried to write, choosing just the right word to express an idea can be difficult. Nevertheless, it is important to choose words carefully, for words can suggest meanings not intended at all; words can also be used to deceive. In order to express ourselves accurately and to understand what other people express, we must be aware that words can camouflage real attitudes; English is full of examples.

Take, for instance, the language of advertising. Advertisers obviously want to emphasize the virtues of their products and detract from the products' faults. To do this, they use carefully chosen words designed to mislead the unwary customer. Carl P. Wrighter in his book *I Can Sell You Anything* has dubbed these expressions "weasel words," which the dictionary defines as words "used in order to evade or retreat from a direct or forthright statement or position."*

Let's say, for example, that the advertiser wants you to think that using his product will require no work or trouble. He cannot state that the product will be trouble free because there is usually no such guarantee; instead, he suggests it by using the expression "virtually," as in this product is "virtually trouble free." The careless listener will ignore the qualifier "virtually" and imagine that the product is no

* *Webster's New Collegiate Dictionary* (Springfield. G&C Merriam Company, 1973), p. 1327.

trouble at all. Another misleading expression is "up to." During a sale a car dealer may advertise reductions of "up to 25 percent." Our inclination again is to ignore "up to" and think that most of the reductions are 25 percent, but too often we find that only a few products are reduced this much. The other day I saw a sign on a shoe store advertising "up to 40 percent off" for athletic shoes. Needing some walking shoes and wanting a good bargain, I went in, only to find that there were only a few shoes marked down by 40 percent; most of the shoes weren't even on sale.

A second example of words that camouflage meaning is euphemisms. A euphemism is defined as "the substitution of an agreeable or inoffensive expression for one that may offend or suggest something unpleasant."*

We often use euphemisms when our intentions are good. For instance, it is difficult to accept that someone we love has died, so people use all kinds of euphemisms for death such as "She passed away," "He's gone to meet his maker," or "She is no longer with us." To defend against the pain of such a reality some use the humorous euphemism, "He's kicked the bucket." To make certain jobs sound less unappealing, people use euphemisms. A janitor is now a "custodial worker" or "maintenance person." A trash man may be called a "sanitation engineer." Such euphemisms are not harmful, but sometimes euphemisms can be used to camouflage potentially controversial or objectionable actions. For example, instead of saying we need to raise taxes, a politician might say we need "revenue enhancement measures." When psychologists kill an animal they have experimented with, they prefer to use the term "sacrifice" the animal. Doctors prefer "terminate a pregnancy" to "abort the fetus."

A final example of language that conveys unintended impressions is sexist language. Sexist language refers to expressions that demean females in some way. For instance, when someone refers to a grown woman as a "girl," the implication is that she is still a child. Therefore, instead of an employer saying, "I'll have my girl type that," what should be said is, "I'll have my assistant (or secretary) type that." Other offensive expressions include "young thing," as in, "She's a cute young thing." The proper term, "girl," should be used in this case, since the "thing" is a young female. Further, the names of many jobs suggest women should not fill these positions. Thus, we use "chair" or "chairperson" instead of the sexist "chairman." Likewise, a "foreman" should be called a "supervisor."

---

* *Webster's New Collegiate Dictionary* (Springfield: G&C Merriam Company, 1973), p. 394.

We must always be careful to choose the words that convey what we really mean. If we do not want to give offense, then we should always be on guard against sexist (as well as racist) language. If we do not want to be misled by advertisements, we must keep our ears open for weasel words. Finally, when we use a euphemism, we should be aware that we are trying to make an idea more acceptable. At times this may be preferable, but let's not forget that euphemisms camouflage reality. After all, "coloring the truth" is still lying.

EXERCISE 7·9   On a separate sheet of paper, answer the following questions about the preceding essay.

1. What is the thesis of this essay?
2. What is the principle of organization of the paragraphs?
3. How many examples does the writer discuss? Are there enough examples?
4. Outline this essay.

Repetition of Key Words and Phrases

The standard transitional expressions are useful for making paragraphs connect logically; however, these phrases used all of the time can become mechanical and repetitious. For variety and for even more smoothness, pick up a key idea, word, or phrase from one paragraph and use it in the sentence introducing the next paragraph.

EXERCISE 7·10   Refer back to the reading "Words That Camouflage" on pages 145–147, and underline the original transitional phrases which start paragraphs 2, 3, and 4 in this essay. Then replace the original phrases that you underlined with the revised transitional phrases provided.

Paragraph 2:
Original transitional phrase:
Take, for instance, the language of advertising.
Revised transitional phrase:
Experts at camouflage are those in advertising.

Paragraph 3:
Original transitional phrase:
A second example of words that camouflage meaning is euphemisms.
Revised transitional phrase:
Just as "weasel words" are used to engender favorable impressions, so are euphemisms.

Paragraph 4:
Original transitional phrase:
  A final example of language that conveys unintended impressions is sexist language.
Revised transitional phrase:
  What many find objectionable today is sexist language.

Although "Words That Camouflage" is coherent without revising the transitional phrases, the revised version flows more smoothly because the transitions are more subtle. A variety of transitions reduces monotony.

Observe how the writers of the essays in Chapters 6 and 7 use transitions between paragraphs:

From "Why People Save Books"

Another reason some people save books is to make a good *impression*. Some think that a library full of the literary classics, dictionaries, and books about art, science, and history make them look well read and therefore sophisticated. Of course, this impression may be inaccurate. Some have never bothered to read the majority of those books at all! In fact, a few people even have libraries with fake books. Also, some people like to reveal to visitors their wide range of tastes and interests. They can subtly reveal their interests in Peruvian art, Indian music, philosophy, or animals, without saying a word.

  While some people may keep books for practical reference and for conveying an *impression*, I suspect that there is a deeper reason.

From "My Favorite Sights"

From the Plaines d'Abraham, it is easy to discover the majestic *Saint Lawrence River*. This beautiful broad river was the open door for our founders. Traveling in canoes, they established the first three cities in the lands drained by the *Saint Lawrence*: Quebec, Montreal, and Trois-Rivières. They must have been impressed with the clear, sweet water, the tree-studded islands, and the banks lined with pine and hemlock. Today, the river is an exceptional waterway extending 1,500 miles into the interior. Like the Mississippi River, it is, in every season, the location for great activities. Although the most important one is commercial, pleasure and sport are considerable: for example, boating, water-skiing, and fishing. These are particularly popular in summer. Furthermore, even though there are 3 to 5 feet of ice on the river in winter, the *Saint Lawrence* is still navigable.

On the north shore of the *Saint Lawrence River*, five miles from Quebec, the famous Montmorency Falls are located.

From "Useless Trifles"

Certainly anyone would also appreciate items that make our lives more *comfortable*, but some of the items for the bathroom border on the absurd. For about $8 you can buy an inflatable pillow to rest against in the bathtub. (It's held secure by suction cups.) An inch-thick foam rubber pad will cushion you from the hard bottom of the tub as you bathe. Of course if it gets mildew on it, it might be better located in the trash can. Finally, you can sit in *comfort* on the toilet on a plush toilet seat cover and listen to music from a radio built into a toilet paper container.

Comfort and convenience are carried to extremes in the area of personal care.

EXERCISE 7·11   Examine the relationship conveyed by the transitions between each pair of paragraphs above. Which transitional phrase demonstrates contradiction? Which conveys similarity? Which transition focuses on the geographical relationship between ideas? How do you know?

EXERCISE 7·12   Study the following sets of paragraphs. Assume that the two paragraphs occur after an introduction. Change the beginning of the second paragraph in each set so that it contains a key word linking it to the previous paragraph.

1. One of the things I do to improve my English is to watch television. This is no doubt one of the most popular techniques that all foreign students use. I find that the situation comedies and detective shows help me improve my listening skills the most because the actors speak very rapidly. Documentaries and news programs help me build my vocabulary because they contain material that interests me. All of the shows help me improve my speaking skills because I consciously try to imitate the way the actors speak, especially the newscasters because they enunciate each word so well.

   I work the crossword puzzles in the daily newspaper. Sometimes I can figure out a word if several of the letters are in it, and sometimes I have to ask somebody. If I cannot finish the puzzle, I keep it until the solution appears in the next edition of the newspaper. Then I look up the words I did not know and write them down. I have learned dozens of new vocabulary words this way, and by doing the puzzles every day, I have found that many of the words reappear, thus reinforcing my knowledge of the new words.

2. One popular mythical character that youngsters in America love is the tooth

fairy. When a child loses a tooth, she puts it under her pillow and during the night the tooth fairy will come and take the tooth, leaving in its place some money. Some children leave their extracted teeth in special boxes to make them easier for the tooth fairy to find. There is no typical description of what the tooth fairy looks like; most kids are content to imagine it as a mysterious benevolent spirit.

The Easter Bunny is a favorite mythical character. During Easter week, children go on Easter egg hunts to find colored and candy eggs hidden in yards and parks. A white bunny, sometimes called Peter Cottontail, has supposedly hidden these treats. In addition, on Easter morning children wake up to find that the Easter bunny has left them a basket full of chocolate eggs, jelly beans, candy eggs—all in a bed of green stuff that looks like grass.

3. One of my favorite neighborhoods in Chicago is Wrigleyville, which is located in the north part of the city. In the heart of Wrigleyville, on the corner of Addison and Clark, sits the wonderful old outdoor Wrigley Stadium, which is the home of the Chicago Cubs. If you are anywhere near the stadium during a game, you might hear the crowd cheer or if you're really lucky, you can hear them singing "Take Me Out to the Ballgame." People who live in apartment buildings next to the stadium can watch ball games from their balconies and rooftops. Stepping out from the stadium, fans can walk to numerous restaurants and enjoy almost any kind of food, from Thai to Mexican to American hot dogs.

   Andersonville is located north of Wrigleyville. It is a small neighborhood that was originally a Swedish settlement. On Clark Street, you can eat Swedish food at Ann Sather's restaurant or take a look at Swedish culture in the Swedish-American Museum Center. Over the years, other ethnic groups have settled in Andersonville, making it a diverse and pleasant community. If you want Greek food, try Andie's restaurant or if you prefer Persian food, try Reza's. Down the street is a charming coffee shop where you can enjoy "caffe latte" and a pastry. In addition, Andersonville has several interesting shops that sell everything from recycled clothing to handmade jewelry and pottery.

Grammar Review

If you want further review of grammatical structures that will help you achieve coherence and grammatical accuracy in your writing, see the Grammar Review Unit. The following sections are designed to coordinate with the example essay:

Gerund and Infinitives, pages 352–358
Noun Clauses, pages 339–344

EXERCISE 7·13 Writing Assignment Select one of the following topics for your writing assignment. Before you begin planning and drafting your essay, use one of the prewriting techniques you learned in Chapter 1 to generate ideas about your topic. Then develop a controlling idea, a thesis statement, and appropriate examples to support your point. Write a plan for the essay and then write the essay.

1. What are some of the unwritten rules that you think cultures use to regulate behavior? Can you think of relevant examples of these rules either in American culture or in some other culture? Write an essay using these examples to support a thesis. You may want to refer to Greene's essay, "How Unwritten Rules Circumscribe Our Lives" (pages 129–131).
2. Has a word or concept from your language been misinterpreted by another language/culture? Write an essay in which you explain the two meanings of the word, supporting your thesis with relevant examples. You may want to refer to Guilbault's essay, "Americanization is Tough on *Macho.*"
3. When you first came to the United States, you were undoubtedly surprised by something. Can you think of examples? Did you find anything particularly difficult to adjust to? Can you think of examples? Choose one of these topics, develop your thesis, and support it with examples.
4. Many groups of people have been victims of prejudice. Write an essay about people you are familiar with who have been victims of prejudice.
5. Clothes can tell a lot about a person. What are some things that you can tell about someone judging from the clothes he or she wears?

EXERCISE 7·14 Assignments from the Disciplines Following are some topics for your final writing assignment which are typical of college writing assignments. For your final writing assignment, you may choose one that you have studied, or consult a textbook or the Internet to find the answer. Then, follow the directions for Exercise 7-13 to write your answer.

1. **From Art history** Paintings by Impressionists such as Claude Monet and Mary Cassat have become very popular because of the beautiful colors and images they painted. Choose a painting which is a good example of Impressionism and use this painting to examine how members of the Impressionistic movement depicted color and light.
2. **From International Business** Select a major regional trading group, such as APEC, ASEAN, EU, NAFTA, or MERCOSUR. In an essay, use this group as an example to explain the advantages and disadvantages of such regional trading groups.

Revision

Peer Review

When you have finished writing the first draft of your essay, give it to a classmate to read and review. Use the peer review checklist in Appendix I to respond to each other's drafts.

Revision Checklist for the Paragraph

Use these questions to help you to give suggestions to your peers and to revise your essay.

1. An example essay supports its thesis with an appropriate number of examples. Does your essay have sufficient examples to support its point?
2. The examples you use to support your thesis should be representative or fair examples. Are your examples fairly chosen?
3. The organization of details and examples in an example essay depends on the subject and the writer's logic. Typical organizing principles are time, familiarity, and importance. Are the thesis and supporting examples logically organized in your essay?
4. Transitions between paragraphs and repetition of key words and phrases help to make an essay coherent. Have you used a variety of techniques to make your essay flow smoothly?

Chapter ⑧ The Comparison and Contrast Essay

Theme

Styles of communication

Goals

Writing

To distinguish between comparison and contrast

To identify points of comparison

To be able to use both patterns of organization to plan and write an essay that compares and/or contrasts

To use typical comparison/contrast transitions to increase coherence

Reading

To learn about and discuss different styles of communication

To understand and explain analogies

Grammar

To review comparisons and adverbial clauses of comparison, contrast, and concession

Getting Started

Journal Writing: Choose one of the following two questions, and write about it in your journal.

1. Remember a time when you had a misunderstanding with someone because of miscommunication. This could be something that happened between you and a friend, a roommate, a family member, or someone at school. Write about the situation and the different ways you and the other person understood the situation.

2. What are the "rules" for conversation in your native language? Who speaks first? How do you show someone that you are being polite? Is age important? How are the rules for conversation in English different from conversation rules in your own language?

CNN® Video Activity: "Workplace Communication: Gender Differences"

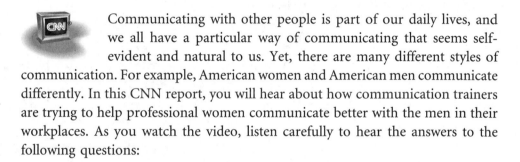 Communicating with other people is part of our daily lives, and we all have a particular way of communicating that seems self-evident and natural to us. Yet, there are many different styles of communication. For example, American women and American men communicate differently. In this CNN report, you will hear about how communication trainers are trying to help professional women communicate better with the men in their workplaces. As you watch the video, listen carefully to hear the answers to the following questions:

1. Why are these seminars, books, and training tapes usually directed at women?
2. When do these communication experts recommend that women should change their communication style?
3. When dealing with different communication styles, what may bring an even better result than changing styles?

Video Follow-up: Brainstorming

Imagine that you work for a company that provides communication training. Your company has decided to develop a communication training seminar and training tape for people who speak English as a second language. Imagine that you and your classmates are the committee in charge of this project. Brainstorm a list of topics that should be covered in the training. Share your list of topics with the class.

Internet Activity: Composition Skills and the Internet

 Use an Internet search tool to find advertisements for communication seminars or training materials. Try the key words "workplace communication training." Find at least two, and then compare the advertisements. Consider the following questions:

1. What communication problems will the training help people to solve?
2. What will workshop participants learn? What will they learn how to do?
3. Are the materials aimed at a particular group, such as women, managers, or members of an ethnic group?

Readings: Styles of Communication

Communicating with other people is part of our daily lives, yet there are many different styles of communication. We all have a particular way of communicating that seems self-evident and natural to us, so we can be surprised, frustrated, or hurt when someone misunderstands us. In the following readings, you will read about the differences in styles of communicating between the two genders (men and women) and between two cultures. As you read, try to answer the following questions:

1. What is the difference between Eastern- and Western-style conversations?
2. What is the difference between men's and women's styles of communicating? In this culture? In your culture?
3. Have you ever been misunderstood because of different styles of communication?

Reading ①

"Conversational Ballgames"
by Nancy Masterson Sakamoto

In the following reading, Nancy Masterson Sakamoto explains the difference between Japanese and American conversational styles. Born in the United States, Sakamoto has lived and taught English in Japan. She is currently professor of American Studies at Shitennoji Gakuen University, Hawaii Institute. The following selection is an excerpt from her textbook, *Polite Fictions* (1982).

Before you read, answer these questions:

1. Consider two cultures you are familiar with. How do communication styles in these cultures differ in their ideas of what is polite and impolite, of who talks first and who second, and of how the conversation should proceed?

2. Do you find it exciting or upsetting when people in a discussion with you begin to agree and disagree with a lot of energy?

3. Do you prefer a conversation in which each speaker has a regular turn to speak, or would you rather that speakers interject each time they have an idea to share?

---

stop

1   After I was married and had lived in Japan for a while, my Japanese gradually improved to the point where I could take part in simple conversations with my husband, his friends and family. And I began to notice that often, when I joined in, the others would look startled, and the conversational topic would come to a halt.° After this happened several times, it became clear to me that I was doing something wrong. But for a long time, I didn't know what it was.

2   Finally, after listening carefully to many Japanese conversations, I discovered what my problem was. Even though I was speaking Japanese, I was handling the conversation in a Western way.

3   Japanese-style conversations develop quite differently from Western-style conversations. And the difference isn't only in the languages. I realized that just as I kept trying to hold Western-style conversations even when I was speaking Japanese, so my English students kept trying to hold Japanese-style conversations even when they were speaking English. We were unconsciously playing entirely different conversational ballgames.

4   A Western-style conversation between two people is like a game of tennis. If I introduce a topic, a conversational ball, I expect you to hit it back. If you agree with me, I don't expect you simply to agree and do nothing more. I expect you to add something—a reason for agreeing, another example, or an elaboration to carry the idea further. But I don't expect you always to agree. I am just as happy if you question me, or challenge me, or completely disagree with me. Whether you agree or disagree, your response will return the ball to me.

5   And then it is my turn again. I don't serve a new ball from my original starting line. I hit your ball back again from where it has bounced. I carry your idea further, or answer your questions or objections or challenge or question you. And so the ball goes back and forth, with each of us doing our best to give it a new twist, an original spin, or a powerful smash.

6   And the more vigorous the action, the more interesting and exciting the game. Of course, if one of us gets angry, it spoils the conversation, just as it spoils a tennis game. But getting excited is not at all the same as getting angry. After all, we are not trying to hit each other. We are trying to hit the ball. So long as we attack only each other's opinions, and do not attack each other personally, we don't expect anyone to get hurt. A good conversation is supposed to be interesting and exciting.

7   If there are more than two people in the conversation, then it is like doubles in tennis, or like volleyball. There's no waiting in line. Whoever is nearest and quickest hits the ball, and if you step back, someone else will hit it. No one stops the game to give you a turn. You're responsible for taking your own turn.

8   But whether it's two players or a group, everyone does his best to keep the ball going, and no one person has the ball for very long.

9   A Japanese-style conversation, however, is not at all like tennis or volleyball. It's like bowling. You wait for your turn. And you always know your place in line. It depends on such things as whether you are older or younger, a close friend or a relative stranger to the previous speaker, in a senior or junior position, and so on.

10   When your turn comes, you step up to the starting line with your bowling ball, and carefully bowl it. Everyone else stands back and watches politely, murmuring encouragement. Everyone waits until the ball has reached the end of the alley, and watches to see if it knocks down all the pins, or only some of them, or none of them. There is a pause, while everyone registers your score.

side by side

11   Then, after everyone is sure that you have completely finished your turn, the next person in line steps up to the same starting line, with a different ball. He doesn't return your ball, and he does not begin from where your ball stopped. There is no back and forth at all. All the balls run parallel.° And there is always a suitable pause between turns. There is no rush, no excitement, no scramble for the ball.

12   No wonder everyone looked startled when I took part in Japanese conversations. I paid no attention to whose turn it was, and kept snatching the ball halfway down the alley and throwing it back at the bowler. Of course the conversation died. I was playing the wrong game.

13   This explains why it is almost impossible to get a Western-style conversation or discussion going with English students in Japan. I used to think that the problem was their lack of English language ability. But I finally came to realize that the biggest problem is that they, too, are playing the wrong game.

14   Whenever I serve a volleyball, everyone just stands back and watches it fall, with occasional murmurs of encouragement. No one hits it back. Everyone waits until I call on someone to take a turn. And when that person speaks, he doesn't hit my ball back. He serves a new ball. Again, everyone just watches it fall.

15   So I call on someone else. This person does not refer to what the previous speaker has said. He also serves a new ball. Nobody seems to have paid any attention to what anyone else has said. Everyone begins again from the same starting line, and all the balls run parallel. There is never any back and forth. Everyone is trying to bowl with a volleyball.

16   Now that you know about the difference in the conversational ball-games, you may think that all your troubles are over. But if you have been trained all your life to play one game, it is no simple matter to switch to another, even if you know the rules. Knowing the rules is not at all the same thing as playing the game.

too late

17   Even now, during a conversation in Japanese I will notice a startled reaction, and belatedly° realize that once again I have rudely interrupted by instinctively trying to hit back the other person's bowling ball. It is no easier for me to "just listen" during a conversation than it is for my Japanese students to "just relax" when speaking with foreigners. Now I can truly sympathize with how hard they must find it to carry on a Western-style conversation.

EXERCISE 8•1 Comprehension/Discussion Questions

1. What happened when Sakamoto first began participating in Japanese conversations? Why?
2. Sakamoto uses two *analogies*, long comparisons of familiar things with unfamiliar things, to ultimately contrast the two styles of conversation. In her first analogy, what does she compare a Western-style conversation to?
3. Explain the analogy. How is a Western-style conversation like a game of tennis?
4. What does she compare an Eastern-style conversation to? Explain the analogy.
5. In drawing the analogies, Sakamoto contrasts the two styles of conversation. Explain the differences in the following:
   a. taking turns
   b. approach to the topic (the ball)
   c. pausing
   d. reactions of participants
   e. determining the score
6. What is the author's thesis? Where in the essay is it stated?
7. In what ways does Sakamoto establish her authority to speak on this topic?
8. In paragraph 17, why are "just listen" and "just relax" in quotation marks?
9. Have you had experience conversing with Asians, especially Japanese? If so, do you agree with Sakamoto's thesis? Is her analysis of Eastern-style conversations accurate? Support your answer.
10. Have you ever been in different "conversational ballgames"? What "rules" were you following? What "rules" was the other person following? What happened in the conversation?
11. Are the conversational rules in your culture more similar to the Western style or the Eastern style described here? Be prepared to explain the similarities and differences between the conversational styles in your culture and another culture.
12. Try to think of an analogy to describe the conversational style of your culture.

EXERCISE 8·2 Vocabulary Development

A. Because the author is comparing conversations to games, she uses some vocabulary associated with tennis, volleyball, and bowling. Some of those words and phrases are listed below. Be prepared to explain their meaning.
   1. *serve* a new ball (par. 5)
   2. a powerful *smash* (par. 5)
   3. *doubles* in tennis (par. 7)
   4. the end of the *alley* (par. 10)
   5. knocked down all the *pins* (par. 10)

B. Following are lists of words associated with various games. Be prepared to explain the meanings of the words. Then add as many words as you can to each list.

   1. Tennis: court, net, racquet, in bounds, out of bounds

   _____

   2. Bowling: strike, spare

   _____

   3. Basketball: court, basket, hoop, tip-off, free throw

   _____

   4. Soccer: field, goal, goal post

   _____

C. Be prepared to explain how to play each of these games.

Reading ②

"Intimacy and Independence"
by Deborah Tannen

In the following excerpt from her book *You Just Don't Understand*, Deborah Tannen examines the different ways that American men and women view decision making. She notes that the different notions of communication that women and men have can lead to conflict between couples. Tannen, a well-known sociolinguist who teaches at Georgetown University in Washington, D.C., bases her research on Americans. Before you read, answer these questions:

1. Do men and women in your culture have different communication styles?
2. What kind of conflicts in communication can occur (a) at home, (b) at work, (c) at school because of differences in male and female communication patterns?
3. Everyone needs both intimacy and independence in his or her relationships, but which do you think is most important?

feeling close to other people

build, bargain to reach agreement

make less important

agreement

position, rank

friend

slang for unimportant talk

subordinate; a person with low status

closely woven together

results, effects

reasonable

1   *Intimacy*° is key in a world of connections where individuals negotiate° complex networks of friendship, minimize° differences, try to reach consensus,° and avoid the appearance of superiority, which would highlight differences. In a world of status,° *independence* is key, because a primary means of establishing status is to tell others what to do, and taking orders is a marker of low status. Though all humans need both intimacy and independence, women tend to focus on the first and men on the second. It is as if their lifeblood ran in different directions.

2   These differences can give women and men differing views of the same situation, as they did in the case of a couple I will call Linda and Josh. When Josh's old high-school chum° called him at work and announced he'd be in town on business the following month, Josh invited him to stay for the weekend. That evening he informed Linda that they were going to have a houseguest, and that he and his chum would go out together the first night to shoot the breeze° like old times. Linda was upset. She was going to be away on business the week before, and the Friday night when Josh would be out with his chum would be her first night home. But what upset her the most was that Josh had made these plans on his own and informed her of them, rather than discussing them with her before extending the invitation.

3   Linda would never make plans, for a weekend or an evening, without first checking with Josh. She can't understand why he doesn't show her the same courtesy and consideration that she shows him. But when she protests, Josh says, "I can't say to my friend, 'I have to ask my wife for permission'!"

4   To Josh, checking with his wife means seeking permission, which implies that he is not independent, not free to act on his own. It would make him feel like a child or an underling.° To Linda, checking with her husband has nothing to do with permission. She assumes that spouses discuss their plans with each other because their lives are intertwined,° so the actions of one have consequences° for the other. Not only does Linda not mind telling someone, "I have to check with Josh"; quite the contrary—she likes it. It makes her feel good to know and show that she is involved with someone, that her life is bound up with someone else's.

5   Linda and Josh both felt more upset by this incident, and others like it, than seemed warranted,° because it cut to the core of their primary concerns. Linda was hurt because she sensed a failure of closeness in their relationship: He didn't care about her as much as she cared about him. And he was hurt because he felt she was trying to control him and limit his freedom.

6   A similar conflict exists between Louise and Howie, another couple, about spending money. Louise would never buy anything costing more than a hundred dollars without discussing it with Howie, but he goes out and buys whatever he wants and feels they can afford, like a table saw or a new power mower. Louise is disturbed, not because she disapproves

of the purchases, but because she feels he is acting as if she were not in the picture.

discuss, check

ideas

restricted
start
open-ended,
unfocused

together with

part of a machine

7   Many women feel it is natural to consult° with their partners at every turn, while many men automatically make more decisions without consulting their partners. This may reflect a broad difference in conceptions° of decision making. Women expect decisions to be discussed first and made by consensus. They appreciate the discussion itself as evidence of involvement and communication. But many men feel oppressed by lengthy discussions about what they see as minor decisions, and they feel hemmed in° if they can't just act without talking first. When women try to initiate° a freewheeling° discussion by asking, "What do you think?" men often think they are being asked to decide.

8   Communication is a continual balancing act, juggling the conflicting needs for intimacy and independence. To survive in the world, we have to act in concert with° others, but to survive as ourselves, rather than simply as cogs in a wheel,° we have to act alone. In some ways, all people are the same: We all eat and sleep and drink and laugh and cough, and often we eat, and laugh at, the same things. But in some ways, each person is different, and individuals' different wants and preferences may conflict with each other. Offered the same menu, people make different choices. And if there is cake for dessert, there is a chance one person may get a larger piece than another—and an even greater chance that one will *think* the other's piece is larger, whether it is or not.

EXERCISE 8·3 Comprehension/Discussion Questions

1. Explain what Tannen means by *intimacy* and *independence*.
2. According to Tannen (par. 1), what is important to women in order to get along with others? to men?
3. In paragraph 2, the author begins with "These differences." What differences is she referring to?
4. In paragraphs 4–6, Tannen gives the example of Linda and Josh. Explain the situation that caused the conflict.
5. Why was Linda upset with Josh?
6. What is Josh's reaction when she protests his actions?
7. Explain the basic difference in their reactions in terms of intimacy and independence.
8. What is the point of the second situation, the example of Louise and Howie?
9. In paragraph 7, Tannen connects different ways of making decisions with communication. What is the connection?
10. In paragraph 8, Tannen says, "Communication is a continual balancing act." What does she mean?

11. In paragraph 8, does Tannen suggest that one style of communication is better than another? Support your answer.

12. In this excerpt, Tannen is discussing American women and men. Do men and women in your culture have similar or different conflicts in communication? Can you give a specific example?

EXERCISE 8•4 Vocabulary Development   Paragraph 1 of the Tannen reading has a lot of abstract words that may make it difficult to understand. In this exercise, you will paraphrase, or state in other words, the sentences in this paragraph. The long sentences are broken down into parts. First paraphrase each part. Then combine the parts to make a complete, grammatical sentence. The first one is done for you.

Sentence 1:

1. Intimacy is key in a world of connections

   Feeling close to other people is the most important thing when society

   emphasizes personal relationships.

2. in a world of connections, individuals negotiate complex networks of friendship.

   _____

   _____

3. they minimize differences

   _____

   _____

4. they try to reach consensus

   _____

   _____

5. they avoid the appearance of superiority

   _____

   _____

6. an appearance of superiority would highlight differences

   _____

   _____

Sentence 2:

   1. In a world of status, independence is the key

      _____

      _____

   2. because a primary means of establishing status is to tell others what to do

      _____

      _____

   3. and because taking orders is a marker of low status.

      _____

      _____

Sentence 3:

   1. Though all humans need both intimacy and independence

      _____

      _____

   2. women tend to focus on the first

      _____

      _____

   3. and men tend to focus on the second.

      _____

      _____

Sentence 4:

   It is as if their lifeblood ran in different directions.

      _____

      _____

Writing

Although details and examples can be used in all kinds of expository writing, not all essay topics are best developed in an example essay pattern. Very often, for example, you are asked to compare and contrast two things, items, or people. In your history class, you might be asked to compare and contrast the Greek and Roman empires; in your biology class, you might be required to compare and contrast DNA and RNA. Comparing and contrasting is a process we all do every day. We compare and contrast to determine the superiority of one thing over another. When we buy a car, for instance, we usually shop around and compare deals. We explain something that is unknown by comparing it to something that is known. We might explain what a barometer is by saying it looks like a thermometer but measures atmospheric pressure instead of temperature. We also compare and contrast when we want to show that two apparently similar things are in fact quite different in important ways or to show that two apparently dissimilar things are really quite similar in significant ways. It might, for instance, be quite enlightening to discover that two very different cultures have some important things in common. We also compare and contrast to show how something or someone has changed, such as California before and after the earthquake in 1994.

We have many reasons for comparing and contrasting, and since the process of comparison and contrast is such a common method of thinking and of developing topics, it is important to write a well-organized comparison and contrast paper. There is one thing to keep in mind, however: With comparison and contrast, the purpose is not just to point out similarities and differences or advantages and disadvantages; the purpose is to persuade, explain, or inform. Think of comparison and contrast as a method of development—not as a purpose for writing.

When you are planning a comparison and contrast essay, there are several points to consider.

Points of Comparison

Let us suppose that you are asked to compare and contrast two people—perhaps two generals, two politicians, or two religious leaders. What would you compare and contrast about them? You could compare their looks, backgrounds, philosophies, the way they treat people, their attitudes toward life, their intelligence, their lifestyles, and so on. The list could continue, but this is just the problem: you would have a list. When comparing and contrasting two things, people, countries, and so forth, especially for a standard 300- to 500-word essay, it is best to restrict the points of comparison to two to four. Therefore, be selective and choose the most significant points for comparison that will support the central idea in your essay. For instance, if you wanted to compare two politicians in order to show that one is better as a public servant, you would not bother comparing and contrasting their tastes in food because this point would be irrelevant.

EXERCISE 8·5 Writing Assignment   Choose one of the following writing assignments.

1. Think of two educational systems that you are familiar with, such as the university system in your country and the system in this country. Brainstorm

a list about the things they have in common—their similarities—and another list about the ways they differ—their differences. From these lists, find three or four general points of comparison.

2. Choose two people or two products (such as two different automobiles, cameras, hair dryers, or stereos), and brainstorm a list of their similarities and differences. From that list, find three or four general points of comparison.

Emphasis on Comparison or Contrast

In a comparison and contrast essay, the emphasis is usually on one or the other; that is, you spend more time either comparing or contrasting, depending on your purpose. If you are comparing two rather similar things, you should acknowledge the obvious similarities but focus on the differences. If you are comparing two obviously dissimilar things, you should acknowledge the obvious contrasts but emphasize the less obvious similarities.

Patterns of Organization

There are two basic patterns of organization for developing the comparison and contrast essay. Although they are called by various names, we refer to them here as Pattern A and Pattern B. To show how these patterns work, let's consider the topic of two automobiles: the Road Runner XL and the Speed Demon 280. Your points of comparison might be the cost of maintenance, performance, and comfort. Using Pattern A, you could organize the essay in this way:

Pattern A (Point-by-Point)

Thesis Statement: The Speed Demon 280 is a better car than the Road Runner XL.

 I. Cost of Maintenance
   A. The Road Runner XL
   B. The Speed Demon 280
 II. Performance
   A. The Road Runner XL
   B. The Speed Demon 280
III. Comfort
   A. The Road Runner XL
   B. The Speed Demon 280

Pattern A—Point-by-Point—is useful for organizing more complex topics. It is also an easy pattern to follow because the comparison-contrast is made clear throughout the essay. A developmental paragraph in a comparison and contrast essay following Pattern A appears to be more complex than a developmental paragraph in an example essay. In the developmental paragraph in the comparison and contrast essay, the writer introduces a topic (the point of comparison), but the topic is broken down into two parts to make the comparison. For example, let us say you were asked to compare the two automobiles, the Road Runner XL and the Speed Demon 280. For one of your points of comparison, you have chosen the cost of maintenance. You have found that the Road Runner XL is expensive to maintain and the Speed Demon is economical. What you have, then, are really two controlling ideas: one for each car. Here is how that paragraph might be developed:

> The Road Runner XL and the Speed Demon 280 differ in cost of maintenance. The Road Runner is rather expensive to maintain. This car gets rather poor mileage, with 23 miles per gallon on the highway and 18 miles per gallon in the city. Moreover, it requires the more expensive premium gasoline. In addition, the Road Runner has to have a tune-up every four months and an oil change every 90 days. The average driver who owns a Road Runner must pay approximately $1,400 a year to keep this car running. The Speed Demon, on the other hand, is quite economical. It gets an impressive 40 miles per gallon on the highway and 35 in the city, and, unlike the Road Runner, the Speed Demon takes the less costly regular gasoline. In addition, whereas the Road Runner requires tune-ups and oil changes, the Speed Demon requires little maintenance. It needs to be tuned up only every 12 months; the oil needs to be changed only every four months. In summary, instead of paying $1,400 per year to keep the car running, the owner of a Speed Demon only has to pay $600, which is significantly less.

This paragraph can be outlined as follows:

I. The Road Runner XL and the Speed Demon 280 differ in cost of maintenance.
   A. The Road Runner is rather expensive to maintain.
      1. Mileage.
      2. Tune-ups.
      3. Oil changes.
      4. Average cost of maintenance.
   B. The Speed Demon is economical to maintain.
      1. Mileage.
      2. Tune-ups.
      3. Oil changes.
      4. Average cost of maintenance.

In this outline, the Roman numeral *I* introduces the point of comparison (the topic); the next point of comparison would be outlined as Roman numeral *II*.

Since the paragraph is rather long, it is possible to break it into two paragraphs, with the second one beginning, "The Speed Demon, on the other hand, is quite economical."

EXERCISE 8·6 Writing Assignments Study the following information about the comfort of the Road Runner XL and the Speed Demon 280 and find a controlling idea about the difference in comfort. Then write a paragraph comparing and contrasting the comfort of the Road Runner and the comfort of the Speed Demon.

THE ROAD RUNNER XL	THE SPEED DEMON 280
1. Spacious interior Ample head and leg room in both front and back.	1. Not as spacious interior Ample head and leg room in front, but cramped in the back (less used).
2. Two people can sit comfortably in the front and three in the back.	2. Two can fit comfortably in front but only two can sit comfortably in back.
3. Uncomfortable seats Although the seats are large, they are vinyl and get hot in spring and summer.	3. Comfortable seats Suede seats are cool in the summer and pleasant all year round.
4. Cooling and heating not ideal The air conditioner does not cool the back seat area; the heater is effective.	4. Excellent air conditioning and heating system The air conditioner cools the entire car rapidly; the heater is equally effective.

This same topic can be developed in another way: Pattern B, called "All of one/ All of the other."

Pattern B (All of One/All of the Other)

Thesis Statement: The Speed Demon 280 is a better car than the Road Runner XL.

 I. The Road Runner XL
   A. Cost of Maintenance
   B. Performance
   C. Comfort
II. The Speed Demon 280
   A. Cost of Maintenance
   B. Performance
   C. Comfort

Note that the points of comparison are the same and that they are discussed in the same order under each section in both patterns of organization. One of the problems with Pattern B, however, is that it is sometimes difficult to remind the reader in the second section of how the points compare or contrast with the points mentioned in the first section. Therefore, generally speaking, Pattern B is more useful for more limited topics.

Read the sample student essay that follows. As you read the essay, determine whether it focuses more on comparison or contrast and which pattern of development it uses.

My Two Brothers

No two people are exactly alike, and my two older brothers, Nhan and Hung, are no exceptions. When I think of them, I think of Rudyard Kipling's words:

> East is East
> West is West
> Never the twain shall meet.

Even though they have the same parents, their considerable differences in looks, personality, and attitude toward life reflect the differences between Eastern and Western cultures.

Like the majority of Asian men, Nhan is short, small, and has a full, moon-shaped face. His smooth white skin and small arms and feet make him look somewhat delicate. Nhan always likes to wear formal, traditional clothes. For example, on great holidays or at family rite celebrations, Nhan appears in the traditional black gown, white pants and black silky headband, all of which make him look like an early twentieth-century intellectual.

In contrast to Nhan, Hung, who is his younger brother by 10 years, looks more like an American boxer. He is tall, muscular, and big-boned. He is built straight as an arrow, and his face is long and angular as a Western character. Unlike Nhan, Hung has strong feet and arms, and whereas Nhan has smooth skin, Hung's shoulders and chest are hairy, large and full. Unlike Nhan, too, Hung likes to wear comfortable T-shirts and jeans or sports clothes. At a formal occasion, instead of wearing traditional formal clothes, Hung wears stylish Western style suits.

Nhan and Hung also differ in personality. I don't know how my father selected their names correctly to reflect their personalities. Nhan's name means "patience," and his patience is shown in his smile.

He has the smile of an ancient Chinese philosopher that Western people can never understand. He always smiles. He smiles because he wants to make the other person happy or to make himself happy. He smiles whenever people speak to him, regardless of whether they are right or wrong. He smiles when he forgives people who have wronged him. Nhan likes books, of course, and literature and philosophy. He likes to walk in the moonlight to think. Nhan also enjoys drinking hot tea and singing verses. In short, in our family, Nhan is the son who provides a good example of filial piety and tolerance.

Hung, on the other hand, does not set a good example of traditional respectful behavior for his brothers and sisters. His name means "strength," but his strength is self-centered. As a result, unlike Nhan, Hung only smiles when he is happy. When he talks to people, he looks at their faces. Because of this, my eldest brother Nhan considers him very impolite. As one might expect, Hung does not like philosophy and literature; instead, he studies science and technology. Whereas Nhan enjoys tea and classical verses, Hung prefers to take sun baths and drink Coca-Cola while he listens to rock and roll music. And like many American youths, Hung is independent; in fact, he loves his independence more than he loves his family. He wants to move out of our house and live in an apartment by himself. He is such an individualist that all the members in my family say that he is very selfish.

My brothers' differences do not end with looks and personalities. Concerning their attitudes toward life, they are as different as the moon and the sun. My eldest brother Nhan is concerned with spiritual values. He is affected by Confucian, Taoist, and Buddhist theories. These theories consider that the human life is not happy. Therefore, if a man wants to be happy, he should get out of the competitiveness of life and should not depend on material objects. For example, if a man is not anxious to have a new-model car, he does not have to worry about how to make money to buy one. Or, if he does not have a car, he does not have to worry about the cost of gas. My oldest brother is deeply affected by these theories, so he never tries hard to make money to buy conveniences.

In contrast to Nhan, my brother Hung believes that science and technology serve human beings and that the West defeated the East because the West was further advanced in these fields. Therefore, each person must compete with nature and with other people in the world in order to acquire different conveniences such as cars, washing machines, and television sets. Hung is affected by the Western theories of real values; consequently, he always works hard to make his own money to satisfy his material needs.

In accordance with the morality of the culture of my country, I cannot say which one of my brothers is wrong or right. But I do know that they both want to improve and maintain human life on this earth. I am very lucky to inherit both sources of thought from my two older brothers.

—Ha Sau Hoa

EXERCISE 8·7   On a separate sheet of paper, answer the following questions about one of the previous essays.

1. What is the thesis of the essay? What are its points of comparison?
2. Does the essay focus more on comparison or on contrast?
3. Which pattern of organization does the writer follow? Why was this pattern selected?
4. Does the essay have topic sentences that state the controlling idea for each point of comparison? If so, what are they?
5. Is the essay unified? Coherent?
6. Is the conclusion logical?
7. Make a detailed outline of the essay.

EXERCISE 8·8 Writing Assignment   Using the preceding essays as a model and the brainstorming notes you made in Exercise 8-5, write a first-draft essay that compares and contrasts two educational systems, two people, or two products.

As you read the essay that follows, try to locate its thesis statement and determine its purpose—that is, why the author is writing about this topic.

My Old Neighborhood

Several years ago, I returned to Washington, D.C., and visited one of my old neighborhoods. I had not been on Nash Street for more than 20 years and as I walked along the street, my mind was flooded by waves of nostalgia. I saw the old apartment building where I had lived and the playground where I had played. As I viewed these once-familiar surroundings, images of myself as a child there came to mind. However, what I saw and what I remembered were not the same. I sadly realized that the best memories are those left undisturbed.

As I remember my old apartment building, it was bright and alive. When I was a child, the apartment building was more than just a place to live. It

related to the years
450 to 1450 A.D.

a large container
slide

natural desire or
behavior
river or stream
a sweet flower

in need of being fixed

writing on walls

was a medieval° castle, a pirate's den, a space station, or whatever my young mind could imagine. I would steal away with my friends and play in the basement. This was always exciting because it was so cool and dark, and there were so many things there to hide among. Our favorite place to play was the coal bin.° We would always use it as our rocket ship because the coal chute° could be used as an escape hatch out of the basement into "outer space."

All of my memories were not confined to the apartment building, however. I have memories of many adventures outside of the building, also. My mother restricted how far we could go from the apartment building, but this placed no restrictions on our exploring instinct.° There was a small branch° in back of the building where my friends and I would play. We enjoyed it there because honeysuckles° grew there. We would go there to lie in the shade and suck the sweet-smelling honeysuckles. Our biggest thrill in the branch was the day the police caught an alligator there. I did not see the alligator, and I was not there when they caught it, but just the thought of an alligator in the branch was exciting.

This is how I remembered the old neighborhood; however, as I said, this is not how it was when I saw it.

Unlike before, the apartment building was now rundown and in disrepair.° What was once more than a place to live looked hardly worth living in. The court was dirty and broken up, and the windows in the building were all broken out. The once-clean walls were covered with graffiti° and other stains.

teenagers

There were no medieval knights or pirates running around the place now, nor spacemen; instead, there were a few tough looking adolescents° who looked much older than their ages.

As for the area where I used to play, it was hardly recognizable. The branch was polluted and the honeysuckles had died. Not only were they dead, but they had been trampled to the ground. The branch itself was filled with old bicycles, broken bottles, and garbage. Now, instead of finding something as romantic as an alligator, one would expect to find only rats. The once sweet-smelling area now smelled horrible. The stench from my idyllic° haven° was heart wrenching.

simple and happy place of safety

I do not regret having seen my old neighborhood. However, I do not think my innocent childhood memories can ever be the same. I suppose it is true when they say, "You can never go home again."

—Floyd Bonner

EXERCISE 8·9   On a separate sheet of paper, answer the following questions about "My Old Neighborhood."

1. What is the thesis? Where is it stated?
2. What is the controlling idea about the apartment building as it was when the author was a child?
3. What is the controlling idea about the apartment building when he visited it 20 years later?
4. What is the controlling idea about the branch as it was when he was a child?
5. What is the controlling idea about the branch as he saw it 20 years later?
6. One of the paragraphs is only one sentence long. What function does that sentence serve?
7. What pattern of organization does the writer use? Why? Does he cover the same points in the first part as he does in the second?
8. Is the essay coherent? Unified?
9. In a couple of places the author uses *would* when referring to the past. What kind of action does "*would + verb*" indicate when referring to the past time?
10. What are some of the expressions the author uses to indicate the change from the past to the present? Reread the essay and underline the expressions and phrases that clarify the changes. (For example, "The *once-clean walls* were covered with graffiti. . . .")
11. Make an outline of the essay.

EXERCISE 8·10 Writing Assignment   Choose one of the following writing assignments. Begin by prewriting, using one of the techniques given in Chapter 1.

1. Have you ever visited a place you had left a long time ago and found it had

changed considerably? Write an essay comparing and contrasting the "way it was" with the "way it is now." Try to formulate a controlling idea about the change. Have things changed for the better? The worse?

2. Before you came to this country, you undoubtedly had certain ideas and expectations about it. After you had been here awhile, did any of those ideas change? Did you find certain things to be different from what you expected? Choose several aspects of your life and experiences in this country and contrast the way you thought they would be with how you find them now.

Composition Skills

Coherence

Transitions for Comparison and Contrast

Transitional expressions give writing coherence; that is, they help to move smoothly from one idea to the next. In addition, a variety of transitions adds interest to an essay. In this lesson, you will practice using transitions that will give a comparison-contrast essay both coherence and interest. Note the transitional expressions used in these sentences:

In contrast to American universities, Lebanese universities have stricter admissions requirements.

American and Lebanese universities *also differ* in graduation requirements.

In Lebanon, *on the other hand,* only one limit exists.

Whereas American students may go part-time, Lebanese students must attend school full-time.

Unlike before, the apartment building was now rundown and in disrepair.

Even though both systems provide a good education, one system makes earning a college degree much easier than the other.

There is quite a large number of transitions that can be used for comparison and contrast. They fall into the following three major groups. Study them carefully and note the necessary punctuation for each type.

1. Transitions in Phrases
   All of the transitions in this group need to be followed by a noun. The phrase in which they occur is often used at the beginning of a sentence and is generally followed by a comma. The following transitions indicate similarity: *similar to, like.* The following indicate difference: *different from, in contrast to, compared with, unlike.* Note the following examples.

Similar to New Orleans, San Francisco attracts many tourists.

Like this American university, a Lebanese university also asked for my high school grades.

Different from the Road Runner, the Speed Demon has comfortable seats.

Compared with New Orleans, San Francisco has a very cold climate. (This means that probably the climate in San Francisco is not really that cold; it is just that the climate in New Orleans is extremely hot.)

Unlike the Road Runner, the Speed Demon is quite economical.

2. Coordinating Conjunctions as Transitions

The coordinating conjunctions *but* and *yet* are often used as transitions to indicate the opposite of what was expected. Coordinating conjunctions occur between two complete sentences and are preceded (but not followed) by a comma. Study these examples:

San Diego is very dry, *but* Houston is not.

The Speed Demon 280 is cheaper than the Road Runner XL, *yet* it has a better air-conditioning system.

Note: Sometimes these conjunctions are used as transitions at the beginning of a sentence:

Several events contributed to my depression last year. *But* my greatest sadness was losing the mathematics contest.

3. Transitional Expressions between Sentences

The transitions in this group generally occur between two independent clauses. When they do, they must be preceded by either a period or a semicolon.

Ecuador ships out a lot of bananas. *In addition,* it is an exporter of oil.

Ecuador ships out a lot of bananas; *in addition,* it is an exporter of oil.

Ecuador exports oil. Moreover, it is a coffee producer.

Ecuador exports oil; *moreover,* it is a coffee producer.

Occasionally, these transitional expressions are used in an independent clause. In this case, the expressions (except *also*) should be set off with commas:

Ecuador ships out a lot of bananas. It is, *in addition,* an exporter of oil.

Ecuador exports oil. It is, *moreover,* a producer of coffee.

Ecuador exports oil. It is *also* a coffee producer.

This group of transitions has the greatest number of words and phrases. Examine them in three parts:

a. Additive Transitions: *first, next, besides, in addition, moreover, furthermore, also, then.* We discussed most of the transitions in this group in Chapters 2 and 4. They can be used to indicate chronological order, to number or list examples, or to add more information to something that was just stated. In comparison-contrast, they can fulfill all these functions.

The tropical rain forest is a beautiful and fascinating place. *Besides,* it is extremely important to our ecosystem.

In addition, the tropical rain forest contains many important species of plants.

Moreover, valuable plant life is threatened.

The rain forest is *also* home to a wide variety of animals.

Also, the rain forest is home to a wide variety of animals.

   b. Transitions to Indicate Similarity: *likewise, similarly, in the same way.* These words are used to indicate a similarity between the items given in the two sentences.

Smog is adversely affecting the trees in the mountains near Los Angeles. *Likewise,* acid rain is harming trees in the northeast.

New Orleans has a big seafood business. *Similarly,* a great deal of fishing and oyster farming is done around San Francisco.

   c. Transitions to Indicate Difference: *on the other hand, conversely, in contrast, however.* These words are used to indicate a difference or a contrast between the items given in the two sentences.

Senator Smith wants to reduce the budget deficit by raising taxes. Jones, *on the other hand,* advocates making more cuts in spending.

New Orleans has hot, humid summers. *In contrast,* San Francisco's summers are cool and windy.

As I viewed these once-familiar surroundings, images of myself as a child there came to mind. *However,* what I saw and what I remembered were not the same.

The expression *on the contrary* is also in this group, but it is very restricted in its use. It indicates that the two ideas being expressed cannot both be true. It is often confused with *on the other hand.* Compare the following:

Jose: It's rather hot today.
Hong: It is not very hot today. *On the contrary,* it is quite cool.
It is not very hot today. *On the other hand,* it is not cool either.

Jose: The Earth is the fifth planet from the sun.
Hong: The Earth is not the fifth planet from the sun. *On the contrary,* it is the third.
The Earth is not the closest planet to the sun. *On the other hand,* it's not the farthest either.

Note that *on the contrary* really means "No, it isn't." Another transition that can sometimes be used in its place is *in fact*.

It is not very cold today; *in fact*, it's quite hot.

EXERCISE 8·11   Fill in the blanks with either *on the other hand* or *on the contrary*, whichever is appropriate.

1. New Orleans does not have a harsh winter _____, it is quite mild.

2. New Orleans does not have a harsh winter. _____, its summers are terrible.

3. New Orleans does not have a large population. _____, it is not a village.

4. Many people think that New Orleans is a large city. _____, it has quite a small population.

5. New Orleans was not originally settled by the Spanish; _____, its first European settlers were French.

6. New Orleans is a big seaport. _____, its manufacturing industry is quite small.

EXERCISE 8·12   Read the following paragraph about the writer Jorge Luis Borges.

Jorge Luis Borges is one of the greatest modern writers in Spanish. Born in Argentina, he was educated in Europe, and in his early days he served as a municipal librarian in Buenos Aires. Borges has written a variety of works, including poetry, essays, film criticism, and short stories. He was at odds with the policies of the Peron government in Argentina in the 1940s and 1950s. After the Peron government was overthrown, Borges became a professor of literature at the University of Buenos Aires. Many of his works have been translated into English and other languages.

For each of the following items, write sentences, using the transitions given, comparing or contrasting Borges with the Japanese writer Yukio Mishima. The first one is done for you.

1. Yukio Mishima is considered one of the greatest modern Japanese writers.

   like   Like Borges, Mishima is considered one of the greatest modern writers.

   also   Borges is a great modern writer. Mishima is also considered a great modern
   writer.

   similarly   Borges is a great modern writer. Similarly, Mishima is considered by
   many people to be a great modern writer.

2. Mishima was educated in his native country of Japan.

   unlike _____

   but _____

   in contrast _____

3. In his early days, Mishima worked for the Finance Ministry.

   in contrast to _____

   whereas _____

   however _____

4. Mishima was a prolific writer, authoring short stories, poems, plays, essays,
   and novels.

   similar to _____

   likewise _____

   like _____

5. Mishima was critical of the Japanese military policies.

   in the same way _____

   similar to _____

   similarly _____

6. Mishima performed as an actor.

   unlike _____

   but _____

   in contrast _____

7. Many of Mishima's works have been translated into English and other languages.

like _____

similar to _____

likewise _____

EXERCISE 8·13 Writing Assignment   In the following essay, transitions have been omitted from the italicized parts. Rewrite the essay using a variety of transitional devices.

When scientists first examined the human brain, they found it to be divided into two halves, or hemispheres, which are nearly identical in appearance, mirroring each other just as the two sides of the body do. When Roger Sperry examined patients whose connection between the two hemispheres—the corpus callosum—was severed, he found that the two sides of the brain seemed to have different functions. Many investigators have studied the differences between the functions of the two hemispheres and found their relationship to be quite complex. Unfortunately, however, most people have tended to overgeneralize. The left brain is supposed to be logical, rational, and analytical, whereas the right brain is supposed to be creative and emotional. The brain's hemispheres are not so simplistically split into two neat divisions. In fact, both halves of the brain participate in almost all our mental activity.

To begin with, both sides of the brain are in operation when we reason. The left brain seems to dominate in the kind of reasoning it takes to translate symbols, recognize abstract differences, and handle algebra and geometry problems. *The left hemisphere may be dominant in these types of reasoning. The right hemisphere also reasons.* The right half functions to integrate information and draw conclusions. *The left hemisphere is dominant in recognizing abstract differences. The right hemisphere tends to recognize sameness.* For example, the right side is where we mediate facial recognition and recognize shapes.

The two hemispheres act as partners in language and communication. It appears that the left hemisphere is dominant when it comes to understanding grammar and syntax, but when it comes to interpreting emotions in communication, the right brain excels. *The right brain can interpret tone of voice and facial expressions. Whenever we use language, both sides of the brain process the information.*

The brain is not totally divided about music. Many people assume that music is mediated solely in the right brain. *That is not so.* It is true that the right brain recognizes chords and melodies and seems to mediate pure and slow tones. *The left hemisphere is also involved in music.* Fast music, such as bluegrass, requires judgments about sequencing and rhythm, and for this the left hemisphere lends its services. When words are involved, again the left brain dominates.

Both halves of the brain are involved in our mental activities. The corpus callosum and other bridges between the two hemispheres obviously serve to integrate the functions of the two halves, which are in constant communication to make sense out of life.

—Information from Richard Thompson, *The Brain: An Introduction to Neuroscience* (New York: W. H. Freeman and Co., 1985) pp. 315–17 and Camille B. Wortman and Elizabeth F. Loftus, *Psychology* (New York: Alfred H. Knopf, 1985) pp. 84–89

EXERCISE 8·14 Writing Assignment Read the following paragraphs. Revise the paragraphs in two ways. First rewrite them using Pattern B. Be sure to divide them into shorter paragraphs. Then rewrite them using Pattern A. Use appropriate transitions. Use the following thesis sentence for your essay.

Thesis Sentence:

There are some interesting parallels between the Roman and Chinese empires even though these empires ended differently.

The Roman Empire ruled the Mediterranean world from about 500 B.C. to about 500 A.D. From a geographic base around Rome, it spread out to include North Africa, the Middle East, and Northern Europe. It developed a higher level of civilization than the areas surrounding it. It had a complex governmental structure and a bureaucracy, while the people surrounding it were barbarians and nomads. These barbarians were a constant threat to the Roman Empire. The leaders of the empire devised three ways to protect the empire. First, they conquered territory whose outer boundaries were natural barriers. Examples are the Rhine and Danube Rivers. They also built fortifications to keep out invaders. They built some, for example, between the Rhine and Danube and between Scotland and England. Third, they used precautionary buffer states, like colonies, which were midway between barbarism and civilization. These all helped to protect the base of the empire, Rome itself. However, toward the end of the empire's rule, some of the buffer states revolted. The final collapse occurred when the German and Slavic barbarians broke through the fortifications. In a short 200 years, the Roman Empire fell to the power of the Germans.

The Chinese Empire grew and remained intact from 221 B.C. to 1911 A.D. From a geographic base around the Yellow River, it spread northward to Peking, west to the Central Plain, and south to Canton. It developed a higher level of civilization than the areas surrounding it. It became a center for art and philosophy, while the people surrounding it were nomads and barbarians. These barbarians, Huns and Mongols, were a constant threat to the empire. The leaders of the empire devised three ways to deal with them. First, they used natural boundaries like the Yellow and later the Yangtze Rivers. They built the incredible Great Wall of China, and they used buffer states that learned much from China, becoming civilized in the process. However, at times the barbarians broke through the fortifications and the buffer states. The barbarians did not destroy the Chinese Empire, however. Because the barbarians admired the superior culture of China, they set up dynasties imitating the Chinese way of life. Examples are the Chau, Yuan, and Manchu dynasties. In other words, the Chinese Empire absorbed its intruders and lived on. The one exception to this was a short rule by the Mongols, Genghis and Kublai Khan from 1215–1279. The subjugated Chinese dynasty reasserted itself shortly, however. The Chinese Empire continued to decline slowly until the Manchu dynasty ended in 1911 and a republic was declared.

—Information from C. Harold King, *A History of Civilization: Earliest Times to the Mid-Seventeenth Century* (New York: Scribner's, 1964)

EXERCISE 8·15 Writing Assignment   Look again at the essays you wrote for Exercises 8-8 and 8-10. Can you make them more coherent by adding appropriate transitions? Revise your essays, trying to use a variety of coherence devices.

Grammar Review

If you want to review grammatical structures that will help you achieve coherence and grammatical accuracy in your writing, see the Grammar Review Unit. The following sections are designed to coordinate with the comparison/contrast essay:

Comparisons, pages 344–349
Adverbial Clauses of Comparison, Contrast, and Concession, pages 331–334

EXERCISE 8·16 Writing Assignment   Choose one of the following writing topics. Before you begin writing, prewrite using one of the techniques you studied in

Chapter 1. From the information you generate, decide on a controlling idea and thesis statement. Then choose the support. Decide whether to use organizational pattern A or B. Then write an essay.

1. In "Conversational Ballgames," Nancy Sakamoto shows the contrast between Eastern- and Western-style conversations. Can you find any differences between conversational styles in this country and in your home country?
2. In "Intimacy and Independence," Deborah Tannen shows that conflicts between men and women can result from different ideas about communication. Do men and women in your culture have different styles of communication?
3. Review the paragraphs about the Roman and Chinese empires in Exercise 8-14. Then write an essay comparing and/or contrasting two periods in your country's history.
4. Review the information about the writers Borges and Mishima in Exercise 8-12. Write an essay comparing and/or contrasting two famous people—two political leaders, two artists, two performers, and so on. Be sure to include a thesis expressing your attitude about the two people.
5. Write an essay comparing or contrasting two different attitudes. For example, you might choose the attitude toward punctuality in the United States compared with the attitude toward punctuality in your country.
6. Write an essay comparing-contrasting your parents' attitude toward something with your attitude toward it.

EXERCISE 8·17 Assignments from the Disciplines   Following are some topics for your final writing assignment which are typical of college writing assignments. For your final writing assignment, you may choose one that you have studied, or consult a textbook or the Internet to find the answer. Then, follow the directions for Exercise 8-16 to write your answer.

1. **From Linguistics**   There are two ways to describe and teach the grammar of the language: prescriptively or descriptively. Compare and contrast these two methods.
2. **From Electrical Engineering**   Compare and contrast the properties and uses of analog and digital signals.

Revision

Peer Review

When you have finished writing the first draft of your essay, give it to a classmate to read and review. Use the peer review checklist in Appendix I to respond to each other's drafts.

Revision Checklist for the Paragraph

Use these questions to help you to give suggestions to your peers and to revise your essay.

1. The purpose of the comparison and contrast essay is to persuade, explain, or inform, not just to list differences or similarities. Is your thesis sentence persuasive? Does it express an attitude?

2. The points chosen for comparison or contrast should be the most significant, interesting, and insightful points to support your thesis. Have you been selective in choosing your points of comparison?

3. Most essays emphasize either comparison or contrast. Which one have you emphasized?

4. There are two basic patterns for organizing a comparison-contrast essay. Have you chosen one of these patterns? Is the organization of your essay logical and consistent?

5. Is your essay coherent; that is, does it flow smoothly?

Chapter **9** The Classification Essay

Theme

Advertising and Consumers

Goals

Writing

To organize and write a classification essay

To use only one principle of classification when dividing members of a group into categories

To use the turnabout method of writing introductions

To use transitions to increase coherence

Reading

To learn about and discuss common health problems

To identify categories in a classification essay

Grammar

To review correlative conjunctions and articles for classification

Getting Started

Journal Writing: Choose one of the following two questions, and write about it in your journal.

1. How does advertising affect you? Do you rely on advertising to give you information about products? How you ever bought something and later discovered that the advertising was misleading?
2. Think of a commercial or advertisement that you especially like or dislike. Why did this advertisement catch your attention?

CNN® Video Activity: "Museum of Product Failures"

 It is estimated that 80 percent of the new products introduced to supermarket shelves each year will not be successful. How can people who work in marketing and product development help to be sure that their products are among the successful ones? Some of them visit the "New Product Showcase" to see products that have already failed so that they can avoid making the same mistakes. As you watch the video, make a note of the reasons why you think each of these products failed:

Product	Reason for failure
Gorilla Balls	_____
Male chauvinist arrogant aftershave	_____
Tanana Banana Suntan oil	_____
Aerosol toothpaste	_____
Black toothpaste	_____
Heavy beer	_____
Wine & Dine dinner	_____
Small Miracle hair care products	_____
Gerber Singles	_____
Garlic cake	_____
Sweater fresh	_____

Video Follow-up: Finding Out More about Products
Visit a store that sells consumer products such as food or health and beauty products. Find one product that you think fits each of the following categories, and explain why you chose it.

	Product	Reason
Most appealing	_____	_____
Least appealing	_____	_____
Funniest name	_____	_____
Best packaging	_____	_____
Worst packaging	_____	_____
Most likely to fail	_____	_____

Readings: Advertising and Consumers

Advertising is everywhere. We see it on television; we hear it on the radio. There are print ads in every newspaper and magazine we read, on billboards, the sides of buses and on many, many Internet pages. Some people rely on advertising to give them information about new products that may meet their needs, but many people believe that advertising doesn't affect them at all. Yet, companies continue to spend billions of dollars on advertising, and students of advertising continue to study persuasive techniques that can be used to reach a company's target consumer.

The following essays explore this relationship between advertising and consumers. In the first essay, "Weasel Words," William Lutz examines the words that many advertisers choose to make misleading but legal claims for products they wish to sell. In "Motivation," Charles Lamb, Jr., Joseph Hair, Jr., and Carl McDaniel introduce Maslow's hierarchy of needs and explain how advertisers can appeal to each type of need to influence consumers' buying behavior. Before you read these essays, consider the following questions:

1. What kind of advertising is the most likely to attract your attention? When you see an advertisement, do you often think about whether or not its claims are true?
2. What influences you to purchase a new product?
3. Think of a new product that has recently been introduced. What kind of need does this product fulfill?
4. In your opinion, do you think advertising is helpful or harmful?

"Weasel Words"
by William Lutz

William Lutz has spent much of his professional life examining the words used in law, politics, and business to discover how words are used to mislead without lying. He has also written extensively to try to educate people about this misleading language, which has been called "double-speak." Lutz defines doublespeak as "language that pretends to communi-cate, but really doesn't. It is language that makes the bad seem good, the negative appear positive, the unpleasant appear attractive or at least tolerable" (*The New Doublespeak*, 1997). In this excerpt from his book *Doublespeak* (1990), Lutz describes one type of doublespeak—"weasel words"—and shows how different types of weasel words are used by advertis-ers to encourage people to buy products. As you read "Weasel Words," try to answer these questions:

1. What are "weasel words"?
2. What benefits do advertisers get from using weasel words in an advertis-ing claim?

---

1   One problem advertisers have when they try to convince you that the product they are pushing is really something different from other, similar products is that their claims are subject to some laws. Not a lot of laws, but there are some designed to prevent fraudulent° or untruthful claims in advertising. Even during the happy years of nonregulation under President Ronald Reagan, the FTC° did crack down on° the more blatant° abuses in advertising claims. Generally speaking, advertisers have to be careful in what they say in their ads, in the claims they make for the products they advertise. Parity claims° are safe because they are legal and supported by a number of court decisions. But beyond parity claims there are weasel words.

2   Advertisers use weasel words to appear to be making a claim for a product when in fact they are making no claim at all. Weasel words get their name from the way weasels eat the eggs they find in the nests of other animals. A weasel will make a small hole in the egg, suck out the insides, then place the egg back in the nest. Only when the egg is examined closely is it found to be hollow.° That's the way it is with weasel words in advertising: Examine weasel words closely and you'll find that they're as hollow as any egg sucked by a weasel. Weasel words appear to say one thing when in fact they say the opposite or nothing at all.

Margin glosses:

dishonest

Federal Trade Commission
discipline
obvious, shameless
claiming a product is equal to other similar products

empty

"Help"—The Number One Weasel Word

3   The biggest weasel word used in advertising doublespeak is "help." Now, "help" only means to aid or assist, nothing more. It does not mean to conquer, stop, eliminate, end, solve, heal, cure, or anything else. But once the ad says "help," it can say just about anything after that because "help" quali-fies° everything coming after it. The trick is that the claim that comes after the weasel word is usually so strong and so dramatic that you forget the word "help" and concentrate only on the dramatic claim. You read into the ad a message that the ad does not contain. More importantly, the advertiser is not responsible for the claim that you read into the ad, even though the advertiser wrote the ad so you would read that claim into it.

4   The next time you see an ad for a cold medicine that promises that it "helps relieve cold symptoms fast," don't rush out to buy it. Ask yourself what this claim is really saying. Remember, "helps" means only that the medicine will aid or assist. What will it aid or assist in doing? Why, "relieve" your cold "symptoms." Relieve only means to ease, alleviate, or mitigate, not to stop, end, or cure. Nor does the claim say how much relieving this medicine will do. Nowhere does this ad claim it will cure anything. In fact, the ad doesn't even claim it will *do* anything at all. The ad only claims that it will aid in relieving (not curing) your cold symptoms, which are probably a runny nose, watery eyes, and a headache. In other words, this medicine probably contains a standard decongestant and some aspirin. By the way, what does "fast" mean? Ten minutes, one hour, one day? What is fast to one person can be very slow to another. Fast is another weasel word.

5   Ad claims using "help" are among the most popular ads. One says, "Helps keep you young looking," but then a lot of things will help keep you young looking, including exercise, rest, good nutrition, and a facelift. More importantly, this ad doesn't say the product will keep you young, only "young *looking*." Someone may look young to one person and old to another.

6   A toothpaste ad says, "Helps prevent cavities," but it doesn't say it will actually prevent cavities. Brushing your teeth regularly, avoiding sugars in food, and flossing daily will also help prevent cavities. A liquid cleaner ad says, "Helps keep your home germ free," but it doesn't say it actually kills germs, nor does it even specify which germs it might kill.

7   "Help" is such a useful weasel word that it is often combined with other action-verb weasel words such as "fight" and "control." Consider the claim, "Helps control dandruff° symptoms with regular use." What does it really say? It will assist in controlling (not eliminating, stopping, ending or curing) the symptoms of dandruff, not the cause of dandruff nor the dandruff itself. What are the symptoms of dandruff? The ad deliberately leaves that undefined, but assume that the symptoms referred to in the ad are the flaking and itching

limits

dry, white flakes of skin in one's hair

commonly associated with dandruff. But just shampooing with *any* shampoo will temporarily eliminate these symptoms, so this shampoo isn't any different from any other. Finally, in order to benefit from this product, you must use it regularly. What is "regular use"—daily, weekly, hourly? Using another shampoo "regularly" will have the same effect. Nowhere does this advertising claim say this particular shampoo stops, eliminates, or cures dandruff. In fact, this claim says nothing at all, thanks to all the weasel words.

8   Look at ads in magazines and newspapers, listen to ads on radio and television, and you'll find the word "help" in ads for all kinds of products. How often do you read or hear such phrases as "helps stop . . . ," "helps overcome . . . ," "helps eliminate . . . ," "helps you feel . . . ," or "helps you look . . ."? If you start looking for this weasel word in advertising, you'll be amazed at how often it occurs. Analyze the claims in the ads using "help," and you will discover that these ads are really saying nothing.

9   There are plenty of other weasel words used in advertising. In fact, there are so many that to list them all would fill the rest of this book. But, in order to identify the doublespeak of advertising and understand the real meaning of an ad, you have to be aware of the most popular weasel words in advertising today.

Virtually Spotless

10   One of the most powerful weasel words is "virtually," a word so innocent that most people don't pay any attention to it when it is used in an advertising claim. But watch out. "Virtually" is used in advertising claims that appear to make specific, definite promises when there is no promise. After all, what does "virtually" mean? It means "in essence or effect, although not in fact." Look at that definition again. "Virtually" means *not in fact*. It does *not* mean

ignore

"almost" or "just about the same as," or anything else. And before you dismiss° all this concern over such a small word, remember that small words can have

results

big consequences.°

gave its opinion

11   In 1971 a federal court rendered its decision° on a case brought by a woman who became pregnant while taking birth control pills. She sued the

violation

manufacturer, Eli Lilly and Company, for breach° of warranty. The woman lost her case. Basing its ruling on a statement in the pamphlet accompanying the pills, which stated that, "When taken as directed, the tablets offer virtually 100% protection," the court ruled that there was no warranty, expressed or

stated or suggested

implied,° that the pills were absolutely effective. In its ruling, the court pointed out that, according to *Webster's Third New International Dictionary*, "virtually" means "almost entirely" and clearly does not mean "absolute" (*Whittington v. Eli Lilly and Company*, 333 F. Supp. 98). In other words, the Eli Lilly company was really saying that its birth control pill, even when taken as directed, *did not in fact* provide 100 percent protection against pregnancy. But Eli Lilly didn't want to put it that way because then many women might not have bought Eli Lilly's birth control pills.

12   The next time you see the ad that says that this dishwasher detergent "leaves dishes virtually spotless," just remember how advertisers twist the meaning of the weasel word "virtually." You can have lots of spots on your dishes after using this detergent and the ad claim will still be true, because what this claim really means is that this detergent does not *in fact* leave your dishes spotless. Whenever you see or hear an ad claim that uses the word "virtually," just translate that claim into its real meaning. So the television set that is "virtually trouble free," becomes the television set that is not in fact trouble free, the "virtually foolproof operation" of any appliance becomes an operation that is in fact not foolproof, and the product that "virtually never needs service" becomes the product that is not in fact service free.

New and Improved

13   If "new" is the most frequently used word on a product package, "improved" is the second most frequent. In fact, the two words are almost always used together. It seems just about everything sold these days is "new and improved." The next time you are in the supermarket, try counting the number of times you see these words on products. But you'd better do it while you're walking down just one aisle, otherwise you'll need a calculator to keep track of your counting.

14   Just what do these words mean? The use of the word "new" is restricted by regulations, so an advertiser can't just use the word on a product without meeting certain requirements. For example, a product is considered new for about six months during a national advertising campaign. If the product is being advertised only in a limited test market area, the word can be used longer, and in some instances has been used for as long as two years.

15   What makes a product "new"? Some products have been around for a long time, yet every once in a while you discover that they are being advertised as "new." Well, an advertiser can call a product new if there has been a "material functional change" in the product. What is "a material functional change," you ask? Good question. In fact it's such a good question it's being asked all the time. It's up to the manufacturer to prove that the product has undergone° such a change. And if the manufacturer isn't challenged on the claim, then there's no one to stop it. Moreover, the change does not have to be an improvement in the product. One manufacturer added an artificial lemon scent to a cleaning product and called it "new and improved," even though the product did not clean any better than without the lemon scent. The manufacturer defended the use of the word "new" on the grounds that the artificial scent changed the chemical formula of the product and therefore constituted "a material functional change."

experienced

16   Which brings us to the word "improved." When used in advertising, "improved" does not mean "made better." It only means "changed" or "different from before." So, if the detergent maker puts a plastic pour spout on the box of detergent, the product has been "improved," and away we go with a whole new advertising campaign. Or, if the cereal maker adds more fruit or a different kind of fruit to the cereal, there's an improved product. Now you know why manufacturers are constantly making little changes in their products. Whole new advertising campaigns, designed to convince you that the product has been changed for the better, are based on small changes in superficial° aspects of a product. The next time you see an ad for an "improved" product, ask yourself what was wrong with the old one. Ask yourself just how "improved" the product is. Finally, you might want to check to see whether the "improved" version costs more than the unimproved one. After all, someone has to pay for the millions of dollars spent advertising the improved product.

unimportant

17   Of course, advertisers really like to run ads that claim a product is "new and improved." While what constitutes a "new" product may be subject to some regulation, "improved" is a subjective judgment. A manufacturer changes the shape of its stick deodorant, but the shape doesn't improve the function of the deodorant. That is, changing the shape doesn't affect the deodorizing ability of the deodorant, so the manufacturer calls it "improved." Another manufacturer adds ammonia to its liquid cleaner and calls it "new and improved." Since adding ammonia does affect the cleaning ability of the product, there has been a "material functional change" in the product, and the manufacturer can now call its cleaner "new," and "improved" as well. Now the weasel words "new and improved" are plastered all over° the package and are the basis for a multimillion-dollar ad campaign. But after six months the word "new" will have to go, until someone can dream up another change in the product. Perhaps it will be adding color to the liquid, or changing the shape of the package, or maybe adding a new dripless pour spout, or perhaps a _____. The "improvements" are endless, and so are the new advertising claims and campaigns.

put in many places

18   "New" is just too useful and powerful a word in advertising for advertisers to pass it up easily. So they use weasel words that say "new" without really saying it. One of their favorites is "introducing," as in, "Introducing improved Tide," or "Introducing the stain remover." The first is simply saying, here's our improved soap; the second, here's our new advertising campaign for our detergent. Another favorite is "now," as in "Now there's Sinex," which simply means that Sinex is available. Then there are phrases like "Today's Chevrolet," "Presenting Dristan," and "A fresh way to start the day." The list is really endless because advertisers are always finding new ways to say "new" without really saying it. If there is a second edition of [my] book, I'll just call it the "new and improved" edition. Wouldn't you really rather have a "new and improved" edition of [my] book rather than a "second" edition?

Acts Fast

19   "Acts" and "works" are two popular weasel words in advertising because they bring action to the product and to the advertising claim. When you see the ad for the cough syrup that "acts on the cough control center," ask yourself what this cough syrup is claiming to do. Well, it's just claiming to "act," to do something, to perform an action. What is it that the cough syrup does? The ad doesn't say. It only claims to perform an action or do something on your "cough control center"? I don't remember learning about that part of the body in human biology class.

20   Ads that use such phrases as "acts fast," "acts against," "acts to prevent," and the like are saying essentially nothing, because "act" is a word empty of any specific meaning. The ads are always careful not to specify exactly what "act" the product performs. Just because a brand of aspirin claims to "act fast" for headache relief doesn't mean this aspirin is any better than any other aspirin. What is the "act" that this aspirin performs? You're never told. Maybe it just dissolves quickly. Since aspirin is a parity product,° all aspirin is the same and therefore functions the same.

a product that is the same no matter what the brand name is

Works Like Anything Else

21   If you don't find the word "acts" in an ad, you will probably find the weasel word "works." In fact, the two words are almost interchangeable in advertising. Watch out for ads that say a product "works against," "works like," "works for," or "works longer." As with "acts," "works" is the same meaningless verb used to make you think that this product really does something, and maybe even something special or unique. But "works," like "acts," is basically a word empty of any specific meaning.

Like Magic

22   Whenever advertisers want you to stop thinking about the product and to start thinking about something bigger, better, or more attractive than the product, they use that very popular weasel word "like." The word "like" is the advertiser's equivalent of the magician's use of misdirection. "Like" gets you to ignore the product and concentrate on the claim the advertiser is making about it. "For skin like peaches and cream" claims the ad for a skin cream. What is this ad really claiming? It doesn't say this cream will give you peaches-and-cream skin. There is no verb in this claim, so it doesn't even mention using the product. How is skin ever like "peaches and cream"? Remember, ads must be read literally and exactly, according to the dictionary definition of words. (Remember "virtually" in the Eli Lilly case.) This ad is making absolutely no promise or claim whatsoever for this skin cream. If you think this cream will give you soft, smooth, youthful-looking skin, you are the one who has read the meaning into the ad.

23   The wine that claims "It's like taking a trip to France" wants you to

think about a romantic evening in Paris as you walk along the boulevard after a wonderful meal in an intimate little bistro. Of course, you don't really believe that a wine can take you to France, but the goal of the ad is to get you to think pleasant, romantic thoughts about France and not about how the wine tastes or how expensive it may be. That little word "like" has taken you away from crushed grapes into a world of your own imaginative making. Who knows, maybe the next time you buy wine, you'll think those pleasant thoughts when you see this brand of wine, and you'll buy it. Or maybe you weren't even thinking about buying wine at all, but now you just might pick up a bottle the next time you're shopping. Ah, the power of "like" in advertising.

24   How about the most famous "like" claim of all, "Winston tastes good like a cigarette should"? Ignoring the grammatical error here, you might want to know what this claim is saying. Whether a cigarette tastes good or bad is a subjective judgement because what tastes good to one person may well taste horrible to another. Not everyone likes fried snails, even if they are called escargot. (*De gustibus non est disputandum,** which was probably the Roman rule for advertising as well as for defending the games in the Colosseum.) There are many people who say that all cigarettes taste terrible, other people who say only some cigarettes taste all right, and still others who say all cigarettes taste good. Who's right? Everyone, because taste is a matter of personal judgement.

25   Moreover, note the use of the conditional "should." The complete claim is "Winston tastes good like a cigarette should taste." But should cigarettes taste good? Again, this is a matter of personal judgement and probably depends most on one's experiences with smoking. So the Winston ad is simply saying that Winston cigarettes are just like any other cigarette: Some people like them and some people don't. On that statement R. J. Reynolds conducted a very successful multimillion-dollar advertising campaign that helped keep Winston the number-two-selling cigarette in the United States, close behind the number one, Marlboro.

EXERCISE 9·1 Comprehension/Discussion Questions

1. What is the definition of a weasel word?
2. How many weasel words does Lutz explain? Find each kind and explain it.
3. How does Lutz support the definition he gives of each weasel word?
4. What is Lutz's attitude toward advertising? How do you know?
5. What is the importance of the court case explained in paragraph 11?
6. In paragraph 15, Lutz says that a manufacturer must make "a material func-

---

* There's no disputing matters of taste.

tional change" to a product in order to use the word "new" in advertising. What is "a material functional change"?

7. What are the "synonyms" for the word "new" which are described in paragraph 18? Why would advertisers want to use these words instead of the word "new"?

8. The claim described in paragraph 19 says that a cough syrup "acts on the cough control center." What is the cough control center?

9. In paragraph 22, advertisers are compared to magicians. Why does Lutz make this comparison? Do you think that it is a valid comparison? Why or why not?

10. What is the author's purpose in writing this article? Do you believe he has been successful?

11. Do you think it is important to analyze advertisers' claims in the way that Lutz suggests? Why or why not?

12. Look at advertising or a product package. How many weasel words do you find? Are there any that aren't mentioned in this article? Reinterpret the advertising claims with the true meaning of the weasel words as Lutz does in his article. How does the meaning change?

13. If you could pass new laws about advertising, what laws would you pass? What laws do you think a specialist in marketing or advertising might suggest?

EXERCISE 9·2 Vocabulary Development   Synonyms. In paragraph 4, Lutz lists several words that **do not** mean the same thing as "help." He points out these words since advertisers often imply that help does mean these things. Be sure you understand the real meaning of each word, then write an advertising claim for products of your choice using the correct meaning of each of these words. Do not use the word "help" or other weasel words. Then, as a class, examine whether you think it is possible for a product to live up to these claims.

1. conquer _____

2. stop _____

3. eliminate _____

4. end _____

5. solve _____

6. heal _____

7. cure _____

Internet Activity: Composition Skills and the Internet

 Many Web pages have advertisements on the pages called "banner ads." Because these ads are usually rather small, they often use only a few words to try and attract your attention and get you to "click through" to the advertiser's Web page. Examine 10 different banner ads and make a list of any weasel words that are used on these banner ads. Discuss the weasel words you found with your classmates.

Reading ②

"Motivation"

by Charles Lamb, Jr., Joseph Hair, Jr., and Carl McDaniel

In this excerpt from the college textbook *Marketing* (1998), Charles Lamb, Jr., Joseph Hair, Jr., and Carl McDaniel introduce Maslow's hierarchy of needs and explain how advertisers can appeal to each type of need of influence consumers' buying behavior. As you read this passage, try to answer these questions:

1. What are the characteristics of each category of needs Maslow has identified?
2. Why do advertisers need to understand consumer needs?
3. Give an example of each type of consumer need and explain how a given product, such as a restaurant, a car, or clothing might fulfill each of these needs.

---

1   By studying motivation, marketers can analyze the major forces influencing consumers to buy or not buy products. When you buy a product, you usually do so to fulfill some kind of need. These needs become motives when aroused sufficiently. For instance, suppose this morning you were so hungry before class that you needed to eat something. In response to that need, you stopped at McDonald's for an Egg McMuffin. In other words, you were motivated by hunger to stop at McDonald's. Motives are the driving forces that cause a person to take action to satisfy specific needs.

2   Why are people driven by particular needs at particular times? One popular theory is **Maslow's hierarchy of needs,** (shown in the figure on page 195), which arranges needs in ascending° order of importance: physiological, safety, social, esteem, and self-actualization. As a person fulfills one need, a higher level need becomes more important.

3   The most basic human needs are *physiological*—that is, needs for food,

rising

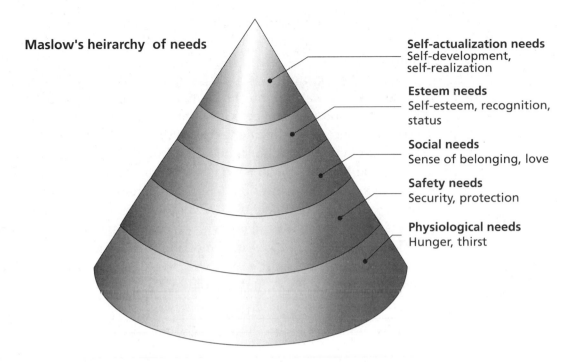

Maslow's heirarchy of needs

Self-actualization needs
Self-development,
self-realization

Esteem needs
Self-esteem, recognition,
status

Social needs
Sense of belonging, love

Safety needs
Security, protection

Physiological needs
Hunger, thirst

drinking quickly

water, and shelter. Because they are essential to survival, these needs must be satisfied first. Ads showing a juicy hamburger or a runner gulping° down Gatorade after a marathon exemplify the use of appeals to satisfy physiological needs.

4 *Safety* needs include security and freedom from pain and discomfort. Marketers often exploit consumer's fears and anxieties about safety to sell their products. For example, Volvo ad campaigns have featured testimonials from real people who believe they survived terrible car crashes because they were driving a Volvo. Consumer demand for products containing Vitamin E

rising very quickly
slows down

prevent

have been soaring° following several scientific studies that suggest the vitamin inhibits° agents that attack cells and cause deterioration. Marketers have promoted other studies that conclude vitamin E may also help ward off° degenerative ailments such as heart disease and cancer and some symptoms of aging.*

equals

5 After physiological and safety needs have been fulfilled, *social* needs—especially love and a sense of belonging—become the focus. Love includes acceptance by one's peers° as well as sex and romantic love. Marketing managers probably appeal more to this need than to any other. Ads for clothes, cosmetics, and vacation packages suggest that buying the product can bring love. The need to belong is also a favorite of marketers. Nike promotes its Air Jordan athletic shoes, for instance, as not just plain old sneakers; they're part

* Matt Murray, "Americans Eat Up Vitamin E Supplies," *Wall Street Journal,* 13 June 1996, pp. B1, B8.

fashion statement, part athletic statement. Lace them up, and the wearer looks cool and plays cool—just like Michael Jordan, the shoe's spokesperson and namesake.[†]

6 Love is acceptance without regard to one's contribution. Esteem is acceptance based on one's contribution to the group. *Self-esteem* needs include self-respect and a sense of accomplishment. Esteem needs also include prestige, fame, and recognition of one's accomplishments. Mont Blanc pens, Mercedes-Benz automobiles, and Neiman Marcus stores all appeal to esteem needs.

7 The highest human need is *self-actualization.* It refers to finding self-fulfillment and self-expression, reaching the point in life at which "people are what they feel they should be." Maslow felt that very few people ever attain this level. Even so, advertisements may focus on this type of need. For example, American Express ads convey the message that acquiring its card is one of the highest attainments in life. Likewise, the U.S. Armed Forces' slogan urges young people to "Be all that you can be."

EXERCISE 9•3 Comprehension/Discussion Questions

1. According to this reading, why do people buy products?
2. Explain the relationship between needs and motives.
3. What are the five categories of human motivations, according to Maslow's theory? Explain each category and give an example.
4. According to this reading, which is the most common motivation that humans experience? Which is the most common motivation targeted by advertisers? Why do you think this is so?
5. Do you agree with Maslow's classification? Can you think of any other categories of motivation? Should any of these categories be combined? Why or why not?
6. What attitude do these authors display toward advertising? How do you know? Compare the attitude of the author of "Weasel Words" with the attitude of these authors.
7. Why should marketers and advertisers study consumer motivation? How does this knowledge help them to do their job?
8. Why is the diagram of Maslow's hierarchy of motivation shaped like a pyramid? What part of the theory does this shape convey?
9. Gather three advertisements from TV, a magazine, a newspaper, or the Internet. For each advertisement, identify which motivation(s) have been targeted. Why do you think the advertiser chose to make this appeal?
10. Which levels of motivation have you generally satisfied in your life? Which

[†] Maria Mallory and Kevin Whitelaw, "The Power Brands," *U.S. News & World Report,* 13 May 1996, p. 58.

level are you currently striving to achieve? Which level do you think most people you see each day are trying to achieve?

EXERCISE 9·4 Vocabulary Development   **Definition quiz.** In this and other textbooks, authors give students clues about words which are important. Studying these vocabulary words can help you to prepare for exams. Imagine that you will be given a quiz on the information in "Motivation," and you know that your instructor will ask you to write definitions in your own words. Which seven words from this passage would you study? Why did you choose these? Write these words on the lines below, and give a definition of each word. Remember to use your own words. Do not copy a definition from the reading.

_____

_____

_____

_____

_____

_____

_____

Writing

The patterns of exposition are really ways to organize thoughts, to develop ideas in an organized fashion so the reader can follow them easily. Some topics are best developed as example essays; others are best developed as comparison and contrast essays. This chapter pursues another common pattern of exposition: classification and division. This pattern, like process analysis and cause-and-effect analysis, is used for analyzing topics.

When analyzing a subject, you break it down into parts to study or determine the relationship of the parts or the nature of the parts. For example, analyzing an engine involves examining the parts to see how they make the engine run. If you were analyzing the United States government, you would probably begin by dividing the government into its three branches—the legislative, executive, and judicial—and then by studying how these branches operate to make up the government. If you were studying psychology and were interested in dreams, you would probably begin by sorting the dreams into categories that share common characteristics, and by so doing you might learn something about the various kinds of dreams. Taking one thing—such as the government—and breaking it down into parts is analysis by division; taking a large group of things—such as governments—and separating the group into categories is analysis by classification. Since classification and division are very similar processes of analysis, and since as patterns of exposition they are even more similar, the general rhetorical term *classification* is used in this text to refer to the general pattern.

The Principle of Classification

When you classify, you divide the members of a group into categories whose members share similar characteristics. But on what basis do you assign the members to categories? When you classify, you need a principle of classification—a guideline for your classifying procedure. For example, the students in your English class might be classified according to the languages they speak natively: Spanish speakers, Vietnamese speakers, Japanese speakers, Dutch speakers, Arabic speakers, and so on. However, including a group such as "hard-working students" disrupts the classification by switching principles of classification. Members of the "hard-working" group could also be members of any of the other groups. Using more than one principle in this way causes categories to "overlap"; that is, the members of one category could also fit into one or more of the other categories. Just what principle of classification to choose is up to you. There are any number of principles available; the important thing to remember is to *use only one principle of classification* in an essay.

EXERCISE 9·5   Study the following classification groups. Underline the category that does not belong. The first one is done for you.

1. Automobiles: two-door, four-door, station wagons, economy.
2. Police officers: detectives, sergeants, lieutenants, captains.
3. Transportation: on land, by water, by air, by train.
4. Rivers: long, dangerous, short.
5. Drugs: stimulants, depressants, illegal.
6. Exercise: aerobic, muscle building, swimming.
7. Fiber: soluble, insoluble, fruit.
8. Languages: Semitic, Indo-European, ancient.
9. Teachers: well-prepared, easy graders, hard graders.
10. Clouds: high clouds, middle clouds, white clouds, low clouds.

Any number of principles of classification are available for a topic. To illustrate, consider the topic *students*. This topic could be classified according to:

1. How many credits the students have completed: first-year students, sophomores, juniors, seniors.
2. Age: under 18, 19–25, 26 and older.

3. Majors: biology, history, science, and so forth.
4. Level of intelligence: brilliant, intelligent, average, below average.
5. Where they sit in class: front row, back row, side walls, middle.
6. Attitude toward school: a place to improve one's general knowledge, a place to socialize, a place to learn a trade.
7. Style of dress: formal, semiformal, casual.

Most of the principles of classification are of three types: (1) *degree* (inferior to superior—for example, rating students from poor to excellent); (2) *chronology* (dividing the subject according to time periods); and (3) *location*. These are common types of principles, but not all principles are these types.

EXERCISE 9·6   Study the following subjects and categories. In each blank, write the principle of classification. The first one is done for you.

1. Teachers: those who dress conservatively, those who dress fashionably, those who dress in a variety of styles.

   The teachers in this school can be classified according to *the way they dress.*

2. Teachers: those with bachelor's degrees, those with master's degrees, those with PhDs.

   The teachers at our school can be classified according to _____

   _____

3. Students: residents, nonresidents.

   The students at this university can be classified according to _____

   _____

4. Burns: first degree, second degree, third degree.

   Burns can be classified according to _____

   _____

5. Snakes: those that swallow the prey live, those that inject poison into the prey, and those that squeeze the prey to death.

   Snakes can be classified according to _____

   _____

6. Smokers: those who smoke because of nervousness, those who smoke to look sophisticated, those who smoke out of boredom.

   Smokers can be classified according to _____

   _____

7. Readers: those who read voraciously, those who read regularly, those who read sporadically, and those who read as rarely as possible.

   People who read can be classified according to _____

   _____

8. Readers: those who read very difficult material, those who read moderately difficult material, those who read only light material.

   Readers can be put into categories according to _____

   _____

9. Drivers: reckless, careless, careful, overly careful.

   Drivers can be classified according to _____

   _____

10. Instructors: professors, associate professors, assistant professors, instructors.

    Instructors can be classified according to _____

    _____

Making the Classification Complete

Once you have decided on a principle of classification, check to see if the classification includes all members of the group. For instance, if you are classifying the students in a class, the categories might cover each and every one of the students in that class, if at all possible. If the students in a class were classified as brilliant or stupid, an obvious group—the average students—would be left out. To avoid omitting members and oversimplifying the analysis, then, it is generally a good idea to divide the group into more than two categories. For most college essays, three or four categories are the average.

When you divide a large group into categories whose members share common characteristics, there will be some members that do not fit perfectly into a category. For instance, you might classify politicians as liberals or conservatives, but since some politicians may be liberal concerning some issues and conservative concerning others, it would be wise to admit any variations or complications in the classification. It is also a good idea to note what the primary characteristics of the members are. For instance, do these politicians vote conservatively most of the time? If so, then placing them in the conservative category and mentioning that they vote liberally on some issues could be justified.

EXERCISE 9·7   Return to Exercises 9-5 and 9-6, and determine if the categories given there are complete.

Internet Activity: Composition Skills and the Internet

 A census counts the people living in the country and gathers demographic information which is used by government, advertisers, and others to predict national trends. So much information is collected that it is necessary to classify it in some way. Visit the U.S. Census Bureau Web site at www.census.gov to browse through information from the most recent census. Then answer these questions:

1. How are the answers to the questions classified?
2. What principles of classification are used?
3. In your opinion, are these classifications complete?

EXERCISE 9·8 Writing Assignment   Evaluate television programming to determine the quality of the programs. Since the topic *television programming* is rather broad, narrow it down to a particular type of show, such as news programs, detective shows, or children's programs. Make a list of all the television shows in that group. Then sort through your list to find groups that share common characteristics. Rewrite the list, clustering the shows into groups. Make sure that a show that appears in one group cannot fit into another group. Write out the principle of classification. Remember to keep in mind your purpose in classifying these programs. If you prefer, choose radio programs, movies, or books.

Organizing the Classification Essay

After deciding on the principle of classification and dividing the group into categories, you need to discuss each of those categories. In the developmental paragraphs, it is useful to devote one paragraph to each category. When discussing the category, include the following points:

1. Identify the group. If it has a special name, identify it.
2. Describe or define the category. What are the general characteristics of the members of this category? Once you have established what the category is according to your classification, discuss the common characteristics of the members.
3. Give examples: Often it is helpful to illustrate the characteristics (which are generalizations, by the way) by giving one or two examples of typical members of the category.

In the second and subsequent developmental paragraphs, add another point:

4. Distinguish this category from the other categories. Discuss the characteristics of the second category by comparing and contrasting them with those of the first category. Doing this will help to distinguish between the categories. How does group 1 really differ from group 2? (For coherence, as in comparison-contrast, try to discuss the characteristics in the same order as the previous group.)

In these respects, classification papers are really a combination of example essays and comparison-contrast essays. Therefore, you will need the expository skills you have been developing.

Introducing the Categories

In an introductory paragraph, it is often a good idea to introduce the categories by mentioning the names of the groups. The thesis statement for the classification essay can be one that simply introduces the classification and the categories:

The teachers in this college can be classified according to the way they dress: those who dress formally, those who dress semiformally, and those who dress casually.

There are basically three types of burns: first degree, second degree, and third degree.

Drugs fall into three categories: stimulants, depressants, and hallucinogens.

Although there is no law that says the categories must be identified in the introduction, identifying them will help keep the essay organized.

When you name the categories in the introduction, express them in parallel structure: that is, express them in the same parts of speech. If you identify a category using a clause, then all of your categories should be identified using clauses.

There are *those who like movies, those who hate movies,* and *those who are indifferent toward movies.* (clauses)

There are basically three types of bus drivers: *friendly, indifferent,* and *mean.* (adjectives)

The students in this class fit into the following categories: *the minis, the middies,* and *the maxis.* (nouns)

Most people respond in one of three ways: *eagerly, indifferently,* or *reluctantly.* (adverbs)

As you read the following essay, determine whether it contains the characteristics of a good classification paper: a single principle, well-defined categories, good examples, categories expressed in parallel structure, and completeness.

Cold Remedies

Cold remedies have a long if not glorious history. Pliny the Younger, a first-century A.D. cold expert, advised "kissing the hairy muzzle of a mouse." Sixteen hundred years later, colonial Americans fought colds by applying kerosene plasters to the chest or by stuffing a dirty sock with salted pork and onion and then wrapping it about the neck. While today's remedies smell better, they still do not cure the common cold. However, they are an improvement over past cold remedies and can relieve some of the symptoms. But the cold sufferer should beware. Most of the cold products contain up to seven different drugs. Since people differ greatly in their cold symptoms, users of these multidrug remedies often end up paying for unnecessary drugs that increase the risk of side effects. Thus, it may be a good idea for cold sufferers to look for effective single-ingredient drugs. These drugs can be classified according to the symptoms they are targeted to alleviate.

The first type of cold remedy is for congestion, which is the most common cold symptom. Decongestants reduce the swelling of the mucous membranes in the nose, resulting in easier breathing and better drainage. There are two kinds of decongestants: topical and oral. Topical decongestants, which include sprays and drops, work rapidly, but there is a potential problem. If used too much, they can cause "rebound congestion," which means worse congestion than there was originally, so they should be used sparingly. Examples of topical decongestants include Dristan and Neo-Synephrine, which contain the active ingredient phenylephrine; Afrin, which contains oxymetazoline; arid Neo-Synephrine II, which contains xylometazoline. Oral decongestants, such as Sudafed and Oramyl, both of which contain pseudoephedrine, take longer to be effective but don't produce rebound congestion. However, potential side effects include dry mouth, sleep disturbances, and an increase in blood pressure.

While most cold sufferers have congestion, only a little over a third suffer from the aches and pains so often mentioned in commercials; in fact, only about 25 percent suffer from headaches, 10 percent from muscle pain, and 1 percent from mild fever. The three standard pain-relieving ingredients for aches and pains include aspirin, acetaminophen, and ibuprofen. Products whose primary ingredient is aspirin include Bayer, Bufferin, Norwich, and St. Joseph aspirin. There is one caution about aspirin. Studies have shown a link between aspirin and Reye's syndrome, a rare but potentially fatal illness that strikes children and teenagers. Therefore, children and teens should not be given aspirin when they have cold symptoms. Alternatives to aspirin include acetaminophen, which is the main ingredient in Datril and Tylenol, and ibuprofen, which is the active ingredient in Advil and Nuprin.

About half of cold sufferers also have a cough. Cough remedies approach this symptom in different ways. Suppressants act on the brain to depress the cough reflex. For this purpose, products such as Benylin DM and Pertussin 8-Hour Cough Formula contain dextromethorphan. Another active ingredient used is diphenhydramine, found in Benylin. However, since this is an antihistamine, it can cause drowsiness. The main problem with cough suppressants is that it may not be wise to suppress the cough, particularly for people with lung ailments. Medicated lozenges, on the other hand, act locally on the throat to ease coughs. Lozenges, such as N'Ice Sugarless Cough Lozenges, which contain more than 5 milligrams of menthol, may help. Expectorants, in contrast to suppressants, supposedly help liquefy and loosen phlegm, making it easier to cough up. Guaifenesin is the active ingredient in Robitussin.

Finally, the last major symptom of the cold is the one that occurs first—the sore throat. About 50 percent of cold sufferers get a sore throat. There are many medicated lozenges and sprays available for such relief: Chloraseptic Sore Throat Spray, which contains phenol compounds; Spec-T Sore Throat Anesthetic Lozenges, made with benzocaine; Sucrets, made with Hexylresorcinol; and N'Ice Sugarless Cough Lozenges, whose active ingredient is menthol. Since a sore throat is also symptomatic of other illnesses, if the sore throat persists one should see a doctor.

While it may be easier to purchase a cold remedy that contains multiple ingredients, it may not be wise. The prudent cold sufferer should consider remedies targeted for specific single symptoms. Nevertheless, all sufferers should remember that there is no cure for the common cold; it will still have to run its course. Finally, when in doubt, people with colds should always consult their physicians.

—adapted from "Cold Remedies: Which Ones Work Best?"
Consumer Reports, January 1989, pp. 8–11

EXERCISE 9•9   On a separate sheet of paper, answer the following questions about the essay "Cold Remedies."

1. What is the thesis?
2. What seems to be the writer's purpose for writing about these kinds of cold remedies?
3. What is the principle of classification?
4. What are the characteristics of the decongestants?
5. What is the controlling idea about the cough remedies?
6. What are the characteristics of cough remedies?
7. Do the examples the writer uses to illustrate the categories seem appropriate?
8. Does the conclusion appear to be logical?
9. Write an outline of this essay.

EXERCISE 9•10   In Exercise 9-8, you were asked to make some notes about television programs. Using the preceding essay as a model, make the first draft of an essay on that topic.

Composition Skills

Introductory Paragraphs

The Turnabout

In Chapter 6, you learned how to compose one of the most common types of introductory paragraphs, what is often called the "Funnel." This approach to opening essays is a good one, but of course it is not the only way writers can introduce their essays. Another common approach is what we call the "Turn-about." This type of introduction opens with a few sentences summarizing a point of view that is actually the opposite of the writer's own thesis. By the end of the introduction, the writer makes a complete turnabout and presents his or her thesis—the opposite of what he or she started out with. This technique is useful when the writer's purpose in the essay is to argue a point or to clear up a commonly held misconception.

Like the Funnel, the Turnabout opens generally and congenially, but unlike the Funnel, the Turnabout has this dramatic shift in ideas. In other words, in the Turnabout, the writer sets up the opponent's view for attack. You have already seen some examples of this type of introduction, such as the introductory paragraph by Habeeb Al-Saeed on page 111 in Exercise 6-4. In the following introductory paragraph from Exercise 6-3, the writer opens with a statement about the generally held view that watching television is a worthwhile pastime, but by the end of the paragraph, she presents the opposing view for her thesis.

> We live in an era where television is the national pastime. Since the invention of the television set, people have been spending more of their free time watching television than doing anything else. Many of the television addicts feel that this particular pastime is not a bad one; indeed, they argue that people can learn a great deal watching television. I am sure that if you look long and hard enough, you can probably find some programs that are educationally motivating. But, for the most part, I say that watching television is a waste of time.
>
> —Pamela Moran

Professional writers often use the Turnabout introduction as well. Study the following introduction to an article in a popular magazine:

> In the struggle for existence, individual animals that are best adapted to their environment are more likely to survive and procreate. Their offspring inherit the adaptive traits, which after many generations spread throughout the species. That, in a nutshell, is Darwin's theory of evolution by natural selection. But for some years now there has been evidence that a struggle for existence also takes place on a completely different level, one that Darwin couldn't have dreamed of: the level of individual genes. While eggs or sperm are being formed, some genes seem to outmaneuver others and thus manage to appear in more than their fair share of the offspring. Because this behavior benefits the genes themselves, and not necessarily the organisms that carry them, the genes are called selfish.
>
> —from "Killer Gene," *Discover the World of Science*
> December 1988: p. 15

EXERCISE 9·11 Writing Assignment

1. For the draft essay you composed for Exercise 9-10, revise the introduction to make it a Turnabout.
2. Select one of the essays you wrote for an exercise in an earlier chapter. Rewrite your introduction using the Turnabout approach.

Coherence

Transitions for Classification

A classification essay is really a combination of the example and comparison-contrast essays. Therefore, expect the transitions for this type of essay to be generally the same as those for the example and comparison-contrast essays. Review the following transitions:

1. TRANSITIONS TO INTRODUCE CATEGORIES. These are generally additive transitions:

   The *first* group includes those students who dress formally.

   The *next* group includes those who dress semiformally.

   The *last* category includes those who dress casually.

   And *finally*, there is the type that everyone dreads: the negative teacher.

   In *addition* to these two groups, there is another group: the dunces.

2. TRANSITIONS TO SHOW SIMILARITIES AND DIFFERENCES. In a classification paper, it is important to clarify the distinctions between the categories; therefore, make use of the transitions that show similarities and differences (see Chapter 7).

   Unlike the positive teachers, the neutral teachers are not very agreeable.

   However, *like* the positive teacher, the neutral teacher allows for questions.

   Their classes tend to be *more boring than* the positive teachers' classes because they allow less time for discussion.

   Expectorants, *in contrast to* suppressants, supposedly help liquefy and loosen phlegm, making it easier to cough up.

3. TRANSITIONS TO INTRODUCE EXAMPLES. Chapters 4 and 6 discuss how to use transitions to introduce examples. The same transitions are used for the classification essay.

   A good example of a positive teacher is my French teacher, Monsieur Poirot.

   An excellent example of a negative teacher is Dr. Wollen.

   One day, *for example*, when one student asked him to repeat his explanation, he became quite angry.

   Professor Hilton is *typical* of the neutral teacher.

4. TRANSITIONS TO SHOW THE IMPORTANCE OF THE CATEGORY. It is a good idea to indicate if an example or a category is more or less significant than the others. Indicate, too, the relative size of the category.

> *Of the three types of teachers*, the negative teachers are the least agreeable. Fortunately, this group is *in the minority*.

EXERCISE 9·12 Writing Assignment   Study the following essay. The original version contained transitions that have been omitted from this version. Rewrite the essay to include transitions wherever necessary.

Kinds of Hotels

Hotels are found in every country and city of the world and even in communities with few inhabitants. That's why the hotel industry ranks high among the largest worldwide industries. Today, the lodging industry offers many new alternatives for the traveling public. Some properties offer luxury accommodations; others offer budget accommodations; while still others accommodate the need of travelers to be away from home. Whatever the reason, there are many different kinds of hotels and they can be classified according to their size, facility, type, price, or service. Generally, we can classify these hotels into three large groups based on location.

Airport hotels accommodate the air traveler. Because air travel has become more common, this kind of hotel has become more popular. The principal distinction is that it is located near airports. It is very convenient to the traveler. Its guests include passengers with short stay-overs or cancelled flights and travelers who are in business. The length of stay is between one to three days for the guests. These kinds of hotels provide a limited level of service, and the rates are usually between low to medium. The Hilton, the Marriott, and the Holiday Inn are large chains that have hotels near airports. Best Western and the TraveLodge are among the smaller hotel chains.

Downtown hotels, also called commercial hotels, are located near large office complexes and retail stores in the major metropolitan areas. Their primary markets are in the business industry. The downtown hotels are near business destinations for daytime activities and are close to the city's entertainment centers for nighttime activities. This combination is attractive to people attending meetings and conventions. Although the primary market for these hotels is the business traveler, many tourists use them as well. The length of stay for the guests is between three to five days and rates can run between medium to high, depending on the hotel. The downtown hotels have a variety of services such as room service, a coffee shop, a formal dining room, laundry services, a gift shop, and a swimming pool. The downtown Hyatt-Regency is a well-known hotel in this category.

There are also the resort hotels located near the beaches, mountains, or spas. Resort hotels are destinations or parts of a destination complex, and their primary clients are vacationers and recreation-minded people. Guests in these resorts can spend from one week to an entire season. The resort hotels must provide guest entertainment. Because the resort guests expect to be entertained right on the premises, they are willing to pay higher rates. The level of service is much higher than what an airport or downtown hotel offers. These complexes are designed with the family and children in mind. The most famous of these is the Walt Disney World Resort, which includes not only the theme park but also all varieties of water sports, campgrounds, and golf courses.

There may be a few other general areas where hotels are located, such as along the interstate highways, but most of them are located near airports, in the downtown areas, and in resort areas.

—adapted from an essay by Carlos Palacio

EXERCISE 9•13 Writing Assignment

1. What is the thesis of the essay "Kinds of Hotels"?
2. Make an outline of the essay.

Grammar Review

If you want to review grammatical structures that will help you achieve coherence and grammatical accuracy in your writing, see the Grammar Review Unit. The following sections are designed to coordinate with the classification essay:

Correlative Conjunctions, pages 349–351
Adjective Clauses Reduced to Participial Phrases, pages 303–305

EXERCISE 9•14 Writing Assignment   Choose one of the following topics for a classification essay. To generate ideas, prewrite using one of the techniques you learned in Chapter 1. Then, find a logical principle around which you can formulate your thesis. As you develop your categories, use specific details and examples to illustrate the classes.

1. Using the preceding essay as a model, write an essay classifying some other type of building or business for another purpose, such as banks, hospitals, restaurants, or gas stations. Be sure to include transitions and examples.

2. Classify types of exercise programs, diets, or diseases.

3. You have received a letter from a friend back home asking you about your friends here. In your response, you have decided to classify your friends.

4. In your psychology class, your professor has decided to have you analyze your own dreams in a report that will be a part of a larger report by the entire class on dreams. Write an essay classifying your dreams. What types of dreams do you have?

5. Write an essay classifying jobs in the computer field. This essay can be written for an article in the school newspaper.

6. Choose one of these topics for a classification essay:
   a. Types of lies people tell.
   b. Types of excuses students make up for missing class.
   c. Types of sciences.
   d. Your neighbors.
   e. The books you read.

EXERCISE 9•15 Assignments from the Disciplines   Following are some topics for your final writing assignment which are typical of college writing assignments. For your final writing assignment, you may choose one that you have studied, or consult a textbook or the Internet to find the answer. Then, follow the directions for Exercise 9-14 to write your answer.

1. From Psychology   Psychologists interested in the study of personality often classify people into groups by personality type. In your opinion, what system of classification is best? Write an essay in which you define this system.

2. From Computer Science   Programmers can give instructions through many different computer programs. Write an essay in which you classify these computer programs into three or more groups, using any principle of classification which is appropriate.

Revision

Peer Review
When you have finished writing the first draft of your essay, give it to a classmate to read and review. Use the peer review checklist in Appendix I to respond to each other's drafts.

Revision Checklist for the Classification Essay
Use these questions to help you to give suggestions to your peers and to revise your essay.

1. A classification essay analyzes a subject by breaking it down into its parts to study the nature or relationship of the parts. Does your essay break a subject down into parts?

2. To classify, you must have one principle of classification. What is the principle of classification in your essay?

3. Your classification should include all the members of the group. Is your classification complete?

4. In organizing your classification essay, you need to identify each group, describe or define it, give examples, and distinguish it from the other groups. Is your essay well organized and sufficiently developed?

5. Have you used an interesting introduction for your essay?

6. Is your essay coherent?

© CNN®

Chapter **10** The Process Analysis Essay

Theme

The World of the Internet

Goals

Writing

To plan, organize, and write a process analysis essay

To understand the differences between a directional process and an informational process

To be aware of how the intended audience of an essay affects the information that should be included in the essay

To be able to decide how to divide a process analysis essay into paragraphs

To use the dramatic entrance method of writing introductions

To use participial phrases to increase coherence

Reading

To learn about and discuss the world of computers

To identify the steps in a process analysis essay

Grammar

To review adverbial clauses of time reduced to participial phrases, adverbial clauses of purpose, and conditionals

Getting Started

Journal Writing: Do you remember the first time you used a computer? Choose one of the following questions, and answer this question in your journal.

1. How did you learn to use a computer?
2. How do you use computers in your everyday life?
3. What are your feelings when you use a computer? Do computers make you feel excited? Nervous? Powerful? Weak?

CNN® Video Activity: "Profile of a Communications Software Company"

 Hilgraeve is a small computer company which has found a niche making communications software for the Windows operating system. In this CNN report, the founders of Hilgraeve talk about what has made their company successful in the past, and what they believe they must do to be successful in the future.

Watch the report and make a list of suggestions you think the founders of Hilgraeve would make to someone starting their own computer company.

Video Follow-up: Using the Internet

One of the founders of Hilgraeve suggests that an advantage of small company is that it can change quickly. Visit Hilgraeve's Web site <www.hilgraeve.com> and surf through company information such as products, mission and events. Does it seem to you that Hilgraeve has changed since the CNN report?

Reading: The World of the Internet

Computers, the Internet, and a part of the Internet called the World Wide Web have become important parts of our daily lives. At work, school, and home, people search the Web to find information use E-mail to communicate with colleagues, professors and friends and family. In the following readings, you will learn more about how the Internet and these applications work as well as the history behind their development. As you read, try to answer the following questions:

1. How does E-mail travel from the computer of the person who sent it to the receiver's computer?
2. How long has the Internet existed? How was it created and developed?
3. What are some of the most important applications used on the Internet?

Reading

"The Life of E-Mail"
by Alan Phelps

This magazine article explains the process through which an e-mail travels from the sender's computer to the receiver's computer. Before you read, answer these questions:

1. Have you ever used e-mail? How quickly does e-mail travel from one computer to another?
2. Explain the process of sending e-mail.

1   Address. Subject. Message body. It's all there. Now just run a quick spelling check, and hit the Send button.

2   From here on out, the e-mail message has left your hands. The forces of the Internet take over as the magical mystery tour begins. It can get somewhat complicated out there, but the basic steps are easy enough to understand. . . .

3   The first stage in the journey of an e-mail message is simply getting out of your computer. That might entail° stuffing it through° a modem on a dial-up 'Net connection or through a network adapter card on a local-area network (LAN). Either way, the message text must be converted into a form that can be stuffed through the available medium. For networks, that could be a variety of languages. With dial-up connections, the modem must transform your computer's digital code into the analog noises that can be transmitted over phone lines.

4   Weaving its way through phone or network cables, our message arrives at computers run by the ISP° or network administrator. What happens next depends upon, to an extent, which type of data is being sent. An e-mail message, for example, is sent to an outgoing mail server computer. The standard format for outgoing mail is Simple Mail Transport Protocol (SMTP), which is why many e-mail programs want to know the name of your "SMTP server."

5   The SMTP computer shoves the message, now encoded according to the Transmission Control Protocol/Internet Protocol (TCP/IP) protocol, onto the 'Net with a push toward the first nearby router computer. At this point, our data is divided into numerous packets, each carrying a small fragment of the message along with the address of your recipient. Here, they bid adieu° to one another, promising to meet again one day.

6   Routers are the traffic cops of the Internet, monitoring the flow of packets around the system. They read the destination information in each packet and send it scooting off toward the next router in the right direction. If the preferred router happens to be malfunctioning° or otherwise out of service, the packet will be sent on a more circuitous° path. Other routers encountering° the packet perform the same service.

Glossary (margin):
involve
pushing something through a small space

Internet Service Provider

good-bye (French)

not working
indirect
meeting

7   Eventually, depending on network traffic and luck, the packet reaches the destination ISP computer. There it meets with its brother and sister packets from back home and is reconstituted° into the original message. The text is then stored until it is downloaded by your friend. For most people using ISPs, this step happens on a computer known as Post Office Protocol (POP) mail server. POP3 is the standard for receiving and storing Internet mail.

put back in its
original form

8   When recipients check their mail, the POP3 server sends the messages on down to the e-mail client program through the modem/phone line or network card/network connection. A cute noise might play, indicating new mail in your friend's inbox. So goes the life for Internet data.

EXERCISE 10·1 Comprehension/Discussion Questions

1. What is the process described in this essay?
2. What are the steps in this process?
3. Find the thesis statement in this article.
4. In paragraph 3, the author identifies two possible ways an e-mail message can "get out" of a computer. What are they? How are they different?
5. The e-mail is divided into "packets." What is a packet? How is it possible for all of the packets to arrive at the same destination?
6. The author says, "Routers are the traffic cops of the Internet." Explain the meaning of this sentence.
7. What will happen if one of the routers isn't working properly?
8. In paragraph 7, the author writes, "Eventually, depending on network traffic and luck, the packet reaches the destination ISP computer." Which do you think is more important in determining when and if the packet will reach the destination computer? Why do you think the author includes luck as a factor in this step of the process?
9. Throughout the article, the author tries to "personify" the e-mail message, or give it human-like qualities. How does the title help to personify the e-mail message? What other methods of personification are used in the article?
10. Did you find this article interesting? How does the author try to make this process analysis more interesting to read?

EXERCISE 10·2 Vocabulary Development   In this article, the author uses a number of colloquial, or informal, words and expressions. These expressions help to give the essay an informal, conversational tone, as if the writer is actually talking with the reader. These informal expressions also help to make the essay interesting because they are specific. Although colloquial expressions are appropriate in informal writing, they are often inappropriate in formal academic writing.

Some of the informal expressions used in this article are given here. You will discover that a number of them refer to the way computers move an e-mail message from one computer to another. For each expression, write a short definition, and then write an original sentence.

1. has left your hands (par. 2)

_____

2. stuffing it through (par. 3)

_____

3. shoves (par. 5)

_____

4. with a push toward (par. 5)

_____

5. bid adieu (par. 5)

_____

6. send it scooting off toward (par. 6)

_____

7. send it on down (par. 8)

_____

Reading ②

"A Brief History of the Internet and the World Wide Web"
by G. Michael Schneider and Judith Gersting

In this selection from a computer science textbook, the authors recount the development of the Internet and the World Wide Web. Before you read, try to answer these questions.

1. Have you ever used the Internet? If so, what did you use the Internet for?
2. What is the difference between the Internet and the World Wide Web?
3. What do people use the Internet for today?
4. When do you believe the Internet was first developed?

to change completely

spreading
working with others

effect

1   In the words of its designers, "The Internet has revolutionized° the computer and communications world like nothing before. It is at once a worldwide broadcasting capability, a mechanism for information dissemination,° and a medium for collaboration° and interaction between individuals and their computers without regard for geographic location." This very strong statement is quite accurate; the Internet has changed the way people learn and study, search for information, and exchange thoughts and ideas. In the coming years it will have an even greater impact°—on the way we shop, get our news, are entertained, conduct financial affairs, and talk with friends and family. There is no doubt that the Internet has had and will continue to have

very important

a profound° effect on society, and in this section we highlight the development and growth of both the Internet and the World Wide Web. (Much of the information in the following pages is taken from the 1997 article "A Brief History of the Internet," written by its original designers and available on the World Wide Web.*)

The Internet

2   Surprisingly, the Internet is not a recent development but an idea that has been around for more than 30 years. The concept took shape during the early and mid-1960s and was based on the work of computer scientists at M.I.T. and the RAND Corporation in the United States and the NPL Research Laboratory in Great Britain. The first proposal for building a computer network was made by J.C.R. Licklider of M.I.T. in August 1962. He wrote his colleagues a memo entitled (somewhat optimistically) "The Galactic Network," in which he described a globally interconnected set of computers through which everyone could access data and software. He convinced other researchers at M.I.T. of the validity of his ideas, including Larry Roberts and Leonard Kleinrock. From 1962 to 1967 they and others investigated the theoretical foundations of wide area networking, especially such fundamental° concepts as protocols, packet switching, and routing.

basic

given responsibility for

3   In 1966 Roberts moved to the Advanced Research Projects Agency (ARPA), a small research office of the Department of Defense charged with° developing technology that could be of use to the U.S. military. ARPA was interested in packet-switched networking because it seemed to be a more secure form of communications during wartime. (Traditional dial-up telephones were considered too vulnerable,° because the failure of the central phone switch would completely cut all voice communications.)

unprotected

4   ARPA funded a number of network-related research projects, and in 1967 Roberts presented the first research paper describing ARPA's plans to build a wide area packet-switched computer network. For the next two years, work proceeded on designing the required network hardware and software. The first two nodes of this network, called the ARPANET, were constructed at UCLA and the Stanford Research Institute (SRI), and in October 1969, the first computer to computer network message was successfully sent. (Unfortunately, unlike Neil Armstrong's famous "A small step for man . . ." statement, the contents of that first Internet message have been lost to history.) Later that year, two more nodes were added (UC-Santa Barbara and the University of Utah), and by the end of 1969, the budding° four-node network was well off the ground.°

growing

was already developing

5   The ARPANET grew quickly during the early 1970s, and it was formally demonstrated to the scientific community at an international conference in

---

*B. Leinter, V. Cerf, D. Clark, R. E. Kahn, L. Kleinrock, D. Lynch, J. Postel, L. Roberts, and S. Wolff, "Brief History of the Internet," http://www.isoc.org/internet-history, February 20, 1997.

1972. It was also in late 1972 that the first "killer app" (critically important application) was developed—electronic mail. It was an immediate success and caused an explosion of growth in people-to-people traffic rather than the people-to-machine traffic that had dominated the first three years of network usage.

6   The success of the ARPANET in the 1970s led other researchers to develop similar types of computer networks to support information exchange in their specific scientific area: HEPNet (High Energy Physics Network), CSNet (Computer Science Network), MFENet (Magnetic Fusion Energy Network), and SPAN (Space Physics Access Network). Furthermore, corporations had started to notice the success of the ARPANET and began developing proprietary° networks that they planned to market to their customers: SNA (Systems Network Architecture) at the IBM Corp. and DECNet from the Digital Equipment Corporation. The 1970s were a time of rapid expansion of networks in the academic and commercial communities.

privately owned

7   Farsighted researchers at ARPA, especially Robert Kahn, realized that this rapid and unplanned proliferation° of independent networks would lead to incompatibilities° and prevent users on different networks from communicating with each other, a situation that recalls the problems that national railway systems have sharing rail cars because of their use of different gauge track. Kahn knew that to achieve the maximum benefits of this new technology, all computer networks would need to communicate in a simple, transparent° fashion. He developed a concept called **Internetworking**, which stated that any WAN is free to do whatever it wants *internally*. However, at the point where two different networks meet, both must use a common addressing scheme and identical protocols—that is, they must speak the same language. Essentially Kahn wanted to create a "network of networks."

spread
problems working together

easy to learn or understand

8   This is the same concept that governs the design of the International telephone system. Every country is free to build its own international phone system in whatever way it wants, but all must agree to use a standardized worldwide telephone numbering system (country code, city code, phone number), and each must agree to send and receive telephone calls outside of its borders in a universally recognized format that has been standardized by the worldwide telephone regulatory agency. Thus any telephone subscriber in the world can call any other without worrying about the internal differences in telephone service in different countries. . . .

9   Kahn and his colleagues . . . along with Dr. Vinton Cerf of Stanford, began working on these problems in 1973, and together they designed the solutions that were to become the framework for the Internet—the global network of interconnected networks.

organized from higher function to lower

• Addressing. Cerf and Kahn created a global, hierarchical° addressing scheme that uniquely identifies a computer user located anywhere in the world. Most of us have seen these addresses, which look like the following:

ABSmith@MyComp.Csci.UoT.edu

- Protocols. Cerf and Kahn also designed a standardized set of communications protocols called TCP/IP, an acronym for Transmission Control Protocol/Internet Protocol. These protocols described the rules and procedures that networks would use for addressing, message formats, routing and error control, and they are the "glue" that allows different networks to communicate with each other. TCP/IP was to become the "common language" spoken by networks around the world.

10   During the late 1970s and early 1980s, work proceeded on implementing° and installing TCP/IP on the new hardware devices that were beginning to appear in the marketplace, such as personal computers connected to LANs. It is a real tribute to° the power and flexibility of the TCP/IP protocols that they were able to adapt to a computing environment very different from the one that existed when they were first created. Originally designed to work with time-shared mainframe computers of the 1970s, they were successfully implemented on PCs and workstations connected by LANs, the computing environment of the 1980s and 1990s.

11   By the early 1980s, TCP/IP was in widespread use around the world. Even networks that internally used other communication protocols implemented TCP/IP to exchange information with nodes outside their own network community. At the same time, exciting new applications appeared that were designed to meet the needs of researchers around the world. For example, **Telnet** is a software package that allows users to log on remotely to any other computer on the network and use it exactly as though they were local, without having to pay for an expensive long-distance telephone call. **FTP**, an acronym for **file transfer protocol**, is a way to move files around the network quickly and easily. Along with e-mail (still wildly popular), these and other new applications added more fuel to the superheated° growth of computer networks.

12   With TCP/IP becoming a de facto° network standard, a global addressing scheme, and a useful set of applications, the infrastructure° was now in place for the creation of a truly international network. The Internet, in its modern form, had begun to emerge.

13   However, although many of the technical problems had been addressed and solved, the Internet had not yet had a significant impact on the general populations for one very important reason: In order to use the original ARPANET, you needed to obtain° a research grant from the U.S. Department of Defense (DoD)—not something most people have. Thousands of people were using the Internet by the early 1980s, but they were almost exclusively physicists, engineers, computer scientists, and other academic researchers.

14   There was one last step needed, and it was taken by the National Science Foundation (NSF) in 1984. In that year the NSF initiated a project whose goal

starting to use

sign of the quality of

fast and active
real, accepted
basic, supporting systems

get

was to bring the advantages of Internet technology to the entire academic and professional community, regardless of discipline or relationship with the DoD. NSF planned and built a national network called **NSFNet**, which used TCP/IP technology identical to that developed for the ARPANET. This new network interconnected six NSF supercomputer centers with dozens of new regional networks set up by the NSF. (Actually, NSFNet itself was only the **backbone network**—the transcontinental links that interconnected the regional networks.) These new regional networks included thousands of users at universities, government agencies, libraries, museums, and medical centers. NSFNet also included a direct link to the ARPANET. Thus, by the mid-1980s, the emerging "network of networks" had grown to include many new sites, and even more important, a huge group of new first-time users, such as students, university administrators, librarians, museum staff, politicians, and urban planners.

15   At about the same time, other countries began developing wide area TCP/IP backbone networks like NSFNet to interconnect their own libraries, schools, research centers, and government agencies. As these national networks were created, they were also linked to the growing internetwork, and its user population continued to expand. For the first time since the development of networks, the technology had begun to have an impact on the wider community . . . .

16   Some time in the late 1980s, the term ARPANET ceased to be used because . . . the ARPANET was now only one of many networks belonging to a larger collection. (By 1990 this collection had grown to 3,000 separate networks and a quarter of a million computers.) People began referring to the entire interconnection of computers . . . as "the Internet," though this name was not officially adopted for many years. The formal acceptance of the term **Internet** by the U.S. Government occurred on October 24, 1995.

immediate
multiplied quickly

17   Like the ARPANET before it, the Internet became an instantaneous° success and grew exponentially.° By the middle of 1993, it had already grown to 20,000 separate networks, about 1.3 million host computers, and roughly 5 to 7 million users, and its size was doubling every year. In fact, it had become so successful that the NSF decided that it was time to get out of the "networking business." The goal of the NSF is to fund basic research, not to become involved in ongoing commercial enterprises. In April 1995, NSFNet

stopped working

closed up shop.° The money that was saved was distributed to the regional networks so they could buy Internet connectivity from private venders such as America Online. The exit of the U.S. government from the networking business created a new business opportunity for firms called **Internet service providers**, companies that offer the Internet access capabilities once provided by networks such as the ARPANET and NSFNet.

simple, modest

18   From a humble° beginning of four universities in 1969, by the middle of 1998 the Internet had grown to more than 29,000,000 computers located in just about every country in the world . . . . The Internet has been one of the biggest

success stories in moving research out of the laboratory and into the wider community. What began as the wild idea of a few dedicated researchers has, in only 30 years, grown into a global communication infrastructure moving countless trillions of bits of data among millions of people. It has adapted time and time again—to changes in usage (from research and academic to commercial), changes in hardware environment (from mainframes to PCs and networks), and changes in scale (from thousands of nodes to tens of millions).

19   Amazingly enough, however, the Internet is still undergoing massive growth and change, this time from the most important new application since e-mail: the World Wide Web.

The World Wide Web

20   Tim Berners-Lee, a researcher at CERN, the European High Engergy Physics Laboratory, first came up with the idea for the World Wide Web in 1989. Because physics research is usually done by teams of people from different universities, he wanted to find a way to allow scientists throughout Europe and North America to exchange quickly and easily information such as research articles, journals, and experimental data. Although they could use the Internet and services such as FTP and e-mail, Berners-Lee wanted to make sharing easier and more intuitive° for people not familiar with or comfortable with computer networks. To accomplish this, he designed and built an information-sharing system using a concept called **hypertext**, a collection of documents connected by pointers, called **links** . . . . Berners-Lee's system eventually came to be called the World Wide Web.

easy to guess

21   Most documents are read linearly from beginning to end, but users of hypertext documents (which are called **pages** in Web parlance)° are free to navigate the collection in whatever order they want by traversing° the links to move from page to page. Berners-Lee reasoned that the idea of hypertext matched up quite well with the concept of networking and the Internet. Hypertext documents could be files stored on the millions of machines of the Internet, and a link would be the name of a page and the Internet address of the machine where that page is stored.

jargon, vocabulary
crossing

22   A hypertext link refers to a **URL**, an acronym for **Uniform Resource Locator**, and it is the worldwide identification of one specific Web page . . . . When a user clicks on a link, the network uses TCP/IP protocols to establish a connection between the user's machine and the remote machine whose Internet address is pointed at by the URL. When the connection is established, the requested page is transferred to the user's machine and displayed on the screen, all of which happens automatically. The package that handles the identification and fetching° of pages and their display on the screen is called a **Web browser**; Netscape and Microsoft Internet Explorer are two of the best known. The first graphical browser (Mosaic) was developed in 1993, the year that many people consider to mark the beginning of the Web . . . .

going and getting

23   The Web's colorful graphics and simply "point and click" method of getting information has made it the Internet "killer app" of the 1990s and beyond. It has become the vehicle for bringing the capabilities of networking to the entire world. No longer must a user be a student or a faculty member at a university, a curator of an art museum, or the librarian of a major research library. The Web has brought the power of the Internet to everyone—from toddlers to senior citizens and from kindergarten students to PhDs. For most people, the World Wide Web *is* the Internet.

EXERCISE 10·3 Comprehension/Discussion Questions

1. What is the process described in this textbook excerpt? Why is it told in the past tense?
2. Create a timeline to show the steps in this process.
3. Is there a clearly stated thesis? If so, what is it and where does it appear? If not, where and how is it implied?
4. What is the authors' purpose in writing this essay? How do you know?
5. Why was the ARPANET developed?
6. What were the first four nodes on the ARPANET?
7. How was networking different before and after e-mail was developed?
8. Why were standardized networking protocols like TCP/IP necessary?
9. What is the authors' opinion of TCP/IP? How do you know?
10. What was the National Science Foundation's involvement in the development of the Internet? Why was this such a crucial step?
11. There are three major stages in the development of the Internet. What were the names of the network at each of these three stages?
12. What changes did the development of the World Wide Web bring to networking? How did the World Wide Web change the types of Internet users?
13. The essay does not really indicate the exact beginning of the Internet. Identify the several points at which it is possible to argue that the existence of the Internet "began." Which event do you believe marks the "beginning" of the Internet's existence?
14. Read the first paragraph of the essay again. Do you agree with all of the authors' statements and with the quotation from the designers of the Internet? Why or why not?
15. What future do you predict for the Internet?

EXERCISE 10·4 Vocabulary Development   Because this is an introduction to computer science textbook, the authors use a number of computer-related terms. Some of these terms are commonly used in many fields in business, education, and science, because computers are part of daily life in these professions. A few of these terms are specific to computer science. A number of the computer terms in this article are listed below. The number in parentheses indicates the paragraph in which the term first appears. Match them with their definition on the right.

Terms	**Definitions**

Terms

_____ computer network (par. 2)

_____ data (par. 2)

_____ software (par. 2)

_____ protocols (par. 2)

_____ hardware (par. 4)

_____ nodes (par. 4) or hosts (par. 17)

_____ address (par. 9)

_____ install (par. 10)

_____ mainframe (par. 10)

_____ PC (par. 10)

_____ LAN (par. 10)

_____ Internet connectivity (par. 17)

_____ ISP (par. 17)

_____ HTML (par. 19)

_____ URL (par. 19)

_____ navigate (par. 20)

_____ link (par. 21)

_____ Web browser (par. 22)

Definitions

a. to put software into a computer

b. personal computer

c. a set of rules and procedures computers follow when communicating on a network

d. the programs that control a computer

e. Uniform Resource Locator—the name used to locate a Web page

f. The name that identifies a computer user

g. To move from one Web page to another by clicking on links

h. A system of connected computers

i. An individual computer in a network

j. Local Area Network—a network in a relatively small area, like a room or a campus

k. Internet Service Provider—a company that sells access to the Internet

l. Software that can be used to access the World Wide Web

m. Computer equipment and machinery

n. Information stored or transmitted by a computer

o. A powerful computer, often used as the center of a network

p. Hypertext markup language—a computer language used to write documents which include connections to other documents

q. The ability to connect to the Internet

r. A highlighted word or phrase in a Web document that, when clicked, allows the user to connect to another document

Writing

A process is a series of actions leading to an expected or planned outcome. There are two types of process essays: those that instruct or direct and those that explain or analyze. Directional process essays tell how to do something. For example, a directional process might explain how to find an apartment. The purpose of this type of essay is to clarify the steps in the procedure so that the reader can recreate the steps and the results. An informational process essay explains or analyzes a process—it tells how something works, how something happened, or how something is or was done. For example, you could explain how World War II began or how hurricanes form. The informational process essay has a purpose different from a directional process essay. Its main purpose is to inform, explain, or analyze. The reader is gaining an understanding of the process; he or she does not necessarily expect to be able to recreate the process.

Although process essays that explain or instruct have different purposes, they can be developed using the same pattern of development and organization. In this chapter, then, our concentration is on developing and organizing the process essay.

Planning the Process Analysis Essay

When you are planning your essay, you should bear in mind the following advice:

Be aware of the audience. When you are planning a process essay, your first question should be, "What do my readers know about my topic?" Identifying the audience is important in deciding what to include and what to omit in the essay. For instance, suppose that you decided to explain how to paint a room to an inexperienced audience—people who have never before painted a room. You would have to be very specific and assume that the readers know little or nothing about the process. However, if your audience is made up of professional or experienced painters, you would have to approach the assignment differently. In this case, you would probably explain a special technique that your audience may not be aware of.

In general, though, you should assume that readers know little about the topic being explained, but have the same general knowledge you do. For instance, it can be assumed that most people know what a paintbrush is, but it cannot be assumed that your readers know which kind of brush is best to use with a certain type of paint.

Order the steps chronologically. Since a process paper describes a sequence of steps leading to some preconceived end, it is important that the steps be discussed in the order that they occur; in other words, the steps should be arranged in chronological order. This principle of organization is the same as the one used for narration (see Chapter 3). In a process essay, ordering ideas chronologically is vital, especially if readers are to be able to recreate the process. The only time to break from chronological order is when you explain some unfamiliar term or give some word of advice or caution.

EXERCISE 10·5   Think of a process that you are familiar with: for example, how to get a visa, how to develop a photograph, how to wait on a customer. Brainstorm a list of the steps in the process. When you have finished brainstorming, arrange the steps chronologically.

Make sure that the process is complete. Whether you are explaining how to do something or how something was done, make sure to include all the steps in the process. Obviously, if you are explaining how to do something and leave out one of the steps, your readers will not be able to recreate the process and get the same result. A good way to test the thoroughness of the steps of a process is to have someone follow each step exactly as explained.

Let us say, for example, that you wanted to write an essay for the campus International Student Association's newsletter about how to get a driver's license. You can assume that the audience is the international student who has probably recently arrived in the United States and does not yet have a driver's license. You might list the steps as follows:

1. Go to the Motor Vehicle Department in your area.
2. At the Motor Vehicle Department, the first thing you will do is take a vision test.
3. After that, you will take a written test.
4. Then you will take a driving test.
5. Finally, you will pay the fee.

Is this list complete? Certainly, these are the major steps involved, but there are many other things that the reader will need to know to get a driver's license. The following is an example of the expanded list of steps.

1. First obtain a pamphlet with the driving rules from the Motor Vehicle Department. You can do this by telephoning them at 555-3333 and asking them to mail you the pamphlet.
2. Study the pamphlet carefully.
3. Before you go to the Motor Vehicle Department, be sure that your car is in proper working order.
4. Bring your birth certificate or your passport with you.
5. Bring $30 in cash.
6. Have a friend drive you to the MVD on Main Street and Vine Avenue. You can park at the rear of the building.

7. Get in the line marked "Driver's License Exam."
8. Fill out the information on the card they give you.
9. Take the vision test.
10. Then take the written exam.
11. If you pass, then you will take the driving test.
12. If you pass that, you can pay the fee of $30.

This version is certainly more thorough than the original list, but it is still incomplete. For example, it would be a good idea to give the reader some more instructions about taking the written and the driving tests. Can you think of any other specific steps that should be included?

EXERCISE 10•6   Using the list of steps you made for Exercise 10-5, test its thoroughness by having someone follow the steps you have outlined. Now revise the list to make it more complete.

Internet Activity: Composition Skills and the Internet

 Many people post "how to" information on the Internet. For example, one search found over 300 pages about "how to tie a tie." Find a "how to" page by doing an Internet search for the phrase "how to" or "how to make" or "how to build." Look carefully at the instructions provided. Do the instructions pass the test for thoroughness? How could they be improved?

Be sure to define new or unfamiliar terms. This is especially true for process essays that give instructions. Sometimes a process description may introduce a word or phrase that the reader might not understand. Since it makes little sense to have the reader attempt to complete a process without understanding the particular terms involved, always define what he or she might not know. If you are explaining how to repair a flat tire, for example, you might have to describe or define what a lug wrench is; otherwise, the reader would not know which tool is being discussed and could not continue with the process. In the example of the process of getting a driver's license, it might be necessary to explain the meaning of a few terms that will be used during the test, for example "oncoming traffic" or "Class A License":

> When you are filling out the form, check the box that says "Class A." A Class A license is for those who want to drive automobiles, not trucks or motorcycles.

Warn your reader of difficulties in the process. When planning a process essay, try to anticipate what problems the reader might have in understanding or recreating the process. If one step is particularly difficult, warn the reader of this. Be sure to warn the reader of what not to do as well. For example, if you are explaining how to get a driver's license, it is a good idea to warn the reader about some of the tricky things that might come up during the driving test. Perhaps you should warn your reader to practice parallel parking before going to take the driving test, or advise the reader to fill out the forms carefully and to ask questions if he or she is confused. You might also advise the reader what to do if the car stalls.

EXERCISE 10·7 Go back over the list you revised for Exercise 10-6. Add definitions of new or unfamiliar terms and warnings of difficulties in the process.

Explain the purpose of a step when necessary. A process essay is more than just a list of steps. Expect that the reader wants to understand the process, whether he or she will attempt to recreate it or merely to read it. Therefore, you should explain the rationale behind the steps when the rationale is not obvious. In other words, try to explain—if only briefly—the purpose of the step. This kind of explanation is especially useful when the reader may skip the step because he or she thinks that it does not serve any real purpose. For example, in step 3 of the driver's license process (page 225), explain why the reader should see to it that the car is in proper working order. (For example, the driver may get a citation for having a brake light out.)

Try to make your thesis statement persuasive. A thesis statement for a process essay does not have to have a strong central idea; in fact, it can be as simple as, "There are three major steps involved in changing a flat tire." However, since the essay has as its underlying purpose more than just a listing of steps (those steps should be explained and analyzed), it is a good idea to have a thesis that contains a strong central idea. The thesis statement might be, "Changing a flat tire is really quite easy." This statement will require showing that the process is indeed easy. However, if the thesis is, "Changing a flat tire is a horrible experience," it would be necessary to show how horrible the process is.

EXERCISE 10·8 Go back over the list of steps you have been working on in the three preceding exercises. Formulate a thesis statement that contains a central idea about the process you are describing.

Organizing the Process Analysis Essay

One of the more difficult aspects of writing a process essay is deciding where to divide the essay into paragraphs. Generally speaking, most processes break down into a beginning, middle, and end. Here are a few pointers for dividing process steps logically into paragraphs:

1. *Introduction.* The introductory paragraph should introduce the topic and establish the purpose for writing the process. The reader should understand why the process is being described and in what situations the process is used.

2. *Developmental paragraphs.* The actual description of the process usually begins in the first developmental paragraph. However, if you are describing how to do something and the process requires that the reader obtain some items first, then you may need to point out in the first developmental paragraph what items are needed.

   The actual steps of the process usually can be divided into three or four major steps. For example, if you were explaining how to change a flat tire, the first section could deal with getting the car jacked up; the next section could deal with removing and replacing the tire; and the last section could deal with removing the jack. In most cases, each major section can be described in a separate paragraph. Note, too, that the topic sentence in a process essay is often implied rather than stated directly.

3. *Conclusion.* How to conclude a process essay depends on the type of process being described. Often the conclusion discusses the results of the process. Take special note of the conclusions in the model process essays in this chapter.

EXERCISE 10•9   Think of a persuasive thesis for the driver's license process. Then break down the steps on pages 225–226 into logical groups.

EXERCISE 10•10   Using the process you have been working on in the preceding exercises, break down the steps into logical groups.

Now that you are familiar with some of the major points concerning process essays, let us look at the following process essay. Observe the paragraphing, locate the thesis, and determine if there is a central idea and if that idea is carried out in the process. Also, try to find explanations, examples, warnings, and definitions in the essay. Finally, note if the process description is complete.

Studying Math

Math is probably the most difficult course for most people. However, I think that what makes math difficult is the power that the term *mathematics* has upon people's minds. Most students are afraid of not passing because of the reputation the course has of being hard. The study of math needs lots of concentration and practice, but it isn't really hard; it just deals with the relationship and symbolism of numbers and magnitudes. What is the most difficult part of math? Working problems progressively, probably. How should students study math in general? They should follow some guidelines, like the ones I have prepared, in order to feel less nervous about the subject.

Concentration is the first thing that a student should acquire before even trying to think about studying math. Full concentration is needed to study math, as well as to be free of any thoughts outside the study of math. Preparing to study starts the concentration because at that moment the student starts to think about what he or she is going to cover or what he or she will need in order to solve some problems. Also, a student should be completely rested, because if a student is tired, he or she may end up taking a lot longer to accomplish what he is supposed to.

In order for the student to understand the material involved, the student should read all sections completely. I think the most appropriate way of doing this is first by reading a section completely. Then, the student should analyze that section, and he or she should take all the formulas and write them down on a separate sheet in order to memorize and analyze them completely. Right after this, the student should take a break of about ten minutes in order to be relaxed to work some of the problems given in the section. Most students do all the problems at once, but I don't think that is the appropriate way. A student should only do the problems he can figure out. If he can't do one of the problems in the section, he should leave it and go on to the next one. Then the student should take another short break. After that, he is ready to read the next section and follow the same procedure.

Right after a student has read all sections, he or she should look at the problems that he or she couldn't do. The student should try again to work them out, but only to a limit. The student shouldn't have to think more than five or ten minutes to figure out what is going on. Instead, a student should take those problems to the professor in order to get a complete understanding of the problems. If a student takes too much time to do a problem, he or she will get burned out and will end up hating the material.

Then right after the student has finished all sections, he should start doing the problems in the review section in order to have a better understanding and to increase his or her speed while working out a problem. At this stage, the student should find a partner to work with. Believe it or not, working with a partner helps a lot, because if a problem comes into action, there are two minds that will solve the problem easily.

Math can be difficult if an individual thinks that it is difficult. But if a student follows some of my guidelines, I'm sure that he or she will do well and will like the material.

—Igor Gonzalez

EXERCISE 10·11   On a separate sheet of paper, answer the following questions about "Studying Math."

1. What is the thesis? The central idea?
2. Does the author establish a need for this process? If so, where?
3. Look at the paragraph divisions. Why does the author divide up the steps as he does?
4. What is the controlling idea for paragraph 2?
5. Is there a topic sentence for each paragraph? If not, is it implied?
6. Why should you take frequent breaks?
7. Is this essay unified? Coherent?
8. Are the steps clearly explained? Is the process complete?
9. Who is the audience?
10. Is this essay a directional or informational process explanation?
11. What verb tenses are used in this essay? Underline them in the essay.
12. Outline this essay.

EXERCISE 10·12 Writing Assignment   Using the brainstorming notes you started in Exercise 10-5, write the first draft of your process essay.

Now let us look at a different kind of process essay. As you read "Cognitive Development," try to determine whether it's an informational or directional process explanation. Also, take note of the verb tenses used by the author. If you are not familiar with the meaning of the word *cognitive*, refer to your dictionary before reading the essay.

Cognitive Development

When I was talking to my three-year-old niece on the telephone, I asked her if she liked preschool. I heard nothing. I asked her again, but still there was no response. Then her mother took the telephone and told me that my niece had been nodding her head to indicate "yes." At age three, my niece was not able to understand that I could not see what she could see or do while she was on the phone talking to me. This kind of observation of children led the great Swiss psychologist Jean Piaget to conclude that children are not born with a cognitive structure. He argued that children's cognitive understanding of the world emerges with experience; in other words, it develops. Knowledge, then, is a process rather than a "state." A child knows or understands an object by interacting with it, and from this interaction he expands his ability to comprehend. According to Piaget, just as all children grow and mature physically in the same basic sequence, they

also develop cognitively in a process that is the same for all children, regardless of cultural upbringing.

Piaget called the first stage that children go through the sensorimotor period, which extends from birth to around age two. The child develops a "sense" of the objects around her by her "motor," or physical, action on the objects. Her understanding of the world is limited to her physical actions on the objects in her world. For example, newborns have certain reflexes, such as sucking and grasping a finger that touches their hand. From these reflexes, the infant begins to learn about and recognize objects, and she can generalize to other objects. At about eight to 12 months, the infant is able to act intentionally and even plan her actions. If she kicks hard enough, the rattle in the crib will make the noise she wants to hear. An important developmental milestone during this stage is what Piaget terms object permanence. By the end of this stage, the infant recognizes that an object continues to exist even when she cannot see it or touch it. For instance, a person who walks behind a screen is still there even though the infant cannot see her.

Object permanence is the beginning of the child's awareness that people and objects exist independent from him, but this is only the beginning. The achievements of the sensorimotor stage just prepare him for the next stage, called the preoperational period, lasting from about age two to seven. During this stage, a child perceives and interprets the world in terms of self. He cannot comprehend that another person sees objects differently. He thinks other people see and hear what he does. Thus, my three-year-old niece nodded her head to indicate "yes" because she assumed I could see her. During this stage, Piaget describes children as being rigid in thought. They base their conclusions on one obvious factor or feature of an object. For instance, if a bowl of water is poured into a tall jar, the child will conclude that the tall jar has more water because its level is higher. But toward the end of this period, the child is beginning to learn about objects in a new way. For instance, he begins to understand that water poured from the bowl into the tall jar is still the same water; that is, an object can change its shape but still be the same basic object. A good example is that a child now understands that if a person puts on a mask he or she is still the same person. The child is developing representational thought.

This increasing flexibility prepares the child for what Piaget called the concrete operational period. From about seven to 11 years old, a child makes great strides in her cognitive development. She develops the ability to make mental transformations with regard to concrete objects. A child begins to comprehend the concepts of reversibility, compensation, and addition and subtraction. Piaget uses the concept of conservation to illustrate this development. If you pour the water back from the tall jar to the bowl, during this stage the child can understand that the amount of water that was in the jar is the same as what's in the bowl, even though the water levels are different. She can understand that the width of the bowl makes up—or compensates for—its lack of height. The child also understands that no water has been removed or added.

In the next stage, called the formal operational period, from about 11 to 15 years old, the child develops more sophisticated reasoning abilities. He can reason now; he can see more logical relationships between objects and can think more systematically before acting. In other words, he can think in more abstract terms; he can use information from the past to predict consequences. One game that requires such skills is chess. During this stage of development, a child can learn not only the rules and movements involved but also can use strategies.

Refinement of cognitive skills continues on into adulthood, but Piaget felt that the development of structure of thought is achieved by about age 15. After that, the content and quality of thought may develop. Although not all researchers in cognitive development agree with Piaget's scheme and all of his conclusions, he can be credited for having a tremendous impact on our understanding of how children develop their understanding of the world around them. Children are not miniature adults who reason as adults do; they understand and interpret their environment in terms of their cognitive development. This is important to realize if we want to understand our children and ourselves better.

—Information from Patricia H. Miller,
Theories of Developmental Psychology
(New York: W. H. Freeman, 1983), pp. 30–66

EXERCISE 10·13   On a separate sheet of paper, answer the following questions about "Cognitive Development."

1. What kind of process is being analyzed in this essay?
2. What is the central idea about the process of cognitive development?
3. What is the topic of paragraph 2?
4. What does Piaget mean by object permanence? Can you give another example?
5. During which stage does the child make a lot of progress?
6. What do you think the writer's purpose is for writing this essay?
7. Does the conclusion logically follow?
8. What verb tense is used frequently? Is it active or passive?
9. Make an outline of this essay.

Composition Skills

Introductory Paragraphs

The Dramatic Entrance

The two types of introductions that you have been writing, the Funnel and the Turnabout, are good approaches to beginning essays. However, as your writing skills improve, you should strive not only for sentence variety but also for variety in essay openings as well. A dramatic, humorous, or otherwise interesting opening will generate interest in the reader. It is important, after all, to capture the reader's attention. The type of introduction that serves this purpose can be called the "Dramatic Entrance."

There are various ways to make a Dramatic Entrance. One way is to describe a scene that introduces your reader to the subject of your essay. Note how this writer opens an article on carbohydrates and depression:

On May 16, 1898, the intrepid Arctic explorer Frederick A. Cook made the following notation in his journal: "The winter and the darkness have slowly but steadily settled over us. . . . It is not difficult to read on the faces of my companions their thoughts and their moody dispositions. The curtain of blackness which has fallen over the outer world of icy desolation has also descended upon the inner world of our souls. Around the tables . . . men are sitting about sad and dejected, lost in dreams of melancholy from which, now and then, one arouses with an empty attempt at enthusiasm. For brief moments some try to break the spell by jokes, told perhaps for the fiftieth time. Others grind out a cheerful philosophy; but all efforts to infuse bright hopes fail."

We now know that the members of the Cook expedition were suffering from classic symptoms of winter depression, a condition related to a recently described psychiatric disorder, known as seasonal affective disorder, or SAD.

—Richard J. Wurtman and Judith J. Wurtman,
"Carbohydrates and Depression," *Scientific American*
Jan. 1989: p. 68. © 1989 by Scientific American, Inc.
All rights reserved.

For process papers, it is often useful to begin with a description of a scene that establishes the need for a process explanation. Observe here how one student uses a description to set up a process paper:

The rain pours down as if running from a faucet, lightning streaks across the dark restless sky, and thunder pounds the roof and walls of the house. All of a sudden the wind kicks up. Trees sway madly back and forth; loose objects are picked up and thrown all around. The house creaks and moans with every gust of wind. Windows are broken by pieces of shingle from a neighbor's roof or by loose objects picked up by the wind. Power lines snap like thread. The unprepared house and its occupants are in grave danger as the awesome hurricane approaches. Had they prepared for the hurricane, they might not be in such danger. Indeed, careful preparation before a hurricane is essential to life and property.

—Donald Landry

EXERCISE 10·14   On a separate sheet of paper, answer the following questions about Donald Landry's introductory paragraph.

1. How is this description organized? Is it organized chronologically, spatially, or both? Why has the writer selected this pattern of organization?
2. What is the process that will be explained?
3. Does the introduction establish a need for the process?

EXERCISE 10·15 Study the following process topics. Select one and brainstorm a list of steps in the process and plan the essay. When you begin drafting, try to write an introduction that is a Dramatic Entrance.

1. How to do a particular job.
2. How to study for a particular course.
3. How something is made (you choose).
4. How something works.
5. The life cycle of an insect.
6. How to use a particular computer software package

Coherence

Participial Phrases

Since process analysis essays are organized chronologically, like narrations, many of the transitional devices discussed in Chapter 3 are used: sequence markers (*first, next, after that*, and so forth) and adverbial clauses of time. To achieve even more coherence in chronologically developed essays, participial phrases can be used to indicate the sequence of actions between clauses. Participial phrases not only make writing more coherent, they also add variety in sentence structure, thus improving the writing. Note the following examples:

> After typing the message, he sent the e-mail message to his friend.
> Having finished the written test, you must wait to take the driving test.
> Having been asked, the witness will describe the person.

Adverbial clauses of time are used to clarify the time relationship between the action in one clause and the action in another. Adverbial clauses of time are used when you combine two independent clauses, making one subordinate, or dependent. Adverbial clauses of time can be reduced to participial phrases when the subject of the adverbial clause is the same as the subject of the independent clause. Study the following examples:

First the e-mail is sent to the outgoing mail server. Then the message is divided into packets and sent toward a nearby router computer. (TWO INDEPENDENT CLAUSES)

After the e-mail has reached the outgoing mail server, the message is divided into packets and sent toward a nearby router computer. (ADVERBIAL CLAUSE + INDEPENDENT CLAUSE)

After reaching the outgoing mail server, the message is divided into packets and sent toward a nearby router computer. (PARTICIPIAL PHRASE + INDEPENDENT CLAUSE)

Having reached the outgoing mail server, the message is divided into packets and sent toward a nearby router computer. (PARTICIPIAL PHRASE + INDEPEN-DENT CLAUSE)

Using participial phrases will give your writing coherence.

Grammar Review

If you want to review grammatical structures that will help you achieve coherence and grammatical accuracy in your writing, see the Grammar Review Unit. The following sections are designed to coordinate with the process essay:

Adverbial Clauses reduced to Participial Phrases, pages 310–313
Adverbial Clauses of Purpose, pages 334–336
Conditionals, pages 376–379

EXERCISE 10·16   Choose one of the following topics for a process analysis essay. First, decide if you want to write a directional process or an informational process. Then generate ideas, using one of the prewriting techniques you learned in Chapter 1. Then make a list in chronological order of the steps involved in the process. Make sure the process is complete. Define any unfamiliar terms and give the reader appropriate warnings. Be sure to use appropriate transitions.

1. Write an essay explaining how to prepare and eat one of your favorite foods.
2. Explain how to repair something, such as sewing on a button or changing a car tire.
3. Think of a hobby or sport that you enjoy doing and know well. Explain how to prepare for or participate in this activity. Write the essay assuming your audience has not done this activity before.
4. Imagine that you have been asked to write an essay to help people to prepare for a natural disaster (such as a flood, storm, or the like).
5. Choose one of the topics suggested in Exercise 10-15.

EXERCISE 10·17 Assignments from the Disciplines   Following are some topics for your final writing assignment which are typical of college writing assignments. For your final writing assignment, you may choose one that you have studied, or consult a textbook or the Internet to find the answer. Then, follow the directions for Exercise 10-16 to write your answer.

1. From Physical Sciences   In science labs, students often have to write reports of laboratory experiments that are performed to demonstrate or test certain principles of physics. Write an essay analyzing the process one would follow when doing one of the following laboratory experiments: (a) determine the mechanical advantage of a pulley system, (b) measuring the focal length of

convex and concave lenses, (c) measure the effect of a catalyst on a chemical reaction.

2. From Human Resource Management   A company is only as good as its employees, therefore it is vital to recruit, hire, and retain the best employees possible. Write an essay describing a typical recruitment process used to locate and hire the best person for the job.

3. From Theater   Staging a play involves much more than putting actors in costumes and helping them learn their lines. Write an essay describing the process of designing and staging one of these elements of the stage design: (a) set design, (b) lighting design, (c) costume design.

Revision

Peer Review

When you have finished writing the first draft of your essay, give it to a classmate to read and review. Use the peer review checklist in Appendix I to respond to each other's drafts.

Revision Checklist for the Paragraph

Use these questions to help you to give suggestions to your peers and to revise your essay.

1. A process analysis essay either tells how to do something or explains how something happens. Have you chosen an appropriate subject—process—for your essay?

2. In writing a process analysis essay, you need to be aware of your audience, to order the steps of the process chronologically, to make sure your explanation of the process is complete, and to define any new or unfamiliar terms for your readers. Have you accomplished these tasks in your essay?

3. Your process analysis essay should warn your reader of difficulties in the process, explain the purpose of a step where necessary, and make a persuasive thesis statement. Does your essay perform these functions?

4. Does your essay have an interesting introduction?

5. Is your essay coherent?

Chapter **11** The Cause-and-Effect Analysis Essay

Theme

Academic Achievement

Goals

Writing

To organize and write a causal analysis essay

To organize and write an effect analysis essay

To diagram, outline, and write a causal chain essay

To distinguish between immediate and remote causes and effects

To avoid confusing chronological and causal relationships

To use a relevant quotation to introduce an essay

To use transitions for cause and effect to increase coherence

Reading

To learn about and discuss academic achievement

To identify causes and/or effects described in an essay

To determine the author's purpose in writing an essay

Grammar

To review adverbial clauses of cause and result, unreal conditionals, and articles

Getting Started

Journal Writing: Choose one of the following two questions, and write about it in your journal.

1. Imagine that a new college student has asked you how to be successful. What advice would you give to this student? What is the most important thing that a student must do in order to be successful?

2. What challenges have your college studies already brought to you? How have you met these challenges? What challenges do you expect to encounter in the future?

CNN® Video Activity: "The Success of Xavier College Pre-Med Students"

 Xavier College has gained a reputation for preparing African-American students for medical school. In this video, you will hear some of the reasons why Xavier students experience such success. As you listen, make a list of (1) the causes for Xavier students' success and (2) the effects a Xavier education can have on a student's future.

Causes of Xavier students' success	Effects of a Xavier education on a student's future
_____	_____
_____	_____
_____	_____
_____	_____

Video Follow-up: Using Campus Resources
Find out what resources your campus offers to help students to be successful. You may want to visit places such as the library and student centers, as well as academic advisors. Collect any information they have about their services to share with your classmates, or invite someone who works at one of these offices to talk to your class about academic success.

Internet Activity: Composition Skills and the Internet

 Locate the address for your school's Web page, and spend some time "surfing" the page. Try to determine what resources for student success at your school have a presence on the Internet. Report the results of your search to your classmates.

Readings: Academic Achievement

While there are many reasons why students decide to go to college, most students want to complete their classes and chosen degree successfully; however, many things about a student's background and habits can contribute to this success or help to prevent it. The following essays investigate what causes students to be successful. As you read, ask yourself these questions:

1. What kind of behavior do you think causes a student to be successful?
2. What can cause an otherwise good student to do poorly in college or university?
3. What values in a society or family can help students to be successful?

Reading ❶

"Surfing's Up and Grades Are Down"
by Rene Sanchez

This report from the *Washington Post National Weekly Edition* examines the effects that computers have on college students' education and lives. In general, Sanchez reports positive effects, but she finds growing concern about Internet addiction, which can cause students to get low grades and even drop out of college. As you read this article, try to answer the following questions:

1. What are some of the negative effects that computers can have on students' academic success? What are some of the positive effects of computers?
2. What do some school counselors suggest might be the causes of Internet addiction in college students?
3. Do you think Internet addiction is really a problem for students? Should schools be responsible for helping to prevent this problem, or are there other more important problems on college campuses?

1   A new campus support group called "Caught in the Web" is being formed at the University of Maryland to counsel students spending too much time on computers.

2   At the Massachusetts Institute of Technology, students unable to break their addiction to playing computer games on campus terminals have new help. At their request, the university will deny them access whenever they try to sign on.

3   Faculty studying the freshman dropout rate at Alfred University in New

York have just found that nearly half the students who quit last semester had been logging° marathon, late-night time on the Internet.

spending

4   Nationwide, as colleges charge into the digital age with high-tech libraries, wired dormitories, and computerized coursework, faculty and campus counselors are discovering a troubling side effect: A growing number of students are letting computers overwhelm their lives.

5   It is hardly a crisis on any campus—yet. Some college officials say it is merely a fad,° and not nearly as harmful as other bad habits students often fall prey to° on campuses—such as binge drinking of alcohol. But concern over the issue is spreading.

short-lived fashion

become a victim of

6   Some universities now are imposing° limits on the time students spend each day, or each week, on campus computers. Other colleges are debating whether to monitor the time students spend on computer games and chat rooms, then program a warning to appear on their screens when it gets excessive.

setting

7   Some college counselors are creating workshops on the subject and planning to include them in freshman orientation programs. Others already are urging students not to plunge° into on-line relationships with strangers.

go quickly

8   "More and more students are losing themselves in this," says Judith Klavans, the director of Columbia University's Center for Research on Information Access. "It's very accessible on campuses, and students have time on their hands. We're seeing some of them really drift off into this world at the expense of practically everything else."

9   Campus officials say that communicating on the Internet or roaming the huge universe of information on the World Wide Web holds an especially powerful lure° for many college students because it takes them into a vast new realm° of learning and research, usually at no cost. But for students having trouble establishing social ties° at huge universities, or who are on their own, unsupervised, and facing adult pressures for the first time, it also poses an array of new risks.

attraction

world

connections

10   At the University of California's Berkeley campus, counselors say they are dealing with a small but increasing number of student cases linked to excessive computer use. Some students, they say, are putting too much emphasis on electronic relationships, are neglecting course work, and, in a few instances, are even being swindled° out of money by e-mail strangers they have come to trust.

cheated

11   "There can be a real sense of isolation on a large campus, and for young students or new students, this seems like a safe, easy way to form relationships," says Jeff Prince, the associate director of counseling at UC-Berkeley. "But some go overboard. It becomes their only way to connect to the world. One of the things we're really working on now is helping students balance how many social needs they try to have fulfilled by computers."

12   Linda Tipton, a counselor at the University of Maryland, which limits students to 40 hours a week on campus terminals, says she began noticing some of the same problems arise last year in individual and group therapy sessions.

13   Some of them, she said, spoke of spending more than six hours a day on-line and considered a computerized forum the only setting in which they could express themselves or relate well to others. A few students told her of dropping or flunking° courses partly because they were so preoccupied with the Internet. Others confessed to trying to get multiple computer accounts with the university to circumvent° its 40-hour-a-week rule.

failing

avoid

14   "Obviously this a wonderful tool, and for many students it's perfectly fine," says Tipton, who is trying to form a campus support group and develop a workshop on Internet addiction. "But for others it's becoming a tremendous escape from the pressures of college life. Students can become whomever they want, for as long as they want, and many other things in their lives, like classes, start to suffer."

15   Nathaniel Cordova, a graduate student at Maryland, says his problems are not that severe—but he is nevertheless heeding° Tipton's advice and trying to cut back on the time he spends on computers. And he says he routinely talks to other students on campus also trying to break habits like his.

obeying

16   "I don't think I'm an addict," Cordova says, "But I admit, sometimes I'll be in my office at eight o'clock at night, and then the next thing I know it's three A.M., and I realize I forgot to eat. It's so easy to get drawn in, and not just in research, but talking to people. You tell yourself, 'Okay, just one more link-up.' But you keep going."

17   Other college officials, however, says the concern seems exaggerated.

18   Some say they see few signs of trouble, and others say student interest in computer games or the Web is often intense at first, then fades. One of the venerable° rites° of college, they contend,° is for students to find distractions from their academic burdens. They say this one is much safer than many others causing campus problems.

honored
rituals
say

19   "There will always be something like this on college campuses," says Richard Wiggins, who manages information systems and teachers computer courses at Michigan State University. "In my day, in the 1970s, it was pinball. We played that all the time to get rid of stress. Usually things like this are not that harmful."

20   "For some people, it's just a great new way to waste time," says Jeff Bouher, a senior at George Washington University who spends several hours a day on the Internet. "And college students have always been quite dedicated to wasting time."

21   At M.I.T, Patrick McCormick, an undergraduate who helps administer computer game systems for the university, says he sees both sides of the trend. A few students in his residence hall dropped classes or saw their grades sink,

fell gradually

after they lapsed° into intensive computer use. "But others stay up all night with this stuff and still get 4.0s," he says. "It's very easy to get sucked in, but it isn't always bad."

22   Still, McCormick notes one problem he spots consistently: Classmates who trust virtually everyone they meet, or everything they read, on-line. "Some

hurt

people think if it's on a computer screen, it must be true, and they get burned,"° he says. "You hear them talking about flying their dream lover up, and of course they never show."

23   This spring, Alfred University in upstate New York decided to examine what the students who dropped out last semester had in common. What

caused

prompted° the inquiry was that twice as many students as usual—75, mostly freshmen—did not return for classes there this spring.

24   Every student at Alfred received a campus computer account, which is free. So Connie Beckman, the director of Alfred's computer center, decided to check the account records of all the students who had dropped out. She found that half of them had been logging as much as six hours a day on computer games or the Web, usually late at night. "It was the only thing that

was related

correlated° among so many of them," Beckman says.

25   University officials say they doubt that is the only, or even the primary, reason many of these students quit. But the discovery has led to several new policies.

26   Next fall, for the first time, freshman at Alfred will be told about the dangers of heavy computer use as soon as they arrive on campus. Residence halls, all of which have computer rooms, will each have a full-time, professional counselor to keep a close eye on late-night computer addicts. Other campuses are studying similar moves.

danger

27   "We've dealt with alcohol and drugs; we've dealt with TV and video games. Now this looks like the latest pitfall° for college students," Beckman says. "They're doing this all night instead of doing their homework, or eating, or sleeping. When they're up until five A.M. playing around on the Web, they're not going to make their eight A.M. classes."

Internet Activity: Composition Skills and the Internet

 Do you spend a lot of time using the Internet? How do you know if you are an avid fan or an addicted fanatic? Do a key word search for "Internet addiction" or point your browser to this Web site www.stresscure.com/hrn/addiction.html, and take this quiz to learn if you have a problem with Internet addiction.

EXERCISE 11·1 Comprehension/Discussion Questions

1. In paragraphs 1–3, the article is introduced. How does the author introduce the article? Is it effective? Why?
2. What has been an unexpected effect of the increased use and availability of technology on college campuses?
3. How have colleges responded to students' overuse of the Internet and computer games?
4. What are some of the social reasons why students on college campuses might become overly involved in relationships on the Internet?
5. Not all college officials believe that Internet addiction is a real problem. Why do these officials think students spend so much time using computers and the Internet?
6. What are some of the effects that spending too much time using the Internet or playing computer games can have on a student's life or academic success?
7. Find quotes made by each of the following people. Based on their statements, rank each person's concern about overuse of computers and the Internet on a scale of 1 to 5, with 1 meaning "not serious" and 5 meaning "very serious": (A) Judith Klavans, Columbia University, (B) Jeff Prince, UC-Berkeley, (C) Linda Tipton, University of Maryland, (D) Richard Wiggins, Michigan State University, (E) Connie Beckman, Alfred University.
8. Is the thesis of this article stated or implied? What is the thesis?
9. What is the author's purpose in this article? To inform? Analyze? Entertain? How do you know?
10. What reaction does the author expect from readers? How do you know?
11. In the article, Jeff Boulier is quoted as saying, "For some people it's just a great new way to waste time . . . and college students have always been quite dedicated to wasting time." What does he mean by this statement? What attitude does he display toward the question of whether the Internet can be addictive?
12. Do you ever "waste time" when you should be doing something productive for school or other obligations? What activities do you find yourself doing when you are putting off work or studying? How do you prevent these activities from becoming destructive to your success?

EXERCISE 11·2 Vocabulary Development   Verbs and Nouns + Prepositions. In the English language, it is very common for certain verbs and prepositions to occur together. Sometimes these verb + preposition combinations form a new verb which has its own meaning. These new verbs are called *phrasal verbs*. Phrasal verbs are more frequent in less formal writing. The following phrasal verbs appear in "Surfing's Up and Grades Are Down." Match each phrasal verb on the left with its definition on the right. You will use one definition twice. Then try to use each phrasal verb in a sentence of your own.

_____ sign on

_____ drift off

_____ cut back

_____ get drawn in

_____ get sucked in

_____ fly someone up

_____ dropped out

1. quit
2. wander
3. register, join
4. purchase an airline ticket for someone
5. get involved
6. reduce

Other preposition combinations do not form phrasal verbs. However, often a noun or verb will occur with the same preposition; these combinations are called *collocations*. Learning collocations can help you to understand more quickly when you read, and it can help you to write more accurately. Read these sentences from the article "Surfing's Up and Grades are Down," and try to fill in the correct preposition. Check your answers by looking at the article. Then, paraphrase the italicized phrases in your own words.

1. (par. 7) Others already are *urging students not to plunge _____ on-line relationships* with strangers.

   _____

2. (par. 8) "It's very accessible on campuses, and students *have time _____ their hands*."

   _____

3. (par. 8) We're seeing some of them really *drift off _____ this world* . . .

   _____

4. (par. 8) ". . . _____ *the expense _____ practically everything else*."

   _____

5. (par. 10) At the University of California's Berkeley campus, counselors say *they are dealing _____ a small but increasing number* . . .

   _____

6. (par. 10) . . . of student cases *linked _____ excessive computer use*.

   _____

7. (par. 11) One of the things *we're really working* _____ *now* is helping students balance . . .

_____

8. (par. 11) . . . how many social needs they try to have *fulfilled* _____ *computers.*

_____

9. (par. 21) A few students in his residence hall dropped classes or saw their grades sink, *after they lapsed* _____ *intensive computer use.*

_____

10. (par. 26) Next fall, for the first time, freshmen at Alfred *will be told* _____ *the dangers* of heavy computer use as soon as they arrive on campus.

_____

Reading ②

"Why They Excel"
by Fox Butterfield

In this excerpt from an article written for *Parade* magazine, Fox Butterfield investigates the causes or reasons for the achievement of young Asians in the United States. She finds the causes rooted in the traditional values of their culture. Butterfield, who worked as a journalist in Asian countries for many years, is implicitly suggesting that Americans have something to learn, or remember, from these immigrants. As you read this article, try to answer the following questions:

1. What are the reasons Asian students succeed in school?
2. What values in your culture have helped you to succeed in school?
3. What particular people have helped in your success?

1   Kim-Chi Trinh was just 9 in Vietnam when her father used his savings to buy a passage for her on a fishing boat. It was a costly and risky sacrifice for the family, placing Kim-Chi on the small boat, among strangers, in hopes she would eventually reach the United States, where she would get a good education and enjoy a better life. Before the boat reached safety in Malaysia, the supply of food and water ran out.

2   Still alone, Kim-Chi made it to the United States, coping with a succession

of three foster families. But when she graduated from San Diego's Patrick Henry High School in 1988, she had a straight-A average and scholarship offers from Stanford and Cornell Universities.

3   "I have to do well—it's not even a question," said the diminutive 19-year-old, now a sophomore at Cornell. "I owe it to my parents in Vietnam."

4   Kim-Chi is part of a tidal wave of bright, highly motivated Asian-Americans who are suddenly surging into our best colleges. Although Asian-Americans make up only 2.4 percent of the nation's population, they constitute 17.1 percent of the undergraduates at Harvard, 18 percent at the Massachusetts Institute of Technology and 27.3 percent at the University of California at Berkeley.

5   Why are the Asian-Americans doing so well? Are they grinds,° as some stereotypes suggest? Do they have higher IQs?° Or are they actually teaching the rest of us a lesson about values we have long treasured but may have misplaced—such as hard work, the family, and education?

6   Not all Asians are doing equally well. Poorly educated Cambodian and Hmong refugee youngsters need special help. And Asian-Americans resent being labeled a "model minority," feeling that it is just another form of prejudice by white Americans, an ironic° reversal of the discriminatory laws that excluded most Asian immigration to America until 1965.

7   Fortunately, the young Asians' achievements have led to a series of

people who do nothing but study intelligence quotient; a test to measure intelligence

the opposite of what is expected

intriguing studies. Perhaps the most disturbing [results] have come in a series of studies by a University of Michigan psychologist, Harold W. Stevenson, who has compared more than 7,000 students in kindergarten, first grade, third grade, and fifth grade in Chicago and Minneapolis with counterparts in Beijing; Sendai, Japan; and Taipei, Taiwan. On a battery of math tests, the Americans did worst at all grade levels.

8   Stevenson found no differences in IQ. But if the differences in performance are showing up in kindergarten, it suggests something is happening in the family, even before the children get to school.

9   It is here that the various studies converge: Asian parents are able to instill° more motivation in their children. "My bottom line° is, Asian kids work hard," said Professor Dornbusch, [Professor of Sociology at Stanford].

develop conclusion

fill, inspire

10   The real question, then, is how do Asian parents imbue° their offspring with this kind of motivation? Stevenson's study suggests a critical answer. When the Asian parents were asked why they think their children do well, they most often said "hard work." By contrast, American parents said "talent."

11   "From what I can see," said Stevenson, "we've lost our belief in the Horatio Alger myth that anyone can get ahead in life through pluck° and hard work. Instead, Americans now believe that some kids have it and some don't, so we begin dividing up classes into fast learners and slow learners, where the Chinese and Japanese believe all children can learn from the same curriculum."

courage and a strong spirit

12   The Asians' belief in hard work also springs from their common heritage of Confucianism, the philosophy of the 5th-century B.C. Chinese sage who taught that man can be perfected through practice. "Confucius is not just some character of the past—he is an everyday reality to these people," said William Liu, a sociologist who directs the Pacific Asian-American Mental Health Research Center at the University of Illinois in Chicago.

13   Confucianism provides another important ingredient in the Asians' success. "In the Confucian ethic," Liu continued, "there is a centripetal° family, an orientation that makes people work for the honor of the family, not just for themselves." Liu came to the United States from China in 1948. "You can never repay your parents, and there is a strong sense of guilt," he said. "It is a strong force, like the Protestant ethic° in the West."

developing inward toward the center

value of hard work

14   Liu has found this in his own family. When his son and two daughters were young, he told them to become doctors or lawyers—jobs with the best guaranteed income, he felt. Sure enough, his daughters have gone into law, and his son is a medical student at UCLA, though he really wanted to be an investment banker. Liu asked his son why he picked medicine. The reply: "Ever since I was a little kid, I always heard you tell your friends their kids were a success if they got into med school. So I felt guilty. I didn't have a choice."

15   Underlying this bond between Asian parents and their children is yet another factor I noticed during 15 years of living in China, Japan, Taiwan, and

Vietnam. It is simply that Asian parents establish a closer physical tie to their infants than do most parents in the United States. When I let my baby son and daughter crawl on the floor, for example, my Chinese friends were horrified and rushed to pick them up. We think this constant attention is overindulgence° and old-fashioned, but for Asians, who still live through the lives of their children, it is highly effective.

excessive, too much

16   Can we learn anything from the Asians? "I'm not naive° enough to think everything in Asia can be transplanted," said Harold Stevenson, the University of Michigan psychologist. But he offered three recommendations.

childish, simple-minded

17   "To start with," he said, "we need to set higher standards for our kids. We wouldn't expect them to become professional athletes without practicing hard."

18   Second, American parents need to become more committed to their children's education, he declared. "Being understanding when a child doesn't do well isn't enough." Stevenson found that Asian parents spend many more hours really helping their children with homework or writing to their teachers.

19   And, third, schools could be reorganized to become more effective—without added costs, said Stevenson. Nearly 90 percent of Chinese youngsters said they actually enjoy school, and 60 percent can't wait for school vacations to end. These are vastly higher figures for such attitudes than are found in the United States. One reason may be that students in China and Japan typically have a recess after each class, helping them to relax and to increase their attention spans.

20   "I don't think Asians are any smarter," said Don Lee, a Korean-American at Berkeley. "There are brilliant Americans in my chemistry class. But the Asian students work harder. I see a lot of wasted potential among the Americans."

EXERCISE 11·3 Comprehension/Discussion Questions

1. (paragraphs 1–3) How does the writer introduce the article? Is the introduction effective?
2. In paragraph 4, what is the general reputations of the three universities listed? How do you know from the paragraph?
3. What is the thesis of the article? Where is it first stated?
4. What is the point of paragraph 6? How does it relate to the thesis?
5. What do the scientific studies comparing American and Asian children show? According to researcher Stevenson, why is this so?
6. What is the first cause the writer gives for the Asian students' success?
7. What aspect of Asian culture gives rise to this first cause?
8. What is the second cause the writer gives for the success of Asian students? How is it related to Asian culture?

9. In paragraph 15, Butterfield suggests that methods of child rearing are a factor in explaining the relationship betwen parents and children. Explain the connection.

10. What difference does she note between American and Asian approaches to physical ties between parents and children?

11. What suggestions does Harold Stevenson give to improve American education?

12. Given the last paragraph, what do you think is Butterfield's purpose in writing this article?

13. Summarize Butterfield's overall point. Do you agree with it? Support your answer.

14. What connection do you think exists between hard work and success? Between a strong family and success? Support your answer.

15. Do you think methods of child rearing affect children's success in school? Support your answer.

16. What are some values of your culture that contribute to students' success?

17. In paragraph 6, Asian-Americans are called a "model minority." Explain this term. According to the paragraph, how do some Asian-Americans feel about this term? Is this a stereotype?

18. In paragraph 14, William Liu's son says he didn't have a choice about his major. Do you think that parents push children too hard? Should children be urged to choose their own majors or not? Support your answer.

EXERCISE 11·4 Vocabulary Development   Below are listed some terms that relate to myths or philosophies that underly cultures. Using the library, friends, or other sources, find out what each of these terms means, and write a paragraph in explanation.

1. the Horatio Alger myth (par. 11)
2. Confucianism (par. 12)
3. the Protestant ethic (par. 13)
4. an important myth or philosophy in your culture

Writing

When we classify and divide, we are attempting to impose order on—or perhaps find order in—the world around us, thereby hoping to understand the world we live in. When we analyze a process, we are also seeking to understand something, in this case how a sequence of events leads to an expected outcome. Similarly, when we analyze causes, we are attempting to understand the relationship of events that brought about an outcome, but in this case one that was probably unexpected and not likely to be repeated in exactly the same way. When we analyze effects, we consider the results of some action. Unlike process analysis, the relationship among events in cause-and-effect analysis is not chronological; it is causal: Something causes something else, or many things cause something; something results from something else, or many things result from one thing.

Every day we try to figure out the causes for something. When a problem arises, we start to examine the cause for it. For example, if police cars burst into flames in a large metropolitan police department, officials would immediately investigate to establish the reasons for the incidents. When any significant change in our lives occurs, such as the success of someone or something, we try to look at the factors that contributed to that change. When we identify an emotional problem, psychologists and other concerned people attempt to understand the causes. Understanding causes is not an idle pastime. We need to know why the police cars burst into flames in order to prevent the recurrence. We would like to know what it takes to be successful, so that we can try to be successful. We try to learn the causes of mental disorders so that we can cure the problem the person has. Understanding causes, therefore, is an important analytical process.

Likewise, we try to analyze—or, if the situation warrants it, predict—results, or effects. When a legislative body considers a tax-cut proposal, for example, it must examine the probable results the tax cut will have in the area. Too, as more tropical rain forests are destroyed, observers, scientists, and politicians are becoming increasingly concerned about the magnitude of the problems that the clearing is causing and will cause for the ecology of the world.

In short, then, cause-and-effect analysis is an important analytical skill to develop. Writing the essay that analyzes causes and effects will require examining the topic carefully in order to be complete and logical. In this chapter, then, our focus is the approaches to writing the cause-and-effect essay.

Since student essays are ordinarily between 300 and 500 words in length, generally speaking these essays can only deal effectively and thoroughly with an analysis emphasizing one or the other—causes or effects. And since most topics have more than one cause or effect, our focus here is on cause-and-effect essays that analyze more than one cause or effect. We discuss three types of cause-and-effect papers.

Multiple Causes → Effect

When we analyze the causes of something, we usually find that there are numerous contributing factors, or multiple causes; just how many factors depends on the complexity of the problem. Each cause may or may not be sufficient to produce the effect. Usually, however, we find that it is a combination of the causes that produces the result. Take, for example, the problem of obesity. Obesity is a complex problem, for it does not mean simply overweight. A person is considered obese if he or she weighs 20 percent above the generally accepted desirable weight for his or her height and age, in addition to having a certain amount of excess body fat. A person can be overweight because he or she has large bones, for example, but he or she is not considered obese. What causes obesity? Usually there is not a single cause; rather, a combination of factors leads to obesity:

Hereditary influences
Lack of exercise
Slow metabolic rate   Obesity
Overeating

In this example, we might find that for some people, only overeating and a lack of exercise lead to obesity; for others, a slow metabolic rate might suffice; for still others, hereditary influences might be the culprit. Of course, in the discussion of overeating, one might find that behind it lies a deeper cause: emotional problems. A person might overeat to satisfy emotional deprivation. Or perhaps some people overeat because they have a deficiency in a certain enzyme that researchers believe is a factor in signaling the body to stop eating when it has had enough. And true, a further examination of the topic might yield even more causes, such as social or environmental factors.

In writing your analysis of this topic, then, you could plan to spend about one paragraph on each of the causes; each paragraph, too, would have to provide an explanation of the cause to show how it contributes to the effect. To illustrate, look at how a paragraph explaining the factor of lack of exercise might be developed:

A lack of exercise is one of the major factors contributing to obesity. When we eat, we consume energy (measured as calories). When we exercise, we expend energy or burn up calories. For example, when we run for an hour, we burn up approximately 450 calories, depending on our body size. When the number of calories we consume exceeds the number we burn up, the excess energy is stored in the body in the form of fat. If a person is inactive, it is more likely that he will not burn up all the calories consumed, so obesity can result. Moreover, studies have shown that inactivity can cause an obese person to expend less energy during a certain activity than a nonobese person. This is because inactivity lowers the basal energy rate (the basic minimum rate at which the body burns up energy). Therefore, if an obese person and a nonobese person try to run one mile, the obese person unused to activity will expend less energy because he has a lower basal energy rate.

EXERCISE 11·5   On a separate sheet of paper, answer the following questions about the preceding paragraph.

1. What is the topic sentence? The controlling idea?
2. What kind of support does the writer use to explain the factor?

EXERCISE 11·6   Study the paragraphs that follow. Each one attempts to explain a reason, but not all of the paragraphs are successful. Circle the number of each paragraph that does not adequately explain the reason given in the topic sentence. Explain your choices.

1. One reason I came to the United States was to learn English. English is the most important language in the world. It is the language spoken at the United Nations; it is also the official language of diplomacy. In addition, English is useful in many occupations. For example, air traffic controllers all over the world must be able to speak English. Since English is so important, I decided to come to the United States.

2. Another reason I came to the United States was to go to college. In my country, only a very small percentage of the applicants to the universities get accepted. Since I was unable to get accepted at a university at home, I had to go to a college outside of my country. I chose this university not only because I was able to get accepted, but also because it offers a program that I want to pursue: computer science.

3. One of the reasons for anxiety among American men is their changing role in society. In the past, it was simple. Men were strong, tough, and aloof. The models for these masculine qualities were movie stars like John Wayne, Humphrey Bogart, and Clint Eastwood. Today, however, most women want men to be more sensitive, more gentle, more understanding more like Robert Redford, Dustin Hoffman, and Alan Alda. So men who grew up following the old role model are suddenly told that they are not right, not good enough, and that they should be different. They are being asked to change the way they think about themselves and their concept of manhood, and they are being asked to change in their relationships with women. This shift in expectations calls into question men's sense of who they are and how they relate to others, giving rise to self-doubts and problems of identity. Of course, this uncertainty about their role in society can cause men serious anxiety.

4. The major reason for anxiety among American men is their changing role in society. According to all accounts, this anxiety is pervasive. It is particularly so among men in their 30s and 40s, but it can also affect men in their 50s. One psychologist tells of a 56-year-old man who originally supported his wife's desire to go back to work and get a job. But, when she was promoted to a managerial position and began to travel a lot, the husband began to have anxiety attacks. Many men respond to this anxiety by refusing to commit

themselves in marriage or by taking refuge in the new "macho man," the man who thinks women really do want the strong silent type and he will be that man.

EXERCISE 11·7 Writing Assignment   Select one of the paragraphs in Exercise 11-6 that does not explain the reason adequately. Rewrite the paragraph and explain the reason.

EXERCISE 11·8 Writing Assignment   Choose one of the following topics and brainstorm about causes. Then, circle three or four of the main causes.

1. What causes people to emigrate to the United States?
2. What caused you to come to the United States?
3. What causes people to be successful in school?
4. Select a bad habit that you have. Why do you have that bad habit?
5. Select an idiosyncrasy of a family member or friend. Why does she or he have that peculiarity?

EXERCISE 11·9 Writing Assignment   Select one of the causes that you wrote in Exercise 11-8 and write a topic sentence for a paragraph. Write the paragraph by explaining the cause. Give enough detail and support for your generalization. Use the paragraph on lack of exercise as a model (page 252).

Organizing the Causal Analysis Essay

When you are discussing multiple causes for an effect, you need to be aware of the types of causes you are analyzing. If the causes are unrelated to each other, but all are related to the effect, such as in the case of the obesity example, arrange the paragraphs (causes) according to your own preference. However, the most common organizing principles are *order of familiarity* (obvious to less obvious) and *order of interest* (less interesting to more interesting). These two principles are useful when the causes are of equal significance. When one cause is more significant, use the *order of importance* principle, and place the most important cause last. Remember to identify the most important cause as the most significant.

Causes are not always unrelated, however. Sometimes a cause could not have brought about an effect unless certain *conditions* existed. In this case, the causes are related to each other. For example, the incident that launched Europe into World War I was the assassination of the Austrian heir to the throne, Archduke Franz Ferdinand, on June 28, 1914, by a young Serb nationalist. However, it is generally felt that this incident alone would not have caused the war if certain other conditions had not existed in Europe at that time: economic rivalries, heightened nationalism, imperialism, and so forth. In this kind of causal analysis, the causes that directly precede the effect are called *immediate* causes (sometimes called *direct* causes), and those causes that are further removed in time from the effect are called *remote* causes (sometimes called *indirect* causes). In the case of World War I, the immediate cause was the assassination, but the remote causes were the conditions mentioned earlier, such as heightened nationalism.

Although remote causes are also often the most important ones (as in the case of the World War I example), they are not always the most important or the most reasonable ones. For instance, you might blame the overcrowded conditions in the public schools on overpopulation and overpopulation on the failure of the government to encourage birth control (remote), but a more reasonable explanation might be on the failure of the local officials to provide adequate educational facilities (immediate).

When you are analyzing causes that are not of equal importance or that are immediate and remote, it is generally a good idea to organize the paragraphs beginning with the immediate and proceeding to the remote, or from the less important to the most important.

EXERCISE 11·10   Following are two sets of causes that are given in no particular order. For each set, decide which of these causes are immediate and which are remote. Then organize them into an outline for an essay.

A. Causes for My Fear of the Water
   1. I can't swim.
   2. When I was a child, my mother wouldn't let me go near the water.
   3. I don't like the feeling of being immersed in water.
   4. My mother had an unreasonable fear of the water.
   5. My eyes are very bad. When I take off my glasses in the water, I can't see.
   6. I don't trust the water. I don't think it will hold me.
   7. I associate the water with being disciplined by my mother.
   8. When I was 10 years old, I saw someone drown.
B. Causes for Air Pollution in Los Angeles
   1. There are a lot of cars.
   2. There are a lot of factories and oil refineries.
   3. Weak legislation exists for antipollution devices in factories and refineries.
   4. People remove antipollution devices from their cars.
   5. The lifestyle requires that people live in suburbs a long distance from their work and commute to work.
   6. Air is trapped between the mountains, not allowing the winds to disperse it.
   7. Los Angeles is built in and around hills, so the suburbs are very spread out.

The Thesis Statement for the Causal Analysis Essay
In a causal analysis essay, the thesis statement does not have to be persuasive, since a topic is being analyzed and the central idea is found in that analysis. A

thesis statement for a causal analysis can simply state briefly the causes to be discussed, or it may express the most significant cause. Consider this example:

> Conflicts over money, interfering relatives, and career problems all contributed to the demise of their relationship.

The topic is *the demise of their relationship* and the central idea is *reasons for its demise.*

Now study the following causal analysis essay. As you read, try to determine whether the author is discussing causes of equal significance, causes of unequal significance, or immediate and remote causation.

Causes of Mental Retardation

A couple who is expecting a baby looks forward to the birth of their child with high hopes and expectations. Fortunately, most babies are born in good health, with their brains and bodies intact. Sometimes, of course, a baby is born with physical and/or mental defects. One such defect is mental retardation. There is no single cause of mental retardation, but researchers have uncovered several causes, some of which are preventable.

Brain damage due to genetic conditions is a well-known cause of mental retardation. Most people are familiar with Down's syndrome, which occurs more often in babies whose mothers are over 35 years old. Down's syndrome is caused by the formation of an additional chromosome. The normal number of chromosomes for people is 46; babies born with Down's syndrome have 47. Another chromosome-related cause of mental retardation is a malformation of the X-chromosome. Evidently, the X-chromosome breaks in two, thereby altering the normal development of the fetus. There are also several recessive-gene diseases that result in mental retardation. For example, an infant born with the recessive-gene disease called phenyleketonuria will end up with profound mental retardation because this disease affects the transmittal of information between the cells in the brain, particularly the neurons in the frontal lobes. Fortunately, blood tests can detect this problem at birth, and immediate measures can be taken to limit the damage. Another disorder caused by recessive genes is Tay-Sachs disease, which is found primarily among Jewish families of northeastern Europe ancestry. This disease also affects the nerve cells, though not in the same way as phenyleketonuria. But there are blood tests that can detect carriers, so it can be prevented.

Not all brain damage resulting in mental retardation occurs because of problems in the genetic makeup of the infant. Certain infectious diseases that the mother may contract during pregnancy can adversely affect the developing brain of the baby, particularly if the mother catches these diseases during the first three months of her pregnancy. The most commonly known diseases include rubella (German measles), herpes simplex, and syphilis. Because these diseases are infectious, to a certain extent they are preventable.

Another preventable cause of mental retardation in newborns relates to what the pregnant woman ingests. Certain drugs are known to hinder the development of the baby's brain. In the early 1960s, for instance, some pregnant women suffering from pregnancy-related nausea were prescribed a drug called thalidomide. This drug interfered with the development of the embryo and resulted in physical deformations and mental deficits. These women had no way of knowing at the time what this drug could cause, but now we know that many drugs can adversely affect the development—both physical and mental—of the fetus. The most easily preventable cause of mental retardation is fetal alcohol syndrome. Drinking as little as one or two glasses of wine a week during pregnancy could result in physical and intellectual impairments in the infant. The mother's diet is also important during her pregnancy. Researchers find mental retardation more common among babies whose mothers were malnourished during pregnancy.

Once the child is born, other factors can cause mental retardation, such as head injuries and environmental pollutants, such as mercury and lead. But even before the child is born, the damage may already have been done. Fortunately, much of this damage can be prevented by the pregnant woman. Genetic counseling, caution to avoid infectious diseases, avoidance of drugs, including alcohol, and proper diet can increase the chances that a woman will bear a child whose intellectual functioning will be in the normal range.

—Information from Gerald C. Davison and John M. Neale. *Abnormal Psychology: An Experimental Clinical Approach,* 4th ed. (New York: Wiley, 1986). pp. 407–415

EXERCISE 11•11   On a separate sheet of paper, answer the following questions about "Causes of Mental Retardation."

1. What is the thesis statement?
2. What is the controlling idea of paragraph 2; in other words, what is the reason discussed in that paragraph?
3. What are the controlling ideas in the next paragraphs?
4. Is the writer discussing immediate and remote causes, or are the causes of equal significance?

5. Does the conclusion follow logically?
6. How does the role of the pregnant woman contribute to the prevention of mental retardation?
7. Make an outline of this essay.

A Problem in Reasoning

When discussing causes and effects, be certain that your analysis is logical. One of the logical fallacies—errors in reasoning—to avoid is called *post hoc ergo propter hoc,* a Latin phrase meaning "after this, therefore because of this." This problem in logic occurs when the writer assumes that an incident that precedes another is the cause of that incident: "President X was elected in January. Three weeks later, our nation suffered a severe depression. Therefore, President X caused that depression." This is an example of post-hoc reasoning. In this example, the illogic is clear, but be careful not to confuse chronological order with cause and effect; in addition, be certain to explain clearly the cause-and-effect relationship.

EXERCISE 11·12   Study the following groups of sentences. If the relationship is solely chronological, put "Time" in the space provided; if the relationship is also causal, put "C/E" (for cause/effect) in the blank.

1. _____ Every time I ride my moped to school it rains. I am not going to ride it today, so it won't rain.

2. _____ Chemicals were dumped in the Love Canal area of New York. People who lived in Love Canal have a high rate of cancer.

3. _____ The sun came out. The dew on the grass dried.

4. _____ A meteor was seen in the sky over Los Angeles. An earthquake occurred the next morning.

5. _____ Last winter, an unusually small amount of snow fell in the mountains. This summer, the water supply in the plain below dried up.

6. _____ It rained last Tuesday. Now I have a cold.

7. _____ A strong hurricane formed in the Gulf of Mexico. Tidal waves hit the coast of Texas.

8. _____ There was a severe drop in car sales. Several workers were laid off.

9. _____ I touched a dead fish. The next day I developed pain in my fingers.

10. _____ Ten movies shown in movie theaters this year showed adultery. There is an increase in adultery in our society.

EXERCISE 11·13   Following are some topics for a causal analysis essay. After you choose a topic, brainstorm about causes. Are they multiple causes or factors? Can you distinguish immediate and remote causes? Using this information, decide on the organizational pattern. Be sure to support the causes with details and examples.

1. Develop the topic you wrote on in Exercise 11-7.
2. Choose another of the topics in Exercise 11-8.
3. Give the causes for your particular fear of something.
4. Give the causes for pollution in a particular area or city (either in this country or in your country).
5. Give the causes for a recent social condition or change (for example, a change in men's roles, women's roles, divorce rates, family size, number of smokers versus nonsmokers, amount of stress in children).

Cause → Multiple Effects

Just as an effect can have multiple causes, so can a cause have *multiple effects*. For example, several years ago, most people thought that processed sugar (such as granulated sugar) was a relatively harmless sweetener that produced a pleasant taste, provided a small burst of energy, and perhaps contributed to tooth decay. There was little concern about the seemingly minor effects of eating sugar. But in recent years, our consumption of sugar has increased tremendously; in addition, we have begun to uncover some unpleasant and serious effects of eating so much sugar. Although sugar may not be the sole cause of some of the following more remote effects, research has shown it can contribute to them:

When an analysis is primarily of effects, as in this case, expect to devote a paragraph to each effect. The paragraph would have to explain the relationship between the cause and the effect. Note how the effect of tooth decay is explained in the following paragraph.

> One of the major effects of eating too much sugar is a high incidence of tooth decay. When we eat something with sugar in it, particularly refined sugar, enzymes in the saliva in the mouth begin to work immediately to change that sugar into a type of carbohydrate. As one eats, particles of the sugary food get lodged between the teeth and

around the gums. As the food changes its chemical composition, the resultant carbohydrate provides food for bacteria that begin to eat away at the enamel on the outside of our teeth. This is actually the decaying of the tooth. Now, if this process happens each time we eat sugar, we can see that eating excessive amounts of sugar causes more and more tooth decay. It is true that some tooth decay can be avoided with immediate brushing after eating, dislodging all the particles of food trapped in the teeth. However, sweets are often eaten as snacks between meals and during the day, times when people generally do not brush after eating. Therefore, the dangerous process of tooth decay is allowed to continue . . . .

EXERCISE 11·14   On a separate sheet of paper, answer the following questions about the preceding paragraph.

1. What is the topic sentence?
2. Does the paragraph show how eating too much sugar can result in tooth decay?
3. Is the paragraph unified? Coherent?

EXERCISE 11·15   Select one of the following topics and brainstorm about three or four effects that might come from the cause.

1. What are some of the effects of drinking products that contain caffeine, such as cola and coffee?
2. What are some of the effects of smoking cigarettes?
3. Have you ever witnessed a disaster, such as an earthquake, a hurricane, or a severe storm? What were some of the effects of that disaster?
4. In what ways has coming to the United States affected you?

EXERCISE 11·16 Writing Assignment   Select one of the causes listed in Exercise 11-15. Using your brainstorming about effects, choose one effect, develop a topic sentence and write a paragraph explaining that effect. Use the preceding paragraph about tooth decay as a model.

Organizing the Effect Analysis Essay

The principles for organizing an effect paper are much the same as those for organizing a causal analysis. Like causes, effects can be unrelated (causally) to each other, even though they all stem from the same cause. For instance, when a killer hurricane hits, several effects result: death, property damage, energy failures, and so on. These effects are not necessarily related causally; they were all just caused by the same thing—the killer hurricane. Although effects can be of equal value or importance, usually some are more important than others. In this case, like causes, organize the paragraphs dealing with effects according to order of importance (though focus should be on the more important—or major—ones).

Effects, too, like causes, can be immediate or remote. In the example of excessive sugar consumption, an immediate effect of eating sugar is a boost in energy, but more remote are the blood sugar problems and tooth decay. In this case, the remote effects happen to be the most important. An immediate effect of the earthquake in Soviet Armenia, in 1988, was the death of thousands of people; a more remote effect will be, perhaps, buildings constructed under a safer and more stringent building code. In this case, although the immediate effect is the most important, the remote effect is still worth discussing.

If an analysis, then, is of effects that occur relatively in the same time relationship, with the cause—in other words, they are all basically immediate or remote—it is a good idea to order the effects according to importance. However, if the discussion is of immediate and remote effects, it is a good idea to begin with the immediate and continue to the remote. Reminder: Identify the quality of the effect (immediate, major, and so on) to the reader to clarify the type of effect being discussed.

EXERCISE 11•17   Following are two sets of effects that are given in no particular order. For each set, decide which of the effects are immediate and which are remote. Then organize them into an outline for an essay.

A. *The Effects of Watching Television*
   1. More people get eyestrain.
   2. There is more violent crime in our cities.
   3. People get fat.
   4. There are more divorces.
   5. Husbands and wives do not talk to each other anymore.
   6. People do not enjoy reading anymore.
   7. People are more afraid of each other.
   8. People are lonely.
B. *The Citizens of This City Have Passed Legislation to Lower Property Taxes.*
   (First divide effects into negative and positive.)
   1. Many city employees will lose their jobs.
   2. Police patrols in the suburbs and downtown area will be reduced.
   3. Citizens will have more money to spend on consumer items.
   4. There will not be money for street repair.
   5. The school budget will be reduced.
   6. New business will be attracted to the city.
   7. The park service will not be able to plant new trees along the highways.
   8. The garbage will be picked up only once a week instead of twice a week.
   9. More jobs will open up.
   10. The local high schools will no longer have football teams.

The Thesis Statement for the Effect Analysis Essay

Like a causal analysis essay, the thesis statement for an effect analysis essay does not have to be persuasive. The thesis statement can have a more simply stated central idea:

The tax increase will bring benefits to our city.

Here, of course, the topic is *tax increase*, and the central idea is that it will *bring benefits* to the city.

Now read the following essay, which analyzes effects. As you read, locate the thesis and determine whether the writer has clarified the type of effects being discussed.

Do It!

Some do it to music, some while watching television; others do it in the privacy of their own homes, others in gyms. For some, they do it in the morning, others at night. But no matter where or when, millions of people all over the world do it, and that is exercise. But, unfortunately, millions of people do not get enough exercise. The benefits of regular aerobic exercise are so great that it's a wonder everybody doesn't start on a program today.

Probably the most well-known effect of aerobic exercise can be achieved in a relatively short period of time, and that is improved cardiovascular and pulmonary functions. When a person exercises long and hard enough, the heart pumps faster and blood is circulated well throughout the body. Since the heart is a muscle, exercise serves to strengthen it. As the heart becomes stronger, a person's stamina improves, as well as her energy level. The same is true of the lungs. It doesn't take long to reap these benefits. A person can get such results within a few weeks just by walking briskly for 30 minutes three or four times a week.

Another physical benefit of regular aerobic exercise takes longer to achieve, but it is well worth the effect, particularly for women. Exercise can help prevent the crippling bone degeneration called osteoporosis. Osteoporosis is a gradual process of loss of bone mass that occurs naturally as people age, but it can be halted by regular aerobic exercise. Exercise actually helps increase bone mass and is said to be the best preventive measure to take to avoid osteoporosis.

Just as regular exercise can help people achieve cardiovascular and skeletal fitness, it can also help people improve their emotional fitness. One of the good things about exercise is that it reduces stress. It does this in different ways. By improving one's overall fitness, aerobic exercise makes a person more capable of handling stress because he is less tense. When exercising, blood circulation improves and people burn off the adrenalin that stress causes the body to produce. Another way that exercise helps people handle stress is that after sufficient aerobic exercise, the body produces beta-endorphins, which are natural stress-relieving chemicals. In addition to helping people cope with stress, exercise can also help to alleviate depression.

There are no doubt many other benefits of regular aerobic exercise. It doesn't require that much time or effort to become a healthier person within weeks. Instead of watching television so much, people would be better off cycling or walking.

EXERCISE 11·18   On a separate sheet of paper, answer the following questions about "Do It!"

1. What is the thesis?
2. Does the writer establish a need or purpose for writing this paper?
3. Which kind of effect does the writer begin with?
4. What is the controlling idea in the third paragraph?
5. Why did the writer discuss emotional fitness last?
6. Make an outline of this essay.

EXERCISE 11·19 Writing Assignment   Choose one of the following topics for an essay that analyzes effects. Begin by prewriting: use one of the techniques you learned in Chapter 1 to generate ideas. Then, develop your thesis sentence and support. Be sure to distinguish between major and minor causes or between immediate and remote causes, whichever is appropriate.

1. Choose one of the topics in Exercise 11-15.
2. Analyze the effects of a change in your life. For instance, how has living away from home for the first time affected you?
3. Every family has problems. Perhaps, for example, a family member is unemployed, homesick, depressed, ill, angry, an alcoholic, or physically or mentally disabled. Problems like these affect the other family members. Discuss the effects of a family member's problem on your family.
4. Discuss the effects of a political or social change in your country.
5. Discuss the effects of your parents' values on you.

The Causal Chain

Another type of cause-and-effect analysis is the *causal chain*. Unlike the multiple cause-and-effect analyses, the causes and effects in a causal chain are always directly related; in fact, they are linked. In the causal chain, one effect can become a cause of another effect, which, in turn, can become a cause of another effect, and so on. For example, suppose an overweight smoker is inactive because of shortness of breath. The doctor told her to quit smoking and she did. Soon she was able to breathe more easily; as a result, she felt better physically. She started an exercise program, and as a result of this increased activity, she lost weight. This domino-like chain might be diagramed as follows:

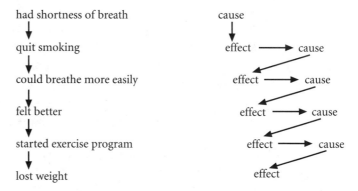

There are two major uses of the causal chain. First, it is sometimes useful for explaining one of the causes in a multiple-cause essay. For instance, in the example of obesity, the cause of overeating could be explained as follows:

The most obvious cause of obesity is overeating. But why do people overeat? One reason is emotional problems. For example, consider the case of Debbie. When Debbie was a child, her parents rewarded her for good behavior with candy and other sweet things. As she grew older, she began to reward herself quite regularly. As a result, she began to gain weight. By the time she was a teenager, Debbie had become rather heavy. Her weight then became a target for the other young people at school. They teased her unmercifully, as youngsters will do. She was teased so much that she started feeling sorry for herself and consoled herself by eating more and more. She gained more weight, and the vicious cycle continued until her self-image was so bad that she could not really perceive herself as anything but fat; therefore, diets were unsuccessful because she would inevitably get depressed during or after a diet and go on an eating binge to soothe her feelings.

EXERCISE 11·20   On a separate sheet of paper, make a causal chain diagram of the preceding paragraph.

The other major use of the causal chain is used in science to analyze various kinds of cycles, such as biological or chemical chains. Study the following essay, which analyzes a causal chain. Determine if the cause-effect relationship is clarified and explained.

Upsetting the Balance of Nature

The members of a living community exist together in a particular, balanced relationship, or ecosystem. One animal species eats another animal species, which in turn eats another. Over the years, a balance is worked out among the plants and animals in a community, and it remains basically stable. It is like a huge puzzle with all of the pieces in their proper places. However, at times this balance in nature is disturbed, resulting in a number of possibly unforeseen effects. Perhaps a disease results in the near extinction of one species, leaving another species with no natural predator. The result can be a terrific increase in that one species' population. This could further result in the devastation of a shared food supply, which could in turn affect another species. It is possible for the disruption in the balance of nature to have natural causes: disease, drought, fire. Sometimes, however, human beings intervene in a natural environment, perhaps only slightly and with good intentions. The result is the same. The balance of nature becomes unbalanced and results in an entire chain reaction of unforeseen and unwanted effects.

A good example of this occurred in the Antilles in the 1870s. Sugar cane was a major crop there, but rats were eating and nesting in the cane, causing a great deal of damage. The mongoose, a one-and-a-half-foot-long mammal of the East Indies, was known to be an excellent rat hunter. Several males and females were imported in 1872, and laws were established that forbade the killing of them or their offspring. The mongoose flourished in the Antilles. After ten years it had multiplied abundantly and had significantly reduced the rat population. Consequently, damage to the cane fields was greatly reduced. It seemed that the scheme to add another piece to the ecological puzzle in the Antilles had been successful.

However, that is not the end of the story. The influence of the mongoose did not stop there. As the rat population decreased and the mongoose population increased, the mongoose needed to enlarge its menu. It attacked young pigs and goats, game, poultry, and began to destroy bananas, maize, and pineapples. Because the mongoose could not be hunted, its numbers increased rapidly, and it became a terrible pest. All of the indigenous animals suffered damage. The mongoose learned to enjoy the native birds, snakes, lizards, and turtles and their eggs. Now, it was specifically these animals that kept the local insect population in check. There were in the ecosystem of the Antilles a number of beetles, borers, and other insects that lived on and in the sugar cane. Until that time, they had not caused significant damage to the cane because they were the natural food of so many local animals that kept their numbers down. However, as the birds, snakes, lizards, and turtles disappeared, the insect population began to increase. With no natural predators to keep them in check, the insects began to do more and more damage to the cane fields.

Finally, the people of the Antilles realized that the introduction of the mongoose had caused a finely and delicately balanced system to go awry. The law against killing the mongoose was rescinded, and the mongoose population was reduced. Gradually, the different members of the plant and animal community came back into balance with each other and equilibrium was reestablished. However, the human members of the community would not soon forget that a single change in an ecosystem can cause a chain reaction that results in completely unforeseen and sometimes unwanted effects.

—adapted from Karl von Frisch, *Biology: The Science of Life*
(New York: Harper & Row, 1964)

EXERCISE 11·21   On a separate sheet of paper, answer the following questions about "Upsetting the Balance of Nature."

1. What is the topic of the essay? What is the central idea?
2. What is the incident in the Antilles an example of?
3. Is this causal chain logical; that is, is the relationship among the causes and effects clearly and logically presented?
4. Does the conclusion logically follow?
5. Make an outline of this essay.

EXERCISE 11·22   Following are two sets of information, each giving the steps in a causal chain. What is the causal chain in each one? Devise a topic sentence for each set of information, and write a paragraph explaining the causal chain. (You may need to add steps.)

A. *Disaster in Southern California*
   1. Summers are hot and dry.
   2. In fall, high winds come from the desert.
   3. Forest fires begin and spread.
   4. In spring, heavy rains fall.
   5. In spring, mudslides and floods occur.
B. *Poverty*
   1. People lack capital.
   2. They buy items on credit.
   3. They pay high interest on credit accounts.
   4. This reduces their capital and puts them in debt.
   5. They buy more items on credit.
   6. This reduces their capital even more; it puts them further in debt.

EXERCISE 11·23 Writing Assignment   Choose one of the following topics for an essay that develops a causal chain. First, think through the chain carefully. Do not leave out any important steps. Develop a thesis sentence and outline. Then write an essay.

1. Choose a chain from one of the sciences: for example, a biological food chain.
2. Reread the preceding essay on the balance of nature. Write an essay describing an upset in the balance of nature that you are familiar with.
3. Choose a chain from geography. What has happened to the land in a particular area?
4. Choose a social problem like alcoholism, poverty, divorce, overpopulation, teenage pregnancy, or teenage drug use.

Composition Skills

Introductory Paragraphs

The Dramatic Entrance

In Chapter 10, we learned how a description of a scene can be used to open an essay. There are, of course, other approaches to use for a Dramatic Entrance. For instance, your essay can begin with a particularly interesting example that illustrates your thesis or is pertinent to your topic; or it can open with an effect if your paper is analyzing causes or with a cause if it is analyzing effects. Note how the writer, Anastasia Toufexis, uses interesting examples in the following opening to her essay on mother-and-son relationships.

Industrialist Andrew Carnegie's mother begged him not to marry until after she died; he waited one year after her death and finally wed at fifty-two. Dwight Eisenhower interrupted planning of the Allied invasion of France in May 1944 to send a Mother's Day greeting to Ida Eisenhower in Kansas. When Franklin Roosevelt was quarantined with scarlet fever at boarding school, his distraught mother Sara climbed a ladder each day to peer through the window of his room to check on his recovery. Actor James Dean explained his troubled life this way: "My mother died on me when was nine years old. What does she expect me to do? Do it all alone?"

The cord that unites mother and son may be Western society's most powerful bond, yet attitudes toward the relationship are either murky or coated over with cliche. "We think we're comfortable with it, but culturally what we get are caricatures," argues Carole Klein, a longtime observer of the dynamics of family relationships . . . .

—Anastasia Toufexis, "The Most Powerful Bond of All,"
Time 1 Oct. 1984: p. 86

When you are writing an essay that analyzes causes, you might consider opening with an effect, or vice versa. Look at how student writer Carolyn Udell opens her essay in which she analyzes the causes and effects of her fear of cockroaches: she describes a dream—one of the effects of her fear.

Roaches

Roaches crawling all over the walls, all over the floor, pouring into the bedroom door, where can I run? I jump on top of the bed. They follow me up. Oh, my God, they're starting to fly all around me . . . . "Oh, it was just a dream." Vile and repugnant are two of the best words used to describe the most despicable creature on earth, the roach. The Bible portrays the devil as a serpent in the Garden of Eden. However, I am sure that God meant the roach to play the part. My feelings for these creatures are of spasmodic disgust, but especially fear.

I am not sure when this fear started, somewhere back in my early childhood. As far back as I can remember, I have never had the desire to touch a roach. The first thing I think of when a person says the word *roach* is its abhorrent looks. Their prehistoric appearance makes me cringe. The dark brown color reminds me of something dirty and gives me a feeling of disgust, which is exactly what a roach is— disgusting, with its long, skinny, black feelers protruding from its head, always moving and twitching in an erratic way, no matter if it is squatting still or scurrying away beneath your feet. This is certainly an immediate cause of my fear.

Maybe the fear stems from the fact that they will eat anything, including the dead body of another animal, humans not excluded. This fact makes them seem disease-ridden. Every disease ever known to man or imagined by man can be caught from a roach, or so it seems.

Granted, some of the fear I have for these parasites might be learned from my mother. You would think you could call good ole Mom to the rescue when you spot a big two-inch roach on the wall and count on her to take care of it for you, but this is not so with my mother. Oh, she may come when you call her all right, but when she spots the two-incher on the wall, she hands me the can of Raid and runs for cover.

Another thing about roaches is that they are nocturnal insects. This may be an indirect cause of my fear of them, but maybe not. A psychiatrist might evaluate it this way. Roaches are nocturnal creatures. People are afraid of the night and associate it with evil things. Therefore, I, ultimately, am afraid of roaches. Now, I do not know how valid this is, because I am not afraid of roaches because of the night. It is more like I am afraid of the night because of roaches. I do not know why, but roaches seem to be scarier at night.

Anyway, it all comes down to this. This nightmare I recounted earlier is just an example of the many bad dreams I have had as a kid and still do have, occasionally. These dreams are a direct result of my fear of roaches. I imagine them crawling on my bed and all over me. These dreams leave me wide awake, scared to death, and unable to go back to sleep.

I can't walk into a dark room without some trepidation. I could not stand to touch one of these things. This would leave me a mental case. The only way I can kill a roach is with Raid. This kind of apprehension makes life very difficult for me when I am roughing it or camping out. I'll lie there in my sleeping bag in my tent and I will not budge, with my can of Raid by my side and a light on, of course. An actual encounter with a roach, and I lose my sense of logic. I become unable to function in a controlled manner. I remember one time when I was down in the French Quarter in New Orleans, and if roaches are manufactured somewhere, that's the factory. Anyway, I was walking through a doorway when this big black roach crossed my path. He started flying—right from the floor into midair—at me! I almost died. I did not know whether to run backward or make a dive for the floor. This would have gone on, running backward contemplating a dive for the floor, until I was all the way to Baton Rouge, had not the roach decided to divert its course.

In a controlled situation, such as that of a classroom, I am mentally as well as physically agonized. I saw a roach in a class once, about a chair ahead of me. I did not want to make a scene and start screaming, especially since the roach was not that big. My mind was telling me to get up calmly and casually stroll away. However, my body was wanting to jump up and run. It was a terrible strain on me. I did manage to walk a far enough distance back without making a scene.

There is one way and only one way to overcome this fear. And that is to walk up boldly to the biggest, blackest roach I can find and grasp it with both hands, and hold it firmly. It would only take a minute. Then, all the bad dreams would stop. I would have confidence when I entered a dark room. And my mental and physical state of being would bear no strain. . . ."Oh, no! A roach! Quick! Raid!"

—Carolyn Udell

EXERCISE 11·24   On a separate sheet of paper, answer the following questions about the essay "Roaches."

1. What is the writer's purpose in analyzing this topic?
2. What is the thesis statement? Is it stated directly or is it implied?
3. Is the essay primarily a causal analysis, an effect analysis, or both?
4. Why is "Oh, it was just a dream" in quotation marks (par. 1)?
5. Is the introduction inviting; that is, does it make you want to read the rest of the essay? Explain.
6. What is the topic of paragraph 2? The controlling idea?
7. Does the writer focus on immediate or remote causes?
8. What purpose or function does paragraph 6 serve?
9. What is the topic of paragraph 7?
10. What does the example of the incident in New Orleans illustrate?
11. Does the writer discuss immediate or remote effects primarily?
12. Does there seem to be any hope that the writer will overcome her fear of roaches?
13. Does the writer seem to be serious about this topic? What clues do we get that she has a sense of humor about her fear?
14. What does "granted" at the beginning of paragraph 4 refer to?
15. Make an outline of this essay.

The Relevant Quotation

Another frequently used approach to opening essays is what we call the Relevant Quotation. An essay with this type of introduction opens with a quotation by an authority on the topic or by someone who says something relevant to what is discussed in the essay. Sometimes writers begin with a famous quotation and then work it into their topic. Observe how this writer uses a quotation to introduce an article about the harvesting of saffron in Spain:

> "The saffron is an arrogant flower," begins an old Spanish zarzuela named for this lush, purple blossom. "It is born with the sunrise and dies at sunset." For a couple of weeks in October of every year, in Spain's La Mancha region, the arrogant crocus is harvested frenetically, as fast as it flowers.
>
> For saffron is the world's most precious spice, often rivaling, ounce for ounce, the cost of gold. A pound of its tiny threads—the stigmas, or female organs, of Crocus sativus, an autumn crocus—currently costs well over $2,000. There is such a demand for these little fibers the Spanish call "red gold" that virtually all that is grown will be sold.
>
> —Diane Raines Ward, "Flowers Are a Mine for a Spice More Precious Than Gold," *Smithsonian* Aug. 1988: p. 105

In the following introduction, the author uses a quotation by a famous Englishman to introduce an article about the United States Constitution:

> It took an Englishman, William Gladstone, to say what Americans have always thought: "The American Constitution is, so far as I can see, the most wonderful work ever struck off at a given time by the brain and purpose of man." From this side of the water, however, the marvel has not been so much the unique system of government that emerged from the secret conclave of 1787 as the array of ordered and guaranteed freedoms that the document presented. "Every word of [the Constitution]," said James Madison, the quintessential Founding Parent, "decides a question between power and liberty."
>
> —H. B. Zobel, "How History Made the Constitution," *American Heritage* Mar. 1988: p. 54

EXERCISE 11·25 Writing Assignment   Select one of the following topics and use a Dramatic Entrance or a Relevant Quotation for your introduction. Assume that your essay will discuss causes.

1. An unreasonable fear you have (such as a fear of roaches, flying, heights, or the like).
2. A particular like or dislike you have (such as a passion for a certain sport).
3. The causes of something tragic (such as a hotel fire, a bomb explosion, or an accident).

Coherence

Transitions and Expressions for Cause and Effect

Transitions are important for coherence. In writing cause-and-effect essays, transitions are necessary to introduce causes and effects. In addition to the transitions studied in earlier chapters, there are other transitions that are particularly useful in cause-and-effect essays. Pay close attention to the punctuation required for each type of transition.

Transition in Phrases   The transitions in this group must be followed by a noun. If the phrase containing the transition comes at the beginning of the sentence, it is usually followed by a comma. The following transitions indicate cause: *because of* and *as a result of.* Study these examples:

> *Because of* the possibility of fetal brain damage, pregnant women should not consume alcohol.
> *As a result of* exercising regularly, a person can handle stress better.

Expressions in Sentences   The transitions in this group are verbs that express cause or effect. The following transitional verbs indicate cause: *caused by* and *results from.* Study these examples:

> Premature aging of the skin *results from* too much exposure to the sun.
> Her fear of roaches was *caused by* an early childhood trauma.

The following transitional verbs indicate effect: *cause* and *result in.* Study these examples:

> Lack of exercise can *cause* obesity.
> Walking regularly can *result in* improved health.

Special Note: *the reason is that* . . .
The expression *the reason is that* is often used to introduce a cause. It must be followed by a complete sentence. Note this example:

> Why do people exercise? *The reason is that* they are trying to stay healthy.

Coordinating Conjunctions as Transitions   The coordinating conjunctions *so* and *for* are often used as transitions. *So* indicates a result. However, it is somewhat colloquial and is usually avoided in formal writing. *For* indicates a cause and is quite formal. Study these examples and note the punctuation for coordinating conjunctions:

> The mongoose was protected by law, *so* it increased in number rapidly.
> We stopped at a restaurant, *for* we had not eaten since early morning.

Transitional Expressions Between Sentences   The transitions in this group usually occur between two complete sentences. They must be preceded by either a period or a semicolon. They cannot be preceded by a comma, but a comma often follows them. The following transitions indicate an effect or result: *thus, therefore, consequently, as a result, for this reason.*

> Mathematics and science teachers do not encourage young girls to study science; *thus*, there are not many female scientists.
> She perceived herself as fat; *therefore*, diets were unsuccessful.
> It significantly reduced the rat population. *Consequently*, damage to the cane fields was reduced.
> Debbie ate constantly. *As a result*, she became rather heavy.
> The students were protesting against the food served in the cafeteria. *For this reason*, the president cancelled classes and closed the university.

Note: These transitions can also occur within an independent clause. When they do, they are set off by commas:

> He had exceeded the speed limit. He was, *therefore*, charged a fine.

Grammar Review

If you want further review of grammatical structures that will help you achieve coherence and grammatical accuracy in your writing, see the Grammar Review Unit. The following sections are designed to coordinate with the cause-and-effect analysis essay:

> Adverbial Clauses of Cause and Result, pages 336–339
> Unreal Conditions, pages 377–379
> Articles, pages 313–322

EXERCISE 11·26 Writing Assignment   Choose one of the following topics for a cause-and-effect essay. Begin by generating ideas. Then look at your notes to determine the best support. Be sure to think through the causes and effects carefully. Write a thesis sentence and an outline. Use transitions and specific detail in the essay.

1. Complete the essay you started in Exercise 11-25.
2. Choose another topic from Exercise 11-15, 11-19, 11-23, or 11-25.
3. Discuss the effects of watching television often.
4. Discuss the effects your parents have had on you.
5. Discuss the specific values you hold that have caused you to do something.

EXERCISE 11·27 Assignments from the Disciplines   Following are some topics for your final writing assignment which are typical of college writing assignments. For your final writing assignment, you may choose one that you have studied, or consult a textbook or the Internet to find the answer. Then, follow the directions for Exercise 11-25 to write your answer.

1. From Architecture   Choose one of the following influential architects, and write an essay describing the effects that this person's work has had on twentieth century architecture: (a) Louis Sullivan, (b) Antoni Gaudi, (c) Frank Lloyd Wright, (d) Le Corbusier.
2. From Geology   Write an essay describing the causes of one of the following geologic events: (a) earthquakes, (b) erosion, (c) volcanic eruptions.
3. From Economics   Explain the principle of supply and demand and the effects that changes in supply and demand can have on price.

Revision

Peer Review
When you have finished writing the first draft of your essay, give it to a classmate to read and review. Use the peer review checklist in Appendix I to respond to each other's drafts.

Revision Checklist for the Paragraph
Use these questions to help you to give suggestions to your peers and to revise your essay.

1. A cause-and-effect essay most often focuses on either the causes or the effects of some event or situation. Does your essay focus on either causes or effects?
2. If your essay focuses on causes, have you analyzed the causes sufficiently and in enough detail? If your essay focuses on effects, is your analysis insightful and sufficient? If your essay focuses on a causal chain, are the links in the chain clear?
3. Some common principles of organization for the cause-and-effect essay are order of familiarity, order of interest, and order of importance. Does your essay follow a logical pattern of organization?
4. The thesis statement for a cause-and-effect essay should contain the central idea of the essay. Does your essay have an effective and succinct thesis statement that expresses your central idea?
5. Does your essay have an interesting introduction?
6. Is your essay coherent?

Chapter **12** The Argumentative Essay

Theme

Issues on Campus

Goals

Writing

To develop an arguable thesis

To argue both sides of an issue

To support and explain arguments

To refute opposing arguments

To review cohesion techniques

To organize and write an argumentative essay

Reading

To learn about and discuss controversial issues on university campuses

To identify and evaluate the support a writer provides to defend an argument

Grammar

To review subjunctive noun clauses

Getting Started

Journal Writing: Choose one of the following two questions, and write about it in your journal.

1. What are the important issues now being discussed on your campus? Proposed changes in the entrance requirements? The building of a new student fitness center? An increase in lab fees? Choose an important issue or problem on your campus and explain it. You may want to check the campus newspaper for ideas.

2. What is an important social issue or problem that concerns you and other students you know? Write about this issue or problem and explain its importance. What are people doing about this issue or problem? Is this enough or is more action needed?

CNN® Video Activity: "Campus Activism"

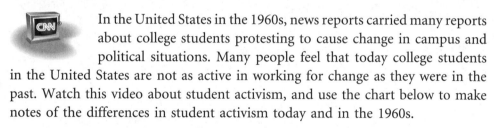 In the United States in the 1960s, news reports carried many reports about college students protesting to cause change in campus and political situations. Many people feel that today college students in the United States are not as active in working for change as they were in the past. Watch this video about student activism, and use the chart below to make notes of the differences in student activism today and in the 1960s.

The sixties	
Today	

Video Follow-up: Investigating Your Campus

To find out more about activism on your campus, choose one or more of the following activities:

- Check your student center, campus bulletin boards, and the campus newspaper for evidence of activism. How much do you find? What issues are important on your campus?
- Attend a meeting of an activist group on campus, and observe how many students attend and what methods of activism they use.
- Read newspapers and watch TV reports about student activism in other countries. What kind of activism do students around the world engage in? How are the issues the same or different?

Reading: Issues on Campus

There are many issues of interest to students and faculty on college campuses. Some people are worried about social, environmental and political problems around the world, and others are concerned about the lifestyles and issues that affect college students daily. The following readings deal with academic issues that are often discussed on college campuses. Before you read, answer these questions:

1. What is your ideal way to learn? Do you prefer classes in which the instructor lectures? Group discussions? Independent student projects? Why?
2. What do the grades A, B, C, D, and F mean to you? Should it be possible for all students in a class to get an A, or should there always be a range of grades given in every class?

Reading ①

"College Lectures: Is Anybody Listening?"
by David Daniels

In this magazine article, David Daniels questions a traditional teaching method: the lecture class. Before you read, answer these questions:

1. Have you had any lecture classes in college? If so, what happened in them?
2. Was lecturing an effective way for you to learn?
3. Do you think your experience in lecture classes is typical?
4. Why might someone object to lecturing as a teaching method? Why might someone defend it?

1   Today, American colleges and universities . . . are under strong attack from many quarters. Teachers, it is charged, are not doing a good job of teaching, and students are not doing a good job of learning. American businesses and industries suffer from unenterprising, uncreative executives educated not to think for themselves but to mouth outdated truisms the rest of the world has long discarded. College graduates lack both basic skills and general culture. Studies are conducted and reports are issued on the status of higher education, but any changes that result either are largely cosmetic or make a bad situation worse.

2   One aspect of American education too seldom challenged is the lecture system. Professors continue to lecture and students to take notes much as they did in the thirteenth century, when books were so scarce and expensive that few students could own them. The time is long overdue for us to abandon the lecture system and turn to methods that really work. . . .

3   One problem with lectures is that listening intelligently is hard work. Reading the same material in a textbook is a more efficient way to learn because students can proceed as slowly as they need to until the subject matter becomes clear to them. Even simply paying attention is very difficult: people can listen at a rate of 400 to 600 words a minute, while the most impassioned professor talks at scarcely a third of that speed. This time lag between speech and comprehension leads to daydreaming. Many students believe years of watching television have sabotaged their attention span, but their real problem is that listening attentively is much harder than they think.

4   Worse still, attending lectures is passive learning, at least for inexperienced listeners. Active learning, in which students write essays or perform experiments and then have their work evaluated by an instructor, is far more beneficial for those who have not yet fully learned how to learn. While it's true that techniques of active listening, such as trying to anticipate the speaker's next point or taking notes selectively, can enhance the value of a lecture, few students possess such skills at the beginning of their college careers. More commonly, students try to write everything down and even bring tape recorders to class in a clumsy effort to capture every word.

5   Students need to question their professors and to have their ideas taken seriously. Only then will they develop the analytical skills required to think intelligently and creatively. Most students learn best by engaging in frequent and even heated debate, not by scribbling down a professor's often unsatisfactory summary of complicated issues. They need small discussion classes that demand the common labors of teacher and students rather than classes in which one person, however learned, propounds his or her own ideas. . . .

6   Smaller classes in which students are required to involve themselves in discussion put an end to students' passivity. Students become actively involved when forced to question their own ideas as well as their instructor's. Their listening skills improve dramatically in the excitement of intellectual give and take with their instructors and fellow students. Such interchanges help professors do their job better because they allow them to discover who knows what—before final exams, not after. When exams are given in this type of course, they can require analysis and synthesis from the students, not empty memorization. Classes like this require energy, imagination, and commitment from professors, all of which can be exhausting. But they compel students to share responsibility for their own intellectual growth.

7   Lectures will never entirely disappear from the university scene both because they seem to be economically necessary and because they spring from a long tradition in a setting that rightly values tradition for its own sake. But the lectures too frequently come at the wrong end of the students' educational careers—during the first two years, when they most need close, even individual, instruction. If lecture classes were restricted to junior and senior undergraduates and to graduate students, who are less in need of scholarly nurturing

and more able to prepare work on their own, they would be far less destructive of students' interests and enthusiasms than the present system. After all, students must learn to listen before they can listen to learn.

EXERCISE 12·1 Comprehension/Discussion Questions

1. What is Daniels' thesis? Where is it located?
2. What reasons does he give to support his thesis?
3. How does he support and explain his reasons?
4. What teaching method does Daniels propose to replace lectures? According to Daniels, what are its advantages? What might be some disadvantages?
5. Do you agree with Daniels' thesis? Why or why not?
6. Imagine that you wanted to support lecturing as a teaching method. What reasons would you give?
7. This essay raises the question of how people learn best. How do you think people learn best? What factors might learning depend on?

Reading **2**

"Let's Put the Excellence Back in the A"
by Elliott Miles

Elliott Miles, a retired educator and university president, discusses a disturbing trend on college campuses: grade inflation. Before you read, answer these questions:

1. In the American education system, what does a grade of A mean? A grade of B, C, D? What about a grade of F?
2. In your university courses, what grades do most students receive?
3. Do you think the grades are distributed fairly?

---

1   Most American universities today still use the traditional grading system of A-B-C-D-F, with A meaning "excellent," B "good," C "satisfactory" or "average," D "unsatisfactory but passing," and F of course "failing." While some feel that this system has shortcomings (too imprecise, too artificial, too arbitrary), it does represent the possible range of a student's work, and most students and faculty members are comfortable—or at least familiar—with it. So far so good. However, American universities since the mid-1960's have increasingly been afflicted by the problem of grade inflation. This refers to the tendency of many faculty members to over-evaluate the quality of a student's work and consequently to assign her/him a grade higher than the work deserves. The reason this practice is called inflation, a term borrowed from economics, is that it resembles paying too high a price for a given item, for example twenty

dollars for a loaf of bread. The problem is common among American universities, including even our most prestigious institutions, such as Harvard. As Craig Lambert reports in his article "Desperately Seeking Summa," the grade of A there accounted for about twenty-two percent of all grades in 1966-67, whereas by 1991-92 it had come to account for forty-three percent—almost double.

2   The trend toward inflated grades began in the mid-1960's probably because that was a time of great unrest on college campuses in the United States. There were widespread student protests against the Vietnam War and civil authority in general, frequently with the enthusiastic support and even participation of the faculty. Under these circumstances, grading standards began to shift for the worse. Faculty members became more and more reluctant to give students a D, let alone an F; the grade of C came to denote a minimal pass, B to represent "satisfactory," and A to mean "better than a B." Today, students and faculty alike have this new, watered-down system in their heads, although their university's official grading policy may be unchanged from previous times.

3   Why is this a problem? After all, a student is unlikely to feel put upon if his/her work is over-valued. However, when a faculty member records that a student has done excellent work (A), when in fact the work might only be pretty good (B) or merely fair (C), that faculty member has committed two faults. First, he/she has told a lie about the student's work, misrepresenting the student's accomplishments. How would we react if the misrepresentation went the other way—if the student had done excellent work, but the faculty member assigned a grade of B or even C? This would strike us all as dreadful, yet faculty members who assign falsely high grades are showing equally flawed judgment. Inaccurate grading is inaccurate grading, no matter which direction it takes.

4   The second fault is that the faculty member has broken faith with all those who will be harmed by the deception. Most obvious among these are the students who really did do excellent or good work. It is grossly unfair to students who earned real A's or B's if their accomplishments are devalued by the lax standards applied to others. To illustrate with an example from the workplace: would it be fair for two employees to receive the same raise when one had done excellent work and the other only mediocre?

5   Grade inflation also harms anyone who must evaluate a student's record, such as admissions officers at other universities and at professional schools. For instance, medical and law schools never have enough spaces for all applicants and hence must choose only the best qualified. When admissions officers evaluate the transcript of a student who received inflated grades as an undergraduate, they get a false idea of that student's past performance as well as his/her potential for future success in a rigorous professional curriculum. For a similar reason, potential employers are harmed when they are presented

with an inflated academic transcript; faced with seemingly equal candidates, they may give a coveted position to a less deserving applicant because they had a false understanding of that person's actual abilities.

6 And finally, our society at large is harmed because grade inflation undermines the integrity of the universities, which is one of our greatest assets. If university faculty members cannot be trusted to give an honest evaluation of each student's academic work, public disillusionment will inevitably set in—and rightly so. The solution to the problem, though difficult, is simple: each faculty member should make a conscious decision to assign grades based on the actual quality of a student's work, realizing that not every student will be able to earn the highest, or even the second highest, grade. One of my former students made the point very concisely in an essay that she wrote on grade inflation: "Let's put the excellence back in the A."

EXERCISE 12·2 Comprehension/Discussion Questions

1. What is grade inflation?
2. According to Miles, what caused this trend?
3. Miles gives a number of reasons why grade inflation is a problem. List them.
4. Is Miles' support for his reasons convincing? Explain your answer.
5. What is the purpose of grades?
6. Do you think grade inflation is a problem? Why or why not?
7. What solution does Miles suggest for this problem? What solution would you suggest?

Writing

Thus far you have been writing essays that are primarily expository, in which the main purpose is to explain or analyze. You have found, too, that narration and description can act as support in this kind of writing. In this chapter, we focus on another type of essay, one that has a somewhat different purpose: to convince or persuade. This is the *argumentative essay*.

An argument ensues when people disagree about something. One side gives an opinion and offers reasons in support of it, and the other side gives a different opinion and offers reasons in support of his or her stand. However, people can disagree about many things that cannot be argued effectively. For example, two people might argue that one flavor of ice cream tastes better than another, but there is no way that either party could convince the other party to change his or her preference. It could, however, be argued that one flavor seems to be more popular; in this case, facts about sales could be cited. Two people might also disagree about the existence of God, but again, it is unlikely that one person could convince the other person to change his or her belief, for religious belief is based on faith, not on logic or verifiable facts. Moreover, two people might disagree about who won the national soccer match in 1998, but if they do some research, the argument would be settled using a fact. Therefore, arguments of preference, belief or faith, and fact are not the type of arguments one can effectively and logically deal with in the formal argumentative essay.

The kind of issue that can be argued logically is one based on an opinion that can be supported by evidence such as facts, examples, the opinion of experts, or logical reasoning. For example, say you wanted to argue that college students should be required to take physical education courses. Those arguing for this proposal would support their opinion with relevant facts and logical reasoning, while those opposed to the change would also give their reasons. This is an issue that has two arguable sides; it is not an argument of belief or faith, preference, or fact.

The Argumentative Thesis: Taking a Stand

Most writing, of course, is improved by having a persuasive edge to the thesis, but for analysis and exposition, that "edge" need not always be sharp. For example, a thesis such as "My first experiences with Americans were traumatic" has a central idea—*traumatic*—but it is not really strongly persuasive, and it is certainly not argumentative. An argumentative essay, however, is one that attempts to change the reader's mind, to convince the reader to agree with the point of view or opinion of the writer. Therefore, the argumentative essay attempts to be highly persuasive and logical.

What is the difference, then, between a thesis with a strong central idea and an argumentative thesis? To begin with, the argumentative thesis takes a side of an issue; frequently, too, it proposes a course of action (often expressed, by the way, with the modal *should*). In the argument for physical education courses, the thesis for a paper on this topic might be, "State University should require all students to take one physical education course each semester." Of course, someone else might argue, "State University should not require students to take physical education courses."

EXERCISE 12·3   Study the following thesis statements. Put an "A" in the blank if the statement is argumentative. Be careful! A statement having *should* as part of the verb is not automatically argumentative.

1. _____ College students should have complete freedom to choose their own courses.

2. _____ Prospective parents should be required to get licenses in order to have children.

3. _____ The building codes in Las Vegas, Nevada, are inadequate.

4. _____ This university has more students than any other university in the city.

5. _____ Students should have a say in the hiring and firing of teachers.

6. _____ Pornographic books ought to be banned from the library.

7. _____ This university should not have a football team.

8. _____ There are many complex reasons for the failure of the police to respond quickly to alarms.

9. _____ The citizens of this state should be allowed to carry guns.

10. _____ The U.S. government ought to allow more immigrants into this country.

The Opposition: Knowing What You Are Up Against

When you write an argumentative paper, more so than with expository or analytical essays, you must be acutely aware of your audience—the reader. Remember, the purpose of an argumentative essay is to convince the reader that your position is the better one. To begin with, assume that the reader disagrees with you. After all, if he or she did not, there would be no cause to argue. Next, remember that although the reader disagrees with you, that does not mean he or she is any less intelligent than you. Therefore, avoid attacking the reader with such statements as, "Anyone who believes all students should take physical education courses must be ignorant or out of touch with reality." Address your reader by writing objectively, logically, and respectfully.

The most important thing to consider about the members of your audience is why they hold their opinion. What reasons do you think they might use to support their opinion? Trying to identify and understand your opponent's point of view is important; if you do not understand your opponent's reasons and you just argue your own reasons, you are not likely to convince the reader at all. For example, let us say that you want to argue for a physical education requirement at your college and you give the following reasons:

1. Students enjoy physical education courses.
2. Students learn valuable social skills and teamwork in physical education courses.
3. Students can study more effectively when they are physically fit.

Your reasons might be very good ones, but these points are probably not the points on which your opposition bases its argument; in fact, your opponents will probably agree with you on these points! At the heart of your opponents' argument is the issue of responsibility: is it the university's job to attend to the physical fitness of students? If you do not address that issue and convince your opponents that physical education courses are appropriate requirements at the college level, then you cannot expect to convince them to agree with you. Once you have argued to the points the opposition holds, then you can further support your case by adding the other reasons mentioned earlier.

EXERCISE 12·4   Read the following thesis statements, and think of the reasons in support of the thesis ("pros") and the reasons against ("cons") it. On separate paper, list as many reasons as you can for both sides. Then circle the reason that you think is the crucial one, the one at the heart of the issue. The first one is done for you.

1. Marijuana smoking should be legalized.

<table>
<tr><td align="center">**PRO**</td><td align="center">**CON**</td></tr>
<tr><td>a. It is a harmless, enjoyable relaxer.</td><td>a. It is an addictive drug.</td></tr>
<tr><td>(b.) The government does not have the right to tell us what we can or cannot consume.</td><td>b. The government should not allow harmful drugs to circulate without control.</td></tr>
<tr><td>c. It is useful as medicine.</td><td>c. People under its influence can harm others.</td></tr>
<tr><td>d. Many people already use it.</td><td>d. Its use leads to use of more dangerous drugs.</td></tr>
</table>

2. A basic core curriculum of liberal arts courses should be required for all students graduating from college.
3. College students should have freedom to choose their own courses.
4. A student convicted of cheating on an exam should automatically be expelled from college.
5. A year of national service, with low pay, should be required of all 18-year-olds in this country.
6. A university education should be free to all high school students with a B grade average.
7. Physicians should be allowed to assist people who want to die.
8. The United States should not restrict immigration or have immigration quotas.
9. The production and sale of cigarettes should be made illegal.
10. Air bags should not be required in cars.

Supporting and Explaining the Reasons

There are a number of ways to support your point in an argumentative paragraph. Since the purpose is to convince or persuade, you can use whatever type of organization and support that is suggested by the reason you give. For instance, if you believe that there should be stricter controls over the dumping of chemical wastes, and one of the reasons you give is the pollution that irresponsible dumping has caused, you could discuss the effects of dumping; in addition, you could give examples of dumping grounds that have polluted the environment. You might even explain the process of pollution—that is, how dumping pollutes.

Whatever method of development you use, you will want to use *facts* to support your point. Facts include data that have been objectively proved and are generally accepted, such as historical facts, scientific data, statistics, and so forth. In order to get facts to support your point, you may need to do some library research.

Note how factual details assist in this argumentative paragraph. Here this writer is arguing that the use of pesticides should be restricted and controlled.

There are many reasons for restricting the methods and quantity of pesticides used in farming, but one of the most compelling reasons is that pesticides kill not only harmful insects which destroy crops and damage property, but also those insects which are helpful to farmers

and the environment, such as ladybugs and honeybees.[1] In fact, the case of the honeybee is an excellent example of the damage that pesticides can do. Honeybees must pollinate more than 30% of the food consumed in the United States or the plants simply will not grow.[2] When pesticides are used on food plants, however, the honeybees carry the poison back to their hives with the pollen they have gathered, so the pesticides kill not only one bee, but the entire hive. Today, almost no wild colonies of honeybees remain in the United States, and beekeepers keep only about 3 million hives; this is about half as many as in the past. To keep fruit and vegetable crop yields high, many farmers are finding that they must hire beekeepers to bring honeybees into their farms on trucks to pollinate the crops.[3] Without enough honeybees to pollinate crops, the amount of food we produce will decrease drastically. Therefore, we must restrict our use of harmful pesticides before we discover that we will not have enough food to feed the world's growing population.

EXERCISE 12·5   On a separate sheet of paper, answer the following questions about the preceding paragraph.

1. What is the author's main reason for restricting the use of pesticides?
2. What kind of support is given for this reason?

Another type of support is *examples*. To be effective, the examples you use should be typical, selected from a sufficient number of examples to prove the case (see Chapters 5 and 7). Note the effective use of examples in the paragraph about pesticides. In this paragraph, both the ladybug and honeybee are given as examples, and the example of the honeybee is developed into an extended example. If you use examples from personal experience, be sure that the example is generalizable to a larger group.

You can also use the *opinions of experts* to help support your point. An expert is a person who is particularly knowledgeable about a topic because of his or her research, profession, or experience. You will need to use the proper quotation and citation format for opinions from experts (see Appendix II). Note the use of experts in this paragraph arguing against the legalization of drugs.

There are two drugs that are legal now: alcohol and nicotine. These two legal drugs demonstrate what will happen if other drugs,

---

[1] Joseph M. Winski, "Bees and Ecology," *The Writer's World*, ed. George Arms et al. (New York: St. Martin's, 1978), pp. 361–62.

[2] Green, J. "Are there bees in your clover." (1998). http://users/aol.com/queenbjan/beeclovr.htm Accessed Jan. 16, 1999.

[3] Green, D. "Pollination Century 21 Style." http://www.seedsource.com/garden/pollinat.htm Accessed on Jan. 16, 1999.

like cocaine, are legalized. According to Dr. Herbert Kleber, who is currently with the Center on Addiction and Substance Abuse at Columbia University, "Today ten times more Americans use alcohol and five times more use tobacco than illegal drugs" (DEA, Claim III, 1). He quotes a recent survey stating that 98 million Americans had used alcohol in the previous month and 54 million had used cigarettes, while only 11 million had used illicit drugs (DEA, Claim III, 1). Drug Enforcement Administration figures indicate that currently about half a billion people are addicted to nicotine and 18 million are addicted to alcohol. In contrast, only 5 million are addicted to illegal drugs (Claim IV, 1). These numbers clearly show that if drugs are legal, people are more likely to use them, since, by being legal, they are accepted as being okay by society. Thus, legalizing drugs like cocaine and heroin would most likely result in more drug use and more drug addiction.

—Sabrina Rodriguez

No matter what underlying pattern of development you use, you must show the progression of your logic. Just as it is necessary to explain an example to show its relevance to the generalization, it is necessary to explain the reason to show how it supports the thesis. Look at how a paragraph supporting the thesis "Universities should continue to give football scholarships" is developed.

Giving football scholarships is really just a wise investment on the part of the university. What the university really needs and wants is money in the form of football ticket sales, contributions, and endowments from alumni, and allotments and grants from the state legislature. By giving football scholarships, many smaller, struggling universities, Northeast University for example, can attract talented, sought-after football players. These players build a winning football team, and the university builds a reputation. The university's football games may be on television, and the team may be asked to play in a bowl game. With this publicity, fans and alumni are eager to attend the games, thus boosting ticket sales. Rich alumni, who are proud of their school, give endowments and grants. And for state schools, members of Congress and representatives at the state Capitol are pleased with the publicity the school, and thus the state, receives. As a result, the state's coffers are a little more open and the money flows, enabling the university to pay its faculty, build new buildings, and maintain the quality of its teaching. Yes, the football scholarship is a small investment from which the university hopes to reap big gains.

EXERCISE 12·6   On a separate sheet of paper, answer the following questions about the preceding paragraph.

1. What is the topic sentence for the paragraph? Where is it located?
2. What is the reason the author gives for universities spending funds on football scholarships?
3. What underlying pattern of development does the author use to support her reason—examples, cause, effect?
4. Do you think the writer could improve this paragraph by giving some details?

Internet Activity: Composition Skills and the Internet

 Many people and organizations use the Internet as a way to post their opinions and arguments. Find a Web page which is argumentative. Read the page carefully, and answer these questions about the page:

1. Does the author effectively support his or her argument with facts and examples?
2. What method(s) of development does this author use to make the argument?

EXERCISE 12·7   Study the following sentences, which give reasons. For each one, decide what kind of development you would use to explain the reason. For example, would you explain with the use of examples and/or factual detail? Would you explain a process? Would you discuss causes or effects? Would you compare and contrast?

1. One reason that we should legalize marijuana is that the government could collect taxes on its sale.

   _____

2. One reason we should not legalize marijuana is that its use leads to the use of more dangerous drugs.

   _____

3. We should not build more nuclear power plants because of the potentially devastating effects they could have if they break down.

   _____

4. Requiring parents to get licenses in order to have children would help to reduce child abuse.

   _____

5. One of the advantages of having a football team is that it boosts student morale.

   _____

6. One reason the university should have a day care center is for the convenience of students and staff.

   _____

7. All students should be required to take a foreign language because it will broaden their education.

   _____

8. One reason we should restrict students' use of computers is that overuse can lead to addiction.

   _____

9. One reason we should ban smoking cigarettes in bars and restaurants is to protect the health of the employees.

   _____

10. An important reason that we should restrict handgun sales is to keep guns away from children.

   _____

EXERCISE 12·8 Writing Assignment   Using one of the reasons from Exercise 12-4 or 12-7, write a paragraph explaining and supporting that reason.

Refuting and Conceding the Opposition

In an argumentative essay, you should refute opposing arguments. It is this characteristic that is more particular to the argumentative essay than to expository essays. Since there are two sides to the issue, and since you—the writer—want to convince the reader that you are right, not only must you prove your own case, but you should also prove that the opponent is wrong, or at least that your points are more valid or significant. *Refute* means to prove wrong by argument or to show that something is erroneous. In refutation, you will deal with the opponent's reasons and show that yours are more valid or superior. However, if the opponent makes some valid points, you will want to concede them, or agree that they are valid, and then go on to argue your own points.

The following paragraphs show how to refute and concede arguments. The first paragraph sets up an argument; the second paragraph both concedes valid points and refutes the main argument.

> One reason people over 75 should not be allowed to drive is that they are a hazard on the road. By that age, most people's vision and

hearing have deteriorated; thus, they cannot see cars, pedestrians, and traffic signs as well as they could in their youth. In addition, they have slower reaction times. This is particularly problematic because while driving, one must be constantly on the alert to the need to stop or swerve suddenly to avoid a collision. These physical and mental impairments lead to a lot of accidents. In fact, if we compare on a per-mile basis the elderly with other age groups of drivers, it turns out that the elderly are involved in 25 accidents per 100 drivers. This is second only to the group aged 24 and under.

Now observe how this point is refuted and the valid points conceded:

My opponents argue that people over 75 should not be allowed to drive because they are a hazard on the road. While it is true that the accident rate per mile driven is high for the elderly, the fact is that the elderly simply do not drive as much as those in other age groups; consequently, the actual number of accidents in this age group is the lowest among all the younger age groups. Moreover, while it is also true that their abilities to see, hear, and react are not as sharp as they were when they were younger, this does not necessarily have to make them hazardous on the road. In fact, elderly drivers can be trained to compensate for their deficiencies by taking special driver's education courses designed for them.

EXERCISE 12·9 Writing Assignment   For Exercise 12-8, you wrote a paragraph supporting and explaining a reason. Now write a paragraph that refutes that reason. If you need to concede a valid point, do so.

Organizing the Argumentative Essay

There are a number of ways to organize the argumentative essay. Here are several patterns.

Pattern 1

| Paragraph 1. Introduction. | Introduce the issue/problem and your thesis. |

| Paragraph 2. Background Information (optional). | For some topics, you may need to give additional information, define terms, and explain whatever the audience needs to know to understand the issue. |

Paragraph 3.	Reason 1. You will probably have one reason per paragraph. Two to four reasons are typical for an argumentative essay.
Paragraph 4.	Reason 2.
Paragraph 5.	Reason 3.
Paragraph 6.	Reason 4.
Paragraph 7. Refutation.	Refute your opponent's most important reason.
Paragraph 8. Conclusion.	Here you can summarize, demand action, suggest a solution, or predict an outcome.

Note: You may also refute your opponent's main argument before you begin your reasons.

Pattern 2

Paragraph 1. Introduction.	Introduce the issue/problem and your thesis.
Paragraph 2.	Same as Pattern 1.
Paragraph 3.	Opponent's argument 1 with your refutation. Begin the paragraph with a short summary of your opponent's argument and spend most of the paragraph refuting it.
Paragraph 4.	Opponent's argument 2 with your refutation.

Paragraph 5.	Opponent's argument 3 with your refutation.
Paragraph 6.	Opponent's argument 4 with your refutation.
Paragraph 7. Conclusion.	Same as Pattern 1.

Read the following essay. Note if the writer clearly states the case or issue under discussion; locate the thesis; evaluate the support and the argument. Is it convincing?

Science: Who Needs It?

At our school, all students are required to take a minimum of six courses in the natural sciences: three in the biological sciences and three in the physical sciences, regardless of the student's major. Students majoring in the humanities often have to struggle to get through these demanding courses and their grade-point averages usually suffer as a result. It has been suggested that the requirements be modified, reducing the number of natural science courses required so that students can take more courses directly related to their majors. As a humanities major, I admit this would make college life a lot easier for me, but I still oppose the measure because natural science courses provide us with a crucial part of our education.

Students majoring in the humanities usually object to taking such science courses because they claim the courses are irrelevant to their majors. "What good will physics do me when I'm teaching Spanish?" a friend of mine asked. It's true that physics, chemistry, biology, and the like may not have a direct application to most careers in the humanities, but this objection ignores one of the key issues of a university education. A university is not simply a training facility; it is an institution of higher learning where students are educated, not merely trained. Even the term *university* implies that it's a place to obtain a general knowledge base; a university education means the student has been educated in many subjects. Since part of our universal knowledge is science, it is and logically should be a part of the university curriculum.

Humanities students might accept this argument and agree that they should take some natural science, but not as many courses as are now required. They might suggest a one-semester course in biological science and a one-semester course in physical science, along with perhaps one semester of math for non-majors. This, they argue, would expose them sufficiently to the universe of science. If the point of a university education were merely to expose students to a variety of subjects, then I might agree. But a university education implies more than mere exposure. After all, people can be exposed to subjects by watching television. Again, the purpose of going to a university is to get an education. What does that mean? It means more than just training and exposure; it means that students learn enough to become critical thinkers in the various disciplines. It means that they should gain enough understanding of the sciences, humanities, social sciences, and the arts to be able to discuss issues in these areas intelligently and to be able to question other people's views rather than just accept what people tell them.

One or two semesters of general science cannot sufficiently educate students in this field. What one learns in natural science courses is more than mere factual information. One learns to think critically, to approach problems logically, to use reasoning. And this takes time. It takes work. It takes studying different areas of science and applying the general principles in laboratory situations.

Developing a critical ability in science is important, but why? In addition to providing the student with a universe of knowledge, an understanding of science is vital in our highly technological society. We are all confronted with issues involving nuclear waste, chemical pollutants, medical advances, exploration in space, and so forth. In order to make intelligent decisions—in fact, even to be involved in the decision-making process—people need to have an understanding of these issues that goes beyond mere "exposure." Otherwise, the uneducated become mere puppets who, out of ignorance, can but nod in agreement with anyone who professes expertise.

Science courses, then, provide us not only with knowledge that is crucial for intelligent functioning in our society, but they also provide us with the opportunity to develop our critical, logical reasoning skills. Although these courses are difficult for the non-science majors, they are a necessary part of a university education.

EXERCISE 12•10   On a separate sheet of paper, answer the following questions about "Science: Who Needs It?"

1. What is the issue discussed by the writer?
2. What is the thesis statement?

3. What are the writer's main arguments?
4. Where does the refutation begin in the essay? What is the first point that the writer refutes?
5. Does the writer refute all possible objections to the thesis? Can you think of any objections someone might make?
6. Does the writer concede any points? Which ones? Are there others the writer should concede? What are they?
7. Is the argument convincing? Why, or why not?
8. Does the conclusion logically follow?
9. Make an outline of this essay.

EXERCISE 12·11 Writing Assignment   In Exercises 12-8 and 12-9, you wrote paragraphs supporting and refuting a topic. Now develop more reasons for your topic and write the first draft of an essay.

Composition Skills

Coherence Review

Good writing must be coherent: that is, one idea must follow logically and smoothly from the previous one. A number of ways to achieve coherence have been noted earlier. In writing essays, whether they are expository or argumentative, always strive to use a variety of techniques for achieving coherence. Let us review them briefly.

1. *Repetition of key words, synonyms, and pronouns.*
2. *Coordinating conjunctions and correlative conjunctions.* The coordinating conjunctions *and, but, or, for, nor, yet,* and *so* join two independent clauses and are usually preceded by a comma.

   We went to the game, *but* we did not get good seats.

   The correlative conjunctions *not only . . . but also, either . . . or, neither . . . nor, both . . .* and *also* join two independent clauses.

   Not only do we object to what he said, but we *also* object to how he said it.

3. *Subordinate clauses.* Subordinate clauses (adverbial, adjective, and noun clauses) use a subordinating conjunction at the beginning of a subordinate clause to join the subordinate clause to an independent clause. Subordinate clauses effectively show the relative importance of the two sentences. Use the following kinds of subordinate clauses:

a. Adjective clauses using *who, whom, which, that, whose, when,* and *where*:

The boy *whose father is a doctor sits behind me in class.*

b. Adverbial clauses of time using *while, as, when, whenever, before, after, until as soon as, since, from the moment that*:

From the moment that I saw her, I was infatuated.

c. Adverbial clauses of comparison-contrast using *while* and *whereas*:

Maria is interested in dancing, *whereas Sonia is interested in gymnastics.*

d. Adverbial clauses of concession using *although, though, even though*:

Although nuclear power is dangerous, it is necessary to provide us with enough electricity to meet our needs.

e. Adverbial clauses of purpose using *so that*:

We arrived early *so that we could get a good seat.*

f. Adverbial clauses of condition using *if*:

If the pump breaks, you will need to go to the service station.

g. Adverbial clauses of cause using *because* and *since*:

We went to the concert *because we were curious.*

h. Adverbial clauses of result using *so/such . . . that*:

The letter was *so illogical that I could not understand it at all.*

4. *Transitional words and phrases.* For the most part, transitional words and phrases are attached to the beginning of a sentence and are preceded by a period or semicolon. They do not really join two sentences together, but indicate the relationship between the two sentences. Note the relationship that the transitions denote:

Chronological Order:

first	after that
second	last
next	finally

Example:

for example

for instance

to illustrate

Addition:

also   in addition

furthermore   besides that

Conclusion:

in conclusion   to conclude

finally   in summary

Comparison-Contrast:

likewise   conversely

similarly   in contrast

in the same way   however

on the other hand on the contrary

similar to   different from

like   in contrast to

EXERCISE 12•12 Writing Assignment   The following paragraphs are not coherent. Rewrite them using any of the coherence devices that we have studied.

Women should not be drafted for combat duty. It is not practical. The army needs to set up two facilities for everything. It needs to set up two sleeping quarters, two sets of showers, and two latrines. The actual amount of work and supplies involved in setting up camp is doubled. More supplies and equipment in the field slows down troop movement considerably. Our troops would lose any advantage they would have for surprise attack. We need an incredible amount of backup support for men. It is not practical to double that in wartime.

Women are not strong enough emotionally. Women are not strong enough physically. It takes a lot of strength and courage to be in actual physical combat. You need to be strong enough to kill people without any pangs of regret. Women could be strong. Women are sheltered. They are not taught to be strong. Men are taught to be strong. Women could not stand to see their best buddy get hit by a shell and die in front of their eyes. Women are not strong enough to handle killing and dying. Maybe they could be strong enough emotionally. They are not strong enough physically. Most women could not throw ninety-pound ammunition cases into a truck all day. Most women could not win in close hand-to-hand combat against a man. Women do not have the strength for combat duty.

EXERCISE 12·13 Writing Assignment   Choose one of the following writing topics for an argumentative essay. For some of them, you may need to do some library research. If you use outside sources, be sure to use quotations and citations properly (see Appendix II).

1. In the reading on college lectures, David Daniels argues against lecturing as a teaching method. Write an essay that argues for it. Or think of some other teaching method that is controversial and argue for or against it.
2. In his essay on grade inflation, Elliott Miles argues for the traditional grading system. In your essay, argue against it. Or think of some other aspect of grading about which you can take a stand.
3. Think of a controversial issue on your campus and argue for or against it.
4. Select one of the topics in Exercise 12-3, 12-4, or 12-7 that you did not choose earlier.
5. Choose one of the following topics.

   Should all companies require on-the-job drug testing?
   Should standardized tests be required of all students at the high school and
       college level?
   Should people be required to have a license to drink alcohol?
   Should rock music be censored?
   Should school children with AIDS be identified?
   Should businesses be responsible for their packaging materials that pollute
       the environment?
   Should the Internet be monitored or censored? By whom?

6. In the editorial section of the newspaper, editors express their own opinions on topical issues, and in letters to the editor, readers express their opinions. Write an essay that argues against the opinion expressed either in an editorial or in a letter to the editor. In your introductory paragraph, summarize the article you are arguing against ("In his article on inflation, Mr. X contends that . . . ."). You may wish to review indirect speech and noun clauses in the Grammar Review Unit.

EXERCISE 12·14 Assignments from the Disciplines   Following are some topics for your final writing assignment which are typical of college writing assignments. For your final writing assignment, you may choose one that you have studied, or consult a textbook or the Internet to find the answer. Then, follow the directions for Exercise 12-13 to write your answer.

1. From Education   Researchers disagree on the best method of teaching reading to children. Some argue for the whole language approach, while others support the phonics approach. Take a position on this issue using relevant research for support.
2. From Political Science   "All people are created equal, and the goal of society should be to make sure that everyone has equal opportunity in life." Write an essay in which you agree or disagree with this statement.
3. From Ecology and Agriculture   Some experts feel that more food should be organically grown to protect the environment, while others believe that pesticides can be used safely and must be used to feed the world's growing population. Write an essay about this issue using facts from research to support your position on this issue.

Revision

Peer Review

When you have finished writing the first draft of your essay, give it to a classmate to read and review. Use the peer review checklist in Appendix I to respond to each other's drafts.

Revision Checklist for the Argumentative Essay

Use these questions to help you to give suggestions to your peers and to revise your essay:

1. An argumentative essay attempts to convince or persuade the reader. The subject for an argumentative essay should be an opinion that can be argued logically and supported by evidence. Have you chosen an appropriate argumentative subject? Have you explained the issue or case sufficiently?
2. The thesis of the argumentative essay should take a clear stand on the issue. Does your thesis express your stand clearly?
3. An argumentative essay should attempt to refute opposing arguments. Does your essay do so?
4. An argumentative essay should offer logical reasons and support for the writer's opinion. Does your essay do so?
5. Is your essay logically organized?
6. Is it coherent?

Unit Three
Grammar Review

Adjectives (Ch. 4)

Adjectives modify nouns. Single-word adjectives are generally placed before the nouns they modify. Adjectives in English *do not change form* to agree with the number of the noun (an *old* car, some *old* cars). Since it is not unusual when striving to be more specific to use more than one adjective to modify a noun, it is important to review the order of the adjectives before the noun they modify. Study the following chart:

PRE-DETER-MINED NUMBER PRONOUN	ARTICLE	GENERAL ADJECTIVE	SIZE	SHAPE	AGE	COLOR	ORIGIN	NOUNS AS ADJECTIVES		NOUN
								MATERIAL	NON MATERIAL	
Most of	the	pretty	little					rubber		toys
	A	beautiful			antique		Mayan		flower	vase
Some				round		white				discs

Most of the pretty little rubber toys

A beautiful antique Mayan flower vase

Some round white discs

Note: When two or three adjectives are used, each of which belongs to a different class (size, age, etc.), it usually is not necessary to separate the adjectives with commas. But when there are two adjectives of the same class, they should generally be separated with commas:

a big red European automobile

vs.

a deep, peaceful sleep

EXERCISE G·1   Study the following paragraphs. Insert the adjectives in parentheses in their proper order before the nouns they modify.

When I am feeling depressed, my favorite place to go is the lake, where I like to sit under a (*old/tall/oak*) _____ tree overlooking the shoreline. On a (*summer/clear*) _____ day, the (*crystal/blue*) _____ water looks peaceful and calm. The (*foamy/white*) _____ waves gently caress the (*white/sandy*) _____ shore leaving (*wavy/thin*) _____ lines on the sand among the (*little/multi-colored*) _____ shells. While listening to the reassuring whispers of the waves, I also watch the (*white/graceful*) _____ seagulls hovering above the water as they look for (*tasty/small*) _____ fish for their meals. I usually remain under that tree for several hours. When the (*apricot/oval*) _____ sun begins its slow, languorous descent into the horizon, I know that it is time to go home, and I reluctantly leave. But before I go, I take one more look at the (*serene/beautiful*) _____ scene and I feel that this (*short/difficult*) _____ life is worth living after all.

Participles as Adjectives

Adjectives such as *beautiful, tall,* and *soft* are necessary in good writing because they give specific, vivid detail. Two other kinds of adjectives that are useful but also very troublesome are the present participle (*-ing*) and past participle (*-ed*) forms. Although they are actually verb forms, they can be used as adjectives. Note these examples:

> When I am *depressed,* my favorite place to go is the lake.

> Maria is *fascinating.*

Sometimes it is difficult to tell whether you should use the present or past participle as an adjective.

EXERCISE G·2   Read the situations that follow and fill in either the present or past participle in the blanks.

1. John is sitting nervously at the racetrack watching his horse. He wants to see the beginning of the race. He is (excite) _____. He thinks the race will be (excite) _____.

2. Steve just learned that he got a D on his chemistry test. He is (depress) _____. He thinks he got a D because he is not (interest) _____ in chemistry.

3. Today is Monday. Janet just got home from work. Mondays at work are always (tire) _____ so Janet is (exhaust) _____.

4. The movie on television last night showed new discoveries about cancer. The show was (interest) _____.

5. My history teacher always talks in a monotone and never looks at the students. He is the most (bore) _____ teacher I have. All of the students are (bore) _____.

6. Mary's mother has always wanted Mary to finish college. She was (disappoint) _____ when Mary told her that she had quit school. Mary's mother sobbed when she heard the (disappoint) _____ news.

7. John went to the doctor because he had a pain in his chest. The doctor's comments were (reassure) _____ to John. Before the doctor told him that the pain was just heartburn, John had been (frighten) _____.

8. I didn't understand the (confuse) _____ income-tax forms that I got from the government. I was so (worry) _____ about them that I asked my neighbor to help me. However, he gave me a lot of (mislead) _____ information. Finally, I went to a tax consultant who had a (depress) _____ office. He helped me fill out the forms correctly.

EXERCISE G·3   In the following sentences, write either the present or past participle in the blanks. Remember that some past participles are irregular.

1. Last Friday, my friend, Jack, and I spent a (pack) _____ day at the natural history museum.

2. First, we toured the (mount)_____ displays of prehistoric animals.

3. In that section, we saw a huge (stuff) _____ replica of brontosaurus.

4. As we went on, we encountered the displays of (develop) _____ *Homo sapiens.*

5. The Neanderthal man was short and had a (shrunk) _____ head.

6. The Cro-Magnon man was taller and more (advance) _____ physically than the Neanderthal man.

7. Finally, we watched a planetarium show in which countless (wander)

_____ stars and planets filled the sky.

8. After we emerged from the (darken) _____ planetarium, we went

to the (crowd) _____ restaurant to talk over the day's events.

Adjective Clauses Reduced to Participial Phrases

Before you begin this section, you may wish to review Adjective Clauses on pp. 322. Adjective clauses connect two sentences by replacing a noun with a relative pronoun (*who, which, that,* and so on). Certain adjective clauses can be reduced to participial phrases. To reduce an adjective clause—relative clause—to a participial phrase, delete the relative pronoun that is acting as a subject and the form of the verb *to be* that follows the pronoun. This should leave a present participle (an *-ing* word) or a past participle (an *-ed/-en* word). To see how this works, first underline the adjective clauses in the following sentences:

I know the man who John is picking up.

I know the man who teaches at this school.

I know the man who is standing over there.

I know the man who was taken to jail.

I know the man who was being charged with the crime.

Note that in the first two sentences, adjective clauses cannot be reduced. In the first one, the relative pronoun is not the subject of the clause. In the second one, we do not have a form of the verb *to be* or the present participle. A reduction here would result in an incorrect sentence:

I know the man teaches at this school.

(Often, in this type of sentence, the verb can be changed to a present participle "I know the man teaching at this school.") Note the correct sentences when *who* + *is/was* is deleted:

I know the man standing over there.

I know the man taken to jail.

I know the man being charged with the crime.

The sentence with the present participle is reduced from an active verb, whereas the sentences with the past participle (*-ed/-en*) are reduced from passive verbs. (To review the active vs. passive voice, see pp. 372.) Do not confuse the simple past tense verbs with passive. Note this sentence:

The man who walked down the street was a thief.

This sentence does not have a form of the verb *to be*, so it cannot be reduced. Reduction would result in this incorrect sentence:

The man walked down the street was a thief.

However, the sentence that follows is passive, so it has a form of the verb *to be*:

The car that was returned to me was not mine.

It can be reduced thus:

The car returned to me was not mine.

Sometimes the reduction of a clause will leave just the participle after the noun. When the participle tells "which," it remains after the noun:

The woman who is singing is my sister.
= The woman singing is my sister.

The man who was accused is angry.
= The man accused is angry.

However, when the participle tells "what kind of," it is placed in front of the noun. Study these sentences:

Countries that are developing need capital.
= Developing countries need capital.

Plays that are unpublished are often performed.
= Unpublished plays are often performed.

Finally, we should note that both restrictive and nonrestrictive adjective clauses can be reduced. (For a review of restrictive and nonrestrictive clauses, see pp. 326.) Note these examples:

The man giving the lecture is Mr. Brown.
Mr. Brown, giving a lecture on economics, paced back and forth.

A city founded 100 years ago is quite young by European standards.
New York City, founded over 100 years ago, is one of the oldest American cities.

EXERCISE G·4   Review the rules for punctuating restrictive and nonrestrictive adjective clauses on pages 326–327. The same rules apply to participial phrases reduced from adjective clauses. Punctuate the following sentences, inserting commas where necessary.

1. Scientists working in the field of genetic engineering are very excited about its future.
2. The young hikers tired and worn out decided to take a rest.
3. Robots run by computers are being used in most automobile factories.
4. The convict planning his escape requested to work in the fields.
5. The Chinese New Year celebrated by millions of Asians all over the world is a grand event.

EXERCISE G·5   In the following paragraph, underline the adjective clauses and determine if any of them can be reduced to participial phrases. Then rewrite the paragraph using participial phrases where possible.

In order to be healthy, we all need a daily balanced diet. A balanced diet includes eating some foods each day from each of the four major food groups, which include dairy foods, meats, vegetables and fruits, and breads and cereals. The first group, which is dairy foods, obviously includes milk. Other dairy foods that are able to supplement milk to fulfill our daily needs are cheese and ice cream. Although dairy foods are high in animal fat, which is a substance to be avoided, they are widely available in low-fat forms such as skim milk and ice milk. The second major group that is needed for good health is meats, which are used by our bodies to provide protein. Meat can be obtained in a variety of ways, which include beef, pork, fowl, and fish. In recent years, we have been warned to avoid red meats, which are beef and pork, and to concentrate on eating the leaner fish and fowl. Some people avoid all or some of these meats for religious reasons. These people must obtain their protein in other ways.

EXERCISE G·6   Now complete the paragraph in Exercise G-5 by writing about the two final food groups: (1) vegetables and fruits and (2) breads and cereals. Add as much information and detail as you can. Use participial phrases wherever possible.

Adverbials (Ch. 3, 4, 10)

Adverbs of Place

Special Sentence Construction

Adverb of place + verb phrase + subject

Under the desk   *is*   *a basket.*

The normal word order for this sentence is

Subject + verb phrase + adverb of place
A basket   is   under the desk.

However, in all kinds of writing, including descriptive writing, it is common to place the adverb of place in the subject position at the beginning of the sentence. This special sentence construction is useful for achieving coherence, especially if the noun in the adverb of place has been mentioned in the previous sentence:

There is a *ball* under the bench. Next to the *ball* is a bat.

Note: You can, of course, include the "dummy subject" (expletive) *there* in the subject position before the verb:

Next to the ball there is a bat.

In this sentence, if the adverb of place is moved to the end of the sentence, *there* is necessary to fill the subject position.

There is a bat next to the ball.

Since *there* is a dummy subject, the verb agrees with the real subject even though it follows the verb.

There is *a bookcase* in the corner.

There are several *towels* on the rack.

Adverbials of Time and Sequence

These adverbial phrases indicate time or sequence. Note that these adverbial expressions fall into two groups. The first group consists of time expressions of more than one word. They generally introduce a sentence and are followed by a comma. Here is a list of the most common ones:

by + time	*By nine o'clock,* the avenue is lined with people.
at + time	*At around ten o'clock,* the excitement mounts.
after + time	*After eleven o'clock,* the people go home.
before + time	Everyone gets there *before nine o'clock.*
after + noun	*After about an hour,* the parade passes by.
before + noun	*Before the parade,* everyone is excited.
during + noun	*During the morning,* the people have a good time.

The second group of adverbial expressions consists of one-word expressions of sequence. These generally introduce a sentence and are followed by a comma. Here is a list of the most common ones:

First, there is the welcome sound of sirens.
Next, the masked men arrive on horseback.
Second, they wave and the crowd waves back.
Then, a band usually marches by.
Last, the big floats come.
Finally, the parade is over.

EXERCISE G·7   Complete the following paragraphs with the appropriate adverbial expressions of time or sequence from the preceding lists.

My friend, Thuy, who has a private nursing business, has a demanding schedule. She does not work for a hospital or a doctor; instead, she nurses patients in their own homes. Every morning, Thuy gets up _____ 6:00 A.M. and fixes breakfast for her family. _____, she takes her son to school and then goes to her office where she arrives _____ 8:00 A.M. She stays there for about an hour. _____ that time she checks to see if there are any phone messages on the answering machine. She also prepares some coffee or tea. While she drinks her beverage, Thuy reads the mail, studies the files of her patients, and prepares the work assignments for her other nurses. _____ that, she is ready to visit her patients. _____ she sees Mr. West and gives him an injection. Thuy goes to Mrs. Garcia's house to take her blood pressure. After seeing two more patients, she returns to the office where she eats her lunch. _____ time she does clerical work, such as filling out forms for Medicare. She also studies recent medical reports and consults with the doctors, if necessary, of her patients. _____ about two hours, Thuy is ready to visit four or five more patients _____ the afternoon. _____ she returns to the office and checks the reports of her other nurses. _____, after a long day, Thuy gets in her car and heads home.

Prepositions in Time Expressions

Since expressions indicating time sequence are important in achieving coherence and clarity, it is vital to use the correct prepositions in time expressions. Let us review the following prepositions in time expressions.

- *At* indicates a time of day:

  Adult students usually go to school *at night*.

  Most Americans eat lunch *at noon*.

  My first class begins *at eight o'clock*.

- *In* indicates a part of the day, month, year, or season:

  I like to get up early *in the morning*.

  I enjoy eating out *in the evening*.

  Final exams take place *in June*.

- *On* indicates a day:

  In the United States, there is usually no school *on weekends*.

  My brother was born *on May 5, 1970*.

  On the morning of May 5, 1970, my brother was born.

- *By* indicates up to but not later than a point in time:

  I usually get up *by 6:30 A.M.,* sometimes earlier but never later.

  They always try to arrive home *by noon*.

- *During* indicates an amount of time (followed by a noun phrase):

  I have classes *during the day*.

  I sometimes fall asleep *during the biology lecture*.

- *Until* indicates time up to a point, but not limited to that point in time:

  I usually don't get home *until midnight,* rarely before and sometimes after.

  I like to sleep *until noon,* and sometimes I sleep later.

Special Time Expressions: *on time* and *in time*
The expression *on time* indicates the completion of an act at a designated time. It indicates the correct or exact time. If class begins at eight o'clock and you arrive at eight o'clock, you are *on time*. If you must turn in a paper on Friday and you get it on Friday, you have turned it in *on time*.

  We arrived at the concert *on time*.

The expression *in time* indicates the completion of an act during a length of time that has a final limit. If class begins at eight o'clock, and you come any time before eight o'clock or you are there at eight o'clock, you are *in time*. *In time* is often followed by *for* and *to*. Note these examples:

We arrived *in time* for the first race.

We arrived *in time* to watch the first act.

EXERCISE G·8   Fill in the blanks with the most appropriate prepositions.

1. Although we live in New York City now, every year _____ August my wife and I go back to Hong Kong to visit my wife's family. We usually leave _____ a Thursday or Friday and fly to San Francisco. _____ the weekend, we visit our favorite places in San Francisco: Golden Gate Park, Fisherman's Wharf, and Chinatown. Then we leave _____ Monday morning for Hong Kong. _____ the flight, I usually read a book or sleep, but my wife plans the details of our stay. We usually arrive in Hong Kong late Monday night, but sometimes we do not arrive _____ Tuesday. I like to arrive at the airport just _____ time to see the sunrise on Tuesday morning. If our flight is _____ time, my wife's uncle and family are generally at the airport to meet us. We greet each other warmly and then drive to my wife's parents' house. _____ the time we get there, we are chattering with anticipation. Whether it is _____ the morning, noon, or _____ night, the old couple is always waiting quietly to welcome us.

2. Registration at this university occurs _____ the third week of August. It is usually _____ Wednesday, Thursday, and Friday. Depending on the first letter of their last name, students pick up registration materials _____ a certain time. Starting _____ 8:00 A.M., students can pick up their materials _____ their designated time. However, students do not have to pick them up at that time. They can pick them up any time after that time _____ the week of registration. But they should pick them up _____ the end of the week. It is not possible

to pick them up _____ the weekend or _____ the first week of classes.

EXERCISE G·9 Choose five of the following prepositions, and use each one in a sentence correctly. Be sure to use an appropriate time expression:

on   during   in   after   at   by   until

Adverbial Clauses Reduced to Participial Phrases

The three most common types of participial phrases that can be used to reduce adverbial clauses to participial phrases are (1) the present participle (verb + *ing*), (2) the perfect participle (*having* verb + *ed*), and (3) the passive perfect participle (*having been* verb + *ed*). The type of participial phrase used depends on the sequence of actions in the clauses and the verb tenses. Study the following examples of uses of participial phrases reduced from adverbial clauses.

The Present Participle (Verb + *ing*)
This participle can be used to indicate that the action in the participle takes place before, after, or at the same time as the action in the main clause. *After, before,* and *while* can appear before the participial phrase to clarify the time relationship.

Before John went to the store, he went to the bank.

Before going to the store, John went to the bank.

After he goes to the bank, he goes to the store.

After going to the bank, he goes to the store.

While John was going to the store, he saw an automobile accident.

While going to the store, John saw an automobile accident.

When John arrived at the bank, he saw a hold-up in progress.

Arriving at the bank, John saw a hold-up in progress.

After he goes to the service station, he will go home.

After going to the service station, he will go home.

The Perfect Participle (*Having* Verb + *ed*)

This participle is used to introduce phrases in which the action occurs before the action in the main clause. It is not necessary to introduce the phrase with the adverbial *after*. Notice also that cause is sometimes implied in these phrases.

After John made a withdrawal at the bank, he went home.

Having made a withdrawal at the bank, John went home.

After John finishes with his chores, he will feel good.

Having finished with his chores, John will feel good.

The Passive Perfect Participle (*Having Been* Verb + *ed*)

This participle is used when the original clause was in the passive voice. It indicates that the action in the participial phrase precedes the action in the main clause. Again, note that it can also indicate cause.

After the candidate was nominated for the office, he took out a loan.

Having been nominated for the office, the candidate took out a loan.

The students were scared away after they were warned about cheating.

Having been warned about cheating, the students were scared away.

After he was given the chance to reform, the young man robbed a bank anyway.

Having been given a chance to reform, the young man robbed a bank anyway.

Sometimes these clauses can be further reduced by leaving off *having been* and starting the clause with the past participle. (These are often called *absolute constructions.*) Compare these sentences with those preceding:

Nominated for the office, the candidate took out a loan.

Warned about cheating, the students were scared away.

Given a chance to reform, the young man robbed a bank anyway.

Finally, note that if the subject of the sentence first appears in the adverbial clause, it is transferred to the main clause when the adverbial clause is reduced.

The monument was built in 1881. It honored the soldiers.

Built in 1881, the monument honored the soldiers.

EXERCISE G·10   Reduce the following adverbial clauses to participial phrases, and rewrite the sentences in the blanks. Remember to include the subject of the sentence in the main clause. The first one is done for you.

1. Before the female monarch butterfly lays her eggs, it finds a milkweed plant.

    Before laying her eggs, the female monarch butterfly finds a milkweed plant.

2. After the young monarch caterpillar is hatched, it eats the milkweed.

    _____

3. While the caterpillar eats the plant, it continues to grow.

    _____

4. As the caterpillar grows constantly, it sheds its skin several times.

    _____

5. After the caterpillar has been nourished by the milkweed for about three weeks, it spins a chrysalis.

    _____

6. After the green chrysalis has been spun, it is attached to a green leaf.

    _____

7. After the caterpillar has spent a week inside the chrysalis, an exciting transformation takes place.

    _____

8. When the caterpillar emerges from the chrysalis, it is no longer a caterpillar, but a beautiful monarch butterfly.

    _____

9. After the butterfly has been born, it begins to search for flowers in order to sip their nectar.

    _____

10. After the life cycle of the monarch butterfly has been completed, it will begin again.

    _____

EXERCISE G·11 The following paragraph about how to get a job is not as coherent as it should be because it lacks participial phrases for transitions. Rewrite the paragraph, using participial phrases at major transitional points.

You are about to graduate from college, and you want to get a job. How do you go about finding the right job for you? Here is one way to begin your job hunt. First, you need to prepare a resume. A resume is a one- or two-page document that lists brief personal information, the type of job you are looking for, your educational background, your job experience, your interests and hobbies, and your references. You can do your resume yourself on a typewriter or computer or have it done professionally. So, now you have done your resume. Next, you need to decide which prospective employers you are going to send it to. Of course, this depends on your particular job interests. If you are a business major, for example, and want to work in a bank, you will want to make a list of the banks for which you would like to work. And you go ahead and make your list. Then, you will need to draft a generic cover letter to send with your resume to the banks on your list. The cover letter should point up your strongest qualities and present you in a favorable light. It and your resume are your representatives to the prospective employers on your list.

Articles (Ch. 5, 9, 11)

Definite and Indefinite Articles

Because the articles in English (*a, an, the, some*) are troublesome for many students, it is useful to review the use of these articles.

The Indefinite Article

The most common use of the indefinite article *a* (*an* before a vowel sound) is to signal an unspecified item. Note the examples:

She wants a bicycle.

A man is at the door.

A picnic is always fun.

Note that there is not an attempt to make the noun specific. The noun is indefinite. This indefiniteness is indicated in the plural of countable nouns with *some* or with no article at all. When no article is used, the noun itself is emphasized. With *some*, the indefiniteness is emphasized.

She wants *some* bicycles.

Some men are at the door.

Picnics are always fun.

A singular countable noun always requires an article, even if an adjective precedes it:

I need *a* new car.

The only time an article is not necessary before a single countable noun is when another determiner is used instead:

I need this new car.

We need another new car.

However, a noncountable noun cannot be preceded by the indefinite article *a.*

I requested new information.

But *some* can be used with noncountable nouns:

I bought *some* gasoline this morning.

EXERCISE G·12 Put the article *a/an* in the blank if it is needed. If the indefinite article is not necessary, put "O."

1. I used to play ＿＿＿＿＿＿ soccer for my high school team.

2. He gave me ＿＿＿＿＿＿ good advice.

3. This is ＿＿＿＿＿＿ difficult situation.

4. Superman is ＿＿＿＿＿＿ example of a fictional hero.

5. I like ＿＿＿＿＿＿ Indian food because it's spicy.

6. We had ＿＿＿＿＿＿ bad weather last week.

7. ＿＿＿＿＿＿ anecdote is ＿＿＿＿＿＿ type of illustration.

8. We wrote ＿＿＿＿＿＿ book about our travels in Guatemala.

The Definite Article

The definite article *the* signals a specific or particular person, place, or thing. Nouns can be made specific in several ways.

1. The noun has been identified in a previous sentence. When the noun is first mentioned, it is unspecified, so the article *a* may be used. The first mention

of the noun serves to identify it. When it is mentioned a second time, the article *the* is used:

> We bought *a* new car last year. After we got *the* car home, one of its tires went flat.

> I ordered *some* soup from the delicatessen. When *the* soup arrived, it was cold.

2. The noun has a modifying phrase or clause in the sentence that identifies it as a specific item.

> The information that I got *from this book* was helpful.

> The information *in this book* was helpful.

Notice in the following sentence *information* is unspecified; it means information in a general sense. Therefore, no article is used:

> *Information* comes to us in a variety of ways.

In certain situations with a modifying phrase or clause, *the* is omitted. *The* is used with modifying phrases or clauses when the sentence is not a generalization but is about one event:

> *The* cars in the driveway just had their tires stolen.

> *The* luggage in the cars was also stolen.

In a generalization when the modifying phrase or clause limits the noun to one item in a class, *the* is also used:

> *The* car in the driveway is a good one.

However, *the* is often omitted in generalizations (and sometimes must be) when the modifying phrase or clause is not referring to one item in a class but merely serves to narrow down the class. Compare with the previous sentences:

> *Cars* from Germany are quite expensive.

> *Luggage* that is made of leather is also expensive.

3. The situation identifies the noun. When both the writer and reader are familiar with the item that is being referred to, *the* is used. Often there is only one such item.

> *The* holiday season is an exciting, stressful time.

> This information was located on *the* Internet.

> *The* European Renaissance began in Italy in *the* seventeenth century.

4. The noun is specific because it is unique.

> When I look at *the* sky, I am filled with wonder.
> Hurricanes usually come from *the* south.

5. The use of superlatives, ranking adjectives, and ordinal numbers makes a noun specific.

> He was definitely *the* most exciting singer.
> *The* main speaker is next.
> *The* first person in line got the prize.

EXERCISE G·13   Put *a, an,* or *the* in the blanks. If no article is needed, put "O."

1. _____ food is necessary for survival.

2. _____ food we had at that restaurant was excellent.

3. _____ most useful magazines are those that tell you how to do something.

4. We all have _____ need for _____ love.

5. _____ fascinating place to visit is Samoa.

6. All of _____ dogs in _____ neighborhood started to bark when _____ lights went out.

7. Rosa bought _____ new white dress and hat for graduation. Unfortunately, _____ dress was too big.

8. We saw _____ woman with _____ baby on _____ Main Street bus. _____ woman was frantic because _____ baby was sick and crying. _____ passengers could not believe it when _____ bus driver stopped _____ bus and asked _____ woman and baby to get off.

EXERCISE G·14   Study the following paragraph and insert *a, an, the,* or "O" (for no article) in the blanks.

_____ usual answer to _____ obstreperous _____ stream, one that erodes or floods out its banks, is to build _____ dam. But _____ dams cost up to _____ $100,000 apiece, even for

_____ very small streams. Now, _____ Bureau of Land Management (BLM) is cutting _____ costs by using local labor: beavers. For three years, three beavers have been at work on Wyoming's Current Creek, whose spring runoff had yearly gouged out its banks and flooded neighboring farms. There were no trees left for beavers to use, so _____ BLM helped by dragging _____ aspens from _____ distant forest. It also wired _____ truck tires together and laid them across _____ stream, making _____ sturdy _____ foundations for _____ beavers' dams. It worked. _____ beavers restored _____ creek's ecological balance and saved its banks from erosion. _____ dams slowed _____ stream, and nutrient-rich silt has settled behind them. _____ rye grass and _____ willows are coming back along _____ banks, and spring flooding has been regulated; _____ creek now has been widened by about 50 feet. _____ cost to _____ federal government? Less than $3,000.

—adapted from "Toxic Wastes—Another Solution?" *Science Digest*, July 1984, p. 36

Articles with Quantifiers

The following quantifiers indicate a number or amount:

USED WITH PLURAL-COUNT NOUNS	USED WITH NONCOUNT NOUNS	USED WITH SINGULAR-COUNT NOUNS
few (students)	little (money)	one (student)
a few	a little	each
several	some	every
some	much	neither, either
many	any	no
any	all	
most	no	

USED WITH PLURAL-COUNT NOUNS	USED WITH NONCOUNT NOUNS	USED WITH SINGULAR-COUNT NOUNS
all		
no		
both		
two, three, and so on		

Examples:

Some students spoke out about the restrictions.

John has a little money.

Neither student was late.

In these examples, the quantifiers indicate how many or how much of something there is.

Special Note: *a few/a little; few/little*

These words refer to a small quantity or amount of something. *Few* and *little* have a negative meaning. They indicate dissatisfaction.

I have *few* friends. (I am unhappy about it.)

I have *little* time. (I cannot help you.)

A few and *a little* have a positive meaning. They indicate satisfaction.

I have *a few* friends. (And I am happy about it.)

I have *a little* time. (It is enough. I can help you.)

We can add *of the* after all of the quantifiers listed earlier.

Some *of the* students spoke out about the restrictions.

John has a little *of the* money.

Neither *of the* students was late.

Notice that when we add *of the* to the quantifiers with singular-count nouns, the noun becomes plural but the verb remains singular, agreeing with the singular subject (*neither, each,* and so on).

One of the students is late.

Each of the students has agreed to help.

In the lists given previously, there are two exceptions. *Every* must become *every one* and *no* must become *not one* or *none*.

> *Every one* of the apples is rotten. (This means "every single one.")

> *None* of the teachers is coming.

In informal usage, the following is also acceptable:

> *None* of the teachers are coming.

When *of the* is added to the quantifiers listed previously, the meaning changes. Because the definite article was added, there is a definite meaning: part of an already known group or item. In the sentence "Some of the students did the homework," the writer has either mentioned the group of students earlier or assumes the reader is familiar with the group. Perhaps he means: "*Some of the students in our class did the homework.*" In the sentence "*John has a little of the money,*" perhaps he said earlier: "*John and I got some money for mowing the lawn.*"

EXERCISE G·15   Put *of the* in the blanks, if it is needed.

1. Many _____ Americans have started to buy small cars.

2. Most _____ Americans on the trip were from California.

3. On our trip, we visited ten cities. Several _____ cities were using solar power.

4. All _____ people are created equal.

5. Some _____ professional athletes receive critical injuries while playing.

EXERCISE G·16   Rewrite the following sentences, using the quantifiers given in italics. Make any necessary changes. The first one is done for you.

1. Most of the trees are dead because of the drought.

   One <u>One of the trees is dead because of the drought.</u>

2. All of the books on the second floor of the library have been stolen.

   None _____

3. Twelve of the members of Congress contact the president every day.

   Each _____

4. Several of the basketball players are sick.

   Each _____

5. Both of the singers also play the piano.

   Neither _____

EXERCISE G·17   Use *a, an, the,* or *of the* wherever you think necessary in the following paragraphs.

1. I think that high schools and universities should require their students to study foreign language, for educational purposes. In my case, for example, I started to study and learn English at age 13. Even though my mother spoke only English at home and I understood most of it, it was not until I changed to bilingual school that I started to learn more and speak it more fluently.

2. Learning another language offers lot of opportunities, too. Many jobs now require that person know another language. Jobs related to travel, hotels, and airlines are few examples. There are others, such as working with government and in business. One example of this is friend of mine who recently changed jobs. She used to be working in travel agency; she said her knowledge of English made lot of things easier for her. Just few weeks ago, I received letter from her saying that she is now working with U.S. Embassy in Honduras. She said that without English language she wouldn't be working there.

3. As we can see, students should learn second language. There are many advantages, especially when finishing school and job opportunities are great. For me it's great experience. Without knowing English, I wouldn't be working and studying in this university.

   —adapted from an essay by Carlos Palacio

EXERCISE G·18   In the following passage, insert *a, an,* or *the* wherever you think it is required. Before you do this exercise, review the discussion of articles in the previous sections. Rewrite the paragraphs on another piece of paper.

There are three types of honeybees: queens, workers, and drones. Each has its own role in life of hive, and to perform its functions properly each must be able to communicate with other individuals and to respond correctly to their communications. There is only one queen in colony. She is larger than other bees and is only fertile female. Her sole function is laying eggs. Except for brief period in her early adult life, when she leaves hive on few brief nuptial flights and mates with several males, she remains permanently within hive.

Workers are also female, but they are sterile and are smaller than queen. As their name implies, they perform everyday chores around hive—gathering food, feeding larvae and queen, storing surplus food, building hive and adding to it as more cells are needed for new eggs or more food, keeping hive and its inhabitants clean, and defending it against bees from other colonies.

Third type of honeybee is male bee, or drone. Drones have only one function: to mate with queen. They do little else, and except for their participation in mating flight, they lead idle life. During spring and summer, when drones still have some potential use, workers tolerate them, but as autumn approaches, workers drag them out of colony and leave them to die. No new drones are produced until following spring.

Three types of honeybee ensure perpetuation of species. Queen and drones attend to reproduction, and workers do housekeeping and care for eggs, larvae, pupae, queen, and drones. For all this to work properly, each bee must "know" what is needed from it. Some information comes to bee in its heredity—whether it is male or female—and this information is already present in egg. Other information comes from bee's environment. What it sees, smells, tastes, hears, or feels determines how it will act at given moment.

—adapted from Joan E. Rahn, *Biology: The Science of Life,*
2d ed. (New York: Macmillan, 1980), p. 39

Articles with Count and Noncount Nouns

In the previous sections, we reviewed some of the uses of articles. Here we review two final uses of articles.

Some nouns can be both countable and noncountable, especially those that come from verbs. The noncount noun indicates the act or thing itself. No article is used with a noncount noun:

Many of us seek a lifetime of *pleasure.*

The count noun refers to the product or result of the action. In this case, the article *a* can be used with a count noun:

It is *a* pleasure to meet you.

EXERCISE G·19 Fill in the article *a/an* if the noun is used in a countable sense.

1. Joyce hates _____ authority.

2. Professor Remby is _____ authority on the Middle East.

3. A parrot learns to speak through _____ imitation.

4. That vase is _____ imitation of an antique French vase.

5. _____ life is often difficult.

6. John has _____ difficult life.

7. "_____ possession is nine-tenths of the law."

8. He considers his violin _____ valuable possession.

It is also possible to use noncountable abstract nouns that have adjective modifiers with the article *a/an*. In these sentences, *a/an* usually means "a type of" or "a kind of." Note this example:

She had a *beauty* not often found in one so young.

Do not confuse this use of *a* with the use of *the* followed by an adjective modifier:

The beauty that he spoke of was not apparent to me.

EXERCISE G·20   Fill in either *a/an* or *the* in the blanks as appropriate.

1. She enjoys _____ atmosphere of gaiety and friendliness.

2. _____ atmosphere at the party was lively and free.

3. _____ distrust he felt after his friend abandoned him was understandable.

4. He feels _____ distrust of people that is inexplicable.

5. _____ popularity of that new song is due to its subject matter.

6. That song has _____ popularity that is hard to explain.

7. He felt _____ loneliness that almost overwhelmed him.

8. _____ loneliness that she felt was overwhelming.

Clauses (Ch. 3, 4)

Adjective Clauses (Ch. 4)

An *adjective clause* (sometimes called a *relative clause*) modifies a noun and, like an adverbial clause, is a dependent clause that cannot stand alone as a sentence; it must be connected to an independent clause. But unlike adverbial clauses, which can be placed either at the beginning or at the end of a sentence, an adjective clause can be placed *only after the noun it modifies*; it can never be placed at the beginning of a sentence. The subordinators that introduce adjective clauses include *who, whom, whose, that,* and *which.* Less common adjective clause subordinators are *when, where,* and *why.*

The subordinators *who, whom, that, whose,* and *which* can function either as the subject or as the object of an adjective clause. Compare:

The Empire State Building, *which is the second tallest building in New York City,* rises 1,250 feet in the air.

The Empire State Building, *which many tourists visit each year,* is the second tallest building in New York.

If the subordinator functions as the subject of an adjective clause, its verb agrees in number with the noun that the subordinator refers to:

Mr. Jones, *who is a marvelous cook,* invited us to dinner.

Bill and Eva Failla, *who are members of the Audubon Social Club,* are avid birdwatchers.

If the subordinator functions as an object in the adjective clause, the verb in the adjective clause agrees in number with its subject:

The house *that you are thinking about buying* has already been sold.

David Marchand, *whom I find unbearable,* has been assigned to my team.

Adjective Clause Subordinators

1. *Who* is used when referring to a person. *Who* is used as the subject of the adjective clause:

   The little girl is playing the violin. The girl is my cousin.
   = The little girl *who is playing the violin* is my cousin.

2. *Whom* is also used when referring to a person, but *whom* is used as an object in the adjective clause:

   My Uncle Boris is a writer. You met him earlier today.
   = My Uncle Boris, *whom you met earlier today,* is a writer.

3. Whose is used to show possession and functions as a possessive pronoun in the adjective clause:

   The artist is coming to our area soon. You adore his paintings.
   = The artist, *whose paintings you adore,* is coming to our area soon.

4. *Which* is used when referring to something other than a person. *Which* can function as the subject or object of an adjective clause:

> He has hideous eyes. These eyes *are* also colorless.
> = He has hideous eyes *which are also colorless.*
>
> You see the books here. These books are special.
> = These books *which you see here* are special.

5. *That* can be used when referring to a person, an animal, or a thing. *That* can function as the subject or the object of an adjective clause.

> I have really enjoyed the book. You gave me the book for my birthday.
> = I have really enjoyed the book *that you gave me for my birthday.*
>
> The trees are going to be cut down soon. The trees line Main Street.
> = *The trees that line Main Street* are going to be cut down soon. (Also: The trees *that are going to be cut down soon* line Main Street.)

6. *When* means approximately *"in which time"* or *"at which time."* Note the word order in this clause: *when* + subject + verb.

> My friends are still talking about the day. On that day I fell in the river.
> = My friends are still talking about the day *when I fell in the river.*

7. *Where* can be used to mean approximately *"at which place"* and introduces the adjective clause: The word order is *where* + subject + verb.

> Tourists in New Orleans visit the Old Mint. At that place United States currency used to be made.
> = Tourists in New Orleans visit the Old Mint *where United States currency used to be made.*

8. *Why* means *"for which"* when used to introduce an adjective clause: Again, the word order is *why* + subject + verb.

> You have not given me any reason. For which reason should I go out with you?
> = You have not given me any reason *why I should go out with you.*

EXERCISE G·21   Study the following sets of sentences carefully. Combine each set into one sentence using an adjective clause. Be careful to select the appropriate adjective clause subordinator. Note that there may be more than one way to combine the sentences.

1. The human eye is a remarkable optical instrument.
   The eye consists of very specialized structures.

   _____

   _____

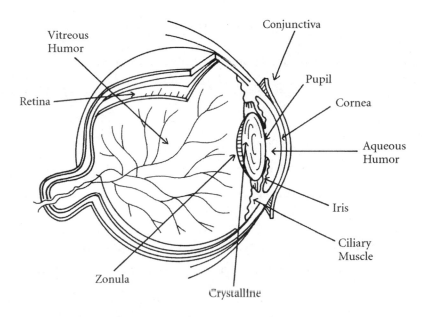

2. On the outside of the eye is the conjunctiva.
   The conjunctiva is a membrane.
   The membrane lines the inner surface of the eyelid and the outer surface of the front of the eyeball.

   _____

   _____

3. Behind the conjunctiva is the cornea.
   The cornea forms the image of an object.

   _____

   _____

4. The cornea is provided nutriment by the aqueous humour.
   The aqueous humour is located behind the cornea.

   _____

   _____

5. The colorful part of the eye is the iris.
   The iris helps control the amount of incoming light.

   _____

   _____

6. In the middle of the iris is the pupil.
   The pupil is really a hole.
   Light passes through this hole to the lens.

   _____

   _____

7. The crystalline lens is elliptical in shape.
   The lens helps the cornea bend the image.

   _____

   _____

8. On the sides of the lens are the ciliary muscle and zonula.
   These structures make the lens change shape, so the image changes in size.

   _____

   _____

9. Behind the lens is a big cavity.
   The cavity contains the vitreous humour.
   The vitreous humour is a clear, colorless jelly.

   _____

   _____

10. At the back of the cavity is the retina.
    The retina is a thin layer of interconnected nerve cells.
    These cells convert light to electrical pulses.

    _____

    _____

Punctuation of Restrictive and Nonrestrictive Adjective Clauses

Sometimes adjective clauses are set off by commas and sometimes they are not:

The trees *that line Main* Street are going to be cut down soon.

David Marchand, *whom I find unbearable,* has been assigned to my team.

The primary function of the clause determines the punctuation: to restrict the class of the noun it modifies or simply to add information about the clause. There are two types of adjective clauses: *restrictive* and *nonrestrictive*.

- *Restrictive adjective clauses: no commas.* Although all adjective clauses modify nouns, some adjective clauses serve mainly to *identify or define* the noun—in other words, to distinguish that noun from all other nouns in its class. If the clause serves this purpose, it is called *restrictive* and requires *no commas.* Look at the sentence cited earlier:

> *The trees that* line Main *Street are going to be cut down soon.*

- *Nonrestrictive adjective clauses: commas.* When the adjective clause is used primarily to provide additional information about the noun, the adjective clause is considered unessential for identifying the noun. This type of adjective clause is called *nonrestrictive* because it does not serve to restrict the class to which the noun belongs. Nonrestrictive adjective clauses require commas.

> David Marchand, *whom I find unbearable,* has been assigned to my team.

Special Note: *that* to Introduce Adjective Clauses

That is always used in restrictive clauses; therefore, *that* adjective clauses are not set off by commas.

EXERCISE G·22   In the following sentences, insert commas where appropriate.

1. My mother whom I love very much has decided to go to college.
2. One of the reporters who was assigned to South America was not able to go.
3. The cars that were parked along one block of Wilshire Boulevard were ticketed for illegal parking.
4. The man who played the Frankenstein monster in several movies was Boris Karloff.
5. Olaus Romer who was Danish was responsible for the first measurement of the velocity of light in 1676.

Adverbial Clauses of Time (Ch. 3)

Before discussing adverbial clauses, we should review some terms.

> *clause* — a clause is a group of words consisting of at least a *subject* and *verb.*
>
> *independent clause* — an independent clause can stand alone as a sentence.
>
> *dependent clause* — although a dependent clause has a subject and verb, it cannot stand alone because it does not express a complete thought. Dependent clauses begin with such words as *because, since, although, after, when, before, while, whereas, who,* and *why.* Dependent clauses must be attached to independent clauses.

subordinator, — these terms refer to adverbials that make a clause
subordinating conjunction   dependent, such as *when, because, although.*

Adverbial clauses are dependent clauses and must be attached to an independent
clause. Adverbial clauses can come at the beginning or at the end of the independent
clause. Look at these examples:

Sub + s + v
Before he leaves for the office,

s   +   v
he always reads the newspaper.

s   +   v
He always reads the newspaper

Sub + s + v
before he leaves for the office.

Note that when the adverbial clause comes at the beginning of the sentence, it
is often followed by a comma. However, if it comes at the end, there is no comma
separating it from the independent clause.

The adverbial clause is used to make the relationship between two clauses
clearer and tighter. An adverbial clause of time clarifies and tightens the time
relationship of two clauses. For example, look at the time relationship between
these sentences:

First I go to the store. Then I go home.

To make this passage flow more smoothly and to tighten the relationship of the
actions, these two clauses can be combined, making one an adverbial clause and
leaving one an independent clause:

After I go to the store, I go home.

Adverbial clauses of time, however, do not express just time alone; they express
time in relation to the independent clause in the sentence. The time in the
adverbial clause of time can occur simultaneously with, before, or after the time
in the independent clause. Let us review the time sequence in adverbial clauses
of time.

1. *While, as, during the time that, when, whenever.* The adverbial clause subordinators listed here indicate that the action in the adverbial clause occurs during
   the same time period as the action in the independent clause.

   • *While, as*—These subordinators often indicate that an action is in progress;
     therefore, the progressive tenses are frequently used with them. When
     the progressive is used in this adverbial clause, the simple tenses (simple
     present, simple past) are often used in the independent clauses.
   • *As the ranger* <u>was issuing</u> *us our permit,* he <u>warned</u> us of the bears.
     As I <u>am sitting</u> there at the table, I <u>look</u> around for a way to escape.
     I held the flashlight while *my brothers* <u>were setting</u> *up* the tent.

- *During the time that*—This expression is similar to *while* and *when*. Both the progressive and simple tenses can be used with this expression, depending on the action conveyed.

  During the time that we remained in the tent, I was very frightened.

- *When*—This subordinator indicates a point in time or a repeated or habitual occurrence; therefore, the simple tenses are generally used with it. Sometimes, however, the progressive tenses are used with it when it is used to mean "while."

  It was dark *when my two brothers and I arrived at the station.*

- *Whenever*—Unlike the other subordinates in this group, *whenever* usually takes only the simple tenses because it indicates a repeated or habitual action. (It means "each time that, every time that.")

  Whenever you call my name, I come running to you.

- Sometimes *whenever* can indicate that the action in the independent clause is future but is expected to be repeated.

  Whenever you call me up, I will come over immediately.

- When used with the past tense, *whenever* indicates that something happened regularly in the past.

  Whenever I was in trouble as a child, my mother would call me by my full name.

2. *Before, after.* These subordinators are used to indicate that the time in the adverbial clause occurs before or after the action in the independent clause.

   After we had put on our hiking boots, we set off down the trail. (First we put on our boots. After that, we set off down the trail.)

   Before we set off down the trail, we put on our hiking boots.

   Before the parade begins, the people stroll in the street.

In sentences like the first two, where there are two *past* actions and a sequence is established, the past perfect tense (*had* + past participle) can be used to indicate the *earlier* of the two actions. However, it is common practice to use the simple past tense in the adverbial clause.

   After we put on our hiking boots, we set off down the trail.

3. *Until, till, up to the time that.* These subordinators indicate that the time in the adverbial clause signals the end of the time in the independent clause.

> I stayed in my tent *until it was light outside.* (Then she left the tent.)

> "You cannot go outside *until you finish your spinach,*" the mother told her child.

4. *Since, ever since, from the moment (time) that.* These subordinators are used to indicate that the action in the independent clause began at the moment indicated in the adverbial clause and continues in the present. The simple past is usually used in the adverbial clause; the perfect tenses are used in the independent clause.

> *Ever since I was a child,* I have had the tendency to get angry easily.

> *From the moment I first saw her,* I have been in love with her.

5. *As soon as, the moment that, when, once.* These subordinators are used to indicate that the action in the independent clause will take place *upon completion* of the action in the adverbial clause. *When* is used less frequently in this way; if you want to make it clear that the action in the independent clause will take place right after the action in the adverbial clause, use *as soon as* or *the moment that.*

> *As soon as we arrived at a small clearing,* we began to set up camp.

> I turn on the television set *the moment that I get home.*

> *Once I arrive in Hong Kong,* I am going to visit my friend's parents.

Note: *Once* can also be used to mean "after."

Special Verb Tense Note

In adverbial clauses of time, the present tense is used even though the time indicated is future:

Before you *begin* to write your paper, you need to think about it.

I am going to stay here until he *arrives.*

We are giving him a party after he *returns* from Japan.

EXERCISE G·23   Read the following paragraphs about a Chinese folktale. Rewrite the paragraphs and combine the sentences using adverbial clauses of time. Be careful to use the appropriate subordinators. The first one is done for you. Your revised version should contain the following subordinators:

while	until	after
when	whenever	as soon as

(1) The night is clear and you can see shadows on the moon.

When the night is clear, you can see shadows on the moon.

> **(1)** *The night is clear and you can see shadows on the moon.* According to an old Chinese folktale, they are the shadows of the cinnamon tree in the moon. This tree came to be because of the laziness of an immortal, Wu Kang.
>
> Wu Kang was in charge of guarding the dragon. However, he was lazy. **(2)** *He drank wine and he often allowed the dragon to run away.* One day he went to Mount K'un Lun. **(3)** *He was there. During that time, he met some of his friends.* They began to drink wine, compose poems, and throw dice. He continued to drink, even after night came. **(4)** *He drank some more and finally, he became completely tipsy.* **(5)** *He saw some fellows playing chess, so he asked to join them.* They advised him to go home because they knew he was being negligent, but Wu Kang offered to wager the dragon's pearl. **(6)** *They played a few moves of the game. Then Wu Kang lost the pearl.* **(7)** *He had wagered and lost the dragon pearl. Immediately, he wagered and lost the mighty dragon.* **(8)** *The Immortals learned of the loss. They were furious.* They immediately sowed a pearl in the ground and a tall cinnamon tree grew from it. **(9)** *The tree reached a great height. After that, they gave Wu Kang an axe and told him to cut off the branches.* **(10)** *He had cut off all the branches. Immediately after that, bigger ones sprouted and grew.* Wu Kang had to cut them off, too. Wu Kang is still there to this day cutting off branches. **(11)** *Now, you see shadows on the moon, and you will know that they are the branches of the cinnamon tree falling down.*
>
> —adapted from *A Harvest of World Folk Tales,*
> ed. Milton Rugoff (New York: Viking, 1968), pp. 193–95

Adverbial Clauses of Comparison, Contrast, and Concession (Ch. 8)

For sentence variety and for even more smoothly flowing sentences, try to use adverbial clauses. Just as adverbial clauses of time are especially useful in narratives, adverbial clauses of comparison, contrast, and concession can be particularly useful in improving coherence in comparison-contrast writing.

- Adverbial Clauses of Comparison: *just as, in the same way that. Just as* (which means the same as *in the same way that*) indicates comparison:

    Just as Borges and Mishima differ in nationality, they also differ in educational background.

So is often used in the main clause following the clause that contains *just as*. Note the inverted subject-verb order:

> *Just as* "weasel words" are used to engender favorable impressions, so are euphemisms.

> *Just as* Bill is a fine student, so is his sister.

> *Just as* some people in the Northern Hemisphere are fortunate to see the northern lights, so are some people in the Southern Hemisphere, who can see the southern lights.

> *Just as* I wrote a letter to the senator, so did Sharon.

- Adverbial Clauses of Contrast: *while, whereas. While* and *whereas* are used to indicate contrast, and like most other adverbial clauses, they can occur at the beginning or at the end of a sentence.

> *Whereas* the northern lights are called the aurora borealis, the southern lights are called the aurora australis.

> The average male (gorilla) cranial capacity is 550 cc, *while* that of the female is about 460 cc.

Note: Unlike most other adverbial clauses that occur at the end of a sentence, *while* and *whereas* require commas before them. Also, note that *whereas* is the preferred subordinator to indicate contrast.

- Adverbial Clauses of Concession: *although, though, even though.* An adverbial clause of concession is a clause that admits a contrast or an unexpected idea. The subordinators roughly mean "despite the fact that." This type of clause is useful for comparison and contrast papers to concede a point. For example, if you are emphasizing contrasts in a paper, it may be necessary to admit that there are similarities. If you are emphasizing similarities, it may be useful to admit that there are apparent contrasts:

> *Although both the Speed Demon 280 and the Road Runner XL are quite similar,* I find they differ in safety features.

In this sentence, the writer is admitting that the two automobiles have similarities, but despite these similarities, they are different. Note these other examples of adverbial clauses of concession:

> *Although villages lack some services,* they still provide a better environment to raise children in.

> He refuses to retire, *even though he is now 70 years old.*

> *Though she was quite tired,* Mary continued to work hard.

As you may have guessed, *though* and *even though* are less commonly used than *although*. *Though* is more common in speech, and *even though* is usually used when the writer wants to be more emphatic than *although*.

Special Note: *even though* **and** *even*

Do not confuse *even though* and *even*. As you have seen, *even though* is a subordinator that introduces an adverbial (and therefore dependent) clause. *Even*, when used as an adverb, is a word used to intensify the meaning of another element in the sentence.

She looked tired, *even exhausted.*

Even John laughed at the joke. (Apparently John does not laugh much at jokes.)

My brother was *even more fanatical than I* about speaking English.

EXERCISE G·24   Read the following paragraphs about high school and college. Then write a sentence or two using the transitions given. The first one is done for you.

Most people like college better than high school. In high school, students have very little homework, maybe only a half hour a night. This means that they do not learn very much. In high school, students are constantly watched by the teachers and school officials. In order to go to the restroom, a student must get permission. If students do not attend classes, the principal will call their parents to check on them. Basically, students are treated as if they are children.

1. In college, students have a lot of homework.

    unlike <u>Unlike high school, in college students have a lot of homework.</u>

    while <u>While students have very little homework in high school, they have quite</u>

    <u>a lot in college.</u>

2. In college, nobody watches the students.

    different from _____

    on the other hand _____

    whereas _____

3. Students do not need permission to go to the restroom.

    unlike _____

    but _____

    while _____

4. No one calls the parents if students do not attend class.

    in contrast _____

    in contrast to _____

    whereas _____

5. Basically, in college students are treated as adults.

    however _____

    whereas _____

    different from _____

    Some college students think college is no different from high school. In college they have to study very hard, sometimes even reading a whole book in one night. They enjoy going to college football and basketball games and cheering for their team. They also enjoy talking with their classmates, who are basically just like them.

6. Students have to study hard in high school.

    just as _____

7. Students enjoy going to high school football and basketball games.

    just as _____

8. Students enjoy talking with their classmates in high school.

    just as _____

For each of the following items, combine the two sentences by using *although* or *even though* as appropriate.

9. High school students have very little homework. They learn a lot during their classes.

    _____

10. There are many rules in high school. They are meant to protect the students.

    _____

Adverbial Clauses of Purpose (Ch. 10)

In writing process and other types of compositions, it is often necessary to include the purpose for a particular step or action. That is, it is necessary to tell why or for what purpose something should be done. The phrase *in order* + infinitive is sometimes used to show purpose, as in, "Light the fire *in order to boil* the water." Often *in order* is left out without any change in meaning, as in, "Light the fire *to boil* the water."

The adverbial clauses of purpose also serve this function. Two conjunctions that introduce adverbial clauses of purpose are *so that* and *in order that*. Study these examples:

Wear gloves *so that* you will not cut your hands.

Put it away immediately *in order that* you will not forget it.

These two conjunctions are used in the same way and have the same meaning. However, *in order that* is more formal than *so that*.

It is important to note that a modal normally follows *so that* and *in order that*. Notice that in the preceding examples the modal *will* is used. This modal is usual in imperative sentences. However, in non-imperative sentences, *would* and *could* are the most common:

He saved his money *so that* he *could* buy a new car.

He did his work early *so that* he *would* not miss his favorite program.

EXERCISE G·25   Answer each of the following questions with two complete sentences. Write one sentence with *in order to* + an infinitive and the other with *so that*. The first one is done for you.

1. For what purpose should you think about your intended major?
   You should think about your intended major in order to choose a university that

   is well qualified and staffed in your major. You should think about your

   intended major so that you can choose the best university with that major.

2. For what purpose should you send for catalogs from different universities?

   _____

   _____

3. For what purpose should you think about your financial situation?

   _____

   _____

4. For what purpose should you find out about financial aid?

_____

_____

5. For what purpose should you find out about part-time jobs?

_____

_____

Adverbial Clauses of Cause and Result (Ch. 11)

Adverbial Clauses of Cause

Because, because of and *since* can be added to sentences to make adverbial clauses of cause. The adverbial clause can come at the beginning or the end of the sentence. When the clause comes at the beginning, it is followed by a comma.

Because these diseases are infectious, to a certain extent they are preventable.

Because of his delightful on-screen personality, Jackie Chan has charmed moviegoers around the world.

I did not speak to him *since* I did not remember his name.

Other transitions which can be used to introduce causes include *thus, therefore, as a result, consequently,* and *for this reason.* These transitions are used to connect two independent clauses. These transitions may begin a sentence which gives the cause of the result in the previous sentence, or they may connect two sentences when the transitional words are preceded by a semicolon and followed by a comma.

The assignment was turned in late. Thus, the professor lowered the student's grade.

Advertising may be very subtle; therefore, many people falsely believe it doesn't affect them.

Arnaud took a writing class. Consequently, his grades in his history class improved.

Women are becoming company managers more frequently; as a result, the rules of business communication have begun to change.

Small children's curiosity can put them in danger. For this reason, parents must monitor them carefully.

EXERCISE G·26   Following are four reasons for liking the study of biology. Write a sentence for each of the transitions given. Some of these transitions introduce adverbial clauses of cause. The first one is done for you.

1. Biology systematically classifies living things.

   because of _I like the study of biology because of its systematic classification of living things._

   so _Biology classifies living things in a systematic way, so I find it satisfies my need for order._

   thus _Biology has a systematic classification of living things. Thus, I find it useful in knowing the names of things._

2. Biology explains the characteristics of living things.

   because of _____

   for _____

   therefore _____

3. Biology explains the interdependence of living things.

   so _____

   as a result _____

   since _____

4. Biology encourages curiosity and research.

   consequently _____

   for this reason _____

   because _____

Adverbial Clauses of Result

Adverbial clauses of result are made by connecting two sentences with *so/such . . . that*. Note how the two sentences are connected in this example:

That building is tall. I cannot climb to the top.

That building is *so* tall *that* I can't climb to the top.

Note carefully the kind of word or phrase that must follow *so/such*:

She is *so* afraid *that* she hands me the can of Raid and runs for cover. [*so* + *adj* + *that*]

That elevator goes *so slowly that* I cannot wait for it. [*so* + *adverb* + *that*]

Johanne likes *so many things that* he cannot decide what to do next. [*so* + *few/many* + *plural noun*]

This car requires *so much gas that* I have decided not to buy it. [*so* + *much/ little* + *noncount noun*]

He gave me *such good advice that* I passed the test easily. [*such* + *adjective* + *noncount or plural count noun*]

It was *such a powerful movie that* I could not forget it. [*such* + *a/an* + *adjective* + *singular count noun*]

Note: The adverbial clause of result always comes at the end of the sentence, so no comma is needed.

EXERCISE G·27   Rewrite the following sentences to use the *so/such* . . . *that* pattern. The first one is done for you.

1. None of the planes could take off because the snowstorm was terrible.

   The snowstorm was so terrible that none of the planes could take off.

2. Because there were many people trapped in the airport, some of them slept on the floor.

   _____

   _____

3. Some of the people did not care about the snowstorm because they were having a good time.

   _____

   _____

4. However, some of the people demanded their money back because they were angry.

   _____

   _____

5. They said that they would never fly again because the airlines were giving bad service.

_____

_____

6. The airline officials explained that because it was snowing hard, the pilots could not see.

_____

_____

Noun Clauses (Ch. 7)

As Direct Objects

The most common use of noun clauses derived from statements is as direct objects. Note the following example:

I think *(that) he is a liar.*

Notice that the conjunction connecting the two sentences is *that. That* can be deleted if the meaning of the sentence remains clear. Next, notice the verb *think.* There are only certain verbs, like *think,* that are commonly followed by noun clauses. (For a complete list, see Appendix IX, page 419.) Some of the most common are: *agree, answer, believe, claim, decide, explain, forget, hear, know, learn, mean, realize, say, think.* A common use of noun clauses is in indirect or reported speech. Normally, quotation marks are used to indicate the *actual* words spoken by someone.

"The strike isn't over yet."

When these words are "reported" or told to a third person, they are often changed into indirect speech:

He said *that the strike wasn't over yet.*

The tense of the main verb affects the tense of the verb in the noun clause. If the tense of the main verb is past, the tense in the indirect statement changes as follows:

1. Present forms change to past:

"We *are* on strike."

He replied that they *were* on strike.

2. Simple past tense changes to past perfect tense:

> "We *went* on strike last week."

> He answered that they *had gone* on strike the week before.

Note: Pronouns and time expressions often must change to conform to the new time relationship.

3. The modals *will* and *can* change to *would* and *could*. When *must* means *have to*, it changes to *had to*.

> "The university *will* not offer more money."

> He asserted that the university *would* not offer more money.

Note: The modals *may, might,* and *should* remain the same.

4. If the noun clause expresses a generalization or historical fact, the tense in the reported statement may remain in the present.

> He said that John *hates* to jog. (a generalization)

> She said that Helena *is* the capital of Montana. (a historical fact)

EXERCISE G·28   You are a reporter for the school newspaper. Your assignment is to write an article about the strike by student workers in the cafeteria. Here is your interview with Ben Foster, the student who organized the strike.

REPORTER'S QUESTIONS	MR. FOSTER'S RESPONSES
"Mr. Foster, just who is on strike here?"	"All of the student workers are."
"How long have you been on strike?"	"Four days."
"Are any of the civil service employees on strike?"	"No, they are not on strike because they already have a satisfactory contract."
"Exactly why are the student workers on strike?"	"It's simple. We need higher wages."
"How much money do you make now? How much are you asking for?"	"Now we get only $3 an hour. That is below minimum wage. We must get at least $5.25 an hour."
"How has the strike affected the people who eat in the cafeteria?"	"The service is slower because there are no student workers to carry the trays or wash dishes. Now the cooks have to do our jobs."
"How long do you expect to continue the strike?"	"We will not go back to work until the administration is willing to negotiate."

On a separate sheet of paper, change all of Mr. Foster's statements into indirect speech. Try to use a variety of verbs to begin the sentences. (Check the list on page 339 or on page 419 for possible verbs.)

Noun Clauses Derived from Questions As Direct Objects

Statements are often used as noun clauses to function as direct objects. Noun clauses derived from questions, often called indirect questions, can also function as direct objects. Look at both "yes/no" questions and "WH-" questions (that is, questions asking *who, what, where,* and so on).

1. *Yes/no questions.* Note the following direct questions:

   "Does Mark like to jog?"

   "Is the president going to cooperate?"

   These yes/no questions are made into indirect questions by adding the conjunction *whether* (or *if*):

   I don't know *whether* (or not) Mark likes to jog.

   He didn't say *whether* the president was going to cooperate.

   Note that when the indirect yes/no question is added to the main clause, the auxiliary *do/does/did* is omitted and the subject and verb revert to statement word order.

2. *WH- questions.* Note the following direct questions:

   "Who is he?"

   "Who is living there?"

   "What does he want?"

   All of these questions can be added to a main clause by omitting the *do/does/did* auxiliary and changing the question to statement word order:

	WH-WORD	**SUBJECT**	**VERB**
I don't know	who	he	is.
I don't know	what	he	wants.
I don't know		who	is living there.

Note the subject-verb agreement with the *do/does* auxilliary is deleted.

   "What does he want?" I don't know what he wants.

EXERCISE G·29   Turn all the reporter's questions in Exercise G-28 into indirect speech. Try to use a variety of verbs to begin the sentences.

Examples:

The reporter asked Mr. Foster who was on strike.

I asked him who was on strike.

As Objects of Prepositions.   Indirect questions can also occur as objects of prepositions. Note the examples:

We are concerned about *whether (or not) he is telling the truth.*

She is interested in *how many people are striking.*

His question about *when to do the report* was ignored.

Subjunctive Noun Clauses

Some types of essays, such as the argumentative essay, conclude with a suggestion or recommendation for future action. A good sentence construction to use for this is a noun clause beginning with *that*.

I recommend that John *go* to the doctor immediately.

We are requesting that all students *take* the test.

Here is a list of the most common verbs used in this pattern:

urge   command   desire   propose   beg   stipulate   advise   require

move   recommend   forbid   suggest   ask   demand   request   insist

There are two other patterns that also advise and suggest, but these are used in more informal situations. The first one is with *should*.

They recommend that we *should arrive* on time.

The second pattern uses the infinitive after a noun phrase. It can be used after the following verbs:

advise   command   request   ask   desire   require   beg   forbid   urge

I strongly urge you *to take* math before chemistry.

We asked him *to consider* his position.

Note that these structures usually include an object for the verb. The subjunctive also occurs after certain adjectives:

advisable   vital   essential   desirable   imperative   good (better, best)
mandatory   important   requisite   necessary   urgent   crucial

Note the following examples:

It is advisable that she not *drive* this car until it is fixed.

It is urgent that Mr. Philo *get* my message today.

As with verbs, there are two other patterns using adjectives that can be used to advise and suggest in informal situations. The first one is *should*:

It is necessary that he *should* become aware of the situation.

The other—and more commonly used—alternative involves the form *for . . . to*:

It is important *for him to be* on time to class.

It is vital *for us to understand* the world situation.

Note that *for* is followed by an objective pronoun or a noun phrase.

EXERCISE G·30 Read the following situations, and write sentences in which you use the words in parentheses to give advice. The first one is done for you.

You are a university counselor. You have just had an hour-long session with two roommates, Lucy and Sandra. Lucy complained that Sandra never washes the dishes and leaves papers, books, and school projects all over the room. She also said that Sandra is always studying and never wants to have any fun or even just sit together and talk. Sandra complained that Lucy ignores her and constantly has friends in the room listening to music and making a lot of noise. She said that Lucy only wants to watch television, go to parties, and isn't concerned at all about her grades in school. The roommates have to live together for another three months. Write sentences of advice to help them learn to live together.

a. (*ask Lucy/Sandra to*) _____

_____

b. (*suggest*) _____

_____

c. (*advisable for . . . to*) _____

_____

d. (*propose*) _____

_____

e. (*important*) _____

_____

Comparisons (Ch. 8)

In the comparison and contrast essay, as well as in some other types of essays, you show how things are alike or different. To do this, you need to use a number of grammatical constructions that show similarities and differences. Following are some of the most important ones to review.

Indicators of Equality or Similarity

1. The following constructions are used to indicate equality or similarity between two items. They are all a part of a complete sentence. Note carefully how they are used:

John's coat	resembles	Bill's coat.
	is the same as	
	is like	
	is the same color (noun) as	
	is similar to	

   For those patterns using the verb *to be,* the two items being compared can be placed at the beginning of the sentence and the comparative adjectives put at the end. Note how the sentences change:

   John's coat and Bill's coat *are* the same.
   alike.
   the same color (noun).
   similar.

   Note: The word *resemble* does not have an adjective form, so it cannot be used in this pattern.

   Intensifiers are words that are used to emphasize or to show finer distinctions in comparisons. Except for *resemble* and *similar (to),* the preceding comparisons often use the intensifiers *exactly* and *just.* They always follow the verb *to be*:

   John's coat and Bill's coat are exactly the same.

2. The construction *as . . . as* is also used to indicate equality or similarity. It can be used in two ways. In the following sentences, two people are being compared:

(with adverbs)	Mark plays	as	forcefully	as Bill (does).
(with adjectives)	Mark is	as	strong	as Bill (is).
(with count nouns)	Mark has	as many	fine qualities	as Bill (does).

(with noncount nouns)   Mark has   as much enthusiasm   as Bill (does).
(with adjective + noun) Mark is   as good   an athlete   as Bill (is).

In the following sentences, two things about one person are being compared:

Mark plays tennis as well as *he plays* football.

Mark is as strong as *he is* tall.

Mark has as many tennis balls as *he has* footballs.

Mark has as much strength as *he has* courage.

In this pattern, the second subject and verb (italicized) are generally included for clarity. The intensifier *just* is common with the pattern *as . . . as*. It always precedes the first *as*:

Mark plays tennis *just* as well as he plays football.

All of these constructions can indicate inequality or dissimilarity by putting *not* in front of them. Study these examples:

Mary does *not resemble* her mother at all.

A computer programmer is *not the same as* a data clerk.

My mother is *not like* my Aunt Agatha.

John is *not the same height* as Tom.

This building is *not similar to* the Empire State Building.

These cars are *not the same size.*

New Orleans and New York City are *not similar.*

Sally is *not as pretty as* Margaret.

Martina Navratilova does *not play as many tennis matches as* she used to play.

Bill can*not swim as well as* he can play pool.

The intensifiers *nearly, exactly,* and *just* are common with the patterns in the first group above. *Resemble* and *similar* are exceptions. The intensifier *very* is common with *similar.* The intensifier follows *not*:

My mother is not *exactly* like my Aunt Agatha.

This building is not *very* similar to the Empire State Building.

The intensifiers *nearly* and *quite* are common with the patterns in the second group. The intensifier precedes the first *as*:

Sally is not *nearly* as pretty as Margaret.

John never has *quite* as much luggage as his wife.

Indicators of Inequality

1. The following construction is used to show the difference between two items. It is also part of a complete sentence. Note its use:

   John's coat is *different from* Bill's coat.

   The comparative adjective can be placed at the end of the sentence:

   John's coat and Bill's coat are *different*.

   The intensifiers *a little, somewhat, much,* and *completely* are useful in this pattern. The intensifier precedes *different*:

   John's coat is *a little* different from Bill's coat.

   Note: The noun *difference* can also be used for inequality. Note its use:

   The major *difference* between the two coats is length.

   There is a great deal of *difference* between you and me.

2. The construction *adjective/adverb* + *-er than* is also used to show difference or inequality. *Adjective/adverb* + *-er than* (like *like* and *as . . . as*) can be used in two ways: to contrast two people in reference to a quality or action or to contrast two qualities or actions in reference to one person. Use this pattern with the following kinds of adjectives and adverbs:
   a. Most one-syllable adjectives and adverbs:

   John is *older than* Bill (is).

   John can kick the ball *farther than* he can throw it.

   b. Two-syllable adjectives ending in *y* or *-ow*:

   John is *lazier than* his sister (is).

   The river is *shallower than* it is long.

Note: The following adjectives and adverbs have irregular comparative forms:

ADJECTIVES	**ADVERBS**
good—better	well—better
far—farther (further)	far—farther (further)
bad—worse	badly—worse

3. The construction *more* [adjective/adverb/noun] *than* is commonly used to show difference. Use this pattern with the following kinds of adjectives and adverbs:

a. Most two-syllable adjectives and adverbs:

Chemistry 101 is *more* basic *than* Chemistry 102 (is).

He plays *more* honestly *than* he does effectively.

b. All adjectives and adverbs with more than two syllables:

John is *more* successful *than* Bill (is).

John works *more* consistently *than* he does efficiently.

c. All adjectives derived from verbs:

John is *more* demanding *than* Bill (is).

John is *more* bored with life *than* he is interested in it.

Use this pattern with count and noncount nouns:

John has *more* books *than* Bill (does).

John has *more* enthusiasm *than* he has intelligence.

The intensifiers *much, a lot* and *a little* are used with the adjective and adverbs discussed in paragraphs 4 and 5. The intensifier precedes the comparative adjective or the word *more*:

John is *much* older than Bill.

John is *much* more intelligent than he is sociable.

The intensifiers *many, a lot,* and *a few* are used with count nouns. The intensifiers *much,* a *lot,* and *a little* are used with noncount nouns. The intensifier precedes *more*:

John has *many* more books than Bill does.

John has a *little* more enthusiasm than Bill does.

Special Note: *less* **and** *fewer*

To indicate a smaller amount or number, we can replace *more* with *less* for use with adjectives, adverbs, and noncount nouns. We can replace *more* with *fewer* for use with count nouns.

This is a *less* exciting movie *than* the one on television.

This class has *fewer* students *than* my history class.

Note: *Than* can also be followed by a clause in more complex sentences.

This is a *less* exciting movie *than* the one we saw last week.

This class has *fewer* students *than* I can ever remember.

EXERCISE G·31   Read the following paragraph about gorillas and the list of statements about chimpanzees. For each item in the list, write a one-sentence comparison of the two animals. Use *same, like, alike, similar, different,* or *difference* as appropriate. The first one is done for you.

> Gorillas belong to the highest order of mammals—the primates. Gorillas have a restricted range; they live either in the mountains of Zaire or in several countries along the west coast of equatorial Africa. A male gorilla averages about 5 feet in height and weighs between 400 and 500 pounds. Females are smaller than males. Gorillas live in family groups. At night, the females and young sleep in a crude nest of twigs and leaves in the trees. Because of his weight, the male sleeps on the ground at the base of the tree. The gorilla's big toe is opposable; that is, it can move freely and pick up objects. Gorillas eat fruits, nuts, and vegetables.

1. Chimpanzees are classified as primates.

   The chimpanzee's classification is the same as the gorilla's classification.

   The classification of the chimpanzee and the gorilla is the same.

   The chimpanzee has the same classification as the gorilla.

2. The chimpanzee's range includes a lot of African countries.

   _____

3. An adult chimpanzee is about 5 feet tall.

   _____

4. An adult chimpanzee weighs up to 140 pounds.

_____

5. Female and young chimpanzees sleep in a nest of twigs in a tree at night.

_____

6. Male chimpanzees sleep in a nest of twigs in a tree at night.

_____

7. The chimpanzee's thumb is opposable.

_____

8. Chimpanzees eat fruit, nuts, and vegetables.

_____

EXERCISE G·32   Compare and contrast the city or town you live in now with another city you are familiar with. Use the constructions *as . . . as* and *-er/more . . . than.* You can add *not* to both of these constructions. Write fifteen sentences on a separate sheet of paper.

Example: San Diego is an *older* city *than* Houston.

Correlative Conjunctions (Ch. 9)

Coordinating conjunctions (*and, but, yet*) can be used as transitions to give writing coherence. Correlative conjunctions can also connect two sentences together, just as regular conjunctions do.

The correlative conjunctions include

both . . . and
either . . . or
neither . . . nor
not only . . . but also

Note how these pairs of words are used in the following sentences:

The Corolla and the Taurus differ *not only* in ride but *also* in mileage.

Both Nhan *and* Hung want to do good things for human beings.

You can take the test *either* on Monday *or* on Wednesday.

It has *neither* a good price *nor* good gas mileage.

Correlative conjunctions add clarity and coherence to writing by signaling the relationship between the two ideas in the sentence. When reading the first one of the pair, the reader immediately knows the second one is to follow and what the relationship between the two ideas is. However, with a regular conjunction in a compound sentence, this relationship is not clear until the reader reaches the second part of the sentence. Compare:

That professor is not a good lecturer, *and* he is not a fair grader.

That professor is *neither* a good lecturer *nor* a fair grader.

The position of the correlative conjunctions in the sentence is important. Each conjunction comes just before the item it is comparing. Further, the grammatical elements that follow correlative conjunctions should be parallel: that is, they should both be verbs, nouns, infinitives, and so on. Study these examples:

Both . . . and

Both *John* and *I* love to ski. (nouns)

John loves both *to ski* and *to dance*. (infinitives)

Either . . . or

Bill will either *take out* the trash or *wash* the dishes. (verbs)

He is not only *rich*, but he is also *talented*. (adjectives)

Note: *Not only* and *nor* can come at the beginning of the clause for emphasis. When they start a clause, a form of the verb *to be* or an auxiliary verb immediately follows it. Note the following examples:

Not only . . . but also

Not only is *he rich, but he* is *also talented*.

Mozart composed not only *for piano*, but also *for violin*.

Mozart not only *composed* for piano, but also *wrote* for violin.

Not only did Mozart *compose* for piano, but he also *wrote* for violin.

Neither . . . nor

I have read neither *the book* nor *the short story*. (nouns)

I have neither *read* the book nor *seen* the movie. (verbs)

Pay attention to subject-verb agreement with *neither . . . nor, either . . . or,* and *not only . . . but also.* With a compound subject, the verb agrees with the nearer part of the subject. Study these examples:

Neither John nor Bill *is* excited about the party.

Either the boys or their sister *is* feeding the dog.

Neither John nor his brothers *are* interested in this book.

Not only Bill but also Mary *is* intending to go with us.

EXERCISE G·33   Combine the two sentences in each item using the correlative conjunction given.

1. (*both . . . and*) Physics is classified as a physical science. Chemistry is classified as a physical science.

   _____

   _____

2. (*neither . . . nor*) We cannot classify mathematics as a biological science. We cannot classify psychology as a physical science.

   _____

   _____

3. (*not only . . . but also*) Botany and zoology are normally considered biological sciences. They are generally requirements for a B.S. degree.

   _____

   _____

4. (*either . . . or*) All liberal arts majors have to take two physical science courses. Instead, all liberal arts majors could take two biological science courses.

   _____

   _____

5. (*not only . . . but also*) In order to graduate, all students in college must take certain required courses. They have to take some electives.

   _____

   _____

Gerunds and Infinitives (Ch. 7)

Gerunds and Infinitives as Subjects

We all are familiar with nouns—persons, places, or things—that act as subjects. However, there are some verb forms in English that can also function as nouns. They are the *-ing* form—or gerund—and the *to + verb* form—or infinitive. In the following sentences, the gerund and infinitive function as nouns in the subject position:

Jogging is good for your circulation.

To find a jogging partner can be difficult.

When the infinitive is the subject, as in the second sentence, it is very common to move it (and its modifiers) to the end of the sentence and place *it* in the subject position: *It* can be difficult *to find* a jogging partner.

If the gerund has a specific subject in front of it, the possessive form is used:

Bill's running down the hall in the dorm disturbs us.

His running down the hall in the dorm disturbs us.

Finally, when the subject of a sentence is a gerund or infinitive, the subject of the sentence is singular and must agree with a singular verb:

The boy's *stealing* the basketballs *is* a serious offense.

EXERCISE G·34   Combine the following sentences, using first a gerund, then an infinitive, and finally *it* in the subject position. Then determine which is the most common usage. The first one is done for you.

1. She takes a math course every semester. This is difficult.

   Taking a math course every semester is difficult.

   To take a math course every semester is difficult.

   It is difficult to take a math course every semester.

2. During the semester, she goes to class every day. This is a good idea.

   _____

   _____

   _____

3. She takes notes as the professor does the sample problems on the board. This is useful.

_____

_____

_____

4. She does the homework problems regularly. This takes time.

_____

_____

_____

5. She turns the homework in every day. This gives her a sense of satisfaction.

_____

_____

_____

6. She gets good grades. This is the best reward.

_____

_____

_____

Gerunds and Infinitives as Objects

As noted earlier, regular nouns are often used as subjects. It is also common to use regular nouns as direct objects (DO):

The coach arranged the *meeting*.

Further, gerunds, and infinitives can function as subjects of sentences. Like regular nouns, after certain verbs, gerunds, and infinitives can also function as objects. Observe the following examples:

He agreed *to run* four miles a day.

He enjoys *playing* tennis.

The number of verbs that can use gerunds and infinitives as objects is limited. For a complete list of these verbs, see Appendix IX. There are several other restrictions on these verbs to keep in mind.

1. The following verbs cannot have a second subject before the gerund or infinitive:

   a. These are some of the most common verbs followed by gerunds: *avoid, enjoy, finish, keep on, practice, resume, quit.*

   > He enjoys *playing* tennis.

   b. These are some of the most common verbs followed by infinitives: *agree, decide, hope, learn, pretend, try, want.*

   > He is learning *to play* tennis.

   c. These verbs can be followed by either gerunds or infinitives: *begin, continue, intend, like, start.*

   > Bill starts *jogging* at 7:00 A.M.

   > Bill starts *to jog* at 7:00 A.M.

   Note: After the verbs *remember* and *stop*, the gerund and infinitive have different meanings:

   > I remember *buying* stamps yesterday. (I bought stamps yesterday and now remember that action.)

   > I remembered *to buy* stamps yesterday. (I bought stamps yesterday because I remembered that I was supposed to.)

   > Anna stopped *visiting* me. (She doesn't visit me anymore.)

   > Anna stopped *to visit* me. (Anna visited me.)

2. The following verbs must have a second subject before the infinitive. Most of the verbs in this class involve one person telling or advising another person.

   a. Here are some common verbs: *advise, permit, remind, tell, warn.*
   He advised *me* to practice for the interview.

   b. After the following verbs, the *to* of the infinitive is deleted:
   (1) Causatives: *have, let, make.*
   (2) Verbs of observation: *feel, hear, notice, see, watch.*

   > Bill *had* the janitor open the door.

   > We *saw* Kim leave the office.

3. The following verbs can occur with or without a second subject: *ask, choose, expect, help, like, want.*

   > I expected *to go* to the track meet.

   > I expected Mario *to go* to the track meet.

Notice that there is a difference in meaning between the two sentences. In the first sentence, the subject of the verb *expect, I,* will perform the action of *to go.* In the second sentence, *I* is the subject of *expect,* but Mario is the subject of *to go.*

EXERCISE G·35   Write either the gerund or infinitive form of the verbs in the blanks. If both are possible, write both. If an infinitive is preceded by a second subject, draw a line under the second subject. Remember to check Appendix IX, pages 415–419, for a list of verbs followed by infinitives and gerunds.

Pedro Reyes is a good example of a young philanthropist. Born in Mexico, Pedro came to the United States with his mother and sister in 1980 when he was six years old. They were hoping (have) _____ a good future. But (achieve) _____ that goal was difficult because they were poor and lived in a part of Los Angeles where there were gangs. In high school, Pedro joined the Youth Community Service Club; this experience changed his life. He decided that he should start (improve) _____ himself and (contribute) _____ to the community. He became interested in helping other people. He has volunteered his services numerous times. In 1987, he encouraged some of his classmates (join) _____ him in helping newly arrived students from Cambodia and South America (adjust) _____ to their new life. He has also helped (lead) _____ outdoor games for the blind at the Braille Institute. This is impressive since he only learned (speak) _____ English fairly recently. In addition, he has kept students from dropping out of school and has discouraged at least one from (join) _____ a street gang. He has also enjoyed (do) _____ other volunteer community work. For example, he once helped (organize) _____ a "Wipe Out Weekend," during which students from all over the Los Angeles area agreed (paint) _____ over the ugly graffiti that can be seen all over the area. He has also spent some of his weekends (clean up) _____ inner-city neighborhoods for the Los Angeles Beautiful group and has even helped (plant) _____ trees around

L.A. He has also volunteered (help) _____ at the Children's Museum (handle) _____ the weekend crowds. Pedro plans (go) _____ to college next year, but he expects (continue) _____ (do) _____ volunteer work. He is truly a "teenager who learned philanthropy as a second language."

—adapted from D. Devoss, "Angels Among Us," *Los Angeles Times Magazine*, December 18, 25, 1988

Gerunds as Objects of Prepositions

There are a number of common expressions and verbs in English that are predictably followed by a certain preposition. These expressions and *verb + preposition* combinations can be followed by gerunds. Some of the most common are the following:

look forward to	plan on	be nervous about	be afraid of
get used to	count on	be excited about	be tired of
be used to	insist on	be concerned about	be capable of
be accustomed to	be interested in	be good at	be accused of

Observe the following examples:

I am looking forward to *seeing* you on Tuesday.

I did not plan on *spending* so much money on my vacation.

The advisor is interested in *helping* him.

The new students were nervous about *living* in the dormitory.

The president is capable of *handling* the situation.

EXERCISE G·36   Write either the gerund or infinitive form of the verb in each blank. If both are possible, write both. Where (P) is indicated, fill in the correct preposition.

Most college students go to college in order to be trained for a particular profession. Many look forward _____ (P) (work) _____ as competent engineers, teachers, or chemists. Before they can begin (work) _____, however, they must find a job. Usually, they are interested _____ (P) (find) _____ a job that offers a good salary and a chance for promotion. The first hurdle for them (jump) _____ is the job interview. Even though they may be well qualified, getting the right job can be difficult if they are not prepared (handle) _____ the job interview. Kim's experience is a good example.

While in school, Kim worked hard to learn his chosen profession, computer science. When a program did not work properly, Kim kept _____ (P) (try) _____ until it did. He never hesitated (ask) _____ his professors about aspects of computer science that he did not understand. He even managed (work) _____ in the computer room on campus to get experience. All of his professors agreed that Kim was a well-qualified graduate.

A month before Kim graduated with a B.S. degree, his advisor encouraged him (sign) _____ up for an interview with a large company. The company needed someone (be) _____ a programming supervisor. Kim thought he would be good _____ (P) (do) _____ that job because he had always enjoyed (work) _____ with people.

A week before the interview, Kim became nervous _____ (P) (make) _____ a bad impression. So, he asked his advisor (give) _____ him some help. His advisor told him (make) _____ a list of possible questions and (practice) _____ (answer) _____ them. He also urged him (not be) _____ afraid _____ (P) (say) _____ anything too controversial. Finally, his advisor assured him that he was capable _____ (P) (handle) _____ the job. Kim thanked his advisor for his encouragement and agreed (practice) _____ (answer) _____ some possible questions.

As Kim waited in the outer office to meet the interviewer, however, all of good advice seemed (fly) _____ out the window. For a brief moment, considered (escape) _____ out the side door. The next thing he he was sitting across the desk from the interviewer trying (remember)

_____ all the answers he had planned _____ (P) (give)

_____. Although he had practiced and was used _____ (P)

(give) _____ the right answers, at the moment he could only stutter and

stammer. To this day, he can only remember that the interview was very short!

You can see that a person can be well qualified for a job but fail (get)

_____ it because he or she is not accustomed _____ (P) (per-

form) _____ in a job interview. Perhaps for students like Kim, how to

manage a job interview should be a required course in college.

Verb/Tense System

The Simple Present vs. The Present Progressive (Ch. 3)

The present tense is often used for narratives and other kinds of writing to indicate that the action takes place habitually or is in the process of occurring. Review the two paragraphs in Chapter 3 (pages 45–46) that describe a typical morning at a Rex Parade. Which present tense is used? As you can see, the simple present tense predominates. Although the simple present tense is generally used in narrations that take place in the present time, occasionally you will need to use the present progressive (*be* + present participle) as well. Study the following passage and observe the use of the two present tenses:

> Much of David's life is centered around his future career. He wants to be a sports announcer, so he is attending the University of California and majoring in communications. This semester, he is taking his first course in broadcasting. Next week, he is giving his first demonstration broadcast, and he is planning to demonstrate his skills in sports announcing. He does not know how he will do; in fact, he worries about it all the time. He does not want to fail, so each night he practices in front of the television while a basketball game is going on. He always records his practice session on a tape recorder. A typical practice broadcast begins like this:
>
> "Good evening, Ladies and Gentlemen, this is David Swenson reporting live tonight from the press booth at the new sports arena in downtown Pleasantville. The arena is filled to capacity tonight, and the fans are anxiously waiting for the game to begin. As you know, the Pleasantville Bears are playing the Hick City Colts. There appears to be a good deal of excitement in the arena tonight! Here they come! The fans are cheering wildly! Yes, folks, this crowd loves its team. The game is about to begin as the players assume their

positions on the court for the tip-off. The referee tosses the ball in the air, and Long Tall Jones, wearing jersey number twenty-two, tips it to his teammate Tommy Evans. Evans races down the court and slips the ball to Raoul Gomez. Gomez breaks through the defensive line, shoots, and he misses! Robinson is there. He catches the rebound and lays that ball in. The crowd is going wild! Pleasantville takes the lead. . . ."

After he finishes the practice broadcast, David plays it back on his recorder and takes notes. Each time he improves his performance.

Although this passage is done in the present tense, the author uses both the simple present tense and the present progressive. Although both describe present time, the simple present and the present progressive convey different actions and times.

The Simple Present Tense

1. The simple present tense is usually used to describe repeated, habitual, or characteristic actions. The adverbs of frequency will help by signaling the need for the simple present, but sometimes those adverbs are not present, even though their meaning is there.

   A band usually *marches* by, playing a popular tune.

   Each night the lonely old lady *feeds* the ducks.

   Each night he *practices* in front of the television.

2. Some verbs, sometimes called *stative verbs,* are almost always used in the simple present form when they are not describing the past. These verbs describe states of being, not actions. These verbs relate sensory perceptions, conditions, judgments, conclusions, emotional states, or states of being. The following are examples of stative verbs:

   wants   see   loves   sounds   appears   seem   think   am/is/are   have/has

   David *wants* to be a sports announcer.

   There *appears* to be a good deal of excitement here.

3. A few verbs are used in the simple present tense even though they describe future actions. Fortunately, not many verbs are in this group, which includes *begin, leave, depart,* and *arrive.* These verbs generally describe acts of arriving and departing, and beginning and ending.

   The game *begins* in ten minutes.

   The plane *leaves* for Bermuda in the morning.

Note: These types of verbs can also be used in the present progressive to convey future actions.

4. The preceding three uses are the most common; however, there are some less common uses of the simple present to be aware of.

   a. The simple present can be used to describe the steps in demonstrations, such as a scientific experiment.

      We first *put* the solution in the flask, and then we *place* the flask in warm place.

   b. The simple present is often used in announcements and in newspaper headlines.

      Floods *destroy* ten homes in the canyon.

      Earthquake *hits* Mexico City.

The Present Progressive Tense

1. The present progressive is used to describe a single action that is in progress at a specific moment, usually the moment of speaking or writing.

   Samson *is studying* the lesson right now.

   The people *are cheering* wildly!

2. The present progressive may also be used to describe an action in progress over a long period of time, even though the action may not be taking place at the moment of speaking or writing. This action, however, is perceived as temporary.

   David *is attending* the University of California. (He may be on vacation at the moment of speaking, but he is still a registered student there.)

   She *is writing* her first novel. (The pen may not be in her hand at this precise moment, but the activity is going on during the present time span and will end at some time in the future.)

3. The present progressive can be used to express a future action, especially when that action is in the near future. Usually, you need adverbials of time to clarify that the present progressive is indicating future time.

   Next week he *is giving* his first demonstration.

   The ship *is arriving* this afternoon at three o'clock.

   We *are taking* the exam later this afternoon.

4. The present progressive can also express the beginning, progression, or end of an action in the present time.

It *is beginning* to get hot.

It *is starting* to rain again.

My writing *is getting* worse.

Note: The verb *to be* is rarely used in the progressive because it describes a general state of being. There are rare instances, however, when you do use the verb *to be* in the progressive:

My child *is being* obnoxious right now. Please excuse him.

In this instance, the progressive is used because the meaning is, "My child is acting obnoxiously right now." The child is not generally obnoxious.

EXERCISE G·37   Read the following passages carefully. Then fill in each blank with the correct present tense: the simple present or the present progressive.

At the end of each semester as final exams (approach) _____, I (have) _____ the same scary dream. I (dream) _____ that I have forgotten to drop a class that I have not attended since the first week of school. I (rush) _____ to the administration building where there (be) _____ always a long line. After nervously waiting in line, I (get) _____ up to the window and (inquire) _____ about dropping the class. The clerk always (tell) _____ me that I (can) _____ not drop the course because it (be) _____ too late. I then (realize) _____ that I (have) _____ to take the final exam. In the next scene, I (sit) _____ in a room in a very old library, which (smell) _____ like dusty books. There (be) _____ several other students who (wait) _____ at tables all around me. Everyone (look) _____ very serious. All of the other students (wear) _____ formal clothes. Suddenly, I (realize) _____ that I (wear) _____ my pajamas. Since I (feel) _____ embarrassed and humiliated, I (try) _____ to conceal my pajamas by sliding down in my chair. As I (sit) _____ there at the table, I (look) _____ around for a way to escape, but it (be) _____ impossible. I cannot do anything because the instructor (start) _____ to pass out the exams. When I (get) _____ my exam

and (read) _____ the questions, my heart suddenly (sink) _____,

for I (find) _____ that I (not know) _____ any of the answers.

In fact, I (not even recognize) _____ any of the material on the exam.

Nevertheless, I try to take the exam. Just as I (start) _____ to write, the

bell (ring) _____. While the bell (ring) _____, I (cry)

_____, "No, no! Please, I need more time!" Then I (wake up)

_____ and (realize) _____ that it is my alarm clock going

off. Thank God it is always just a dream!

The Simple Past vs. The Past Progressive and the Past Perfect (Ch. 3)

To write a good narrative paragraph about something that happened in the past, it is imperative that you review the most common forms of the past tense used in this kind of writing: the simple past, the past progressive, and the past perfect. Although these tenses are not the only ones used in paragraphs written about an event that takes place in the past, they are the most common ones. Study the following paragraph about a memorable and tragic day that the author remembers vividly. Note the author's use of the past tenses.

It started out as a nice enough day. The weather was unusually warm for the third week in November, so I was in a good mood when my mother dropped me off at school. Everything went as usual that morning: the classes were boring and nothing exciting was happening. At noon, I went to the cafeteria for lunch. While I was standing in line with my friends, I noticed that some of the other students were excited about something. Then a girl in line asked me if I had heard that someone had shot the president. I was surprised at this news; however, I figured that it was probably just a minor wound. Suddenly, a voice came over the loudspeaker announcing that the president was dead. There was a hush in the cafeteria. Students stopped eating. No one was moving; it was as if we were all frozen. That afternoon, the teachers did not conduct the classes as usual; in fact, most of the teachers allowed the students to express their feelings about what had happened. Even my old stodgy English teacher did not conduct class as usual. She did not give us the exam that she had planned for that day. After school, I went home. Fortunately, no one was home, for I wanted to be alone. Finally, after three hours of containing my emotions, I began to cry. I was still crying when my mother arrived home. She came into my room, put her arms around me, and said, "This is a sad day for our country." Yes, November 22, 1963, was a sad day, a tragic day that was the beginning of a long, difficult period in American history.

The Simple Past Tense

The simple past tense indicates that an action occurred or a situation existed at a known moment in the past or during a period of time in the past.

> It *was* nearly dark when my two brothers and I *arrived* at the ranger station.

> Everything *went* as usual that morning.

The Past Progressive Tense

The past progressive tense indicates that an action began and continued over a period of time in the past. It is also used to describe an action that is going on at a particular time in the past.

> I *was* still *crying* when my mother arrived.

> No one *was moving* during that time.

The past progressive is often used in adverbial clauses of time with *while* and *as* to indicate an action that occurs at the same time as the action in the independent clause.

> *While* I *was standing* in line with my friends, I noticed that some of the students were excited about something.

> *As* the ranger *was issuing* us our camping permit, he warned us to be careful.

The Past Perfect Tense

The past perfect tense indicates that one past event occurred before another past event. The past perfect is used to describe the event that occurred first.

> She did not give us the exam that she *had planned* for that day.

> After we *had put* on our hiking boots, we set off down the trail.

In strict chronological sequence, or when adverbials make the time relationship clear, the past perfect is often unnecessary. In these cases, the simple past tense is used instead.

> First we *put* on our hiking boots, and then we set off down the trail.

> After we *put* on our hiking boots, we set off down the trail.

However, when the amount of time leading up to the first event is given, the past perfect is necessary.

I *had known* her for three years when she left.

It *had* just *begun* to rain when we got out of the theater.

The past perfect is often used with the expressions *no sooner . . . than* and *hardly. . . when.*

I *had no sooner begun* to work *than* the telephone rang.

We *had hardly started* to fish *when* it began to rain.

EXERCISE G·38

1. Following are some facts about Albert Einstein's life.* Keeping these facts in mind, fill in the correct verb tense for each verb in the paragraphs that follow. Use the simple past, past progressive, or past perfect tense.

   Albert Einstein

   1879—born
   1880—moved to a suburb of Munich
   1889—sent to Leopold Gymnasium (high school)
   1893—read a series of natural science books
   1894—his parents moved to Milan, Italy
   1895—left Munich for Milan
   1896—admitted to Zurich Polytechnic Institute
   1900—graduated from Zurich Polytechnic Institute
   1901—began to publish
   1902—obtained a job in the Swiss Patent Office in Berne

   Albert Einstein was one of the greatest scientists of the twentieth century.

   His theories have affected all of modern science. However, as a child, this

   great man (be) _____ often considered dull and (be) _____

   misunderstood by his teachers.

   Albert Einstein (be) _____ born in Ulm, Germany, on March

   14, 1879. As a child, he (be) _____ taciturn and slow in learning

   to talk. Very often, while other children (play) _____, he (day-

   dream) _____ and (think) _____.

   Although he (enjoy) _____ learning, he (have) _____

* Information from G. J. Whitrow, *Einstein The Man and His Achievement* (London: British Broadcasting Corp., 1967).

problems in school. By the time Einstein (be) _____ twelve, his family (move) _____ to a suburb of Munich, and he (attend) _____ the Leopold Gymnasium there for two years. He did not enjoy learning Latin and Greek grammar or mathematics at school because the standard methods of solving problems (not arouse) _____ his imagination. However, he (like) _____ solving algebra problems in his own way at home. Also, by the time he (be) _____ fifteen, he (read) _____ a number of books on natural science and (develop) _____ an enthusiasm for it. Later in 1895, when Albert (want) _____ a discharge from the gymnasium to join his parents, who previously (move) _____ to Milan, his teacher (help) _____ him get one, telling Albert that he (be) _____ a disruptive influence in the class.

His problems with school (follow) _____ him to Milan. In 1895, he (decide) _____ to go to the famous Polytechnic Institute in Zurich, Switzerland. However, because he (not receive) _____ a gymnasium diploma from his school in Munich, the Institute (refuse) _____ to admit him. He (go) _____ to a gymnasium in Aarau to obtain his diploma. After Einstein (receive) _____ it, the Institute finally (admit) _____ him at the age of seventeen.

While Einstein (study) _____ at the Polytechnic Institute, he again (clash) _____ with the educational system. He often (cut) _____ classes to study more interesting subjects on his own. This (anger) _____ his professors. By the time he (get) _____ his diploma in 1900, he (anger) _____ his theoretical physics professor so much that this professor (prevent) _____ Albert from becoming an assistant at the Institute.

Finally, in 1910, Einstein (begin) _____ to publish his revolutionary ideas. Eventually, the whole world (recognize) _____ his genius.

EXERCISE G·39 Writing Assignment   Study the following list of information. As you will notice, all of the verbs are in the simple present tense. Use this information to write a narrative paragraph in the past time. The times given at the left will help you determine the chronological order; do not mention the times given in your paragraph. In the paragraph, use time-sequence markers and adverbial clauses of time. You must include at least one sentence for each of the following subordinators of time: *while, when, as soon as, after.* If you want to use others, you may. Be sure that the verb tenses accurately describe the time you want to indicate. In addition, the paragraph should have a topic sentence with a controlling idea about this incident. The controlling idea could deal with the lesson that Patrick learned. You can add information if you wish.

Thursday night: Patrick goes to a party instead of studying for his biology exam.

Friday

10:00—The bell rings.
10:00—The instructor distributes the biology exams.
10:02—The instructor reads the instructions for the multiple-choice exam.
10:03—The students begin answering the questions.
10:03–10:50—The students take the exam.
10:03–10:48—The instructor reads a book.
10:05—Patrick looks at the instructor. Patrick looks worried.
10:05—Patrick glances around the room.
10:30—Patrick sees the answers on Mario's answer sheet.
10:03–10:47—Mario writes out his answers.
10:30–10:47—Patrick hurriedly copies Mario's answers.
10:48—The instructor looks up.
10:50—The bell rings.
10:50—The instructor collects the exams.

Monday

10:00—The bell rings.
10:00—The instructor enters the classroom.
10:02—The instructor returns the exams to the students.
10:04—Patrick peeks at Mario's exam and sees an "A" on it.
10:05—Patrick gets his exam with an "F" on it.
10:06—Patrick compares his answers to Mario's answers.
10:06—Patrick sees that his answers are all incorrect. He had copied Mario's answers incorrectly.

Special Verb Usage: *would* + verb and *used to* + verb

Sometimes it is necessary to express actions that are repeated in the past; we can call them *habitual actions,* actions that occur again and again in the past. For such a habitual past action, you can use the expression *would* + a verb.

For example, suppose that every weekend your family went to the park. Your family did this regularly. You could say:

Every weekend my family *would go* to the park.

Although you could say "Every weekend my family went to the park," the use of *would* + a verb emphasizes the repetition of the act.

The expression *used to* + a verb is sometimes used in expressing the habitual past, but this expression is considered more informal.

I *used to* take the bus every day.

Verb Tense Review: The Present Perfect vs. The Simple Past (Ch. 5)

An important verb tense that is useful not only for expository writing but for all kinds of writing is the present perfect tense. Since the time period referred to in the present perfect tense is often the same as in the simple past tense, these two tenses are often confused. Study the following paragraph and note the use of the present perfect and simple past tenses:

> Before I came to the United States to study, I was afraid. I heard from my friends about widespread crime in the United States and about the unfriendliness of Americans. Since my arrival here six months ago, I can say I have been pleasantly surprised. I have not found crime everywhere, and, while not all Americans have been friendly, many of them have. In fact, I have found this country to be as safe and almost as friendly as the one I left. Let me give you an example. One night two weeks ago, I had to walk back to the dorm from a friend's house. It was quite late and the streets were lonely and deserted. As I was walking along, I saw a man walking toward me. I said to myself, "Oh no, this is it." But when the stranger finally got close to me, he just said "hey, man" and kept walking. I realized then that America is not as dangerous as I thought.

The Present Perfect Tense

The present perfect tense (*has/have* + past participle) indicates a state or action that started in the past and continues to the present moment. It indicates that that state or action is relevant to the present time. The duration of the state or action is often indicated or implied.

Since my arrival here six months ago, I can say I *have been* pleasantly *surprised.* (The duration of time here is from the arrival until the present.)

My hometown *has changed* from a friendly small town into a busy modern suburb. (Although the duration of time is not stated, it is implied—from the time I lived there until the present.)

The present perfect tense is also used to indicate an action that has been completed at some indefinite time in the past, usually in the recent past.

The president *has signed* the bill into law. (No specific time of the signing is given, but it was probably recently.)

The present perfect tense is used as well to indicate that an action that occurred in the past has the capability of happening again.

I *have had* three headaches today. (This person will probably have another one.)

There *have been* six hijackings this week. (It is possible that there will be another hijacking).

EXERCISE G·40   In the following paragraphs, fill in the blanks with either the simple past tense or the present perfect tense of the verbs indicated.

Although people (not stop) _____ shopping at the local mall, because of the wide availability of the Internet, a whole new way of doing business, called e-commerce, (develop) _____. In the late 1990s, when people (begin) _____ to get Internet access in their homes, they (start) _____ to shop online. One well-known Internet site, amazon.com, quickly (become) _____ the number one online bookseller, largely because it (be) _____ the first major bookseller online. Another Internet shopping service, buy.com, (made) _____ a name for itself by offering a best price guarantee. This strategy (be) _____ successful so far. Even in their first year of business, buy.com (have) _____ sales of 86 million dollars.

Many other companies (turn) _____ to e-commerce as a way to boost sales. Not all companies make the transition from stores to cyberspace successfully, but many (profit) _____ from e-commerce. Successful cyber-companies (do) _____ several things right. First, they (make)

_____ sure their prices were low enough to attract customers. They (design) _____ easy to use Web sites, and they (acquire) _____ the newest, fastest, and most secure Internet technology.

E-commerce (allow) _____ retailers to reach a global audience without the cost of maintaining stores. It is just one of the many ways the Internet (change) _____ our lives.

Adverbials Used with the Present Perfect and Simple Past Tenses

Note the position of the following adverbs. They usually occur at the end of a sentence. However, for emphasis or variety, these adverbs and adverbial phrases can also be placed at the beginning of a sentence.

PRESENT PERFECT		SIMPLE PAST	
Today	I haven't seen him today.	*Today*	I saw him at school
		Yesterday	I broke my arm yesterday.
This week	It has rained three times this week (year, month)	*Last week*	It rained three times last week
		(This week)	*(month, etc.)*
In my life	I have done some silly things in my life.		
Up to now	He has been successful up to now.		
So far	We have won every race so far.		
Recently	Three shows have been cancelled recently.	*Recently*	Three shows were cancelled recently.
Lately	Have you seen any good movies lately?		
Since	I have lived in New York since May. (This means that I am still living in New York.)		
For	I have lived in New York for three years. (This means the last three years. I am still living in New York.)	*For*	I lived in New York for years. (This means I no longer live in New York. I once lived there.)

The following adverbial phrase can be placed only at the end of the sentence.

Ago	I lived in New York two years ago. (This means I no longer live in New York.)

Note that none of these adverbs—*just, already, yet*—can occur at the beginning of the sentence.

Just can occur only in the middle of the sentence after the first auxiliary verb.

We have *just* eaten dinner.

Already and *yet* can occur in two places: after the first auxiliary verb or at the end of the sentence.

He has *already* finished his homework.

He has finished his homework *already*.

They have not *yet* gone to school.

They have not gone to school *yet*.

EXERCISE G·41   Write the information and relevant dates for each of the following situations. Then write three sentences for each one, using *ago, since,* and *for* and either the present perfect tense or simple past tense as appropriate. The first one is done for you.

1. The first school you attended and the dates you attended it:

   Lakewood Elementary School—1968–1974
   _____

   a. *I first went to Lakewood Elementary School twenty-two years ago.*

   b. *I haven't been there since 1974.*

   c. *I attended that school for seven years.*

2. The next school you attended and the dates you attended it:

   _____

   a. _____

   b. _____

   c. _____

3. Your current school and when you started there:

_____

a. _____

b. _____

c. _____

4. Something you learned to do and when you learned it: _____

_____

a. _____

b. _____

c. _____

EXERCISE G·42   In the following verb tense review exercise, use the tense that you think is most appropriate. You may use any of the verb tenses studied so far.

By the time I reached the middle of my law career, I (become) _____ a workaholic. That (be) _____ two years ago. Then Tim, an old high school friend, (persuade) _____ me to take a break. Together we (plan) _____ a 250-mile walk down the New Jersey and Delaware coasts.

On Day Four of the expedition, I (call) _____ my office and (announce) _____ that I (extend) _____ my vacation a few more days. "You sound like a different person," my secretary (say) _____. By Day Seven of the walk, a remarkable strength and vigor (come) _____ over me.

Tim, meanwhile, (undergo) _____ a dramatic transformation of his own. Before the marathon, he (be) _____ a chain smoker and normally (go) _____ through two or three packs a day. As we (increase) _____ our daily walking distance from eighteen to twenty-five miles, however, he (smoke) _____ fewer cigarettes, and before long he (replace) _____ the smoking habit with the walking habit.

What (happen) _____ to the two of us (be) _____ an example

of what I (call) _____ the natural powers of walking. By merely increasing the amount of daily walking—without regard to technique or exercise regimen—you (benefit) _____ greatly. Research done since 1960 (show) _____ that walking (be) _____ the most efficient exercise for improving overall fitness. It (use) _____ more muscles in a continuous uniform action than most other forms of exercise, and it (remain) _____ accessible to you throughout your life. Since that research, doctors often (use) _____ it as an integral part of medical programs to prevent heart-related diseases and to rehabilitate those already stricken with heart trouble.

If your walking muscles (decline) _____, then your whole body (decline) _____. So you might as well give walking your fullest attention; it (be) _____ the best life insurance policy around.

—adapted from Gay D. Yonker, "Walk Your Way to Health and Fitness,"
Reader's Digest, June 1984, pp. 141–142

The Passive Voice vs. the Active Voice (Ch. 4)

Most writing involves the use of the *active voice,* whether verbs are in the present or past tense. The active voice is used when the subject performs the action directly:

I *bought* a book.

Sometimes, however, when the doer of the action is unknown, or perhaps the doer of the action is unimportant, the *passive voice* is appropriate.

Our house was *built* in 1953.

Who built the house? Perhaps the builder is unknown, or perhaps the writer of the sentence thinks that it is not important to identify the builder. In addition, the passive voice is used when the subject is the main topic of discussion.

The Coopers' spacious living room is neatly *arranged.*

Although the passive voice is used in all kinds of writing, it is particularly useful for descriptive writing, especially descriptions of places.

Study the following passage and observe the use of the passive voice:

One of the most enduring symbols of New York City is the Empire State Building. This famous structure is located on Fifth Avenue in Manhattan. Construction was begun in 1930 and was completed in 1931. This enormous building rises 1,250 feet into the air. It has 102 stories, most of which are used for offices. The Empire State Building was once the tallest building in the world, and became especially famous as the building from which the original King Kong fell. Many tourists who have ridden the elevators to the observation deck have enjoyed a fascinating and unforgettable view of New York City.

EXERCISE G·43 Underline the passive verbs in the preceding paragraph. Why is the passive voice used in this paragraph?

The Passive Voice: Five Points to Review

1. The passive voice always adds a form of the verb *to be* and the past participle to the sentence.

    This famous structure *is located* on Fifth Avenue in Manhattan.

2. Only transitive verbs (verbs with object and indirect objects) can be made passive. With a direct object, the passive voice is formed as follows:

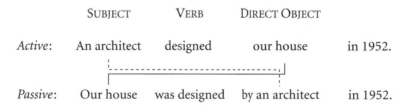

	SUBJECT	VERB	DIRECT OBJECT	
Active:	An architect	designed	our house	in 1952.
Passive:	Our house	was designed	by an architect	in 1952.

In the following example, the indirect object of the active sentence becomes the subject of the passive sentence:

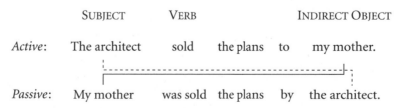

	SUBJECT	VERB		INDIRECT OBJECT
Active:	The architect	sold	the plans to	my mother.
Passive:	My mother	was sold the plans	by	the architect.

Intransitive verbs (verbs that do not take a direct object) *cannot* be made passive. If you are uncertain whether a verb is transitive or intransitive, consult the dictionary. In most dictionaries, directly next to the verb is an abbreviation, either *vt* ("transitive verb") or *vi* ("intransitive verb"). Read the definition of the verb carefully; some verbs can be used as transitive and intransitive verbs, though their meanings change with each use.

With some intransitive verbs, the object of a preposition following the verb may become the subject of the passive sentence.

	SUB	INTRANSITIVE VERB	PREP	OBJECT OF PREP
Active:	They	spoke	to	him about it.
Passive:	He	was spoken	to	about it.

3. The tense of the active sentence is used in the corresponding passive sentence.

> A huge oak tree *dominates* our backyard.
> Our backyard *is dominated* by a huge oak tree.

> They *are building* a subway in my hometown.
> A subway *is being built* in my hometown.

> Someone *is going to consider* John for promotion.
> John *is going to be considered* for promotion.

4. The *by* phrase is often omitted, especially if the information it contains is not specific or important.

> The university *was founded* in 1920. (by John Smith)

5. Although every transitive verb in English has an active form, the passive is especially useful in two situations:
   a. When the doer of the action is unimportant or unknown.
   b. When the subject of the passive sentence is the main topic of discussion.

EXERCISE G·44   Study the following pairs of sentences. For each pair, indicate which sentence is in the appropriate voice. Be prepared to explain the reason for your choice!

1. The new students were lectured to by the counselor about academic honesty.
   The counselor lectured the new students about academic honesty.
2. A sailboat was sailed around the world by me.
   I sailed a sailboat around the world.
3. The four-minute-mile record has been broken several times.
   Someone has broken the four-minute-mile record several times.
4. The dinner will be enjoyed by everyone.
   Everyone will enjoy the dinner.

5. It has been advised by my teacher that we study every night.
   My teacher has advised that we study every night.

Special Note: The Verb *locate*

The verb *locate* poses a problem for many students, for it can be used in both the active voice and the passive voice.

1. When *locate* is used in the *active voice*, it means "to find the location of":

   Jose *located* his sister's house.

2. When *locate* is used in the *passive voice*, it indicates location and is often followed by an adverbial phrase of place (preposition + noun).

   The Empire State Building *is located in Manhattan*.

   The store *is located on the corner of Main and Broad Streets*.

EXERCISE G·45   Read through the following paragraphs and decide which active verbs need to be converted to passive ones. Write the correct verb phrase in the blank. Be sure to keep the tense the same as it is now. For some of the passive verbs, it may be necessary to add *by*.

This smooth, rectangular metal box (sits) _____ in almost every living room in the United States. Cords and cables usually (grow) _____ out of the top, and one side of the box (covers) _____ a piece of gray glass. Some small knobs or buttons (have place) _____ next to the glass. If one of the knobs (pushes) _____ in, a moving picture (appears) _____ in the glass. If another knob (pushes) _____ the volume of the sound that (accompanies) _____ the picture can (control) _____. Although most people (not look) _____ inside the box, the contents of the box (look) _____ like a bowl of spaghetti and meatballs. Hundreds of wires and other components (connected and arranged) _____ to transmit the moving picture. Since it (invented) _____ in the 1920s and (introduced) _____ at the World's Fair in 1939, this nondescript yet magic box (has captured) _____ the imagination of people all over the world. What is it?

Conditionals

Real Conditions (Ch. 10)

In writing a process essay, you often need to tell the reader what might happen if a particular step is not followed. In other words, you need to give advice or warning. To state this warning, you often use a clause beginning with *if*.

> *If you do not stir the white sauce,* it will burn.

> The new putty will not hold *if you do not scrape the old putty off first.*

> *If the glass breaks,* buy another one.

Note that these real conditions are ones that are possible to be realized; they could really happen. Notice also that the *if* clause uses the present tense. In the first two examples, *will* is used in the main clause to indicate future time. In the third example, the imperative is used.

The words *unless* and *otherwise* are also used often to indicate conditions. *Unless* means "if . . . not":

> *If* you do *not* bandage the cut, it will get infected.

> *Unless* you bandage the cut, it will get infected.

Note that *otherwise* is equivalent to the entire *if* clause and is used as a transition between two complete sentences:

> Give me the money. *If you don't give me the money,* I will sue you.

> Give me the money. *Otherwise,* I will sue you.

EXERCISE G·46   The following are steps to follow when someone faints. Give a warning about each of the steps using *if, unless,* or *otherwise.* The first one is done for you.

1. Leave the victim lying down.

   If you leave the victim lying down, he may be able to breathe more easily.
   _____

2. Loosen any tight clothing and keep crowds away.

   _____

   _____

3. If the victim vomits, roll him onto his side or turn his head to the side and, if necessary, wipe out his mouth with your fingers, preferably wrapped in cloth.

   _____

   _____

4. Maintain an open airway.

_____

_____

5. Do not pour water over the victim's face because of the danger of aspiration; instead, bathe his face gently with cool water.

_____

_____

6. Do not give any liquid unless the victim has revived.

_____

_____

7. Examine the victim to determine whether or not he has suffered injury from falling.

_____

_____

8. Unless recovery is prompt, seek medical assistance. The victim should be carefully observed afterward because fainting might be a brief episode in the development of a serious underlying illness.

_____

_____

—American National Red Cross, *Standard First Aid and Personal Safety*
(New York: Doubleday, 1973), p. 174

Unreal Conditions (Ch. 11)

At times in writing about effects, you may want to make a prediction about an effect or a possible effect. For example, you may decide to explain what could have happened or what might have happened if a particular law had not been passed. To make predictions, you may find unreal conditional clauses useful. Let us review them briefly.

Unreal conditions are either impossible to realize or not likely to be realized. In these sentences, a contrary-to-fact condition exists. Study these examples:

Present Time:

If the dam *collapsed,* many acres of good farm land *would* disappear.

Past Time:

If the dam had not collapsed, the farm land *would not have been* flooded.

Past Time with Present or Future Result:

If the law *had passed*, the economy *would be* in better shape now.

Note that for present time, *was* (singular) and *were* (plural) are used in the *if* clause, and *would* or *could* + verb is used in the main clause. For past time, *had* + past participle is used in the *if* clause and *would/could have* + past participle is used in the main clause. Note the combination of the two when the *if* clause is past time but the main clause is the present or future result.

EXERCISE G·47   The following sentences tell something real. Change them to indicate something unreal. The first one is done for you.

1. Some television programs are violent. They can result in increased violence among some viewers.

   If television programs were not violent, they would not result in increased violence

   among some viewers.

2. We have the international Olympic Games. Therefore, we do not have more international violence.

3. We allowed the oil company to build this refinery. Therefore, we have oil pollution now.

4. We pay taxes. Our schools are not closed.

5. This university does not have more student housing. It does not attract more international students.

6. We have to deal with a computer when we pay our bills. Our business transactions have become impersonal.

7. Cigarette smoking is not against the law. Many people get sick from it.

8. The government did not deal with the crisis properly. Inflation has continued at high levels.

EXERCISE G·48   According to one anthropologist, soap operas are so popular in part because they deal with family problems. Read the following plot of the soap opera "Days of Our Lives," which tells the story of the characters Bob, Phyllis, and Julie. Assume that this is real information and that it took place in the past. Then, using this information, write three sentences using unreal conditions.

> Bob and Phyllis were happily married for many years but now Bob has fallen in love with Julie. Bob decides he must leave Phyllis for he no longer loves her. Phyllis becomes distraught; she thinks about killing Julie. Bob proposes marriage to Julie and she eventually accepts, even though she does not love him, for he can provide her with social and financial security. Can their marriage be successful if Julie does not love Bob (and in fact is in love with another)?
> —Susan S. Bean, "Soap Operas: Sagas of American Kinship,"
> *Anthropology for the Eighties*, ed. Johnnette B. Cole
> (New York: Free Press, 1982), p. 163

Example:

If Bob hadn't fallen in love with Julie, maybe he wouldn't have left Phyllis.

1. _____

2. _____

3. _____

Appendices

Appendix I

Peer Review Checklist for Paragraphs

When you have finished writing the first draft of your paragraph, give it to a classmate to read and review. Use the following questions to respond to each other's drafts.

Writer _____

Reviewer _____

Date _____

1. What is the topic of the paragraph? Is it narrowed down enough? Could it be narrowed down further? _____

2. What is the topic sentence of the paragraph? Write it here. (State the topic sentence in your own words if it is implied.)

   _____

3. What is the controlling idea of the paragraph? Is it clear and focused? Do you have any suggestions for improving the controlling idea?

   _____

   _____

4. Is the paragraph unified? Do all of the sentences support the controlling idea? _____
   If not, point out sentences that are irrelevent.

   _____

5. Is the paragraph coherent? Are the ideas logically arranged? Does the paragraph flow smoothly? _____
   If not, suggest ways to improve coherence. _____

   _____

6. What is the most interesting part of the paragraph?

   _____

7. What has the writer done well?

   _____

8. Is this a narrative, descriptive, or expository paragraph?

   _____

   a. Does the writer use appropriate details, events, or examples for this type of paragraph?

      _____

   b. What, if any, additional supporting details, events or examples are necessary?

      _____

   c. Is the organization appropriate for this kind of paragraph?

      _____

Peer Review Checklist for Essays

When you have finished writing the first draft of your essay, give it to a classmate to read and review. Use the following questions to respond to each other's drafts.

Writer _____

Reviewer _____

Date _____

1. Is the introduction inviting? _____

2. What is the thesis of the essay? State it in your own words by completing the following statement: The main point of the essay is that:

   _____

   _____

3. Is the thesis clear and sufficiently narrowed down? _____

4. Do you have any suggestions about the introduction or the thesis?

   _____

5. What is the principle of organization for the essay? _____

   Is it effective? _____ Suggestions on organization:

   _____

6. Has the writer used transitions and key words to give variety and coherence?

   Explain: _____

   _____

7. Does the first developmental paragraph support the thesis? Explain how:

_____

_____

8. Do you have any suggestions about the first developmental paragraph?

_____

_____

9. Answer questions 7 and 8 about the remaining developmental paragraphs:

_____

_____

10. Is this an example, comparison and contrast, classification, process analysis, cause and effect, or argumentative essay? _____

   a. Did the writer use appropriate suppport for this kind of essay?

   _____

   b. Do you have any suggestions about the support the writer used?

   _____

11. Is the development of the essay complete? _____
    Do you have any suggestions about anything the writer should include or eliminate from the essay? _____

12. Is the conclusion logical? Is it interesting? _____

    Do you have any suggestions about the conclusion? _____

    _____

13. What is the best part of the essay?

    _____

14. What part needs the most attention? _____

    _____

You may also answer the questions in the revision checklist at the end of each chapter.

Appendix II

Using Others' Ideas

You have learned that it is important to provide support for thesis statements and topic sentences. Often, in academic classes, you will find it necessary to use the ideas of experts to support your thesis statements and topic sentences. In English, when you refer to the work of others, it is important that you give credit to the author of the original idea. If you do not, it is considered plagiarism, which is a serious academic offense.

To avoid plagiarism, give credit to authors any time you use their *words* or *ideas*. Here are some examples of correct and incorrect ways to use outside sources in your writing:

Suppose a student in a literature class is writing an essay on the true identity of William Shakespeare, and she believes that Edward de Vere, the Earl of Oxford, was the real writer of the Shakespearean plays. In one paragraph, the student plans to write that the Earl of Oxford was treated as though he were a writer, even though he is rarely listed as the author of any literary works. To support this assertion, she wants to use the information underlined in this paragraph:

> By adopting the pseudonym William Shakespeare, Oxford would have provided himself, his family, and the crown with the means of preventing the public from looking to the court of the Shakespeare playwright. That the "secret" was something of an open one in certain literary circles seems confirmed by Oxford's receipt of more dedications by his fellow Elizabethans than any other contemporary contributor to the art of letters, even though he published nothing under his own name after 1576. By contrast, no one ever dedicated a thing to anyone named William Shakespeare.
>
> —Wright. D. (1999). "The Lie with Circumstance."
> *Harper's*. p. 43

Here are some incorrect, plagiarized uses of these words and ideas:

Wrong

> In Elizabethan times, other famous writers wrote about the Earl of Oxford as though he were a well-known literary figure. This fact is confirmed by Oxford's receipt of more dedications from his fellow Elizabethans than any other contemporary contributor to the art of letters, even though he published nothing under his own name after 1576.

This use of Daniel Wright's words is plagiarism because his words are copied and he is not given credit.

Wrong

> In Elizabethan times, other famous writers wrote about the Earl of Oxford as though he were a well-known literary figure. In fact, Oxford received more dedications from his fellow writers than any other author of that time, even though, after 1576, he didn't publish anything under his own name.[1]

This use of Daniel Wright's idea is plagiarism, because even though the student gave Wright credit, she has simply rearranged his words.

Wrong

> In Elizabethan times, other famous writers wrote about the Earl of Oxford as though he were a well-known literary figure. In fact, many authors who were contemporaries of the writer of the Shakespearean plays dedicated their work to Oxford, even though the last work on which his name appears was written in 1576.

This is plagiarism of Wright's work, because the author used Wright's idea *and did not give him credit.*

Here are some proper ways to use Daniel Wright's words and ideas:

Quotation

> "In Elizabethan times, other famous writers wrote about the Earl of Oxford as though he were a well-known literary figure. This fact is confirmed by Oxford's receipt of more dedications from his fellow Elizabethans than any other contemporary contributor to the art of letters, even though he published nothing under his own name after 1576."[1]

This is acceptable because Wright's words are placed inside quotation marks and he is given credit for them.

Paraphrase

> In Elizabethan times, other famous writers wrote about the Earl of Oxford as though he were a well-known literary figure. In fact, many authors who were contemporaries of the writer of the Shakespearean plays dedicated their work to Oxford, even though the last work on which his name appears was written in 1576.[1]

---

[1] Wright D. (1999). "The Lie with Circumstance." *Harper's* p. 43.

This is acceptable use of Wright's idea, because the idea is paraphrased correctly and the original author is given credit.

In these examples, the form of citation is the one recommended by the American Psychological Association (APA). There are many other systems of citation, including those recommended by The Modern Language Association (MLA) and Chicago Manual of Style. All systems, however, include the author, date, title of the work, and page numbers. For books, the publisher and place of publication is included. For magazines, the title of the magazine and volume number are included. Before writing a paper for a class, always ask what citation format your teacher wants you to follow. If you are unfamiliar with the format, most libraries and bookstores have copies of the style manuals mentioned above, and you may be able to find citation formatting information on the Internet as well.

Appendix III

The Definite Article with Place Names

USE *THE* WITH:	DO NOT USE *THE* WITH:
All plural names: the United States, the Canary Islands, the Sierra Nevada Mountains, the Great Lakes	The names of continents: Europe, Asia, South America
All names containing of: The Gulf of Cadiz, The University of Illinois, the Republic of South Africa	
The names of these countries: the Congo, the Sudan	The names of countries: Japan, Venezuela, Haiti, Australia
The names of countries containing the words *Union, United,* and *Commonwealth:* the Soviet Union, the British Commonwealth	
The name of this city: the Hague	The names of cities and states: Seoul, Caracas, Louisiana, Florida
Groups of Islands (see the first section above): the British Isles, the Aleutian Islands (The word *islands* may be omitted—the Philippines.)	The name of a single island: Victoria Island, Long Island
Most bodies of water (rivers, seas, oceans, channels, canals, gulfs, straits): the Saint Lawrence River, the China Sea, the Atlantic Ocean, the Persian Gulf, the Bering Strait (the words *river, sea,* and *ocean* may be omitted—the Pacific)	The names of lakes and bays: Lake Michigan, Manila Bay
The names of mountain ranges: the Rocky Mountains (the word *mountain* may be omitted—the Alps)	The name of a single mountain: Mount Everest, Bald Mountain
The names of peninsulas: the Iberian Peninsula	
Distinct geographic areas using *north, south, east,* and *west:* the East, the Midwest, the Far East	

The names of libraries and museums: the Louvre, the Confederate Museum

The names of universities and colleges (unless part of the actual name): Harvard University, Rocky Mountain College; BUT: The Ohio State University

The names of avenues, streets, and boulevards: Fifth Avenue, Main Street, Pontchartrain Boulevard

The names of parks: Central Park, Audubon Park

The Definite Article with Other Proper Nouns

USE *THE* WITH:	DO NOT USE *THE* WITH:
	The names of holidays: Christmas, New Year's Day, Easter
All names containing *of:* the President of the United States	
Titles of officials: the king, the secretary of state, the prime minister	Titles of officials when the name accompanies the title: President Clinton, King Hussein, Prime Minister Major
Names of historical periods or events: the Middle Ages, the Civil War, the Manchu Dynasty, the Second World War	
Official documents and acts: the Monroe Doctrine, the Louisiana Purchase, the Magna Carta, the Equal Rights Amendment	Names with roman numerals: World War II
Branches of the government and political parties: the Judicial Branch, the Republican party	
Names of organizations and foundations: the United Nations, the Carnegie Foundation, the YMCA	
Law enforcement groups: the army, the navy, the marines	

Appendix IV

Punctuation Problems

Fragments

A fragment is a part of a sentence that has been punctuated as a complete sentence. It is usually a dependent clause or a phrase.

> The man who is coming over to fix the washer and dryer this morning. (adjective clause)

> Whether the legislature passes the bill or not. (noun clause)

> The woman singing the lovely, haunting refrain. (participial phrase)

> The beauty of the lake, the quiet solitude, the starlit night, and the lovely smell of the pine trees. (nouns and phrases)

A fragment can be corrected by attaching the dependent phrase or clause to an independent clause.

> The man who is coming over to fix the washer and dryer this morning is charging $50 an hour.

> I do not care whether the legislature passes the bill or not.

> The woman singing the lovely, haunting refrain walks in the park every evening.

> I was enthralled with the beauty of the lake, the quiet solitude, the starlit night, and the lively smell of the pine trees.

Comma Splices and Run-on Sentences

A comma splice occurs when two independent clauses are joined by a comma. A run-on sentence occurs when two independent clauses are written as one sentence with no punctuation at all.

> The local tire plant shut down for the holiday, as a result, everyone had two weeks off.

> We walked over to the waterfall slowly then we sat down to admire the beauty of the falls.

Comma splices and run-ons can be corrected in four main ways.

1. Use a period to make two complete sentences.
2. Use a semicolon between the two clauses.
3. Use a comma and a coordinating conjunction.

4. Use a subordinator to make a dependent clause; attach it to the independent clause.

> The local tire plant shut down for the holiday. As a result, everyone had two weeks off.

> The local tire plant shut down for the holiday; as a result, everyone had two weeks off.

> We walked over to the waterfall slowly, and then we sat down to admire the beauty of the falls.

> After we walked over to the waterfall slowly, we sat down to admire the beauty of the falls.

Rules for Punctuation

The Period

1. Use a period at the end of a statement or command.

> The government has promised to reduce inflation.

> Pick up the lug wrench.

2. Use a period after abbreviations.

> A.M.   Mr.   U.S.   B.C.

The Comma

1. Use a comma to separate independent clauses joined by a coordinating conjunction.

> We went to the campsite as soon as we arrived, but it was already full.

> Note: If the clauses are quite short, the comma may be omitted.

> He studied hard and he passed the test.

2. Use a comma to separate words, phrases, or clauses in a series.

> We took our tent, our sleeping bags, food, and fishing poles.

> He drinks milkshakes in the morning, in the afternoon, and in the evening.

> We enjoyed ourselves before we took the boat ride, while we were on the boat ride, and after we left the lake.

3. Use a comma after introductory phrases or clauses.

Because we had wanted to see all of the interesting sights in the city, we agreed to spend our entire vacation there.

With the worst of the winter over, the people began to make plans for spring.

Note: If the clauses or phrases are quite short, the comma may be omitted.

After we arrived we had a beer.

4. Use a comma after transitional words and phrases, mild interjections, and *yes* and *no*.

On the other hand, no effort has been made to help the stranded people.

Oh, I do not think that is the answer.

Yes, he said he was coming.

5. Use commas to set off nonrestrictive clauses and phrases and appositives.

President John F. Kennedy, who was assassinated in 1963, was an eloquent speaker.

The boat, tied securely to the dock, rode out the storm well.

Mr. Benninger, a well-known physicist, received the key to the city.

6. Use commas to set off contrastive elements or elements that interrupt a sentence.

We chose the moderately priced one, not the most expensive one, because we were short of funds.

It is a good idea, therefore, to study this book thoroughly before the test.

7. Use commas to set off absolute constructions. (An absolute phrase is a noun followed by a modifier. It modifies a whole sentence, not a particular element in the sentence.)

Night falling, the lights of the town slowly began to appear.

8. Use commas in direct address and quotations.

He said, "Mary, did you steal the money?"

9. Use commas with degrees, titles, dates, places, addresses, and numbers.

Mr. Ross Charleston, M.F.A., is the chairman of the English Department.

Mr. Cyrus Leary, chairman of the board, made a number of changes in policy.

We decided to have the wedding reception on Friday, October 8, because of our vacation.

We arrived in this country in May of 1979.

We arrived in this country on May 24, 1979.

The water in Chicago, Illinois, comes from Lake Michigan.

They sold over 100,000 pounds of rice in 1979.

Please send it to Mr. Harold Bobbs, 1230 Smith Place, New Orleans, Louisiana 70124.

Note: As in the preceding example, there is no comma placed between the state and the zip code.

10. Use a comma to prevent misreading.

Inside, the building was beautiful.

Before eating, the dog barked three times.

The Semicolon

1. Use a semicolon between two main clauses that are not joined by a coordinating conjunction.

This floor polish does not work; I have already tried it.

2. Use a semicolon between coordinate elements with internal commas.

After we arrived, Mr. Buris, the manager of the plant, showed us the main assembly lines; but he neglected to show us the warehouse where most of the products, waiting to be shipped overseas, are stored.

3. Use a semicolon between items in a series when the items themselves contain commas.

Present at the meeting were Charles Jones, chairperson; Lydia Jones, vice-chairperson: and Roger Smaltz, treasurer.

The Colon

1. Use a colon between two independent clauses when the second one explains the first.

There is only one thing to say: He did not deserve it.

2. Use a colon to introduce an appositive.

> "There are three sources of belief: reason, custom, inspiration."
>
> —Blaise Pascal

3. Use a colon to formally introduce a quotation.

> Kennedy eloquently reminded us: "Ask not what your country can do for you; ask what you can do for your country."

4. Use a colon in a time reference, after the salutation of a formal letter, in biblical references, and in bibliographical entries.

> 1:30 A.M.
>
> Dear Dr. Runch:
>
> Genesis 6:2
>
> New York: Macmillan, 1980

Note: Do not use a colon after a linking verb or preposition.

Incorrect:

> Present at the meeting were: Mr. Jones, Mr. Osgood, and Ms. Blake.

Correct:

> Present at the meeting were Mr. Jones, Mr. Osgood, and Ms. Blake.

The Dash

1. Use a dash to indicate a sudden interruption in thought.

> He confessed to the crime—but why?

2. Use a dash to set off abrupt parenthetical elements (particularly ones containing commas).

> He took the letter angrily—or was he really happy?—when the letter carrier arrived.
>
> We saw him huffing, puffing, and snorting—trying to break loose.

3. Use a dash to set off an appositive or a brief summary.

> There is one poem I love more than any other—"The Waste Land."
>
> Persistence, agility, and strength—all of these are needed to learn tennis.

Parentheses

1. Use parentheses to enclose a loosely related comment or explanation.

    The car (it had been purchased only the day before) needed new brakes, a tune-up, and new tires.

2. Use parentheses to enclose figures numbering items in a series. The government tried to (1) increase employment, (2) reduce inflation, and (3) cut taxes.

Brackets

1. Use brackets to enclose editorial corrections or additions in a quotation.

    Dirkson reports: "When we came upon him [General Lee], we found that he had been badly wounded in the leg."

2. Note that the word *sic* in brackets means that the preceding word is an error and that the error appeared in the original.

    The editor asserted: "When I read the Bibel [sic], I was enlightened."

Quotation Marks

1. Use double quotation marks to enclose a direct quotation.

    He said, "I cannot study anymore."

    Note: Indirect speech is not put within quotation marks.

    He said that he could not study anymore.

2. Use single quotation marks to enclose a quotation within a quotation.

    May reported, "When Bob said, 'I cannot see you anymore,' my sister was heartbroken."

    Smith argues that, "Hamlet's 'to be or not be be' has an entirely different meaning."

3. Use quotation marks to set off titles of songs, poems, short stories, articles, essays, chapters in longer works, paintings, and statues.

    My favorite song is "Raindrops Keep Falling on My Head."

    He recites "Mending Wall" for each of his classes.

    Have you read "The Blue Stocking" yet?

    Note: Quotation marks are essentially used to enclose short works of art. For longer works of art, use italics (or underlining).

4. Use quotation marks to denote a special meaning of a word.

> Her "pet" was a small round stone.

5. Put commas and periods inside quotation marks.

> He answered, "I cannot watch television tonight."

> Although he answered with a "yes," he did not seem enthusiastic.

6. Put colons and semicolons outside quotation marks.

> I am always sad when I see "The End"; it means the movie is over.

7. Put question marks, dashes, and exclamation points that are part of a quotation inside the quotation marks. Put question marks, dashes, and exclamation points that are not part of a quotation outside the quotation marks.

> Her father asked, "What time will you be home?"

> Did he just say, "We will not have school tomorrow"?

> He shouted, "Help! I cannot get out!"

> Do not shout "help"!

Italics

Italics are a special kind of print found in most publications. The letters in italics slant to the right. In handwritten or typed papers, use underlining for italics.

1. Use italics for the titles of books, magazines, newspapers, periodicals, plays, motion pictures, longer musical compositions, and other works published separately.

> *The Grapes of Wrath* (book)

> the *Atlantic Monthly* (magazine)

> the *New York Times* (newspaper)

> *TESOL Quarterly* (periodical)

> *Rocky* (motion picture)

> *The Iceman Cometh* (play)

> *The Rite of Spring* (musical piece)

2. Use italics for ships, trains, and airplanes.

> the *Queen Elizabeth* (ship)

> the *Zephyr* (train)

> the *Spirit of St. Louis* (airplane)

3. Use italics for foreign words and phrases that have not yet been accepted into English.

> The *piece de resistance* was his poached fish with hollandaise sauce.

4. Use italics to call attention to words as words and letter as letters.

> The word *fluffy* reminds me of a cloud.

> The teacher said, "Now put the letter *X* in the margin."

Note: This is an ineffective method of emphasis if it is overused.

The Apostrophe

1. Use the apostrophe to indicate possessive.
   a. For all proper nouns, add apostrophe and *s.*

   > the girl's book

   > Jesus's birth

   > Charles's house

   > Kansas's weather

   b. For plural nouns, add an apostrophe after the plural *s.*

   > The boys' books

   c. For compound words, use the apostrophe after the last word.

   > his mother-in-law's house

   > everyone's concern

   d. For joint possession, use the apostrophe after the last noun. For individual possession, use the apostrophe after both nouns.

   > Charley and Bill's car

   > Sheila's and May's cameras

2. Use the apostrophe to form the plural of letters.

> Only two A's were given in the class.

Note: Omit the apostrophe to form the plural of numerals and words referred to as words.

> There were three 12s in the average.

> Her two-page essay included twenty-five *of courses.*

Note: Omit the apostrophe when forming the plural of abbreviations, numbers, and periods of time expressed in years.

SATs

VCRs

fours

1990s

3. Use the apostrophe to indicate the omission of a letter or number.

wouldn't

Jack-o'-lantern

the '60s

The Hyphen

1. Hyphenate a compound of two or more words when it is used as a modifier before a noun.

He is a well-liked politician.

He is well liked.

Note: Do not use the hyphen when the first word of the group is an adverb ending in -*ly*.

a half-eaten apple

a partly eaten apple

Note: Certain words are permanent compounds. They always use a hyphen. Consult your dictionary to determine which words are permanent compounds.

She is old-fashioned.

2. Hyphenate spelled-out compound numbers from twenty-one through ninety-nine.

sixty-four

eighty-three

3. Hypenate words of more than one syllable when they occur at the end of a typewritten line, when necessary. Hyphenate according to accepted syllabification. Consult your dictionary to determine where the syllable breaks are. Do not divide words of only one syllable, and do not set off single letters. Do not

divide words that already contain a hyphen elsewhere. Attempt to hyphenate in the approximate middle of the word.

Correct:

satis-faction   water-melon

Incorrect:

bou-ght   prett-y

Numbers

1. Spell out numbers that can be written in one or two words.

   one million

   forty-three

2. Use figures for other numbers.

   145

   2 1/2

   $456

3. Use numerals for figures in a series and for tabulations and statistics.

   Bill weighed 180 pounds; Steve, 150 pounds; and John, 100.

   He bought 125 pencils, 30 erasers, and 6 pens.

4. Use figures for street numbers, page references, dates, percentages, money, and hours of the day with A.M. and P.M.
   But:

101 Main Street	Tenth Street
Look at page 45.	We arrived on January 10, 1980.
I have twenty pages ready.	The interest was 15 percent.
We paid $15 for the tickets.	He gets up at 7:30 A.M.
He got up at seven o'clock.	

   Note: Do not use figures to begin a sentence. Spell out the number or rephrase the sentence.

Appendix V

Rules for Capitalization

1. Capitalize the first word in a sentence.

   Where did he go?

2. Capitalize the pronoun *I*.

   Although he said so, I did not believe him.

3. Capitalize proper names and nouns used as proper names.
   a. Capitalize a title preceding a proper noun.

      President Bush

      Dr. Gonzalez

   b. Capitalize the names of people and races.

      Bob

      Luis Marcos

      Oriental Caucasian

      African-American

   Note: Do not capitalize the words *black* and *white*.

      The blacks and whites in our neighborhood are well integrated.

   c. Capitalize the names of religions, deities, and sacred terms.

      Catholic

      Moslem

      Buddhist

      God

   d. Capitalize geographic locations.

      New York

      Mont Blanc

      the Ohio River

e. Capitalize the words *north, south, east,* and *west* when they refer to a section of the country usually considered to constitute a region.

> the Midwest
>
> the South

f. Capitalize nationalities and names of languages.

> Vietnamese   Spanish   French   Japanese

g. Capitalize the complete names of specific churches and buildings.

> the Statler Hotel
>
> the First Baptist Church

h. Capitalize the days of the week, months, and holidays.

> Wednesday
>
> August
>
> the Fourth of July

i. Capitalize the specific names of college courses (as the name would appear in the college catalog).

> I am taking French, American History 102, and a science course.

j. Capitalize all the words in a title except articles, prepositions, and conjunctions. Capitalize articles, prepositions, and conjunctions if they are the first or last word in the title or if they are of five or more letters in length.

> *Gone with the Wind*
>
> "We're Through with Heartache"
>
> "He Comes In"

k. Capitalize nouns, adjectives, and prefixes in temporarily hyphenated compounds.

> The Twentieth-Century Ideal   But: Twenty-five Brave Men

l. Capitalize the names of documents, historical events, and organizations.

> The Bill of Rights
>
> the Vietnam War
>
> the National Organization for Women

Note: Do not capitalize the names of the seasons: spring, summer, fall, winter.

Appendix VI

Noun Plurals

Most nouns in English become plural by adding an *s* to the singular form:

SINGULAR	**PLURAL**
girl	girls
boy	boys

Some words, however, become plural by adding *es* to the singular form. This is generally true for words ending in *s, sh, ch, ss, zz,* or *x.* Note these examples:

SINGULAR	**PLURAL**
plus	pluses
ash	ashes
watch	watches
class	classes
buzz	buzzes
ax	axes

Words that end in a consonant plus *y* make the plural by changing the *y* to *i* and adding *es.*

SINGULAR	**PLURAL**
industry	industries
company	companies
city	cities
baby	babies

However, words that end in a vowel—*a, e, i, o,* or *u*—plus *y* form their plural by adding *s* only.

SINGULAR	**PLURAL**
boy	boys
highway	highways

Words ending in one *z* often make the plural by doubling the *z* and adding *es.*

SINGULAR	**PLURAL**
quiz	quizzes

For words ending in a consonant plus *o,* usage varies. Some words make the plural by adding *es* only.

SINGULAR	PLURAL
veto	vetoes
hero	heroes
tomato	tomatoes

Other words become plural by adding *s* only.

SINGULAR	PLURAL
auto	autos
memo	memos
pimento	pimentos

And some words can be made plural in either way.

SINGULAR	PLURAL
motto	mottoes or mottos
zero	zeroes or zeros

Words ending in *fe* form their plurals by changing *f* to *v* and adding *es.*

SINGULAR	PLURAL
wife	wives
half	halves
knife	knives

The following are exceptions to this rule:

SINGULAR	PLURAL
belief	beliefs
roof	roofs

Some nouns have special plural forms. They do not add *s* or *es* to form the plural. Note the following examples:

SINGULAR	PLURAL
man	men
woman	women
child	children

SINGULAR	PLURAL
tooth	teeth
foot	feet
mouse	mice
goose	geese
ox	oxen
person	people (or persons)

Some words do not conform to any of the English rules for forming plurals but form their plurals in other ways. Note the following examples:

SINGULAR	PLURAL
medium	media
criterion	criteria
datum	data
crisis	crises
axis	axes

Some words do not change form in the plural. The form for singular and plural is the same.

SINGULAR	PLURAL
sheep	sheep
fish	fish
deer	deer
moose	moose

Some words that always end in *s* are singular in meaning. These words are considered singular, not plural. They include:

news	politics
economics	athletics

Appendix VII

Subject–Verb Agreement

The verb of a sentence must agree in number with its subject. Singular subjects take singular verbs and plural subjects take plural verbs. The agreement pattern for the present tense is as follows:

	SINGULAR	PLURAL
First person	I want to go to a movie.	We want to go to a movie.
Second person	You want	You want
Third person	He wants	They want
	She wants	
	It wants	

As you can see, the form of the verb is the same for all persons except for the third-person singular. Here the verb adds an *s* (or *es* in some cases) in order to agree with the subject. In addition to the pronouns given, the subject could be any singular noun for which you could substitute those pronouns. Exceptions to this pattern are the verbs *to be* and *have,* which change in other persons as well.

	TO BE		HAVE	
	SINGULAR	PLURAL	SINGULAR	PLURAL
First person	I am	We are	I have	We have
Second person	You are	You are	You have	You have
Third person	He is	They are	He has	They have
	She is		She has	
	It is		It has	

In order to make the verb agree in number with its subject, you must first determine which noun or pronoun is the subject of the sentence. There are several instances when the subject may not be apparent.

1. Sometimes the subject is separated from the verb by intervening words, phrases, or clauses.
   a. Prepositional phrases often follow the subject but never contain the subject.

   The student by the window likes to talk.

   The cars in the parking lot have their windows open.

b. Adjective clauses often come between the main subject and verb of a sentence. Note that there are instances of subject-verb agreement in this case. The main subject and verb of the sentence must agree and the verb in the adjective clause must agree with its antecedent, or the word before the relative pronoun.

MAIN SUBJECT	RELATIVE PRONOUN	VERB	MAIN VERB
The girls	that	live next door	like to sing.

2. Sometimes subjects and verbs are reversed.
   a. Sentences beginning with *there* have reversed word order.

   V   S
There are a lot of students here for the test.

   V S
There is a man waiting to see you.

   b. Sometimes subjects and verbs are reversed for stylistic purposes.

   V   S
Here comes the plane!

   V   S
Hardest hit by the tragedy was the mother of the family.

After you have determined which noun in the sentence is the subject, you must decide if it is singular or plural. Most nouns in English become plural by adding an *s* to the noun:

SINGULAR	PLURAL
girl	girls

1. Some nouns change their form in order to indicate plural:

SINGULAR	PLURAL
man	men
woman	women
child	children

The plural forms of these nouns—*men, women, children, people*—agree like this:

S   V
The people dislike the commercials on television.

2. Some nouns, called collective nouns, are usually considered singular, but may, in some cases, be considered plural. These nouns take a singular verb when they refer to a group as a unit. Note the collective nouns (italic) and the singular verbs (bold) in the following sentences.

> My *family* **writes** to me every month.

> Our *class* **wants** to go to the museum.

> The *team* for our school **wears** red and white jerseys.

> The *faculty* **elects** a senate every year.

> The *committee* **needs** to have another meeting.

These nouns may take plural verbs when they refer to individuals or parts of the group. However, this is more formal and less common usage. Note these examples:

> The faculty disagree on certain parts of the issue.

> The committee argue among themselves concerning the best course of action.

Note: You can clarify these sentences by using the word members as the subject:

> The members of the faculty disagree on certain parts.

> The members of the committee argue among themselves concerning the best course of action.

3. Nouns that are plural in form but singular in meaning take singular verbs. These nouns include *news, politics, economics, electronics, physics,* and *athletics.*

> The news on television is not very complete.

> Economics is an interesting field of study.

4. When words such as *each, either, neither, one, everybody,* and *everyone* are used as subjects, they take singular verbs.

> Neither wants to finish the work.

> Each of us has a good idea.

> Everybody in our class wants to go to the play.

> One of them has to do it.

5. When words such as *all, any, half most, none,* and *some* are used as subjects, they can take either singular or plural verbs, depending on the context.

All of the people dislike the new tax.

All of the money is gone.

6. A sentence that has two subjects joined by *and* requires a plural verb.

My sister and my father watch television every night.

The company and the bank disagree about the loan.

7. Singular subjects joined by or *either . . . or,* or *neither . . . nor* usually take a singular verb.

John or Paul buys groceries for the family every week.

Either the president or the vice-president answers every letter.

Neither anger nor happiness ever shows on his face.

If one of the subjects is singular and the other is plural, the verb agrees with the one closest to the subject.

Mr. Smith or his sons go every day to pick up the mail.

Neither the students nor the teacher understands the new schedule.

Appendix VIII

Principal Parts of Irregular Verbs

SIMPLE FORM	PAST FORM	PAST PARTICIPLE FORM
be	was, were	been
bear	bore	born
beat	beat	beat
become	became	become
begin	began	begun
bend	bent	bent
bet	bet	bet
bind	bound	bound
bite	bit	bitten
bleed	bled	bled
blow	blew	blown
break	broke	broken
breed	bred	bred
bring	brought	brought
build	built	built
burst	burst	burst
buy	bought	bought
catch	caught	caught
choose	chose	chosen
come	came	come
cost	cost	cost
creep	crept	crept
cut	cut	cut
do	did	done
dig	dug	dug
draw	drew	drawn

SIMPLE FORM	PAST FORM	PAST PARTICIPLE FORM
drink	drank	drunk
drive	drove	driven
eat	ate	eaten
fall	fell	fallen
feed	fed	fed
feel	felt	felt
fight	fought	fought
find	found	found
fit	fit	fit
flee	fled	fled
fly	flew	flown
forbid	forbade	forbidden
forget	forgot	forgotten
forgive	forgave	forgiven
freeze	froze	frozen
get	got	gotten
give	gave	given
go	went	gone
grind	ground	ground
grow	grew	grown
hang	hung	hung
have	had	had
hear	heard	heard
hide	hid	hidden
hit	hit	hit
hold	held	held
hurt	hurt	hurt
keep	kept	kept
know	knew	known

SIMPLE FORM	PAST FORM	PAST PARTICIPLE FORM
lay	laid	laid
lead	led	led
leave	left	left
lend	lent	lent
let	let	let
light	lit	lit
lose	lost	lost
lie	lay	lain
make	made	made
mean	meant	meant
meet	met	met
pay	paid	paid
put	put	put
quit	quit	quit
read	read	read
ride	rode	ridden
ring	rang	rung
rise	rose	risen
run	ran	run
say	said	said
see	saw	seen
seek	sought	sought
sell	sold	sold
send	sent	sent
set	set	set
shake	shook	shaken
shine	shone	shone
shoot	shot	shot
shut	shut	shut

SIMPLE FORM	PAST FORM	PAST PARTICIPLE FORM
sing	sang	sung
sink	sank	sunk
sit	sat	sat
sleep	slept	slept
slide	slid	slid
speak	spoke	spoken
speed	sped	sped
spend	spent	spent
spin	spun	spun
split	split	split
spread	spread	spread
spring	sprang	sprung
stand	stood	stood
steal	stole	stolen
stick	stuck	stuck
sting	stung	stung
strike	struck	struck
swear	swore	sworn
swim	swam	swum
swing	swung	swung
take	took	taken
teach	taught	taught
tear	tore	torn
tell	told	told
think	thought	thought
throw	threw	thrown
understand	understood	understood
wake up	woke up	woken up
wear	wore	worn

SIMPLE FORM	PAST FORM	PAST PARTICIPLE FORM
weave	wove	woven
weep	wept	wept
win	won	won
wind	wound	wound
wring	wrung	wrung
write	wrote	written

Problem Verbs

Some verb forms are particularly troublesome. Note carefully the following forms:

begin	began	begun
choose	chose	chosen
fall	fell	fell
feel	felt	felt
throw	threw	thrown
write	wrote	written

The following sets of verbs have similar forms but are used in different ways.

1. *Lie/lay/lain/lying* means "to recline." It is intransitive, so it takes no object.

   I *lie* down every afternoon.

   I *lay* down yesterday.

   I *have lain* down many times.

2. *Lay/laid/laid/laying* means "to put." It is transitive, so it needs an object.

   Lay the book over there.

   He *laid* it there yesterday.

   He *has laid* it there before.

3. *Sit/sat/sat* means "to sit down." It is intransitive (takes no object).

   I *sit* in the same chair every day.

   I *sat* here yesterday.

4. *Set/set/set* means "to put something down." It is transitive, so it needs an object.

> *Set* the dishes on the table.

> He *set* the books over there.

5. *Lose/lost/lost* means "to misplace." It is transitive.

> I always *lose* my shoes.

> I *lost* them two weeks ago.

6. *Loosen/loosened/loosened* means "to relax something." It is transitive.

> He *loosened* his shoes.

Note: The term *loose* is an adjective.

> I like *loose* clothing.

Appendix IX

Verbs and Their Complements

Verb Followed by an Infinitive

S   V   INF
This man happens to be my husband.

agree	hope	appear	intend	arrange	learn
ask	manage	attempt	mean	beg	need
care	plan	choose	promise	decide	refuse
desire	request	endeavor	seem	expect	tend
fail	threaten	get	try	guarantee	used
happen	want	have	wish		

Special Expression

I can(not) stand *to sit* here like this!

We can(not) bear *to see* him suffer.

Verb Followed by a Noun Phrase + Infinitive

S   V   INF
I do not want you to go now.

advise	engage	persuade	allow	expect
appoint	forbid	pick	ask	force
prefer	assign	get	prepare	authorize
hate	push	beg	help	raise
call	hire	rely on	cause	inspire
remind	challenge	instruct	request	choose
intend	require	command	invite	select
contract	lead	send	convince	like
teach	dare	love	tell	depend on
meant	tempt	desire	name	train
direct	need	trust	drive	notify
urge	elect	oblige	want	employ
order	warn	enable	pay	wire
encourage	permit	write	phone (also telephone)	

Verb Followed by a Gerund

```
 s     v    GER
Children enjoy learning new things.
```

admit	enjoy	picture	resent	advise	escape
postpone	resume	appreciate	feel like	put off	resist
avoid	finish	protest	risk	can't help	get
around to	practice	save	confess	get out of	quit
stop	consider	imagine	recall	succeed in	debate
include	recommend	suggest	delay	keep on	regret
take up	deny	mention	relate	welcome	discuss
mind	remember	work at	dislike	miss	report

understand

Verb Followed by a Gerund or an Infinitive

```
 s     v    INF
He continued to serve the Queen.
```

```
 s     v     GER
He continued serving the Queen.
```

(can) afford	dread	regret	attempt	forget	remember
begin	hate	(can) stand	bother	intend	start	choose
like	stop	continue	neglect	try	deserve	prefer

Special Note

Some verbs change their meaning when they are followed by a gerund or an infinitive.

John stopped *to pet* the dog. (John's intention in stopping was to pet the dog.)

John stopped *petting* the dog. (He ceased the action of petting.)

I remember *to lock* the doors each night. (The action of locking comes after the action of remembering.)

I remember *locking* the doors last night. (The action of locking comes before the action of remembering.)

Verbs Followed by a Noun Phrase + Gerund

The broadcasters reported the spaceship's landing.
(s) (v) (GER)

admit	hate	recall	applaud	imagine
recommend	appreciate	like	regret	approve
mention	remember	concede	mind	report
deny	miss	risk	disapprove	picture
save	enjoy	prefer	salute	forget
protest	welcome	depend on		

Verb-Preposition Combination Followed by a Gerund or Noun Phrase + Gerund

The officer forgot about John's breaking the law.
(s) (v) (PREP) (NP) (GER)

John forgot about breaking the law.
(s) (v) (PREP) (GER)

admit to	cry about	look forward to	agree on
decide against	object to	allude to	decide on
pay for	approve of	depend on/upon	plan on
argue about	wonder about	refer to	argue against
end with	rely on	ask about	fight about
speak about/of	balk at	figure on	start with
begin with	forget about	talk about/of	believe in
hear about	tell about	care about	inquire about
think about/of	center on	insist on	lie about
confess to	laugh about	count on	worry about
warn against/of/about		dream about/of	

Special Note

As a general rule, most verb-preposition combinations are followed by a gerund. Beware, however, of confusing the infinitive *to* with the verb-preposition combination requiring *to* as part of the verb.

Adjective-Preposition Combination Followed by a Gerund

s v ADJ PREP GER
We are sick of sailing.

Special Note

When an adjective is followed by a preposition, it is usually followed by a gerund.

accustomed to	cynical about	proud of
addicted to	delighted about	resigned to
afraid of	sad about	amazed at
disturbed about	satisfied with	angry about
excited about	sick of	famous for
slow at/about	anxious about	fond of
sold on	ashamed about	glad about/of
sorry about	aware of	good at
successful at	bad at	good about
superb at	bored with	happy about
surprised at/about	capable of	hesitant about
tired of	careful about	impressed with
unaccustomed to	clever at	interested in
undecided about	confident of	new at
upset about	opposed to	used to
concerned about	pleased about	worried about
conscious of	disappointed about	annoyed about/with
confused about		

Adjective Followed by an Infinitive

s v   ADJ   INF
I am delighted to go with you.

able	fun	reluctant	afraid	glad	sad
anxious	good	slow	apt	happy	smart
ashamed	hard	sorry	bound	inclined	stupid
careful	kind	strange	certain	likely	supposed
delighted	nice	sure	depressing	pleased	surprised
disturbed	possible	terrible	eager	predicted	welcome
easy	prepared	willing	expected	qualified	wise
foolish	quick	wonderful	free	ready	wrong

Special Note

Some adjectives occur with *it* as the subject.

It is nice to stay at home on weekends.

It is nice of him to stay with the family.

Adjectives in this group include the following:

depressing	kind	stupid
easy	likely	strange
expected	nice	supposed
foolish	possible	sure
free	predicted	terrible
fun	sad	wise
good	smart	wrong
hard		

Verbs That Can Be Followed by a Noun Clause

s   v   NC
He declared that he loved her.

acknowledge	discover	maintain	retort	admit	doubt
mean	reveal	advise*	estimate	mention	say
agree	expect	note	see	announce	explain
notice	sense	answer	fear	notify	shout
anticipate	feel	order*	show	argue	forbid*
point out	signify	arrange*	forget	predict	state
ask*	gather	prefer*	suggest*	assert	guarantee
presume	suppose	assume	guess	pretend	suspect
believe	hear	promise	swear	charge	hint
protest	teach	claim	hope	prove	tell
comment	imagine	read	think	conclude	imply
realize	trust	decide	indicate	recall	understand
declare	infer	recommend*	urge*	demand*	inform
regret*	vow	demonstrate	insist*	relate	whisper
deny	know	remember	write	determine	learn
request*					

* Subjunctive noun clauses: The verb stays in the base from and does not change for conjugation or tense.

Appendix X

Sample Business Letters

The following sample letters are from Guffey, M.E. (1997). *Essentials of Business Communication.* Cincinnati, Ohio: South-Western Publishers.

Letter of Thanks

4029 Lewiston Drive
Logan, UT 84321
May 12, 199x

Professor and Mrs. Cliff Brighton
340 Overlook Avenue
Logan, UT 84322

Dear Professor and Mrs. Brighton:

Thanks for inviting the other members of our business club and me to your home for dinner last Saturday.

The warm reception you gave us made the evening very special. Your gracious hospitality, the delicious trout dinner with that superb chocolate mousse and the lively discussion following dinner all served to create an enjoyable evening that I will long remember. Perhaps we did not resolve the issue of exorbitant executive salaries, but we certainly thrashed it out.

I appreciate the opportunity you provided for us students to become better acquainted with each other and with you.

Cordially,

Adam W Miller

Adam W. Miller

Letter of Application

1770 Hawthorne Place
Boulder, CO 80304
May 23, 199x

Mr. William A. Caldwell
Director, Human Resources
Del Rio Enterprises
Denver, CO 82511

Dear Mr. Caldwell:

Since I have focused my education and training on sales and marketing, your advertisement for an assistant product manager, appearing May 22 in Section C of the *Denver Post,* immediately caught my attention.

Your ad states that the job includes "assisting in the coordination of a wide range of marketing programs as well as analyzing sales results and tracking marketing budgets." A recent internship at Ventana Corporation introduced me to similar tasks. I assisted the marketing manager in analyzing the promotion, budget, and overall sales success of two products Ventana was evaluating. My ten-page report examined the nature of the current market, the products' life cycles, and their sales/profit return. In addition to this research, I helped formulate a product merchandising plan and answered consumers' questions at a local trade show. This brief but challenging introduciton to product management convinced me that I could be successful and happy in a marketing career.

Intensive coursework in marketing and management, as well as proficiency in spreadsheets, databases, and the Internet, has given me the kind of marketing and computing training that Del Rio demands in a product manager. Moreover, I have had retail sales experience and have been active in campus organizations. I'm confident that my academic preparation, my marketing experience, and my ability to work well with others qualify me for this position.

After you have examined the enclosed resume for details of my qualifications, I would be happy to answer questions. Please call me to arrange an interview at your convenience so that we may discuss how my marketing, computing, and interpersonal skills could contribute to Del Rio Enterprises.

Sincerely,

Carolyn A. Crockett

Carolyn A. Crockett
Enclosure

Letter That Makes a Request

235 Providence Drive
Logan, UT 84325
August 14, 199x

Bravo Computer, Inc.
2308 Borregas Avenue
Sunnyvale, CA 94088-3565

Ladies and Gentlemen:
SUBJECT: RETURN OF MALFUNCTIONING BRAVO COMPUTER
Please tell me how I may return my malfunctioning Bravo Pentium 33
computer to you for repair.

I am sure you can solve a problem that puzzles my local dealer. After about 45
minutes of normal activity, the screen on my Bravo suddenly fills with a
jumble of meaningless letters, numbers, and symbols. Computers For You, the
dealer from whom I purchased my Bravo, seems to be unable to locate or
correct the malfunction.

Although I am expected to have my computer serviced locally, my dealer has
been unable to repair it. I am confident you can solve the mystery and that
you will repair my Bravo quickly.

Sincerely yours,

Pauline LeBlanc

(Mrs.) Pauline LeBlanc

Letter That Refuses a Request Tactfully

Premier Sound Sales
3091 Geddes Road
Ann Arbor, MI 48104
Phone: (313) 499-2341
Fax: (313) 499-5904

May 24, 199x

Mr. Russell L. Chapman
4205 Evergreen Avenue
Dearborn, MI 48128

Dear Mr. Chapman:

You're absolutely right! We do take pride in selling the finest products at rock-bottom prices. The Boze speakers you purchased last month are premier concern hall speakers. They're the only ones we present in our catalog because the're the best.

We have such confidence in our products and prices that we offer the price-matching policy you mention in your letter of May 20. That policy guarantees a refund of the price difference if you see one of your purchases offered at a lower price for 30 days after your purchase. To qualify for that refund, customers are asked to send us an advertisement or verifiable proof of the product price and model. As our catalog states, this price-matching policy applies only to exact models with USA warranties.

Our Boze AM-5 II speakers sell for $749. You sent us a local advertisement showing a price of $598 for Boze speakers. This advertisement, however, described an earlier version, the Boze AM-4 model. The AM-5 speakers you received have a wider dynamic range and smoother frequency response than the AM-4 model. Naturally, the improved model you purchased costs a little more than the older AM-4 model that the local advertisement describes. Your speakers have a new three-chamber bass module that virtually eliminates harmonic distortion. Finally, your speakers are 20 percent more compact than the AM-4 model.

You bought the finest compact speakers on the market, Mr. Chapman. If you haven't installed them yet, you may be interested in ceiling mounts, shown in the enclosed catalog on page 48. We value your business and invite your continued comparison shopping.

Sincerely yours,

Mark L. Johnson

Index